NATIONALITY AND STATELESSNESS UNDER INTERNATIONAL LAW

Written by leading experts, Nationality and Statelessness under International Law introduces the study and practice of 'international statelessness law' and explains the complex relationship between the international law on nationality and the phenomenon of statelessness. It also identifies the rights of stateless people, outlines the major legal obstacles preventing the eradication of statelessness and charts a course for this new and rapidly changing field of study.

ALICE EDWARDS is Senior Legal Coordinator and Chief of the Protection Policy and Legal Advice Section at the UN High Commissioner for Refugees (UNHCR), Geneva.

LAURA VAN WAAS is the founder and manager of the Statelessness Programme at Tilburg Law School, the Netherlands.

NATIONALITY AND STATELESSNESS UNDER INTERNATIONAL LAW

Edited by
ALICE EDWARDS AND LAURA VAN WAAS

CAMBRIDGE
UNIVERSITY PRESS

CAMBRIDGE
UNIVERSITY PRESS

University Printing House, Cambridge CB2 8BS, United Kingdom

Cambridge University Press is part of the University of Cambridge.

It furthers the University's mission by disseminating knowledge in the pursuit of
education, learning and research at the highest international levels of excellence.

www.cambridge.org
Information on this title: www.cambridge.org/9781107032446

© Cambridge University Press 2014

First published 2014

Printed in the United Kingdom by Clays, St Ives plc

A catalogue record for this publication is available from the British Library

Library of Congress Cataloguing in Publication data
Nationality and statelessness under international law / edited by
Alice Edwards and Laura van Waas.
pages   cm
Includes bibliographical references and index.
ISBN 978-1-107-03244-6 (hardback)
1. Stateless persons–Legal status, laws, etc.   2. Citizenship.   3. Statelessness.
I. Edwards, Alice, editor.   II. Waas, Laura van, 1981– editor.
K7128.S7N38 2014
342.08′3–dc23
2014022527

ISBN 978-1-107-03244-6 Hardback

CONTENTS

CONTRIBUTORS

JORUNN BRANDVOLL currently works as a Protection Officer with UNHCR as part of the Syrian refugee response in Qobayat, Lebanon. Prior to her current position, she worked for more than six years for the UNHCR Division of International Protection in Geneva, Switzerland, specializing in issues related to nationality and statelessness, most recently as a Legal Officer in the Statelessness Unit from 2009 to 2013. She has been employed by UNHCR since 2003. During this period she has also been based in Azerbaijan and Darfur. She holds an M.Sc. in Russian and Post-Soviet Studies from the London School of Economics and Political Science, a Master's degree in Political Science from the University of Oslo and a Master of Studies in International Human Rights Law from the University of Oxford.

RYSZARD CHOLEWINSKI works for the International Migration Programme of the International Labour Organization (ILO) in Geneva. Prior to joining ILO in 2010, he was Senior Migration Policy and Research Specialist in the Migration Policy and Research Department of the International Organization for Migration (IOM) in Geneva (2005–2010). Prior to this, he was Reader in Law at the University of Leicester (1992–2005). He has served in a consultative capacity to other international organizations such as the Council of Europe, the Office of the United Nations High Commissioner for Human Rights and UNESCO as well as to a number of non-governmental organizations. Ryszard has published widely on international and European migration law and policy, including *Migrant Workers in International Human Rights Law: Their Protection in Countries of Employment* (1997); *Borders and Discrimination in the European Union* (2002); *The Legal Status of Migrants Admitted for Employment: A Comparative Study of Law and Practice in Selected European States* (2004); and *Study on Obstacles to Effective Access of Irregular Migrants to Minimum Social Rights* (2005). More recently, he co-edited *International Migration Law: Developing Paradigms and*

Key Challenges (Asser Press, 2007) and co-authored the *Handbook on Establishing Effective Labour Migration Policies in Countries of Origin and Destination* (2006), a joint publication of the IOM, Organization for Security and Co-operation in Europe (OSCE) and ILO. He was also Co-Editor-in-Chief of IOM's *World Migration 2008: Managing Labour Mobility in the Evolving Global Economy*. Ryszard holds a doctoral degree (LL.D.) from the University of Ottawa, a Master in Laws degree (LL.M.) from the University of Saskatchewan and a Bachelor of Laws degree (LL.B.) from the University of Leicester.

GERARD-RENÉ DE GROOT is Professor of Comparative Law and Private International Law in Maastricht, Aruba and Hasselt. He studied Law at the Rijksuniversiteit Groningen (Netherlands) and at the Westfälische Wilhelmsuniversität Münster (Germany). Since 1982, he has taught Private Law, Comparative Law and Private International Law at Maastricht University, where he obtained the degree of Doctor iuris and was appointed as Professor. He has published extensively on comparative law, private international law, legal education, problems of legal translation, the law of property and nationality law. He is a consortium member of the European Union Democracy Observatory on Citizenship, contributing a number of comparative studies of nationality legislation, including on birthright citizenship. He has worked closely with the Council of Europe in the development of regional standards relating to the regulation of nationality, including in the role of Scientific Expert of the Council of Europe's Group of Specialists on Nationality. He recently prepared a paper on 'Preventing Statelessness among Children: Interpreting Articles 1–4 of the 1961 Convention on the Reduction of Statelessness and Relevant International Human Rights Norms' for UNHCR, helping to guide an Expert Meeting on the same question in May 2011.

ALICE EDWARDS is the Senior Legal Coordinator and Chief of the Protection Policy and Legal Advice Section at UNHCR in Geneva, where she is responsible *inter alia* for shaping UNHCR's doctrinal positions, as well as standard-setting, litigation, research, and human rights liaison. She was previously on the law faculties of the universities of Oxford and Nottingham (2006–10); was the expert adviser to the CEDAW Committee on questions of displacement and statelessness; and the lead amicus in a brief to the US Supreme Court on statelessness (*Flores-Villar* v. *United States of America*, 2010). She has taught statelessness courses at masters level and has delivered short courses on the subject for practitioners. In 2010, she was awarded a British Academy Small Grant to pursue research into statelessness questions. Her other publications include *Human Security and Non-Citizens: Law, Policy and International Affairs* (Cambridge University Press, 2010) and *Violence against Women under International Human Rights Law* (Cambridge University Press, 2011), work related to which she was awarded the Audre Rapoport Prize for Scholarship on the Human Rights of Women. She currently enjoys the privileges of being Research Associate at the University of Oxford's Refugee Studies Centre, Research Fellow of St Anne's College, Oxford and Fellow of Nottingham's Human Rights Law Centre. She holds a B.A, LL.B (Hons) from the University of Tasmania, an LL.M (Distinction) in Public International Law from the University of Nottingham, and Ph.D. from the Australian National University, studying under an Australian Postgraduate Award.

MATTHEW J. GIBNEY is University Reader in Politics and Forced Migration and Fellow of Linacre College, Oxford. He is a political scientist who has written widely on issues relating to refugees, migration control, citizenship and deportation from the perspectives of normative political theory and comparative politics. He is a graduate of Monash University in Melbourne, Australia and completed an M.Phil. and a Ph.D. at Cambridge University, where he was a Commonwealth Scholar. He has taught politics at the universities of Monash, Cambridge, Toronto and Harvard. His work has been published in the *American Political Science Review*, the *Georgetown Immigration Law Journal*, *Government and Opposition* and a range of other journals.

RADHA GOVIL works as a Legal Officer in UNHCR's Division of International Protection, focusing on issues relating to nationality and statelessness. She holds an LL.B. and a BA from the University of Melbourne and a Master's in Public International Law from the London School of Economics and Political Science. Radha has led the work of the Statelessness Unit on addressing gender discrimination in nationality laws. She has conducted participatory discussions with women and their families affected by such discrimination and has helped coordinate the efforts of UN Agencies and NGOs to launch an International Campaign to End Gender Discrimination in Nationality Laws in 2014.

GÁBOR GYULAI works as Refugee Programme Coordinator and trainer at the Hungarian Helsinki Committee, in Budapest. He has in recent years done extensive research and published studies on protection mechanisms available for stateless persons and the dimensions of populations affected by statelessness in several European countries and the USA. He is a regular lecturer and trainer on statelessness at various international and national courses on refugee law or international protection. He participates in a global expert consultation process on statelessness under the auspices of the UNHCR and collaborates with the Open Society Justice Initiative as a consultant on statelessness-related issues.

NIAMH LENAGH-MAGUIRE (BA, LL.B. (Hons) (ANU)) is Counsel in the Office of General Counsel at the Australian Government Solicitor. She is an SJD candidate at the Australian National University College of Law, where her research focuses on federalism, citizenship and constitutions.

MARK MANLY is Head of the Statelessness Unit within the Division of International Protection at UNHCR in Geneva. He previously worked as a legal officer in the same unit. Upon joining UNHCR, he served as a training officer with the Costa Rica-based Regional Legal Unit from 2001 to 2003 and then as a UNHCR Protection Officer in Colombia until 2006. Mark has also worked as a human rights observer with the UN Human Rights Verification Mission in Guatemala from 1995 to 1998 and in 2000 served as human rights officer in the OSCE Mission in Kosovo. Mark holds an LL.M. in International Human Rights Law from Essex University.

SOPHIE NONNENMACHER is a migration policy specialist. She has been working for the IOM since 2000 on labour migration issues at its head-quarters in Geneva, Switzerland. At the end of 2009, she moved to the IOM Bangkok Regional Office to take up the position of Head of the Regional Counter-trafficking Unit for South East Asia. In 2011, Ms. Nonnenmacher assumed the position of Senior Regional Policy & Liaison Officer for Asia and Pacific. She specializes in various aspects of international migration, developing additional expertise on workers' mobility as manifested in GATS Mode 4 and other regional free trade arrangements, on the nexus between migration and development as well as on irregular migration, human trafficking and smuggling issues. In her present capacity, she is developing regional strategies and supporting the development of migration policy in the region. Ms. Nonnenmacher holds Masters' degrees in International Cooperation and Development from the Department of Political Science, University of Paris 1 (Sorbonne) and in Social Anthropology from the School of Higher Studies in Social Sciences, Paris.

KIM RUBENSTEIN is Professor and Director of the Centre for International and Public Law (CIPL) in the ANU College of Law, Australian National University. Kim's current research projects are at the cutting edge of the intersection between public and international law as the co-series editor of the Cambridge University Press five-volume series *Connecting International with Public Law*. Her public law work spans constitutional and administrative law, and also includes her expertise in citizenship law and her international law work concentrates on the status of nationality. Kim is a graduate of the University of Melbourne and Harvard Law School where the Sir Robert Menzies Scholarship to Harvard, a Fulbright postgraduate award, and a Queen Elizabeth Jubilee Trust award supported her. In addition to her scholarly work, Kim has contributed to the greater community through media work and public community education. She was a member of the Independent Committee appointed by the Minister for Immigration and Citizenship to review the Australian Citizenship Test in 2008 and she has appeared three times in the High Court of Australia on citizenship matters, with her work cited in various judgments of the court.

LAURA VAN WAAS is Senior Researcher and Manager of the Statelessness Programme, an initiative of Tilburg Law School in the Netherlands, which is dedicated to research, training and outreach on statelessness and related issues. Among the Statelessness Programme's current work is a detailed study of statelessness in the Middle East, in collaboration with the Open Society Justice Initiative and a research project aiming to map the link between statelessness and human trafficking, funded by the US Department of State Bureau for Population, Refugees and Migration. Laura's doctoral thesis, entitled *Nationality Matters – Statelessness under International Law* (Intersentia, 2008), is an in-depth analysis of the international normative framework relating to statelessness. After gaining her Ph.D., Laura was employed as an expert by UNHCR to work on several successive statelessness projects. She has drafted public information materials, developed training programmes and delivered training on statelessness. She has undertaken comparative research of statelessness situations in the Middle East and North Africa as well as South East Asia. While based in UNHCR's Beirut and Bangkok offices respectively for these projects, Laura helped the agency to build capacity to address statelessness by providing further training and directly advising on strategy development. In 2011, she developed a module on Statelessness for the University of Oxford's Refugee Studies Centre's International Summer

School in Forced Migration. She has also conducted research on behalf of Plan International on the link between irregular migration, birth registration and statelessness.

INETA ZIEMELE has been Judge at the European Court of Human Rights since 2005 and Professor of International Law and Human Rights at the Riga Graduate School of Law, Latvia. She holds a Ph.D. from the University of Cambridge, an M.I.L. degree from the University of Lund and a law degree from the University of Latvia. She is a member of the Executive Board of the European Society of International Law and an expert on the Constitutional Law Committee created by the President of the Republic of Latvia. She is the founding editor of the Baltic Yearbook of International Law and was Editor-in-Chief from 2001 to 2005. She has worked for the Parliament of Latvia, the Prime Minister's Office and the Council of Europe. Her publications include *State Continuity and Nationality: The Baltic States and Russia* (Martinus Nijhoff Publishers, 2005).

ACKNOWLEDGEMENTS

This project started when I was at the University of Oxford, as Lecturer in International Human Rights and Refugee Law at the Refugee Studies Centre. I would like to thank the British Academy for a small grant which prompted the exploration of some of the issues in this publication, and to the Oppenheimer Fund for some seed funding into research assistance. Thank you to Marina Sharpe for being my research assistant in the early stages of this project and for her immaculate collection and filing of materials on nationality and statelessness. I need to thank Laura, my co-editor, for coming to the rescue of this project when I moved to take up my current position at UNHCR in Geneva as Senior Legal Coordinator and Chief of the Protection Policy and Legal Advice section. The project has been an immensely enjoyable one, and it would not have happened without her. A great deal of debt is owed to the excellent contributions and the amazing patience of our many contributors. Thanks also to Finola O'Sullivan, Elizabeth Spicer and the rest of the team at Cambridge University Press for their positive support of this project and its evolution; as well as the Statelessness Unit at UNHCR, in particular Mark Manly for his openness to new arguments in the statelessness area and keen eye for errors(!). I am also particularly pleased that all of our royalties from this book will help support statelessness projects around the world.

A.E.

From first hearing of Alice's plans for this edited collection, I was impatient to see and use the finished product, since it would engage prominent international experts to jointly fill a significant gap in the literature on statelessness. My own contribution was initially to be limited to a chapter on the UN statelessness conventions, which I studied closely in the context of my doctoral research. To my delight, however, I had the opportunity to become more closely involved in the project and join Alice as co-editor. I have learned a great deal from her over the course of this collaboration and have also cherished the opportunity to delve into detailed nitty-gritty and enthusiastic discussions with her on the state of stateless-ness law today. It has been a great pleasure to work together and I hope this will not be the last chance to do so. I would also like to thank Monica Neal for willingly giving up so much of her time alongside her studies to assist with editing the contributions in this volume. A big thank you is also due to my colleagues at the Statelessness Programme at Tilburg Law School, whose enthusiasm for exploring and understanding state-lessness knows no bounds and whose sense of humour is unmatchable. And to Mark and Dylan – thank you for never letting a day pass without a good dose of grinning and giggles, and for being such great motivational coaches for the whole Statelessness Programme team.

Laura

ABBREVIATIONS AND ACRONYMS

1930 Hague Convention	League of Nations Convention on Certain Questions Relating to the Conflict of Nationality Laws 1930
1951 Convention or 1951 Refugee Convention	Convention relating to the Status of Refugees 1951
1954 Convention or 1954 Statelessness Convention	Convention relating to the Status of Stateless Persons 1954
1961 Convention or 1961 Statelessness Convention	Convention on the Reduction of Statelessness 1961
1967 Protocol	Protocol relating to the Status of Refugees 1967
ACHPR or African Charter	African Charter on Human and Peoples' Rights 1981
ACHR	American Convention on Human Rights
ACRWC or African Child Rights Charter	African Charter on the Rights and Welfare of the Child 1990
CEDAW	Convention on the Elimination of All Forms of Discrimination against Women 1979
CEDAW Committee	Committee on the Elimination of Discrimination against Women
Children's Committee	Committee on the Rights of the Child
CHR	Commission on Human Rights
CJEU	Court of Justice of the European Union
CRC	Convention on the Rights of the Child 1989
CRPD	Committee on the Rights of Persons with Disabilities
ECHR	European Convention on the Protection of Human Rights and Fundamental Freedoms 1950

ECmHR	European Commission on Human Rights
ECN	European Convention on Nationality 1997
ECOSOC	Economic and Social Council
ECtHR	European Court of Human Rights
ExCom	Executive Committee of the High Commissioner for Refugees Program
HRC	Human Rights Committee
I-ACmHR	Inter-American Commission of Human Rights
I-ACtHR	Inter-American Court of Human Rights
ICCPR	International Covenant on Civil and Political Rights 1966
ICCS	International Commission on Civil Status
ICERD	International Convention on the Elimination of All Forms of Racial Discrimination 1965
ICESCR	International Covenant on Economic, Social and Cultural Rights 1966
ICJ	International Court of Justice
ICRMW	International Convention on the Protection of the Rights of All Migrant Workers and Members of their Families 1990
ICRPD	International Convention on the Rights of Persons with Disabilities 2006
ILC	International Law Commission
ILO	International Labour Organization
IOM	International Organization for Migration
MWC	Committee on the Rights of Migrant Workers and Members of their Families
NGO	Non-governmental organization
OHCHR	Office of the United Nations High Commissioner for Human Rights
OSCE	Organization for Security and Co-operation in Europe
PCIJ	Permanent Court of International Justice
PRWA or Protocol on the Rights of Women in Africa	Protocol to the African Charter on Human and Peoples' Rights on the Rights of Women 2000
UDHR	Universal Declaration of Human Rights 1948
UNCAT	United Nations Convention against Torture and Other Cruel, Inhuman or Degrading Treatment or Punishment 1984

UNGA	United Nations General Assembly
UNHCR	United Nations High Commissioner for Refugees
UNRWA	United Nations Relief and Works Agency for Palestine Refugees in the Near East
UPR	Universal Periodic Review

∼

Introduction

ALICE EDWARDS* AND LAURA VAN WAAS

'International statelessness law' is the clear runt of the international legal regime. So much so, in fact, that it has yet to truly assert itself as a field of study in its own right – unlike, for instance, international refugee law, international human rights law or even 'international migration law'. Yet international statelessness law deals with a plethora of fascinating and fundamental questions about the interactions between States, the relationship between people and their governments, and the aspirations versus the limitations of the contemporary human rights framework. As such, international statelessness law has much to contribute to our understanding of the functioning of the modern international legal system.

With at least 10 million stateless people around the world,[1] the sheer weight of numbers also demands that we pay closer attention to international law relating to statelessness and renew efforts to interpret and apply it. These 10 million people, lacking a legal identity, are largely invisible and forgotten, yet their suffering is real and, at times, acute. To be cast adrift by every country is a powerfully distressing state of being: 'I feel like nobody who belongs to nowhere. Like I don't exist.'[2] Moreover, statelessness interferes with the enjoyment of a wide range of civil, cultural, economic, political and social rights, which, despite the great aspiration of international human rights that they are to be enjoyed by all human beings equally and thus transcend citizenship categories, this is yet to become reality.

> In Burma we are forced to build roads. We are forced to build jetties and piers and we are forced to build military camps and move all of the military equipment. We are forced to work sentry duty at night. If we doze

---

* The views expressed in this Introduction are the personal views of the author and do not necessarily reflect those of the United Nations or the UNHCR.
[1] UNHCR, *Global Trends 2012: Displacement. The New 21st Century Challenge,* June 2013, available at www.unhcr.org/51bacb0f9.html, last accessed 9 May 2014.
[2] Stateless woman from Ukraine whose story was captured by Greg Constantine as part of the photography series *Nowhere People,* available at www.nowherepeople.org, last accessed 9 May 2014.

off from exhaustion we are beaten. When we wake up we are beaten. And when we are beaten we are made to give away a chicken to pay for our punishment. My father was a farmer and had some land but it was confiscated by the military to build a military camp. I can remember working in the field with my father. When they confiscated our land we cried, but we had no way to say anything.[3]

While the stateless in Myanmar are one of the world's most oppressed groups, disenfranchisement and lost livelihoods are recurring themes for most of the world's stateless people from Kuwait's Bidoon, to Kenya's Nubians, to those rendered stateless due to state dissolution or individual deprivation of nationality. Promoting the study of international statelessness law is key to addressing their plight and preventing new groups and individuals from being exposed to the same problems in future.

The phenomenon of statelessness, or the lack of recognition as a national of any State, is intrinsically linked to broader questions surrounding the regulation and content of nationality. The study of statelessness law, therefore, necessarily goes hand-in-hand with an exploration of nationality law. This is reflected in the title and contributions to this volume, which set out and critique the main legal frameworks relevant to nationality and statelessness matters, with a particular focus on where these intersect. It is hoped that through this book, a modest contribution is made to examining and answering some of the most important legal questions around nationality and statelessness, and that it will encourage practitioners, scholars and students to take up the study of statelessness and lead to its reduction, or even eradication, once and for all.

Although the regulation of nationality remains largely within the exclusive domain of States, statelessness has been on the international agenda since the United Nations was founded. The Secretary-General's 1949 *Study of Statelessness* was a defining moment in the positioning of the UN in the aftermath of the Second World War, in which statelessness was recognized as being connected to genocide, armed conflict, persecution and racism.[4] Ultimately, however, statelessness took a back seat to what were considered the more pressing needs of the Second World War's refugees.[5]

---

[3] Account of the plight of the stateless Muslim minority, commonly known as the Rohingya, from Northern Rakhine State in Myanmar as told in Greg Constantine, *Exiled to Nowhere. Burma's Rohingya,* 2012, part of the *Nowhere People* book series.

[4] United Nations, *A Study of Statelessness*, UN Doc. E/1112 (August 1949).

[5] For more on the relationship between refugee law and statelessness law, see A. Edwards and L. van Waas, 'Statelessness' in G. Loescher, E. Fiddian-Qasimeyah, K. Long and N. Sigona (eds.), *Oxford Handbook on Refugee and Forced Migration Studies* (Oxford University Press, 2014).

Today, questions around nationality and statelessness are increasingly on international and national agendas and the dedication of an edited collection to the intersection of nationality and statelessness is therefore timely, if not long awaited. The break-up of the Soviet Union and the former Yugoslavia in the 1990s gave rise to renewed questions around nationality in the context of state succession[6] and saw the agreement of new legal instruments.[7] Resolving nationality questions and avoiding statelessness have also been fundamental to ending the conflicts between Ethiopia and Eritrea,[8] and have been central to the peace negotiations between South Sudan and Sudan and the transition of the south into independent statehood in 2011.[9] Clearly questions over statehood are central to the resolution of the Palestinian question, and in due course the framing of the State of Palestine's nationality legislation will be pivotal.

Armed conflict as a cause and consequence of statelessness is well documented. In many parts of the world, there are cases of the deliberate administrative removal of members of minority ethnic groups from the citizenship registers, or the official deprivation of nationality by legislative enactment. In some cases, these situations have given rise to human rights claims to restitution of nationality and compensation.[10]

---

[6] On the Soviet Union, see G. Ginsburgs, 'Soviet Citizenship Legislation and Statelessness as a Consequence of the Conflict of Nationality Laws' (1966) 15(1) *Int'l & Comp. L. Qty* 1–54; G. Ginsburgs, 'The "Right to a Nationality" and the Regime of Loss of Russian Citizenship' (2000) 26(1) *Rev. Central & East European L.* 1–33; I. Ziemele, *State Continuity and Nationality: The Baltic States and Russia. Past, Present and Future as Defined by International Law* (Leiden: Martinus Nijhoff Publishers, 2005). On the former Yugoslavia, see R. Mullerson, 'The Continuity and Succession of States, By Reference to the Former USSR and the Yugoslavia' (1993) 43 *Int'l & Comp. L. Qty* 473–93; Working papers of the Europeanisation of Citizenship in the Successor States of the Former Yugoslavia, CITSEE Project, based at the University of Edinburgh, available at www.citsee.ed.ac.uk/.

[7] See, e.g., European Convention on the Avoidance of Statelessness in Relation to State Succession 2006, ETS 200, 15 March 2006 (not yet entered into force).

[8] See, e.g., K. Southwick, 'Ethiopia–Eritrea: Statelessness and State Succession' 32 (2009) *Forced Migration Review* 15–17.

[9] See, e.g., 'Peace and Security Council Should Protect the Right to a Nationality in Sudan', International Refugee Rights Initiative and the Open Society Foundation, 28 January 2011, available at: www.refugee-rights.org/Publications/2011/CRAI_PSC_Sudan_PressRelease_Jan2011[1].pdf; UNHCR, 'Khartoum Symposium Discusses Citizenship Ahead of Referendum', *News Story*, 9 November 2010, available at: www.unhcr.org/4cd981529.html, last accessed 9 May 2014.

[10] See, e.g., *Kuric and Others* v. *Slovenia*, ECtHR, Applic. No. 26828/06, Grand Chamber Decision 26 June 2012; Human Rights Watch, *The Horn of Africa War: Mass Expulsions and the Nationality Issue* (2003); African Commission on Human and Peoples' Rights, *Malawi African Association and Others* v. *Mauritania*, Comm. Nos. 54/91, 61/91, 98/93, 164/97–196/97 and 210/98, 11 May 2000.

As nationality is the principal gateway to political participation, the spread of multi-party democracy has put an increasing strain on access to nationality in some countries, while opening it up in others. In the former, disenfranchisement through statelessness can therefore be an attractive tool for those who seek to gain or hold onto power.[11] The Arab Spring has also demonstrated how the extreme politicization of nationality policy can contribute to generating new cases of statelessness through the deliberate deprivation of nationality,[12] as well as to opening new doors to the resolution of long-standing situations of statelessness.[13]

Ethnic, racial and gender discrimination are at the source of many governmental actions to deprive individuals of their nationality. Apart from discrimination against ethnic minorities in respect of nationality laws, women and children may be disproportionately affected by statelessness. Women continue to be discriminated against in the enjoyment of the equal right to a nationality, and in turn they may be unable to pass on their nationality to their children.[14] Lack of birth registration and other

---

[11] Consider the case of Kenneth Kaunda, former President of Zambia, who was effectively declared stateless in 1999 by the country's High Court after his political opponents called his nationality into question. 'Founder of Zambia is Declared Stateless in High Court Ruling', *New York Times*, 1 April 1999. See also C. Pouilly, 'Africa's Hidden Problem', *Refugees Magazine*, Number 147, Issue 3, 2007; J. Goldston, 'Holes in the Rights Framework: Racial Discrimination, Citizenship and the Rights of Noncitizens', *Ethics and International Affairs* 20 (2006) 321–47;

[12] 'Bahrain Revokes 31 Opposition Activists' Citizenship', BBC News Middle East, 7 November 2012, available at: www.bbc.co.uk/news/world-middle-east-20235542, last accessed 9 May 2014.

[13] Consider Decree No. 49 issued by President Assad of Syria in March 2011, in response to protests early in the Syrian crisis, paving the way for the naturalization – after fifty years of statelessness – of the country's stateless *Ajanib* Kurds. Z. Albarazi, 'The Stateless Syrians', SSRN, 2013, available at: http://papers.ssrn.com/sol3/papers.cfm?abstract_id=2269700. Consider also the repeated promises by the Kuwaiti authorities, following ongoing protests by members of the country's stateless Bidoon population, to take measures to address their situation. C. Hilleary, 'In Kuwait's Arab Spring, Bidun Fight for Citizenship', Middle East Voices, 23 January 2012, available at: http://middleeastvoices.voanews.com/2012/01/in-kuwait%E2%80%99s-arab-spring-bidun-fight-for-citizenship/; Human Rights Watch, 'Kuwait: Promises, Mostly Unfulfilled, on Citizenship', 5 February 2012, available at: www.hrw.org/news/2012/02/05/kuwait-promises-mostly-unfulfilled-citizenship. All websites last accessed 9 May 2014.

[14] A. Edwards, Displacement, Statelessness and Questions of Gender Equality under the Convention on the Elimination of All Forms of Discrimination against Women, UNHCR, Legal and Protection Policy Research Series, POLAS/2009/02, Geneva, August 2009, available at www.unhcr.org/4a8d0f1b9.html, last accessed 9 May 2014; International Law Association, Committee on Feminism and International Law, Rapporteurs C. Chinkin and K. Knop, Final Report on Women's Equality and Nationality in International Law (2000).

administrative obstacles to acquiring nationality,[15] as well as systems of nationality acquisition based on patrilineal descent further risk stateless-ness in children.[16] International adoption and surrogacy arrangements also pose an additional challenge to guaranteeing the right to a national-ity for children.[17]

Statelessness has also been raised as an issue in the climate change debates around the status of persons who may no longer have a phys-ical territory upon which to live should it submerge under rising tides.[18] Meanwhile, governments are increasingly interested in who is and who is not a national, especially in the post-9/11 security environment,[19] as well as in relation to questions around irregular migration. The latter has caused particular problems for persons with no 'effective nationality', or 'who cannot prove or verify their nationality.'[20] Attempted deportations of long-staying and permanent residents have also raised legal issues around the meaning of nationality in today's world.[21] Not all of these issues were

---

[15] See, e.g., Human Rights Watch, '"Illegal People": Haitians and Dominico-Haitians in the Dominican Republic' (2002), available at: www.hrw.org/reports/2002/domrep/ last accessed 9 May 2014; Inter-American Court of Human Rights, *Dilicea Yean and Violeta Bosico* v. *Dominican Republic*, I-ACtHR, Judgment of 8 September 2005, Series C No. 130; African Committee of Experts on the Rights and Welfare of the Child, *Nubian Minors* v. *Kenya*, Communication No. Com/002/2009, 22 March 2011.

[16] See, e.g., J. Bhabha (ed.), *Children without a State: A Global Human Rights Challenge* (Cambridge, MA: MIT Press, 2011); D. Hodgson, 'The International Legal Protection of the Child's Right to a Legal Identity and the Problem of Statelessness' (1993) 7(2) *Int'l J. Law, Pol'y and Family* 255–70. On the practical effects of statelessness in children: J. Boyden and J. Hart, 'The Statelessness of the World's Children' (2007) 21(4) *Children and Society* 237–48.

[17] For a recent example of a case relating to surrogacy arrangements, see 'Stateless Twins Live in Limbo', *The Times of India*, 2 February 2011.

[18] See, e.g., J. McAdam, '"Disappearing States", Statelessness and the Boundaries of International Law' in J. McAdam, *Climate Change and Displacement: Multidisciplinary Perspectives* (Oxford: Hart Publishing, 2010), 105–29.

[19] See cases raising diplomatic protection questions in the terrorism context: *R (on the appli-cation of Abbasi and another)* v. *Secretary of State for Foreign and Commonwealth Affairs and another* [2002] EQCA Civ 1598 (English Court of Appeal); *R (Al Rawi and others)* v. *SSFCA and another (UNHCR intervening)* [2006] EWCA Cov 127 (English Court of Appeal); *Canada (Prime Minister* v. *Khadr)* (2010) S.C.C. 3 (Supreme Court of Canada); *Kaunda and Others* v. *The President of the Republic of South Africa and Others*, Case CCT 23/04 (Constitutional Court of South Africa).

[20] D. Weissbrodt, *The Human Rights of Non-citizens* (Oxford University Press, 2008), at 84. See, further, C. Batchelor, 'Stateless Persons: Some Gaps in International Protection', *Int'l J. Ref. L.*, 7 (1995), 232.

[21] See two Australian cases: *Minister for Immigration and Indigenous Affairs* v. *Stefan Nystrom* [2006], HCA 50, 8 Nov. 2006, which involved an unsuccessful challenge before the High Court of Australia concerning the deportation under 'character grounds'

able to be addressed in this book, but a good portion of them are reflected and discussed.

Nationality and Statelessness under International Law is primarily a legal text, focusing on the legal dimensions of nationality and statelessness, albeit situated within their political context, and introduces the reader to them. The authors hope the book will be a resource for scholars, researchers, legal practitioners and governmental and international policy-makers. It is also geared to students and university teachers, with each chapter being followed by a set of questions to guide self-study or classroom discussion. At the same time, the authors believe it provides an introduction to these issues for scholars and students of other disciplines: in order to successfully contribute to this field of study, a thorough understanding of statelessness as a legal concept is crucial. Contrary to several other works in this area, the book adopts a thematic approach, rather than, for instance, presenting population-specific dilemmas. In this way, the book hopes to offer possible solutions to such challenges through the law. The observations made should therefore be relevant across different countries, regions and contexts.

The book is composed of eleven chapters. The first two contributions comprise an extended introduction to the concepts of nationality and statelessness, from both legal and political-philosophical perspectives. Alice Edwards' chapter provides an overview of the meaning, content and purpose of nationality under international law, including an exploration of the procedural versus the substantive aspects of the right to a nationality. Her chapter asks us to consider whether the 'right to a nationality' is limited only to the right to acquire a nationality and to protections against the arbitrary deprivation of nationality (that is, procedural guarantees), or whether it has, with the growth in human rights, come to mean more than that. Can we, as nationals, expect a certain level of treatment based on that nationality? Within this dichotomy, she deals with the limits on state discretion in conferring or removing a person's nationality, as well

relating to criminality of the relevant legislation of Nystrom, an Australian permanent resident, born in Sweden, but having returned to Australia with his parents less than one month after his birth and who had otherwise never left Australia. He was convicted of 87 criminal offences and had served eight different periods in prison. Another case of Robert Jovicic, who was deported to Serbia in 2004, despite having lived in Australia as a permanent resident since he was two years old and with no ties to Serbia: see 'Court Backs Deportation to Serbia', *The Australian,* 16 December 2006, available at: www.theaustralian.com.au/news/nation/court-backs-deportation-to-serbia/story-e6frg6nf-1111112697067, last accessed 9 May 2014. See also *Jovicic* v. *Minister for Immigration and Multicultural Affairs* [2006] FCA 1758, 15 December 2006.

as what possessing a nationality really means in terms of benefits or privileges. As such, the chapter sets out the overall legal framework governing nationality rights and explores what international human rights law has added to this equation. This is complemented by the subsequent chapter, which gives 'an overview of the normative complexities and political dynamics of contemporary statelessness'. Matthew Gibney discusses the political and practical importance of the possession of citizenship in the modern state-based world for the enjoyment of rights and protections, while also challenging the idea that securing citizenship somewhere – anywhere – is the end-goal. He observes that obtaining citizenship represents the minimum right, but it does not always lead to the enjoyment of rights, nor of political participation. He also gives us insights into the interests states may have in maintaining or perpetuating statelessness, as well as what moral duty exists for states to nevertheless admit stateless people as citizens.

After these broad reflections on the function of nationality and the anomaly of statelessness, Chapters 3–5 delve into the global legal framework on statelessness in greater detail. Van Waas presents the two United Nations' statelessness conventions – the 1954 Convention relating to the Status of Stateless Persons[22] and the 1961 Convention on the Reduction of Statelessness[23] – which were developed specifically with a view to offering protection to stateless persons and prescribing safeguards for the avoidance of new cases of statelessness. Through a discussion of the drafting history of these two pivotal texts, she canvasses their relative strengths and weaknesses. Importantly, she explains the legal definition of a 'stateless person' set out in the 1954 Convention and the distinction between *de jure* statelessness and the emergence of the non-legal, yet popular, concept of *de facto* statelessness, the latter extending the concept of statelessness beyond mere possession of nationality to ideas around the 'effectiveness' of that nationality. She critiques the utility of '*de facto* statelessness' as a construct, arguing in particular that it is not grounded in an international legal framework and is highly ambiguous.

Following van Waas, Chapter 4 by Mark Manly, Head of the UNHCR's Statelessness Unit, turns to discuss one of the primary institutional elements of the UN framework for addressing statelessness, the UNHCR.

---

[22] Convention relating to the Status of Stateless Persons, New York, 28 September 1954, in force 6 June 1960, 360 UNTS 117.

[23] Convention on the Reduction of Statelessness, New York, 30 August 1961, in force 13 December 1975, 989 UNTS 175.

Tracing the history and development of the agency's role in statelessness, as laid down in General Assembly resolutions and conclusions of
UNHCR's own Executive Committee, Manly explains how UNHCR has
come to hold a global, comprehensive and multifaceted mandate, giving
examples of both the operational successes achieved and the ongoing difficulties faced in implementing that mandate. In relation to the latter, the
widely different interpretations of 'stateless person' that exist re-emerges
in Manly's chapter as a factor that impacts on the accepted extent of
UNHCR's mandate, which sits alongside the real problem of identifying
and counting stateless persons, who are often not recorded in government
censuses. Next, in Chapter 5, Gábor Gyulai explores a key question for the
statelessness regime: what is the relationship between the international
legal framework and statelessness-specific status determination and protection mechanisms at the municipal level? In particular, he examines
the necessity of statelessness determination as a precursor to effective
protection and looks at some of the ways in which this has taken shape
in different countries. In canvassing some of the main challenges which
states have to address in this context, he puts forward the basic building
blocks for a functioning protection system, and in essence offers a model
for states. His chapter will be particularly useful to government policy-
makers.

The next set of chapters (6–8) turns to look at three of the most pressing
and pervasive problems in respect of the avoidance of statelessness: securing children's right to a nationality; abolishing gender discrimination in
the enjoyment of nationality rights; and interpreting and applying the
prohibition of arbitrary deprivation of nationality in the context of state
decisions to withdraw nationality from an individual rendering him/her
stateless. In Chapter 6, René de Groot discusses the development and content of the child's right to a nationality under international and regional
human rights law, as well as within the specific parameters of the 1961
Statelessness Convention and numerous Council of Europe instruments
where these norms have been elaborated in greater detail. He explains the
challenges to childhood statelessness through three case studies, focusing on abandoned children, international adoption or surrogacy arrangements, and foundlings. In presenting a complex legal picture, in which
European standards have advanced beyond and filled some of the gaps at
the international level, he proposes a solid set of propositions to address
childhood statelessness. Nonetheless, these are not yet widely accepted at
the international level and may need further codification.

In Chapter 7, Radha Govil and Alice Edwards explore the historical 'gendering' of nationality laws and their impact, in particular in terms of creating and perpetuating statelessness. The chapter focuses on the equal right to nationality, evident in a growing number of international and regional human rights instruments, and its link with statelessness. They point out arguably one of the most stark shortcomings of the 1961 Statelessness Convention: it is not in fact concerned with providing for equal rights to nationality between women and men, or between mothers and fathers, and it does *not* prohibit discriminatory nationality laws. Rather, the 1961 Convention only requires states to permit the passage of nationality from mother to child in circumstances where the child would *otherwise* be stateless. It also says nothing about a right to nationality for women independent of their husbands. The role of the United Nations Convention on the Elimination of All Forms of Discrimination against Women 1979 (CEDAW) as the leading source of international norms on gender equality is thus central to the eradication and elimination of inequality in nationality matters, particularly where this gives rise to statelessness. Last in this set of chapters is Jorunn Brandvoll's contribution, which looks at the meaning of 'arbitrariness' in the context of a deprivation of nationality. Noting that the statelessness regime permits the deprivation of nationality even if it results in statelessness in certain circumstances, Bandvoll departs from a discussion of the relevant provisions of the 1961 Statelessness Convention, but takes a step beyond this framework by considering how developments in human rights law or within relevant regional instruments may now be shaping states' obligations in this area.

In the final three chapters (9–11), the discussion moves away from issues relating to the general functioning of statelessness law and into the realm of how questions of nationality and statelessness are – or should be – dealt with in particular contemporary contexts that pose corresponding challenges. Judge Ineta Ziemele looks at how states regulate nationality matters in the context of state succession, which by its very nature creates significant upheaval and prompts difficult questions about the reconciliation of municipal interests and international obligations. She explores the way in which the international community's interest in avoiding large-scale statelessness has influenced progressive standard-setting in this context. Judge Ziemele also considers the distinct difficulties posed by situations in which state succession entails the transition from an illegal regime, when international law may make conflicting demands in asking both for the non-recognition of the illegal regime (and its effects) and the avoidance of statelessness.

In Chapter 10, Sophie Nonnenmacher and Ryszard Cholewinski delve into the pressures placed on nationality policy by modern patterns of international migration. They consider in particular the manner in which migration is contributing to new cases or a heightened risk of statelessness among different migrant groups. At the same time, they explore the other dimension of the nexus between nationality and migration: where statelessness is acting as a push-factor, triggering migration while also sometimes hampering states' ability to effectively implement their immigration laws. In the final chapter of the book, Kim Rubenstein and Niamh Lenagh-Maguire offer an exposé of the treatment of dual nationals – including case studies of the United Kingdom and Australia – arguing that some nationals (namely dual or multiple nationals) are more vulnerable to denationalization or deportation than others, precisely because they are not at risk of statelessness. This brings them to a broader reflection on the relationship between nationality and 'one's own country', in particular in light of contemporary human rights law, taking the reader full-circle back to the question of the meaning and content of nationality under international law today.

International statelessness law is undeniably receiving increasing attention from students, scholars, researchers, governments, civil society, legal practice and the international community, specifically UNHCR. Yet, as Manly points out in Chapter 4, 'there is nothing even closely resembling an international movement of the kind which currently exist to address child soldiers, landmines, or even refugee rights'. Given the rapid pace of developments on this issue over the past few years, as discussed in many of the contributions presented here, we may nevertheless be on the cusp of such an international movement on statelessness. With the sixtieth anniversary of the 1954 Convention coinciding with the release of this book, it is hoped that the book will inspire many more scholars, students and practitioners to take up the cause of statelessness so that in the coming years, statelessness will become a phenomenon of the past, studied only by historians.

The meaning of nationality in international law in an era of human rights

Procedural and substantive aspects

ALICE EDWARDS

1.1.   Introduction

Nationality defines the legal relationship or 'legal bond'[1] between the citizen/national and her state, based on social facts of attachment, and which gives rise to rights and duties on the part of both sides of that relationship. This chapter is interested in what 'nationality' means as a matter of international law today, particularly with the growth in human rights, which apply, in theory at least, to all human beings, *irrespective of their nationality*. The chapter looks at two aspects of the right to a nationality – procedural and substantive – and explains what these aspects entail. On the procedural side, this chapter examines the regulation of nationality: how is nationality determined, who decides, and what are the limits on states' discretion in conferring or removing one's nationality? On the substantive side, it examines whether there is a 'minimum core substantive content' for nationality to exist. What rights are associated with nationality? It looks at this both from the perspective of the state, and from the perspective of the national. Reflecting on these primary legal questions, the chapter sets out the overall legal framework governing nationality rights and explores what international human

The views expressed in this chapter are those of the author and are not necessarily reflective of those of the United Nations or UNHCR.

[1] European Convention on Nationality 1997, 6 November 1997, in force 3 January 2000, ETS No. 166, Art. 2(a). See also *Dickson Car Wheel Company Case*, Special Claims Commission between the United States and Mexico, *UN Reports*, 1931 vol. IV, 669–91, at 688; *Annual Digest,* 1931–32, Case No. 115, in which it was stated that: 'This [bond of nationality] is the link existing between the law and individuals and through it alone are individuals enabled to invoke the protection of a State and the latter empowered to intervene on their behalf', as referred to in P. Weis, *Nationality and Statelessness in International Law,* 2nd edn (Dordrecht: Kluwer Academic Publishers Group, 1979), 162.

rights law has added to this equation. It is hoped that this chapter will be used as a reference on its own, as well as a guide to the other chapters in this volume.

1.2.   The concept of nationality

The International Court of Justice (ICJ) in the *Nottebohm* case indicated that 'Nationality serves above all to determine the person upon whom it is conferred enjoys the rights and is bound by the obligations which the law of the State in question grants to or imposes on its nationals.'[2] In its most frequently cited passage as to the meaning of nationality, the ICJ held that: '[N]ationality is a legal bond having as its basis a social fact of attachment, a genuine connection of existence, interest and sentiments, together with the existence of reciprocal rights and duties.'[3] Nationality is thus *determined* by one's social ties to the country of one's nationality, and when established, gives rise to rights and duties on the part of the state, as well as on the part of the citizen/national. In turn 'citizenship' is a way to maintain common norms and values of the state as a social and political community.

The modern concept of nationality emerged following the Peace of Westphalia of 1648 and the rise of separate sovereign states.[4] It was essentially a method of classification between those who owed allegiance and those who did not to a particular sovereign, within the new state-based world order. As such, nationality is essentially a matter of domestic law, but it is one with international consequences.[5]

From the perspective of the citizen/national, possessing the nationality of a particular state grants entitlements to a range of goods, services and rights, such as rights to take up residence, participate in public life and to vote, and to consular assistance when abroad. It also includes entitlements to social benefits. Citizens may also be required to perform specific

---

[2] *Nottebohm Case (Liechtenstein v. Guatemala); Second Phase*, International Court of Justice (ICJ), 6 April 1955, ICJ Reports 1955, p. 4; General List, No. 18.

[3] *Ibid.* See also 1997 European Convention on Nationality, Council of Europe, 6 November 1997, ETS 166, which defines 'nationality' as 'the legal bond between a person and a State that does not indicate the person's ethnic origin' (Art. 2).

[4] For more on the historical evolution of the concept of nationality, see Ivan Shearer and Brian Opeskin, 'Nationality and Statelessness' in Brian Opeskin, Richard Perruchoud and Jillyanne Redpath-Cross (eds.), *Foundations of International Migration Law* (Cambridge University Press, 2012), 93.

[5] This has been nicely put by Shearer and Opeskin as 'Nationality is essentially an institution of domestic law but it has consequences in international law', *Ibid.*

civic duties, including the obligation to defend the state against enemies (military service), to pay taxes, or even to vote.[6] Interestingly, some of these rights and duties are no longer applicable only to citizens, but are regularly extended to permanent residents or certain migrant categories. At the municipal level, it has been said that there are as many variations of citizenship as there are states.[7]

As a concept of international law, however, nationality goes beyond the individual rights of the national vis-à-vis her state of nationality. In fact, the bonds of nationality create *duties* upon states vis-à-vis other states, such as the duty to readmit one's own nationals from abroad. The bond of nationality also grants particular discretionary rights to the state of nationality, such as the right of that state to exercise 'diplomatic protection' on behalf of its own citizens/nationals. Other aspects of nationality include procedural safeguards against the arbitrary deprivation or loss of nationality, as well as to some extent shared practices on rules relating to nationality acquisition.

Before moving to explore these aspects more fully, it is important to say a word about terminology, in particular 'nationality' versus 'citizenship', and 'national' versus 'citizen'. For the purposes of this chapter, both terms will be used, although as a chapter centred on international law, the notion of 'nationality' is preferred. There are, however, two general approaches to understanding these terms in international law. The first, more traditional view, is that:

> Conceptually and linguistically, the terms 'nationality' and 'citizenship' emphasize two different aspects of the same notion: State membership. 'Nationality' stresses the international, 'citizenship' the national, municipal, aspect. Under the laws of most States citizenship connotes full membership, including the possession of political rights; some States distinguish between different classes of members (subjects and nationals).[8]

Nationality has been described as giving rise on the part of the state to 'personal jurisdiction over the individual, and standing *vis-à-vis* other States under international law.'[9] Citizenship, on the other hand, is 'the highest

---

[6] Australia, for example, imposes an obligation on citizens to vote in elections, with the penalty of a fine for failing or refusing to do so: Commonwealth Electoral Act 1918.

[7] *Towne* v. *Eisner*, 245 US 418, 423 (1918), per Justice Holmes.

[8] Weis, Nationality and Statelessness in International Law, 4–5.

[9] A. Boll, 'Nationality and Obligations of Loyalty in International and Municipal Law' *Australian Yearbook of International Law* 24 (2003) 37–63, 37, n. 3.

of political rights/duties in municipal law.'[10] A study by the International Law Association also accepts this distinction between the two terms.[11]

The second view, and the one adopted by many international human rights law scholars, including many of the contributors to this book, is that the terms can be used interchangeably. They argue that while the distinction between nationality (international law) and citizenship (municipal law) can be maintained in many contexts, it is also true that there is a close relationship between the two, such that making such a clear distinction is not always necessary or helpful. From a rights perspective, the label is less important than the ability to exercise rights. Such an approach has also been adopted because, as we will see in this chapter, 'Nationality has no positive, immutable meaning. On the contrary its meaning and import have changed with the changing character of States ... Nationality always connotes, however, membership of some kind in the society of a State or nation.'[12] Likewise, the substantive content of 'citizenship' will depend to a large extent on one's country of citizenship.

1.3.   Procedural aspects of nationality

Article 15 of the 1948 Universal Declaration of Human Rights (UDHR) provides that everyone has 'the right to a nationality' and no one shall be arbitrarily deprived of that nationality nor denied the right to change one's nationality. No corresponding obligation on states to grant nationality was elaborated in the UDHR.[13] The transposition of Article 15 of the UDHR into Article 24(3) of the 1966 International Covenant on Civil and Political Rights (ICCPR) limited its application to children, while clarifying that they have a right 'to acquire' a nationality.[14] Again, no corresponding obligation *to grant* nationality to every child born in their

---

[10] *Ibid.*

[11] International Law Association Committee on Feminism and International Law, 'Final Report on Women's Equality and Nationality in International Law' (2000) Report of a conference held in London, International Law Association, London, available at: www.unhcr.org/3dc7cccf4.pdf, last accessed 1 June 2014.

[12] M. O. Hudson and R. W. Flournoy Jr., 'Nationality – Responsibility of States – Territorial Waters, Drafts of Conventions prepared in Anticipation of the First Conference on the Codification of International Law, The Hague 1930', *American Journal of International Law* 23 (1929), Supplement, 21.

[13] Art. 15, UDHR, provides: '1. Everyone has the right to a nationality; 2. No one shall be arbitrarily deprived of his nationality nor denied the right to change his nationality.'

[14] Art. 24(3) of the ICCPR provides: 'Every child has the right to acquire a nationality.' 1966 International Covenant on Civil and Political Rights, New York, 16 December 1966, in force 23 March 1976, 999 UNTS 171.

territory was included, nor protection against the arbitrary deprivation of nationality. Nonetheless, the right to acquire a nationality in Article 24(3) of the ICCPR is not devoid of obligation.

The UN Human Rights Committee has stated, for example, that: 'States are required [by Article 24(3)] to adopt every appropriate measure, both internally and in cooperation with other States, to ensure that every child has a nationality.'[15] This obligation includes the requirement to register every child immediately after birth.[16] A child's right to acquire a nationality is repeated in the 1989 Convention on the Rights of the Child (CRC), which importantly contains a special safeguard against statelessness.[17] The right to a nationality is also affirmed in a wide range of soft law instruments.[18] It could be asserted that the obligation under the CRC is time-bound, since such measures must be undertaken by the state prior to the child reaching majority.[19] Delays in the recognition of a child's right to acquire a nationality by application are permitted in some circumstances,[20] yet, as they can have adverse consequences for the child, including leaving the child stateless for periods of time, it has been argued that Articles 7 and 3 (best interests of the child principle) of the CRC require nationality to be granted either (i) automatically at birth or (ii) upon application shortly after birth.[21]

---

[15] Human Rights Committee, *CCPR General Comment No. 17: Rights of the Child (Art. 24)*, Geneva, 7 April 1989, para. 8.

[16] Art. 24(2), ICCPR provides: 'Every child shall be registered immediately after birth and shall have a name.'

[17] Art. 7, CRC provides: '1. The child shall be registered immediately after birth and shall have the right from birth to a name, the right to acquire a nationality and, as far as possible, the right to know and be cared for by his or her parents.2. States Parties shall ensure the implementation of these rights in accordance with their national law and their obligations under the relevant international instruments in this field, in particular where the child would otherwise be stateless.'

[18] See latest resolutions and conclusions: General Assembly resolution 67/149 of 20 December 2012; Executive Committee (ExCom) Conclusion No. 106 (LVI) – 2010 on Identification, Prevention and Reduction of Statelessness and Protection of Stateless Persons; ExCom Conclusion No. 107 (LVIII) – 2007 on Children at Risk, para. (h), lit. 19.

[19] According to Article 1 of the Convention on the Rights of the Child, a 'child' is defined as: 'a child means every human being below the age of eighteen years unless under the law applicable to the child, majority is attained earlier.'

[20] See Art. 1(2), Convention on the Reduction of Statelessness, New York, 30 August 1961, in force 13 December 1975, 989 UNTS 175 (1961 Statelessness Convention).

[21] UNHCR, 'Guidelines on Statelessness No. 4: Ensuring Every Child's Right to Acquire a Nationality through Articles 1–4 of the 1961 Convention on the Reduction of Statelessness', HRC/GS/12/04, 21 December 2012, in particular paras. 34–5.

According to the United Nations Secretary-General's report on human rights and the arbitrary deprivation of nationality, the right to a nationality implies (i) the right of each individual to acquire, change and retain a nationality; and (ii) that one's nationality cannot be arbitrarily removed.[22] Beyond these two components, the Secretary-General's report does not delve into the question of whether there are any substantive rights associated with the possession of nationality, to which all nationals, regardless of their state of nationality, are entitled to enjoy as a matter of international law. The right to a nationality under international law has thus been crafted and could be classified primarily as a '*procedural right*', covering rights and rules relating to nationality acquisition and deprivation. This chapter now turns to look at some of these procedural aspects of the right to a nationality; the issue of any associated substantive content is considered in Section 1.4.

1.3.1   Modes of nationality acquisition

There are three main methods in which nationality is acquired or conferred by states, namely by descent/parentage (*jus sanguinis* – law of the blood), birth on the territory (*jus soli* – law of the soil) or by way of naturalization (including *jus domicili* or long residence). In each case, the idea is that nationality reflects a link with the state, either through a connection with the territory (*jus soli, jus domicili*) or through lineage such as through a family member who is already a national (*jus sanguinis* including legitimation,[23] adoption, or marriage). This relates to the fact that nationality, as already noted, is a bond of membership that is based on a 'social fact of attachment'.[24] Territorial or family links are commonly viewed as demonstrating such an attachment. There are also modes of nationality acquisition in the specific context of state succession and dissolution, although these are not discussed in this chapter.[25]

---

[22] Report of the Secretary-General to the General Assembly, 'Human rights and arbitrary deprivation of nationality', A/HRC/13/34 (14 December 2009), para. 21.

[23] 'Legitimation' refers to where the father's parentage is legally recognized having the effect of changing or confirming the nationality of the child in systems operating rules of *jus sanguinis* by paternity. For more on these other forms, see I. Brownlie, 'The Relations of Nationality in Public International Law', *British Yearbook of International Law*, 39 (1963), 284–364.

[24] *Nottebohm*, above n. 2.

[25] See ILC, 'Articles on Nationality of Natural Persons in relation to the Succession of States' (1999). See also Ziemele's Chapter 9 in this book.

While there is far more variation in the conferment of nationality via naturalization, there is widespread state practice of nationality conferral at birth using one or a combination of the *jus soli* or *jus sanguinis* approaches. In fact, Manley O. Hudson, the International Law Commission's (ILC) Rapporteur on nationality questions in the 1950s concluded that 'This uniformity of nationality laws seems to indicate a consensus of opinion of States that conferment of nationality at birth has to be based on' either or both of these modes.[26] By 1958, van Panhuys had suggested that the two modes are approved by customary law.[27] They remain the predominant practices.[28]

These two modes of nationality conferral are subject to a number of widely accepted exceptions. As far as the *jus soli* conferral system is concerned, a number of international treaties provide that children born to persons enjoying diplomatic immunity are not automatically entitled to nationality by operation of law.[29] Another exception is in respect of children of 'enemy alien fathers born in territory under enemy occupation'.[30] At the national level, an exception exists in some countries to deny children born to asylum-seekers and irregular migrants the automatic recognition of nationality on the basis of *jus soli*; or an exception requires that they are subject to a *jus sanguinis* link simultaneously.[31] In contrast, as to

---

[26] Report by Mr. Manley O. Hudson, Special Rapporteur, 'Nationality, including Statelessness', A/CN.4/50, *ILC Yearbook* (1952-II), p. 3, at p. 7; cited also in Brownlie, 'The Relations of Nationality in Public International Law', 302–3.

[27] H. F. Van Panhuys, *The Role of Nationality in International Law* (Leydon: A. W. Sythoff, 1959), 160–1.

[28] See, by way of comparison, the laws of states in 1940, 1952 as well as 2010, in which *jus soli* and *jus sanguinis* are used alone or in combination: see *Brief of Amicus Curiae, Scholars of Statelessness in Support of the Petitioner in the Supreme Court of the United States of America, Ruben Flores-Villar v. United States of America*, 24 June 2010, in which the author of this chapter was lead amicus.

[29] See Article 12, League of Nations, Convention on Certain Questions Relating to the Conflict of Nationality Law, 13 April 1930, League of Nations, Treaty Series, vol. 179, p. 89, No. 4137 (1930 Hague Convention): 'Rules of law which confer nationality by reason of birth on the territory of a State shall not apply automatically to children born to persons enjoying diplomatic immunity, in the country where the birth occurs' and 1961 United Nations Conference on Diplomatic Intercourse and Immunities which adopted an Optional Protocol to the Vienna Convention on Consular Relations concerning the Acquisition of Nationality, 24 April 1963, UNTS 469, Article II provides: 'Members of the mission not being nationals of the receiving State, and members of their families forming part of their household, shall not, solely by the operation of the law of the receiving State, acquire the nationality of that State.'

[30] Brownlie, 'The Relations of Nationality in Public International Law', 305.

[31] See, for more, L. van Waas, 'The Children of Irregular Migrants: A Stateless Generation?', *Netherlands Quarterly of Human Rights*, 25 (2007), 437–58; D. A. Martin, 'Citizenship

persons born on ships or aircraft registered under the flag of the conferring state, the *jus soli* rules are generally extended to them.[32]

For countries operating *jus sanguinis* rules, a number of practices that
in the past were considered to be legitimate exercises of discretion in
nationality matters are no longer accepted. Some *jus sanguinis* countries,
for example, trace a child's lineage through paternal lines only, which in
turn deprives a citizen-mother of being able to independently pass her
nationality to her children.[33] At times, such children will be rendered
stateless.[34] A number of states also deprive a woman of her nationality
automatically upon marriage.[35] UNHCR has calculated that there are
some twenty-seven countries that continue to maintain gender discriminatory nationality laws, which are per se in violation of the international
prohibition on discrimination on the basis of sex.[36]

Compared to *jus sanguinis* or *jus soli* rules of nationality conferral, the
granting of nationality by naturalization remains more robustly within
the discretion of states, and has largely remained untouched by international law. Historically, naturalization was based primarily on *jus domicili* principles; in other words, nationality was acquired via long residence

in Countries of Immigration – Introduction', in T. A. Aleinikoff and D. Kluysmeyer
(eds.), *From Margins to Citizens: Membership in a Changing World* (Washington D.C.:
Brookings Institution Press, 2000).

[32] See Art. 3, 1961 Statelessness Convention: 'For the purpose of determining the obligations of Contracting States under this Convention, birth on a ship or in an aircraft shall
be deemed to have taken place in the territory of the State whose flag the ship flies or
in the territory of the State in which the aircraft is registered, as the case may be.' See
also Arts. 17–21 of the International Civil Aviation Organization (ICAO), International
Convention on Civil Aviation ('Chicago Convention'), 7 December 1944 (1994) 15 UNTS.
295, which recognizes the nationality of the flag state over aircraft.

[33] For more on discrimination in the conferral of nationality, see Chapter 7 by Govil
and Edwards in this volume. See also International Law Association Committee on
Feminism and International Law, 'Final Report on Women's Equality and Nationality
in International Law' (2000) Report of a conference held in London, International
Law Association, London, available at: www.unhcr.org/3dc7cccf4.pdf; A. Edwards,
'Displacement, Statelessness and Questions of Gender Equality under the Convention
on the Elimination of All Forms of Discrimination against Women', (2009) Legal
and Protection Policy Research Series, UNHCR, Geneva, available at: www.unhcr.
org/4a8d0f1b9.pdf. Both websites last accessed 1 June 2014.

[34] 1954 Convention relating to the Status of Stateless Persons, 28 September 1951, 360
UNTS 117, Art. 1.

[35] See Govil and Edwards in this volume.

[36] UNHCR, Background Note on Gender Equality, Nationality Laws and Statelessness
2014, 8 March 2014, available at: www.refworld.org/docid/532075964.html, last accessed
1 June 2014. See, in particular, Art. 9 of the 1979 UN Convention on the Elimination of
All Forms of Discrimination against Women.

in the territory. The length of this residency was determined by each individual state. Historically, too, as single nationality was preferred, individuals would usually be required to relinquish their other nationality, or it would cease automatically upon acquisition of their new nationality.

Jus domicili alone is not, however, the only basis of conferment of nationality by naturalization. States have in fact adopted a multitude of rules related to naturalization. An emerging trend in naturalization rules, especially in industrialized countries, is that persons must prove their allegiance to the state in new ways (also noting the demise of compulsory military service). Via knowledge testing, language proficiency and/ or even financial position – usually still coupled with residency periods – potential citizens are asked to demonstrate that they share the values of the state.[37] 'Citizenship testing' has been introduced, for example, in many countries including Australia, Denmark, France, Greece, the Netherlands and the United Kingdom, as an attempt to ensure that only those loyal to the values of the state ('good citizens') are granted nationality. 'Citizenship ceremonies' have been made mandatory in some jurisdictions, in which new citizens are required to swear official allegiance to their new sovereign in a public forum. More restrictive policies in respect of acquiring citizenship based on marriage, including extending qualifying residence periods and/or raising the marriage age for foreign spouses and/or the duration of marriage periods and by removing exemptions from other naturalization requirements, are also observed.[38]

Some of these new, more onerous naturalization practices have emerged against a backdrop of political concern and tensions over the integration of migrants and new citizens, as well as fraud. Another factor is the loosening of the rules relating to dual nationality in many countries – both in the countries of old and new citizenship.[39] In both countries, the motivation of the state in allowing dual nationality is linked as much to economic as to social attachment arguments.[40] Allowing one's

---

[37] R. Bauböck, Eva Ersbøll, Kees Groenendijk and Harald Waldrauch (eds.), *Acquisition and Loss of Nationality: Policies and Trends in 15 European Countries* (Institute for European Integration Research, Austrian Academy of Sciences, Vienna, 2006), p. 1.

[38] *Ibid.*

[39] See Chapter 11 in this book by Rubenstein and Lenagh-Maguire.

[40] Bauböck, Ersbøll, Groenendijk and Waldrauch (eds.), *Acquisition and Loss of Nationality*, p. 1. The authors of this report noted different responses to the phenomenon of migration. They note that '[s]ome States have reacted to problems with immigrant integration by promoting naturalisation and by granting second and third generations of immigrant descent a right to their nationality, while others have made access to nationality more difficult for immigrants and their descendants. Some States have seen an interest

citizens abroad to acquire a new nationality can safeguard remittances and investment in the country of original or first nationality over the long term, while for countries of new citizenship, governments ensure that migrants are rewarded for their economic contribution to society and that such contributions will not be lost to other countries where citizenship rules may be more relaxed.

Long gone are the days for many countries of the 'exclusivity of national identification'[41] of the early twentieth century. In the past, dual nationality was generally thought to create tensions among nation states as loyalty and allegiance would be split between different sovereigns. In particular, it could place competing demands on citizens in terms of military service.[42] Dual nationality was also considered to create challenges to the institution of diplomatic protection (discussed below).[43] In fact, international law relating to nationality was originally focused on questions of dual nationality and reconciling conflicts between nationality laws. While dual or multiple nationality is now more widely accepted,[44] including citizenship of supranational bodies such as the European Union,[45] there remain many countries that do not allow their nationals to hold

    in maintaining ties with their emigrants by allowing them to naturalise abroad without losing their nationality of origin, while others have refused to do so.'

[41] P. J. Spiro, 'Dual Nationality: Unobjectionable and Unstoppable', Centre for Immigration Studies, available at: www.cis.org/node/2939, last accessed 1 June 2014.

[42] See the 1963 European Convention on the Reduction of Cases of Multiple Nationality and Military Obligations in Cases of Multiple Nationality, 6 May 1963, ETS 43, which attempted to set some rules in this regard. Spiro, in 'Dual Nationality: Unobjectionable and Unstoppable', gives the example of Europeans emigrating to the United States of America in the late nineteenth and early twentieth centuries, with their home countries refusing to recognise their new nationality. This in turn led to their prosecution for failing to complete military service by some countries if they returned to their country of origin to visit family.

[43] The classical case is also that of *Nottebohm*, above n. 2 (discussed below).

[44] Spiro, 'Dual Nationality: Unobjectionable and Unstoppable' refers explicitly to the Dominican Republic, Italy, Mexico and Thailand as recent additions to the group of states that recognize dual nationality. He also states that South Korea, India and the Philippines are poised to join the group. See also A. M. Boll, *Multiple Nationality and International Law* (Leiden: Martinus Nijhoff, 2007). See also B. Manby, *Struggles for Citizenship in Africa* (London: Zed Books, October 2009), 7, who lists thirteen countries in Africa that have changed their nationality laws to allow for dual nationality since 1999, with another three allowing it with official permission from the government. She notes, however, that still half of African countries do not permit dual nationality.

[45] Article 17 of the Treaty Establishing the European Community 1957 provides that: 'Citizenship of the Union is hereby established. Every citizen holding the nationality of a Member State shall be a citizen of the Union. Citizenship of the Union shall complement and not replace national citizenship.' See, inter alia, Court of Justice of the European Union, Case C-200/02 – *Zhu and Chen* v. *Secretary of State for the Home Department*, ECR

simultaneously nationality elsewhere. For those that do, and as highlighted above, gaining membership to some countries is becoming more layered and complex.

Dual nationality also appears to come with some risks for the individual. Rubenstein and Lenagh-Maguire in this book argue, for example, that a dual national is more vulnerable to deportation or extradition compared with single-country nationals. It has also been seen, although more research is required in this area, that dual nationals are more likely to have their nationality removed than single nationals, in part because there is no risk of statelessness preventing a state from so doing.[46]

1.3.2   Loss and deprivation of nationality

Nationality may be lost or deprived in a number of ways, either through the operation of law (loss) or through administrative act (deprivation).

2004, I-3887, in which it was held that not only is every person holding the nationality of a Member State a citizen of the EU, but also that it is not permissible for a Member State to restrict the effects of the grant of the nationality of another Member State by imposing additional conditions for recognition of that nationality. Thus, Member States with harsher naturalization criteria are not entitled to withhold the benefits of fundamental freedoms under Community law from Union citizens who have naturalized on easier terms in other Member States. Cf. CJEU, Case C-135/08, *Rottmann v. Freistaat Bayern*, 2 March 2010, which considered whether Austria (state of original nationality granted at birth) might be bound, by virtue of the duty to cooperate with the Union in good faith and having regard to the values enshrined in the 1961 Statelessness Convention and in Article 7(1)(b) of the European Convention on Nationality, to interpret and apply its national law or to adapt it so as to prevent the person concerned from becoming stateless when, as in the case in the main proceedings, that person had not been given the right to keep his nationality of origin following the acquisition of a foreign nationality (in this case German nationality, which had been withdrawn owing to serious fraud on an occupational basis). In that case, the CJEU turned instead to the question of whether Germany had withdrawn his nationality in line with EU and international law, and did not pass judgment on whether Austria was required to grant him nationality [except in noting that that decision also must observe the principle of proportionality], finding that '[57] a Member State whose nationality has been acquired by deception cannot be considered bound, pursuant to Article 17 EC, to refrain from withdrawing naturalisation merely because the person concerned has not recovered the nationality of his Member State of origin. [58] It is, nevertheless, for the national court to determine whether, before such a decision withdrawing naturalisation takes effect, having regard to all the relevant circumstances, observance of *the principle of proportionality requires the person concerned to be afforded a reasonable period of time in order to try to recover the nationality of his Member State of origin*' (emphasis added).

[46] International law generally prohibits the making of persons stateless, which in turn limits the power of states to deprive single-country nationals of their nationality if it would render them stateless: see below in text.

According to the 1961 Convention on the Reduction of Statelessness (1961 Statelessness Convention), the only United Nations treaty where some rules on loss and deprivation of nationality are spelt out, there are various ways in which nationality may be lost or deprived. For example, one may lose one's nationality where the law entails loss of nationality as a consequence of a change in the personal status of a person such as marriage, termination of marriage, legitimation, recognition or adoption.[47] The 1961 Statelessness Convention adds that any loss of nationality as a consequence of any change in personal status shall be conditional upon possession or acquisition of another nationality.[48]

Nationality may also be lost through acquisition of another nationality, or through renunciation of nationality.[49] Renunciation of nationality is the voluntary act of giving up one's nationality for the purposes of acquiring another nationality. It is also called 'expatriation'.[50] Some countries may not allow or do not recognize renunciation of nationality or they may establish administrative procedures that make it impossible or very difficult to complete. Again, the 1961 Statelessness Convention, concerned with reducing the incidence of statelessness, imposes a number of safeguards on states parties to ensure that such loss shall be accompanied by the acquisition of another nationality.[51]

Deprivation of nationality, too, takes many forms. The 1961 Statelessness Convention recognizes that a state may deprive an individual of nationality, for example, because that nationality was acquired by fraud or misrepresentation, even where statelessness may result.[52] Disloyalty to the state or deprivation in the national interest are further permissible deprivations of nationality.[53]

---

[47] Art. 5, 1961 Statelessness Convention.

[48] Art. 5, 1961 Statelessness Convention provides: '1. If the law of a Contracting State entails loss of nationality as a consequence of any change in the personal status of a person such as marriage, termination of marriage, legitimation, recognition or adoption, such loss shall be conditional upon possession or acquisition of another nationality; 2. If, under the law of a Contracting State, a child born out of wedlock loses the nationality of that State in consequence of a recognition of affiliation, he shall be given an opportunity to recover that nationality by written application to the appropriate authority, and the conditions governing such application shall not be more rigorous than those laid down in paragraph 2 of Article 1 of this Convention.'

[49] Art. 7, 1961 Statelessness Convention.

[50] Weis, *Nationality and Statelessness in International Law*, pp. 115–17.

[51] Art. 7, 1961 Statelessness Convention.   [52] Art. 8, 1961 Statelessness Convention.

[53] Art. 8, 1961 Statelessness Convention. Note that for states parties to the Convention, they need to specify that they wish to retain the right to so deprive nationals of their nationality at the time of signature, ratification or accession (Art. 8(3)).

As already noted, a past trend of nationality being removed via acquisition of a new nationality has reduced in significance in many countries as dual and multiple nationality have become more accepted. It remains a form of deprivation in single nationality countries, although the administrative procedures around it will vary. Likewise, deprivation of nationality owing to criminal activities has reduced in at least Europe, although remains a practice in many other countries. Forms of deprivation that are not accepted under international law include the arbitrary or discriminatory deprivation of nationality, such as on grounds of race, ethnicity, religion or political views,[54] or, generally, deprivation resulting in statelessness (these are dealt with next in the section on limits on states' discretion). It remains widely accepted, however, that one's nationality can be removed in cases of fraud or other abuse of process, or if the person joins the military or diplomatic services of another state. These practices are permitted by the 1961 Statelessness Convention in certain circumstances, even where the person may be left stateless.[55]

Finally, nationality may be deprived via 'expiration'. This refers to circumstances where a citizen has taken up residence abroad and their nationality 'expires' after a specified number of years if their passport is either not renewed or the citizen does not return to reside in their country of nationality. This is still the practice in a few countries, but is not widely enforced.

1.3.3 The limits on state discretion in respect of nationality conferral and loss

It has long been held that decisions as to the conferral and loss of nationality are, in principle, a matter within the 'reserved domain' of municipal law, albeit one dependent on the development of international relations.[56] The 1930 Convention on Certain Questions Relating to the Conflict of

---

[54] See, e.g., Art. 9, 1961 Statelessness Convention. On gender discrimination as an arbitrary form of deprivation, see Chapter 7 by Govil and Edwards in this volume.

[55] Art. 8, 1961 Statelessness Convention. See, further, Chapter 8 by Brandvoll in this volume.

[56] *Nationality Decrees in Tunis and Morocco Opinion* (1923) Permanent Court of International Justice (PCIJ) Series B No. 4, 24: 'The question whether a certain matter is or is not solely within the domestic jurisdiction of a State is an essentially relative question; it depends upon the development of international relations. Thus, in the present state of international law, questions of nationality are, in the opinion of this Court, in principle within this reserved domain.' See, further, C. F. Amerasinghe, *Diplomatic Protection* (Oxford Monographs in International Law, 2008), at 4. See also *Nottebohm* above n. 2, at 23.

Nationality Laws (1930 Hague Convention) provided, for example, that: 'It is for each State to determine under its own law who are its nationals'[57] and further that: 'Any question as to whether a person possesses the nationality of a particular State shall be determined in accordance with the law of that State.'[58]

While largely deferring to municipal law, the Permanent Court of International Justice (PCIJ) in *Nationality Decrees in Tunis and Morocco* did acknowledge limits, derived from international law, on the discretion of states in this area:

> For the purpose of the present opinion, it is enough to observe that it may well happen that, in a matter which, like that of nationality, is not, in principle regulated by international law, the right of a State to use its discretion is nevertheless restricted by obligations which it may have undertaken towards other States. In such a case, jurisdiction which, in principle, belongs solely to the State, is limited by rules of international law.[59]

Similarly, the 1930 Hague Convention acknowledges the international law limits on the general rights of states in nationality matters:

> This law [of nationality] shall be recognised by other States in so far as it is consistent with international conventions, international custom, and the principles of law generally recognized with regard to nationality.[60]

One of the growth areas since the Second World War that has had an influence on nationality rights is that of human rights. There is an observable trend towards recognizing the right to nationality as a human right – and not only as a state's right – and it has been accepted that, in matters of nationality, states shall also take individual interests into account. Nationality not only links an individual to a state, it also links individuals to international law.[61]

For example, the Inter-American Court on Human Rights has advised that:

> Despite the fact that it is traditionally accepted that the conferral and recognition of nationality are matters for each State to decide, contemporary developments indicate that international law does impose certain limits

---

[57] Art. 1, 1930 Hague Convention.   [58] *Ibid.*, Art. 2.
[59] *Advisory Opinion No. 4, Nationality Decrees in Tunis and Morocco Opinion* (1923) PCIJ Series B No. 4, at p. 24.
[60] Article 1, 1930 Hague Convention.
[61] Bauböck, Ersbøll, Groenendijk and Waldrauch (eds.), *Acquisition and Loss of Nationality.*

on the broad powers enjoyed by the States in that area and that the manner in which States regulate matters bearing on nationality cannot today
be deemed to be within their sole jurisdiction: those powers of the State
are also circumscribed by their obligations to ensure the full protection
of human rights.[62]

So what are the limits imposed by international law?

Examples of some general principles of international law that are particularly relevant to nationality matters include the obligation not to inter-
fere in the domestic affairs of other states[63] and the right of every state 'to
exist and … to protect and preserve its existence.'[64] Spiro describes these
limits on state practice as when municipal matters impinge on the interests of other states by, for example, 'drawing their membership circles too
broadly – especially when they laid claim to individuals over whom other
States might establish better claims.'[65] The classic example of such interference would be the wholesale and automatic attribution of nationality
by one state over another state's nationals. According to Brownlie, such
situations would prima facie be violations of general principles of international law.[66] This general principle has also been codified in the international and regional laws on state succession.[67]

Apart from these general principles, a number of other limits on a state's
discretion in nationality matters derived either from general principles,
custom or treaty obligations include: (i) the prohibition on the arbitrary
deprivation of nationality; (ii) non-discrimination in nationality matters;
and (iii) the duty to avoid statelessness. These are summarized below.

First, the prohibition on the arbitrary deprivation of nationality is
considered a general principle of international law,[68] also reinforced in

---

[62] Inter-American Court of Human Rights, *Proposed Amendments to the Naturalization
Provision of the Political Constitution of Costa Rica*, Advisory Opinion OC-4/84 of 19
January 1984, Series A No. 4, para 32.

[63] See, e.g., UN General Assembly resolution 2131 (XX), 'Declaration on the Inadmissibility
of Intervention in the Domestic Affairs of States and the Protection of their Independence
and Sovereignty', adopted on 21 December 1965, by a vote of 109 votes to none, with one
abstention.

[64] Preparatory Study Concerning a Draft Declaration on the Rights and Duties of States
(Memo. Submitted by the Secretary-General), ILC, 1948, A/CN.4/2, cited in Brownlie,
'The Relations of Nationality in Public International Law', 295.

[65] P. J. Spiro, 'A New International Law of Citizenship', American Journal of International
Law, 105 (2011), 694, 698.

[66] Brownlie, 'The Relations of Nationality in Public International Law', 295.

[67] See Chapter 9 by Ziemele in this volume.

[68] See GA Res A/RES/50/152, Office of the United Nations High Commissioner for Refugees,
9 February 1996, para. 15, referring to the prohibition of arbitrary deprivation as a fundamental principle of international law.

international human rights law.[69] The Secretary-General's report confirms that states must comply with their human rights obligations when granting nationality.[70] The arbitrary deprivation of nationality generally refers to the withdrawal by the state of a citizen's nationality where it does not serve a legitimate purpose, comply with the principle of proportionality and that is otherwise incompatible with international law.[71]

Second, nationality laws must not be discriminatory. Related to arbitrariness, non-discrimination in nationality laws is a general principle of international law underpinned by many international conventions. Article 9 of the 1961 Statelessness Convention, for example, prohibits the deprivation of nationality on racial, ethnic, religious or political grounds. Likewise, Article 5(d)(iii) of the 1965 Convention on the Elimination of Racial Discrimination provides that depriving someone of their nationality on the basis of race, colour, descent, or national or ethnic origin, is a breach of a state's obligations under the Convention. Moreover, the prohibition on racial discrimination is considered a *jus cogens* norm of international law.[72]

---

[69] Art. 15, UDHR. Relevant provisions in other international human rights instruments include Convention on the Rights of Persons with Disabilities, 13 December 2006, in force 3 May 2008, 2515 UNTS 3, Art. 18(1)(a). According to this treaty, states parties shall ensure that disabled persons are not deprived of their nationality arbitrarily or on the basis of their disability. American Convention on Human Rights (ACHR), 22 November 1969, in force 18 July 1978, OAS Treaty Series No. 36, Art. 20; Arab Charter on Human Rights (adopted 22 May 2004, entered into force 15 March 2008), Art. 29; Commonwealth of Independent States Convention on Human Rights and Fundamental Freedoms, 26 May 1995, in force 11 August 1998, Art. 24. It is worth noting that neither the European Convention on Human Rights nor the African Charter on Human and Peoples' Rights includes the right to a nationality and not to be arbitrarily deprived of it.

[70] See Report of the Secretary-General to the General Assembly, 'Human rights and arbitrary deprivation of nationality', A/HRC/13/34 (14 December 2009), para. 20.

[71] On the meaning of 'arbitrary interference', see, e.g., HRC General Comment No. 16, 'Right to respect of privacy, home, correspondence, and protection of honour and reputation (Article 17)', para. 4: 'In the Committee's view the expression "arbitrary interference" can also extend to interference provided for under the law. The introduction of the concept of arbitrariness is intended to guarantee that even interference provided for by law should be in accordance with the provisions, aims and objectives of the Covenant and should be, in any event, reasonable in the particular circumstances.' In its jurisprudence on the deprivation of liberty, the Human Rights Committee explains that the concept of 'arbitrariness' is 'not to be equated [only] with the law, but must be interpreted more broadly to include elements of inappropriateness, injustice and lack of predictability'. See, inter alia, *Van Alphen* v. *The Netherlands* HRC, Comm. No. 305/1988, 23 July 1990, para. 5.8.

[72] See, e.g., *South West Africa Cases (Liberia* v. *South Africa; Ethiopia* v. *South Africa)* 1962 ICJ Rep. 319.

The 1957 United Nations Convention on the Nationality of Married Women and the 1979 Convention on the Elimination of All Forms of Discrimination against Women (CEDAW) also provide that gender discrimination in nationality matters is prohibited. Article 9 of the CEDAW provides that: '[States] shall ensure in particular that neither marriage to an alien nor change of nationality by the husband during marriage shall automatically change the nationality of the wife, render her stateless or force upon her the nationality of the husband.' Gender-discriminatory nationality laws have been held in a range of jurisdictions to be unlawful under international law,[73] and this form of prohibited discrimination in nationality laws is increasingly acknowledged by international law.[74]

The third area imposing limits on states' discretion in the conferment or loss of nationality is the duty to prevent or reduce statelessness. Nationality and statelessness are intimately interlinked. In fact, the duty to prevent statelessness has been described as a negative right arising from the right to nationality.[75] Gaps in nationality laws or their incomplete or discriminatory application, for example, can lead to statelessness. Statelessness is the fact of having no nationality recognized by any state under the operation of its laws.[76] As a matter of international relations and international law regarding diplomatic protection, Spiro has aptly

---

[73] See, e.g., *The Attorney General of Botswana* v. *Unity Dow*, High Court of Botswana, 1995 (which highlighted how a range of women's human rights with regard to child custody, personal travel and freedom of movement, as well as the child's rights relating to health, education and child support in the country of the mother's nationality, can be undermined when a woman cannot transmit her nationality to her children because of the nationality of their father); *Genovese* v. *Malta*, Application no. 53124/09, Council of Europe: European Court of Human Rights, 11 October 2011 (which found that Maltese provisions discriminated on the basis of descent and being born out of wedlock and thus in violation of Article 14 in conjunction with Article 8 of the ECHR).

[74] Human Rights Council resolution 10/13, Human rights and arbitrary deprivation of nationality, 26 March 2009, paras 2 and 3. For more on gender discrimination in nationality matters, see Chapter 7 by Govil and Edwards in this volume.

[75] J. Blackman, 'State Succession and Statelessness: The Emerging Right to an Effective Nationality under International Law', *Michigan Journal of International Law*, 19 (1998), 1141–94, at 1176.

[76] 'Stateless person' is defined in the 1954 Convention relating to the Status of Stateless Persons as 'a person who is not considered as a national by any State under the operation of its laws', and this definition has been accepted as reflecting customary international law: see p. 49 of the ILC's Articles on Diplomatic Protection with commentaries, 2006, in which it is noted that the definition of 'stateless person' in Article 1 of the 1954 Convention is 'no doubt [to] be considered as having acquired a customary nature'.

described statelessness as 'challenging the international legal system by creating a class of individuals for whose conduct no State would stand responsible, thereby presenting, in theory at least, a gap in the enforceability of international law'.[77] The consequences of having no nationality for stateless persons themselves, as well as for states, are well-known and documented elsewhere in this book.[78]

Provisions on statelessness and its avoidance, prevention and reduction, as well as on the protection of stateless persons, permeate international agreements relating to nationality matters. The 1930 Hague Convention, for example, permits a woman to be deprived of her nationality upon marrying a foreigner *only* when she acquires the nationality of her husband.[79] Likewise the Hague Convention contains safeguards against statelessness in the case of children.[80] The key international and regional instruments governing state formation and succession likewise contain provisions that guard against statelessness.[81] The 1961 Statelessness Convention is dedicated entirely to the reduction of statelessness.

The low, albeit growing, membership of the 1961 Statelessness Convention may argue against an across-the-board acceptance of the proposition that the prevention of statelessness has emerged as a general principle of international law.[82] On the other hand, it has been argued that the underlying principles in the 1961 Statelessness Convention are generally reflected in state practice,[83] even in non-states parties. A global example of near-universal state practice is the Convention on the Rights of the Child, which specifically addresses statelessness in

---

[77] Spiro, 'A New International Law of Citizenship', 709.
[78] See also L. van Waas, *Nationality Matters: Statelessness under International Law* (Antwerp/Oxford/Portland, OR: Intersentia, 2008).
[79] Art. 8, 1930 Hague Convention.
[80] Art. 13, 1930 Hague Convention provided that if a child does not acquire the new nationality of his or her parents in the context of their naturalization, they were to retain their original nationality. See also Article 13 of the 1937 Convention on Certain Questions Relating to the Conflict of Nationality Law, 13 April 1930, League of Nations, Treaty Series, vol. 179, p. 89, No. 4137.
[81] See Report of the Secretary-General to the General Assembly, 'Human rights and arbitrary deprivation of nationality', A/HRC/13/34 (14 December 2009), paras 47–55; International Law Commission, 'Articles on Nationality of Natural Persons in Relation to the Succession of States (With Commentaries)', Supplement No. 10 (A/54/10) (3 April 1999). See also Chapter 9 by Ziemele in this volume.
[82] At the time of writing, there were only fifty-five states parties to the 1961 Statelessness Convention.
[83] See, e.g., Chapter 3 by van Waas in this volume.

children. Likewise, a number of regional treaties reinforce the obligation on states to grant nationality if the person would otherwise be stateless.[84] These trends indicate that the duty to prevent statelessness, at least in respect of children, is emerging as a norm of customary international law.

In sum, nationality rules are domestic matters only in so far as international law (including general principles, custom or international agreements) does not regulate the practice to the contrary, and as long as domestic rules do not otherwise conflict with international law.

1.4. Substantive content of nationality

Having explained the basic rules relating to the acquisition and loss of nationality (or what this chapter has termed the 'procedural aspects' of nationality), this section will now explore whether there is a 'substantive' content of nationality – both from a state's perspective (and thus from the perspective of international law) and from the national's perspective (and from the perspective of individual human rights). Are there any shared substantive aspects of nationality across jurisdictions? Is the state obliged under international law to provide certain rights to its nationals if they hold its nationality? What happens if such rights are not provided? Does this mean that the individuals are not nationals, or only that they have

---

[84] See, e.g., Article 20 of the 1969 American Convention on Human Rights, which provides that every person has a right to a nationality, no one should be arbitrarily deprived of nationality, and a person has the right to the nationality of the state of birth if otherwise stateless. See, too, Inter-American Court of Human Rights, *Dilcia Yean and Violeta Bosico* v. *Dominican Republic*, Judgment of 8 September 2005, Series C No. 130, which held that although states have the sovereign right to regulate nationality, they are responsible for abiding by international human rights standards protecting individuals against arbitrary state action. States are particularly limited in their discretion to grant nationality, the Court held, by their obligations to guarantee equal protection before the law and to prevent, avoid and reduce statelessness. Article 6(3) and (4) of the 1990 African Charter on the Rights and Welfare of the Child contains a similar principle of acquisition of the nationality of the state of birth in cases where there would otherwise be statelessness. The 1997 European Convention on Nationality indicates as a general rule that statelessness shall be avoided, with steps outlined in specific articles on how to ensure statelessness does not occur. This instrument stipulates that after a maximum period of ten years of lawful residence, an individual who was neither born in the state nor descended from a national must be given the opportunity to apply for naturalization, thus potentially facilitating the reduction of statelessness for those who cannot acquire a nationality otherwise. The Convention on the Avoidance of Statelessness in relation to State Succession adopted by the Council of Europe in 2006 is devoted in its entirety to the problem of statelessness.

been deprived of certain rights? The question whether there is a minimum core 'substantive' content of nationality under international law is complex, and has been related to the definition of a 'stateless person'.[85] The answer is far from settled.

1.4.1   The state's perspective

When the concept of nationality was first conceived, it was intended to regulate relationships among and between sovereign states.[86] Only later with developments in international human rights law did its individual dimensions emerge, as discussed next. In the seminal work by Paul Weis of 1979 two functions of nationality under international law are identified: (i) the right of diplomatic protection and (ii) the duty of (re-)admission and residence.[87] Both are claimed as rights and duties of the state, albeit the former is seen as a discretionary right of the state, while the latter has been historically considered primarily a duty exercisable vis-à-vis other states, rather than towards a state's own nationals. The latter is no longer, however, viewed as only a question of states' rights, as it is matched by the international human right of individuals to return to their own country from abroad and to reside there (see below). In understanding the content (and thus whether there is a minimum core content) of the right to nationality under international law, it is important to understand these two components. While this chapter focuses only on these two main aspects of nationality, other authors have argued that there are additional components.[88]

---

[85] The question of whether the right to a nationality has a 'minimum core content' arose during UNHCR's consultations on the status of a stateless person and whether the concept of 'effective nationality' is helpful to that definition: UNHCR, 'Summary Conclusions – Expert Meeting – The Concept of Stateless Persons under International Law ("Prato Conclusions")' (May 2010).

[86] J. Chan, 'The Right to a Nationality as a Human Right: The Current Trend Towards Recognition', Human Rights Law Journal, 12 (1991), 1–14, at 1.

[87] Weis, Nationality and Statelessness in International Law.

[88] Shearer, for example, refers to seven aspects of nationality. In addition to those covered by this chapter, he includes: state responsibility for nationals; allegiance; right to refuse extradition; determination of enemy status in wartime; and exercise of jurisdiction: I. A. Shearer, Starke's International Law, 11th edn (London: Butterworths, 1994), 309. Some of these are challengeable as components of nationality. See Boll, 'Nationality and Obligations of Loyalty in International and Municipal Law', who argues that 'allegiance' or obligation of loyalty is not a concept and principle of international law, but one of municipal law. Others would be subsumed under procedural aspects of the right to nationality.

(i) Diplomatic protection

'Diplomatic protection' is generally described as a right of the state to intervene on behalf of its own nationals if their rights are violated by another state for the purpose of obtaining redress.[89] As the PCIJ stated in *Mavrommatis*:

> [Diplomatic protection] is an elementary principle of international law that a State is entitled to protect its subjects, when injured by acts contrary to international law committed by another State, from whom they have been unable to obtain satisfaction through ordinary channels.[90]

The power of the state is far-reaching, and 'involves the resort to all forms of diplomatic intervention for the settlement of disputes, both amicable and non-amicable, from diplomatic negotiations and good offices to the use of force'.[91] In the first instance, diplomatic protection is exercisable vis-à-vis one's own nationals. As the PCIJ noted in *Panevezys-Saldutiskis Railway*:

> This right [of diplomatic protection] is necessarily limited to intervention on behalf of its own nationals because, in the absence of a special agreement, it is the bond of nationality between the State and the individual which alone confers upon the State the right to diplomatic protection …[92]

The only arguable exception to this nationality link is in relation to refugees and stateless persons, where it is asserted that a state may exercise diplomatic protection on their behalf in the absence of any other state. This position is supported by the ILC's Articles on Diplomatic

---

[89] See Art. 2, 2006 Articles on Diplomatic Protection: 'A State has the right to exercise diplomatic protection in accordance with the present draft articles'. For a comprehensive review of diplomatic protection, see Amerasinghe, *Diplomatic Protection* (who identifies seven basic elements of diplomatic protection, pp. 25–7).

[90] *Mavrommatis Palestine Concessions (Greece v. U.K.)*, 1924 PCIJ (ser. B) No. 3 (August 30), at p. 12.

[91] *Barcelona Traction Case* (Judgment), ICJ Reports, 1970, p. 3, at p. 44, which concerned the question of the protection of a corporate entity: 'The Court would have to observe that, within the limits prescribed by international law, a State may exercise diplomatic protection by whatever means and to whatever extent it thinks fit, for it is its own right that a State is asserting …'. In the literature on the use of force, this practice is sometimes referred to as 'humanitarian intervention', or a separate feature of that, including as part of the right of self-defence: see F. K. Abiew, *The Evolution of the Doctrine and Practice of Humanitarian Intervention* (The Hague: Kluwer Law International, 1990), 30–59; Boll, *Multiple Nationality and International Law*, 135–6.

[92] *Panevezys-Saldutiskis Railway (Estonia v. Lithuania)*, 1938 PCIJ (ser. A/B) No. 76 (February 28), 16.

Protection – Article 2(3) read together with Article 8 – providing that a state may exercise diplomatic protection on behalf of lawfully and habitually resident refugees or stateless persons,[93] although in respect of refugees, a state cannot exercise diplomatic protection as against the refugee's state of nationality. This position is based on policy considerations such that 'Most refugees have serious complaints about their treatment at the hand of their State of nationality, from which they have fled to avoid persecution. To allow diplomatic protection in such cases would be to open the floodgates for international litigation. Moreover, the fear of demands for such action by refugees might deter States from accepting refugees.'[94]

While diplomatic protection, therefore, has an individual dimension in so far as it is an intervention on behalf of a national, the ICJ in *Nottebohm* clarified that ultimately 'Diplomatic protection and protection by means of judicial proceedings constitute measures for *the defence of the right of the State*.'[95] According to the ICJ, it is not, however, an unlimited discretion. It is worth outlining the facts of the case before moving to the Court's position on diplomatic protection.

Friedrich Nottebohm, a continuous resident of Guatemala since 1905 at aged 24, acquired Liechtenstein citizenship at the outbreak of the Second World War in 1939. By doing so, he lost his German citizenship automatically. Guatemala, treating him as a German citizen, extradited him to the United States during the war and confiscated his property. After the war, Liechtenstein sought to challenge these actions on Nottebohm's behalf. The issue before the Court was whether Liechtenstein, Nottebohm's state of nationality, could exercise diplomatic protection on his behalf vis-à-vis Guatemala, which objected to Liechtenstein's overtures. A majority of the ICJ did not accept that the nationality Liechtenstein had conferred on Nottebohm could validly be invoked against Guatemala for the purpose of diplomatic protection, and held instead that both Nottebohm and Liechtenstein had sought to circumvent the laws of war through the loose international rules relating to nationality.[96] In making its findings, the Court examined the basis of Nottebohm's nationality and held, in the oft-quoted passage, that nationality is 'a legal bond having as its basis a

---

[93] International Law Commission, Articles on Diplomatic Protection (2006).

[94] International Law Commission, 'Commentary on the Draft Articles on Diplomatic Protection' (2006), 51.

[95] *Nottebohm* above n. 2, 15–16 (my emphasis).

[96] *Nottebohm* above n. 2, 26. See also Robert D. Sloane, 'Breaking the Genuine Link: The Contemporary International Legal Regulation of Nationality', *Harvard International Law Review* 50 (2009), 11.

social fact of attachment, a genuine connection of existence, interests and sentiments, together with the existence of reciprocal rights and duties'.[97] Finding that Nottebohm did not enjoy such attachments to Liechtenstein, Liechtenstein was denied the right to exercise diplomatic protection on his behalf. This judgment confirmed that diplomatic protection is a right of the state vis-à-vis another state, rather than an individual's right, but it also clarified that legal nationality is a necessary but not sufficient criterion for one's state of nationality to exercise diplomatic protection on one's behalf.

Whether a similar decision would be rendered today is not clear and certainly worth asking. In the background to this case were the exceptional post-war circumstances in which, as synthesized by Rubenstein and Lenagh-Maguire in their chapter in this book:

> In the Court's view neither Nottebohm nor Liechtenstein had acted unlawfully, but Liechtenstein had granted citizenship 'without regard to the concept of nationality adopted in international relations'. While Liechtenstein was entitled to do so, Guatemala did not need to recognise that citizenship as effective nationality for the purposes of providing Nottebohm with diplomatic protection.[98]

In one way the case says nothing more than the international/domestic rules relating to nationality are inferior to the laws of war and international relations. This decision thus permitted the alleged violating state (here Guatemala) from recognizing the right of claim to diplomatic protection from the aggrieved state (here Liechtenstein), even where there was no competing state of nationality (Nottebohm was no longer a German national). The ICJ held that the alleged violating state is immune from the overtures of diplomatic protection if a 'genuine and effective link' has not been established.[99] The ICJ held in essence that 'Guatemala is under no obligation to recognize a nationality granted in such circumstances'.[100] The 'circumstances' in question, according to Sloane, were those of an abuse of diplomatic relations between states.[101]

---

[97] *Nottebohm* above n. 2, 23.   [98] Footnotes omitted.

[99] The final sentence in the judgment is instructive here: Nottebohm acquired Liechtenstein's nationality 'to substitute for his status as a national of a belligerent State that of a national of a neutral State, with the sole aim of thus coming within the protection of Liechtenstein.' *Nottebohm*, above n. 2, at 26.

[100] *Nottebohm* above n. 2, 26.

[101] Sloane, 'Breaking the Genuine Link', Sloane also refers to the case of *Flegenheimer (US v. Italy)*, 14 R.I.A.A. 327 (Italian-US Concil. Comm'n. 1958) to confirm that at the essence

The case also reveals a distinction between national laws on nationality and their consequences under international law. As a matter of international law, the case appears to establish that nationality in the form of diplomatic protection is only exercisable as a state's right if it is conferred based on 'social attachment'. As a matter of the national law of Liechtenstein, Nottebohm was considered a lawful citizen, irrespective of whether he had ever lived in Liechtenstein. For purposes other than diplomatic protection, such as if Guatemala sought to deport him to Liechtenstein, it would be interesting to see if his nationality stood the test. I suspect that the ICJ would find that Liechtenstein is obligated to readmit him, given that he held no other nationality.

The case has been widely criticized[102] and (in part) rejected by the ILC's Articles on Diplomatic Protection, which recognize nationality per se as subject to the laws of the conferring state without mention of the 'genuine and effective link' test established in *Nottebhohm*.[103] Critics of *Nottebohm* have stated that if followed, hundreds of thousands of foreign nationals living or doing business abroad could be deprived of diplomatic protection.[104]

Conversely, where a state has an inadequate interest in the grievance of one of its nationals, it is unlikely to exercise diplomatic protection. There is also a limited right of challenge by the national concerned. This has been confirmed in a number of recent terrorism-related cases. In the cases of *R (Abbasi)* and *Al Rawi and Others*, for example, the United Kingdom's Court of Appeal held that human rights imperatives do not open the executive's conduct of foreign affairs to review under ordinary administrative law principles.[105] The Supreme Court of Canada held similarly in *Omar Khadr* v. *The Prime Minister of Canada*. While holding that the constitutional rights of Khadr, a fifteen-year-old boy held in Guantanamo Bay, had been violated, it stopped short of ordering the government to seek Khadr's return to Canada from Guantanamo Bay (in other words, the government was not obliged to render diplomatic protection).[106] Each of these cases reaffirms Weis' description of diplomatic protection as 'not a legal right, but an extraordinary legal remedy'.[107]

of the judgment in *Nottebohm* is an equality of arms between states, rather than the focus on the 'effective and genuine link', which he claims was in fact mostly *dicta*.

[102] L. F. E. Goldie, 'The Critical Date', *Int'l and Comp. L. Qty*, 12 (1963), 1251; Sloane, 'Breaking the Genuine Link'.

[103] ILC, 'Articles on Diplomatic Protection with Commentaries' (2006), 32–3.

[104] Sloane, 'Breaking the Genuine Link'.

[105] *R (Abbasi)* [2003] UKHRR 76 and *Al Rawi and Others* [2006] HRLR 42.

[106] *Canada (Prime Minister)* v. *Khadr* [2010] 1 SCR 44.

[107] Weis, *Nationality and Statelessness in International Law*, 34.

An exception to the generally held view that diplomatic protection remains an unchallengeable discretion of the state is found in South Africa's Constitutional Court's judgment in *Kaunda*. While accepting the general principle that there is no individual right to diplomatic protection, the Constitutional Court held nonetheless that the decision not to intervene is an act subject to judicial review as an exercise of public power.[108]

As to new developments, Article 19 of the ILC's Articles on Diplomatic Protection declares that a state entitled to exercise diplomatic protection 'should ... give due consideration to the possibility of exercising diplomatic protection, especially when a significant injury has occurred'.[109] While it is too early to suggest that there has been any change in the international legal position on diplomatic protection, South Africa's Constitutional Court's judgment subjecting such decisions to judicial review, plus the ILC's appeal to states to give due consideration to exercising diplomatic protection (even if not mandatory), hint that the future of diplomatic protection may look different to the strict parameters of *Nottebohm*. Only time will tell.

Finally, diplomatic protection needs to be contrasted with the right to consular assistance, which imposes certain obligations in the case of an arrest or detention of a foreign national, in order to guarantee the inalienable right to counsel and due process through consular notification and effective access to consular protection.[110] Individuals have the right to seek consular assistance from their country of nationality and governments are required to provide it. Likewise, access to one's own government officials cannot generally be denied by the host country.[111]

(ii)   The duty of (re)admission and residence

The second function of nationality from a state's perspective is the right – or duty – to readmit its nationals to its territory. Based on the 'territorial supremacy of States', van Panhuys noted that 'The duty to admit nationals

---

[108] *Kaunda* v. *President of the Republic of South Africa* 2005 (4) South African Law Reports 235 (CC), ILM vol. 44 (2005), p. 173.

[109] International Law Commission, 'Commentary on the Draft Articles on Diplomatic Protection' (2006), 29–30.

[110] The distinction between 'diplomatic protection' and 'consular assistance' is an important one. The latter is regulated by Article 36 of the 1963 Vienna Convention on Consular Relations, 596 UNTS 261.

[111] See International Court of Justice, *Avena and Other Mexican Nationals (Mexico* v. *United States of America)*, 31 March 2004, ICJ Reports 2004, 12. The exception to the general rule is likely to be where the states have no diplomatic relations.

[and to allow their residence] is considered so important a consequence of nationality that it is almost equated with it.'[112] As explained by Weis:

> As between national and State of nationality the question of the right of sojourn is not a question of international law. It may, however, become a question bearing on the relations between States. The expulsion of nationals forces other States to admit aliens, but, according to the accepted principles of international law, the admission of aliens is in the discretion of each State – except where a State is bound by treaty to accord such admission.[113]

Weis also points out the exceptions to this general rule, such as expulsion of nationals in connection with conviction for a crime.[114] States can only expel their nationals in cooperation with and with the consent of the receiving state. Meanwhile, the state of nationality is under a duty towards other states to receive back its expelled nationals to its territory.[115] The duty of readmission of one's nationals is thus an obligation of states vis-à-vis other states under international law. It is also clearly one of the defining features of nationality as a matter of international law.

But what if (re)admission is denied? Whether denying a national readmission to his or her state of nationality would consequently lead to the position that the person is no longer considered as a national under international law (provided he or she has no other nationality) will depend on the facts of the case at hand. It could, for example, be indicative of the loss of nationality and that the person is *de jure* stateless (provided he or she has no other nationality). This is to be distinguished from the situation described later in this section (relating to the United Kingdom) whereby a person is recognized as being a national by a particular country but is 'merely' denied the right to reside in certain parts of the territory. Readmission could still take place to the territory of the state, but to certain parts of it, which are within the discretion of the state of nationality. Clearly, too, the ability to readmit one's nationals is an essential exercise of statehood. Likewise, the granting of nationality is linked to the Montevideo Convention criterion of a permanent population.[116]

---

[112] Van Panhuys, 56.

[113] Weis, *Nationality and Statelessness in International Law*, 45.

[114] *Ibid.*

[115] Van Panhuys 55, 56; Weis, *Nationality and Statelessness in International Law*, 46. See, for an early example, Havana Convention on the Status of Aliens, 20 February 1925, OAS Treaty Series No. 34, in force 29 August 1929, Art. 6: 'States are required to receive their nationals expelled from foreign soil who seek to enter their territory'.

[116] Article 1, Convention on the Rights and Duties of States: Montevideo, 26 December 1933, in force 26 December 1934, LoN-3802. See P. Weil, 'Access to Citizenship: A Comparison

Developments in international human rights law confirm the duty of readmission on the state as also being a right of the individual, not least Article 12 of the ICCPR, which prohibits the arbitrary deprivation of the right to re-enter one's country, and equivalent provisions in regional treaties.[117] At the same time, human rights law has arguably extended the obligation of readmission further than the public international legal duty to readmit one's *own nationals*. Human rights case law suggests that this duty is to be exercisable also in favour of habitual residents.[118] In *Stewart* v. *Canada*, for example, the UN Human Rights Committee held that Stewart, a habitual resident of Canada, had the right to re-enter Canada owing to his long residence there and that Canada was considered his 'own country' for the purposes of the right of return.[119] This case directly challenges the exclusivity of nationality and its link with readmission and residence, and, together with the Committee's General Comment No. 27, extends the right of (re)admission and residence to a specific category of long-staying non-nationals. Although this case does not undermine the duty of states to readmit their own nationals, it does appear to extend that duty to other country's nationals, as well as stateless and other persons in specific circumstances.[120] The 1951 Convention relating to the Status of Refugees and the 1954 Convention relating to

---

of Twenty-five Nationality Laws', in A. T. Aleinikoff and D. Kluysmeyer (eds.), *Citizenship Today: Global Perspectives and Practices* (Washington, D.C.: Carnegie Endowment for Peace, 2001), 17–35, at 17 (who argues that 'If territory determines the geographical limits of state sovereignty, nationality determines its population'). In contrast, Crawford states that: 'Nationality is … dependent on statehood, not the reverse': J. Crawford, *The Creation of States in International Law* (Oxford: Clarendon Press, 1979), 40.

[117] See Art. 12: '2. Everyone shall be free to leave any country, including his own; 3. The above-mentioned rights shall not be subject to any restrictions except those which are provided by law, are necessary to protect national security, public order (ordre public), public health or morals or the rights and freedoms of others, and are consistent with the other rights recognized in the present Covenant; 4. No one shall be arbitrarily deprived of the right to enter his own country.' See also Protocol 4 of the ECHR, for example, which provides: 'No one shall be deprived of the right to enter the territory of the State of which he is a national' (Art. 3(2)).

[118] See, for example, *Nystrom* v. *Australia*, Human Rights Committee, CCPR/C/102/D/1557/2007.

[119] *Stewart* v. *Canada*, Human Rights Committee, CCPR/C/58/D/538/1993 (1996) See Chapter 11 by Rubenstein and Lenagh-Maguire in this volume.

[120] UN Human Rights Committee, CCPR General Comment No. 27, Freedom of movement, CCPR/C/21/Rev.1/Add.9, 2 November 1999, which includes: nationals of a country who have been stripped of their nationality in violation of international law; individuals whose country of nationality has been incorporated in or transferred to another national entity whose nationality is being denied them; and other categories of long-term residents, including but not limited to stateless persons arbitrarily deprived of their right to acquire the nationality of the country of such residence.

the Status of Stateless persons arguably reiterate this position, implicitly requiring states parties to readmit refugees and stateless persons to whom they have issued Convention Travel Documents, pursuant to Article 28 of each instrument.[121]

1.4.2   Individual right to a nationality

As a citizen/national, an individual is recognized as a full member of the state, with all its attendant rights and obligations to be enjoyed in full equality and without discrimination. As noted in the introduction to this chapter, citizens also bear the burden of duties, including specifically those relating to military service, the payment of taxes and to participate in public life.

In contrast, non-nationals, including stateless persons, 'often have minimal, if any, access to the kind of basic political and social rights that most citizens take for granted'.[122] Their residency is dependent on municipal laws, including immigration rules and requirements, and they do not always have the right to leave and return at will.[123] Contrary to the aspiration of international human rights law that all rights apply to everyone by virtue of their shared humanity, and regardless of their nationality, there are multiple junctures in which distinctions between nationals and non-nationals are permitted.[124] Clearly, political rights, including the right to vote, to run for elections and to hold public office, which can be exclusively reserved for citizens, are important distinctions.[125] The range of economic, social and cultural rights provided by international human rights law can also be variously restricted under human rights law.[126] Distinctions between nationals and non-nationals are also at times legally permitted where, for example, they 'serve a legitimate State objective and

---

[121] Art. 28, 1951 Convention relating to the Status of Refugees, 189 UNTS 150; Art. 28, 1954 Convention relating to the Status of Stateless Persons.

[122] UNHCR, 'The World's Stateless – Questions and Answers' (2004), 4.

[123] Lawfully staying stateless persons are entitled to a Convention Travel Document, per Art. 28, 1954 Convention, for the purposes of travel abroad.

[124] See General Assembly Declaration on the Rights of Peoples who are not Nationals of the Country in which they Live, UN Doc. 40/144, 13 December 1985. For further discussion of the treatment of non-nationals under international law and in international relations, see: A. Edwards and C. Ferstman (eds.), *Human Security and Non-Citizens: Law, Policy and International Affairs* (Cambridge University Press, 2009); van Waas, *Nationality Matters*.

[125] See, e.g., Article 25, ICCPR.

[126] See, e.g., Article 2(3), ICESCR. 1966 International Covenant on Economic, Social and Cultural Rights, New York, 16 December 1966, in force 3 January 1976, 993 UNTS 3.

are proportional to the achievement of that objective'.[127] It is also accepted that some rights can be limited depending on the category of the non-national.[128]

In practice, differential treatment between nationals and non-nationals occurs for many reasons, mostly around non-implementation of obligations. Many governments, for example, have not domesticated fully their international human rights obligations or they reserve rights only for nationals. Many national constitutions regulate the relationship between the sovereign and its citizens only. Some countries also continue to recognize different citizenship categories, or limit rights depending on how nationality was acquired. Some countries because of historical reasons have various categories of nationality with differing names and associated rights.[129] The United Kingdom, for example, distinguishes between a number of different categories of 'British national', based on its historical imperial power and its many overseas territories, not all of whom enjoy the right of abode in the United Kingdom.[130] The United States of America does not allow citizens to run for president unless they were born in the territory.[131] In parts of the Middle East and Africa, long waiting periods are imposed on those having naturalized before they can exercise political rights.[132] For the purposes of both municipal and international law, these persons are considered to be citizens of their countries of nationality, even though they do not enjoy equal rights. In an ideal world, such differences in citizenship categories would be removed entirely.

---

[127] D. Weissbrodt, *The Human Rights of Non-citizens* (Oxford University Press, 2008), at 45.
[128] Such limits can be imposed on the right to freedom of movement as it applies only to persons lawfully in the territory: Art. 12, ICCPR, provided that such restrictions do not amount to arbitrary deprivation of liberty: Art. 9, ICCPR.
[129] UNHCR, 'Handbook on Protection of Stateless Persons under the 1954 Convention relating to the Status of Stateless Persons' (Geneva, 2014), para. 52.
[130] For more, see L. Fransman Q.C., *British Nationality Law*, 3rd edn (West Sussex: Bloomsbury Publishing, 2011).
[131] Article II, Constitution of the United States of America: The President must be a natural-born citizen of the United States or a citizen at the time of the adoption of the Constitution, at least thirty-five years old and a resident of the United States for at least fourteen years.
[132] On Africa, see B. Manby, *Struggles for Citizenship in Africa* (London: Zed Books, 2009). In the Middle East, Kuwait's nationality law provides for a thirty-year waiting period after naturalization before a person has the right to vote in parliamentary elections, plus determines that naturalized persons cannot (ever) stand as a candidate or be appointed to membership of any parliamentary body (Article 6 of the law). In Jordan, a naturalized national has a five-year wait before being eligible for nomination to a municipal council

In practice, too, the circumstances of stateless persons are a clear example of the very real problems faced by persons who live with no nationality. Stateless persons are politically, socially and culturally marginalized. '[N]ationality is [thus still] critical to full participation in society',[133] both as a matter of law and as a pragmatic fact. The case of dual or multiple nationality also supports the view that: 'The link between the State and the individual that is defined by nationality is still a supreme one, if perhaps no longer an all-encompassing one.'[134] So while international human rights law articulates the basic rights all persons are entitled to enjoy, *regardless* of their nationality, there are still some key rights linked to nationality.

While there is no list of rights to which a national may appeal, it is possible to indicate that there are a number of rights generally associated with holding a nationality by drawing on international human rights norms, summarized as:

- the right to leave one's 'own country' and to re-enter and reside permanently in the territory of the state of one's nationality;[135]
- the right to consular assistance (as discussed earlier), at page 35;
- the right to vote and participate in public life,[136] although, as noted, even here there are some exceptions depending on the type of nationality held; and
- rights to economic, social and cultural advancement.[137]

But what does such a list mean for persons who do not have access to or enjoy these rights in full equality and without discrimination? UNHCR summarized its position on this question in its Handbook on Protection of Stateless Persons:

> Generally, at a minimum, [nationality] status **will be associated with** the right of entry, re-entry and residence in the State's territory but there may be situations where, for historical reasons, entry is only permitted to a non-metropolitan territory belonging to a State. The fact that different categories of nationality within a State have different rights associated with them does not prevent their holders from being treated as a 'national' for

or trade union office and a ten-year wait for eligibility to a political or diplomatic position or any public office prescribed by the Council of Ministers or a member of the state council (Article 14).

[133] CEDAW, General Recommendation No. 21: Equality in Marriage and Family Relations (1994), at 2.

[134] Boll, *Multiple Nationality*, 12.

[135] See n. 117 above.   [136] Art. 25, ICCPR.

[137] See Weissbrodt, *The Human Rights of Non-citizens*, at Ch. 4. See, further, Edwards and Ferstman, *Human Security and Non-Citizens*.

the purposes of Article 1(1) [of the 1954 Convention relating to the Status of Stateless Persons]. Nor does the fact that in some countries the rights associated with nationality are fewer than those enjoyed by nationals of other States or indeed fall short of those required in terms of international human rights obligations. Although the issue of diminished rights may raise issues regarding the effectiveness of the nationality and violations of international human rights obligations, this is not pertinent to the application of the stateless person definition in the 1954 Convention.[138]

While UNHCR's position was developed in relation to the phrase 'not being a national of any State' for the purposes of identifying who is stateless and who is not, a similar approach ought to be taken in relation to more general questions about nationality, not least to ensure consistency in international law. Even though the above-mentioned substantive rights are usually associated with the holding of nationality, the lack of access to or enjoyment of these rights does not change the nationality status of the individual under international law, nor ordinarily under municipal law. Such an approach would also appear consistent with the ICJ's position: the ICJ in *Nottebohm* did not question Mr. Nottebohm's Liechtenstein nationality, even as they decided Liechtenstein was not entitled to exercise diplomatic protection on the basis of that nationality.

The only possible exception may be the case where a state denies an individual of the right to enter, re-enter and reside in its territory (considered as the essence of nationality as a matter of public international law), which could be interpreted as that state effectively denying that the individual is its national. However, this could only be determined on the individual case at hand and considering all the relevant facts. Overall, while different national laws may recognize different categories of citizenship or provide different levels of rights to its various citizens compared to another country, for international law purposes, there are only two relevant categories: being a national or being (*de jure*) stateless.[139]

1.5. Conclusion

This chapter has sought to understand the meaning of nationality in an era of human rights. The right to a nationality was discussed from two aspects: as a *procedural right* – derived from the right to acquire a

---

[138] UNHCR, 'Handbook on Protection of Stateless Persons under the 1954 Convention relating to the Status of Stateless Persons' (Geneva, 2014), para. 53.

[139] UNHCR, 'Summary Conclusions – Expert Meeting – The Concept of Stateless Persons under International Law ("Prato Conclusions")' (May 2010) para. 11.

nationality and not to be arbitrarily deprived of that nationality, as well as the established international rules regarding the acquisition and loss of nationality; and in terms of *substantive content*, which looked at the range of rights ordinarily associated with the possession of nationality/ citizenship. It was observed that there is no agreed substantive minimum content of nationality as a matter of international law, not least because it turns so heavily on conditions and rules in the state of nationality. It further found that the inability of nationals to enjoy human rights in their country of nationality does not as a rule have a bearing on the recognition of their nationality under either municipal law or international law. The right to nationality, as it is expressed as a human right, remains largely framed as a *procedural* right.

The chapter did note, however, that each state of nationality has: (i) a duty to admit and readmit its nationals from abroad and allow them to reside in its territory, and (ii) a discretionary right to provide diplomatic protection to its own nationals (and arguably also to refugees and stateless persons), the former drawing parallels with the human right of nationals to leave their country and to return to it from abroad. This chapter also saw that while the general idea that nationality falls within the 'reserved domain' of states is still largely correct, state sovereignty is subject to other rules of international law, not least those derived from international human rights law. In particular, states may not arbitrarily deprive an individual of nationality, which means that governmental decisions must be proportionate and pursue a legitimate objective, concepts which are drawn from international human rights law; may not discriminate against particular individuals or groups in decisions regarding nationality conferral or deprivation; and have a general duty to prevent statelessness in their decisions on nationality. States retain discretion, however, in the rules they apply regarding nationality acquisition especially by way of naturalization.

Questions to guide discussion

1. Is there a definition of nationality under international law? How would you explain the concept?
2. Does the right to a nationality contain only procedural aspects, or substantive content, or both? Is this analytical division between procedural and substantive aspects a useful one?
3. What are the three general modes of nationality acquisition? How can nationality be lost?

4. To what extent is the conferral or loss of nationality within the 'reserved domain' of the state? What are the three main limits imposed by international law? How established are these limits?

5. Discuss the ICJ's decision in *Nottebohm*. Do you think it would be differently decided today? Is so, why?

6. Do the developments in international human rights law suggest we are moving towards agreement by states on the minimum core substantive content of nationality? What is your view?

2

Statelessness and citizenship in ethical and political perspective

MATTHEW J. GIBNEY

In a well-known article defending open immigration, the political theorist Joseph Carens once unflatteringly compared modern citizenship to a feudal status. National citizenship, he said, 'is assigned at birth, for the most part, not subject to change by an individual's will and efforts; and it has a major impact upon a person's life standards'.[1] Yet the plight of one group of people in the contemporary world – the stateless – suggests that there may be at least one thing worse than holding a feudal status, and that is holding no status at all. To lack any state in which one claims nationality or full membership (citizenship) is a recipe for exclusion, precariousness and dispossession.

Despite its profound impact upon the lives of the people affected, the issue of statelessness has, with some notable exceptions, been largely ignored by scholars, practitioners and government officials in the decades since World War II. This neglect, which stands in stark contrast to the international attention focused on refugees, asylum seekers and immigrants (in their various incarnations), is particularly notable because the current estimated number of stateless people in the world – over 10 million – is comparable to the total number of refugees at 15 million.[2] Arguably, the position of the stateless in the shadows of international society merely reflects their abject disempowerment. That said, there has been a flourishing of interest in statelessness in the last few years, buoyed by new scholarship,[3] commissioned reports,[4] and a commitment by

---

[1] J. Carens, 'Migration and Morality: A Liberal Egalitarian Perspective' in B. Barry and R. Goodin, (eds.), *Free Movement* (London: Harvester Wheatsheaf, 1992), 26.

[2] See UNHCR, *Global Trends 2013* and UNHCR *Global Appeal 2014*.

[3] C. Sawyer and B. K. Blitz (eds.), *Statelessness in the European Union: Displaced, Undocumented, Unwanted* (Cambridge University Press, 2011); K. Staples, *Retheorising Statelessness: A Background Theory of Membership in World Politics* (Edinburgh University Press, 2012).

[4] B. K. Blitz and M. Lynch (eds.), *Statelessness and the Benefits of Citizenship: A Comparative Study* (London: Geneva Academy of International Humanitarian Law and Human Rights

international bodies, organizations and states to engage with the issue. This new interest is important not only because it offers the possibility of encouraging collective action to reduce statelessness, but also because the issue of statelessness raises important normative and political questions about the international order of states itself.

As a *normative* issue, the existence of statelessness brings into question the very legitimacy of the international state system. Put simply, a key claim at the centre of statelessness as a moral issue is this: if there is going to be a world exhaustively divided between states – if people are to have no choice but to live under the coercive rule of one state or another – then everyone should be able to claim citizenship and its corresponding rights somewhere. This is a claim that unites political and moral scholars as diverse as civic republicans, natural law adherents, communitarians and liberals. As the legal scholar John Finnis has recently written: 'Whoever and wherever one may be, one is both entitled and bound to regard one-self as belonging to … [a state]: statelessness is an anomaly, a disability, and presumptively an injustice.'[5] Nonetheless, if statelessness is indeed morally unacceptable, there is only limited agreement on how the duties of individual states to rectify it ought to be formulated.

As a *political* issue statelessness challenges one to understand the dynamics behind the exclusion from national membership of substantial numbers of people. Statelessness is not a new issue. Indeed, in 1951 Hannah Arendt described the stateless as the 'most symptomatic group in contemporary politics' because they symbolized the triumph of the exclusivity of the nation over the civic inclusion of the state.[6] Yet it is a problem that has hitherto survived the development of an international order of human rights in the post-World War II period. Why is it that states have not only tolerated the existence of statelessness but in some cases acted to create it?

In this chapter, I aim to provide an overview of the normative complexities and political dynamics of contemporary statelessness. Unlike the other chapters in this book, which discuss nationality and statelessness from the perspective of international law, I approach these subjects from a political theory perspective and hope to add a layer of analysis not reflected elsewhere in the book. More specifically, I have three major goals.

---

and International Observatory on Statelessness, 2009); Equal Rights Trust, *Unravelling Anomaly* (London: Equal Rights Trust, 2010).
[5] J. Finnis, 'Nationality, Alienage and Constitutional Principle', Oxford Legal Studies Research Paper No. 08/2008 (2008), at 30.
[6] H. Arendt, *The Origins of Totalitarianism* (London: Andre Deutsch, 1986), 77.

First, to illustrate why statelessness is commonly conceived of as 'bad' and thus something to be avoided and minimized; in so doing, I will show how statelessness is informed by an implicit normative conception of what states ought to provide to their citizens. Second, I will offer an account of the 'uses' of statelessness for governing elites in order to understand better why, despite its negative consequences, statelessness is produced and maintained over time. Third, I consider how we might conceptualize the duties of states to rectify statelessness. I will discuss two different accounts of the injustice inflicted by statelessness: one stresses responsibilities to the stateless qua stateless people; the other recognizes responsibilities to them by virtue of their role as unrecognized citizens. I argue that the most convincing account of state duties may be one that articulates a right to membership in a way conceptually unrelated to statelessness.

My examination here also aims to highlight a paradox. The possession of citizenship may (often) provide individuals with a particularly secure grounding for their rights and entitlements in the contemporary world, but it also enchains people, as Carens suggested above, to particular territories, reinforcing egregious patterns of global inequality and mocking consent-based governance. Statelessness brings to our attention not only the dangers of not possessing citizenship, but also the profound problems posed by the international order of states in which the status of citizenship is nested.

It should already be obvious that I am using the term 'stateless' as shorthand for both a lack of nationality and of citizenship (full membership in the state). Hence, while I acknowledge that the categories of nationality and citizenship are analytically separate, I combine them in the discussion that follows.

2.1.   Statelessness in normative and descriptive context

Before I proceed, it is important to explore the concept of statelessness to bring out its implicit normativity. In purely *descriptive* terms, statelessness can be defined as a situation in which an individual (or a group of people) has no membership in any state whatsoever. This account of statelessness has the virtue of picking out a range of groups who have been stripped of their citizenship (e.g. Jews in Nazi Germany) or who are born without a nationality (e.g. the children of the Bidoon in the United Arab Emirates). However, understanding statelessness in this way tells nothing about why one should be concerned about the phenomenon.

Describing someone as stateless in descriptive terms provides no more reason for incorporating them into state membership than describing someone as a non-Christian does for converting them to the path of Jesus. Statelessness is merely one amongst a number of ways of categorizing certain individuals or groups. However, in its practical use statelessness is a concept that typically secretes an (implicit) *normative* agenda: to be stateless is perceived to be suffering a *loss* or a *deprivation*. In its broadest terms, this deprivation is of 'State protection'.[7] To be stateless is not to enjoy various rights and entitlements guaranteed by states to their nationals, including the right lawfully to reside somewhere on the earth's surface.

The descriptive term and the normative components of statelessness stand in an uncomfortable relationship to each other. While the descriptive term seems to pick out a relatively confined and clearly demarcated section of the world's population (those without legal citizenship anywhere), the normative component is far more expansive. The category of people who lack the goods associated with state protection certainly includes the formally stateless, but it is not exhausted by it. A person may possess state membership in name (hence they are not *descriptively* stateless) and yet their nationality and citizenship may not deliver to them the kinds of goods, rights and entitlements membership ought to provide (making them *normatively* stateless). These are what are sometimes called the *de facto* stateless.[8]

There are a variety of ways of becoming normatively (or *de facto*) stateless in the contemporary world. An individual might, like the undocumented migrant, be out of the territory of her state of membership and lack protection because she is unable for some reason to avail herself of the protection of the state in which she is residing (perhaps because she fears deportation). Alternatively, someone may never have left his national territory but, because of the unwillingness or incapacity of his state, experiences an existence that is tantamount to statelessness in its absence of basic protections and rights. This is the situation of many internally displaced people, oppressed minorities and marginalized social groups. The elasticity of the term stateless is evident in the sociologist Margaret Somers' controversial use of the term to describe

[7] J. Bhabha (ed.), *Children Without a State: A Global Human Rights Challenge* (Cambridge, MA: MIT Press, 2011).

[8] For a discussion of the notion of *de facto* statelessness from the perspective of international law, see also the contribution by van Waas in this volume at Chapter 3.

the experience of black Americans who were displaced by Hurricane Katrina. She argues that the 'social exclusion' and 'expendability' of this group, evidenced by the US government's failure to respond to their plight, showed that '[these Americans] were no longer in any meaningful sense citizens; they were now, in effect, stateless people'.[9] This is not a use of the word 'stateless' that would be likely to be endorsed from a legal perspective.

Refugees, individuals who are persecuted by their own state, are yet another group who might be conceptualized as normatively stateless. In international law such people have access to a distinctive regime built around the 1951 UN Convention relating to the Status of Refugees (1951 Convention), yet their practical separation from the stateless – and particularly what we may call the *de facto* stateless – is a matter of vicissitudes of history and institutional arrangements more than a matter of conceptual distinctiveness. Indeed, in her famous 1951 exposition on refugees in the *Origins of Totalitarianism*, Hannah Arendt treated the stateless and the refugee as synonyms: both were cast adrift from state protection.[10]

In what remains of this chapter, my concentration will be on the formally stateless, i.e. those people that have no membership in a state anywhere. This focus does not reflect a belief that there is any normative difference or significance between *de jure* and *de facto* statelessness, less still that international attention should focus on the former more than the latter. For, as I have shown above, the reason statelessness matters for individuals (if not necessarily for states) is because state membership is a valuable guarantor of certain goods, rights and entitlements. Once we acknowledge this, it seems difficult to justify distinguishing between those who do not have these goods guaranteed because they have no state whatsoever and those who do not enjoy them because their state is ineffective, absent or simply malign, even if the distinction is an evident one in international law. Indeed, I suggest below that the moral responsibilities of states to stateless people may best be conceptualized through an approach indifferent to whether one has no state at all or simply an absent or ineffective state.

---

[9] M. R. Somers, *Genealogies of Citizenship: Markets, Statelessness, and the Right to Have Rights* (Cambridge University Press, 2008), 114.

[10] Arendt, *The Origins of Totalitarianism*.

2.2. The undesirability of statelessness

I have suggested that there is an implicit assumption that statelessness is a normatively undesirable state of affairs, but why is it considered so? One answer is that it leaves individuals vulnerable to insecurity and rights violations. But this is only part of the reason why statelessness has traditionally been considered a problem or a 'bad'. To get a richer picture of the problem of statelessness it is important to consider the problems posed by statelessness across different levels of agency: in particular, the international state system, the individual state, and stateless persons themselves.

In terms of the *international state system*, statelessness is a bad to be avoided primarily because it risks exacerbating international tensions and disorder. Statelessness creates people who are, by definition, out of place, somewhere where they have no right to be. Adapting Zygmunt Bauman's pithy description, the stateless are 'gatecrashers' in the back-yards of others,[11] and thus people whose presence is unlikely to be viewed with equanimity. International tension is particularly likely to result when their situation has come about because of the deliberate actions of a state attempting to rid itself of unwanted peoples (e.g. by stripping citizenship or not recognizing as members sections of their populations). A prime example of such international tensions were those set in train by the mass denationalization of their foreign resident citizens by Communist Russia and Nazi Germany in the 1920s and 1930s respectively. The actions created floating populations of unwanted foreigners that states were unwilling to integrate but could not expel. The stateless showed the truth of Arendt's observation of the 1940s that 'whether we like it or not we have really started to live in One World'.[12] In a world exhaustively divided between states, the membership decisions of states are radically interdependent. Statelessness is thus often a challenge of 'order management' in the international system.[13]

Statelessness also creates problems for *individual states*, potentially challenging their ability to control and order their subject populations. Statelessness undermines the ability of states to expel unwanted foreigners (who will take them?) and thus shape the boundaries of inclusion. It is therefore unsurprising that the United Kingdom, for example, has

---

[11] Z. Bauman, *In search of Politics* (Stanford University Press, 1999), 195.
[12] Arendt, *The Origins of Totalitarianism*, 296.
[13] P. J. Spiro, 'A New International Law of Citizenship' (2011) 105 *Am. J. Int'l L.*, 694.

recently criminalized the actions of asylum seekers who destroy their passports. This act of destruction aims to obscure asylum seekers' membership of a state – mimicking a situation of statelessness – to prevent Britain from deporting them.

The presence of statelessness also demonstrates a population who lack a reason (beyond the threat of force) for yielding to the state's authority, yet unlike other non-citizens cannot be deported. If the rights, entitlements and privileges that states grant to citizens are seen as ways that obedience to rule is achieved, the stateless – who live in the state but do not receive the benefits of citizenship – are easily interpreted as potentially dangerous and disloyal. More radically, the stateless may be perceived as offering a potentially subversive vision of a life beyond membership in the state. Agamben's view of the refugee as 'nothing less than a border concept that radically calls into question the principles of the nation State and, at the same time, helps clear the field for a no longer delayable renewal of categories'[14] seems equally applicable to the concept of statelessness. Governing elites, whose power is vested in national institutions, are unlikely to welcome such a 'renewal', or take kindly to its supposed harbingers.

Yet if statelessness is a problem for the state system and individual states it is most of all a problem for those *individuals* who lack membership. Statelessness not only tracks patterns of social and political exclusion, it creates circumstances of vulnerability and precariousness in its own right. In a famous 1958 United States' Supreme Court decision, *Trop* v. *Dulles*, which limited the ability of the US government to strip citizenship as a punishment, the court described the experience of statelessness:

> [Loss of all citizenship] strips the citizen of his status in the national and international political community. His very existence is at the sufferance of the country in which he happens to find himself. While any one country may accord him some rights …, no country need do so, because he is stateless … In short, the expatriate has lost the right to have rights.[15]

Hannah Arendt, whose writings the court drew upon in its judgement, went further in her famous work of 1951, *Origins of Totalitarianism*. She argued that the stateless were victims of not one loss but of three: the loss of a home, the loss of government protection and the loss 'of a place in the world which makes opinions significant and actions effective', a

---

[14] G. Agamben, 'We Refugees', *Symposium*, 49(2) (1995), 114–19, at 117.
[15] United States Supreme Court, *Trop* v. *Dulles*, 356 US 86, 31 March 1958, at section II.

shared political community in which to act, initiate and form views of a common world.[16]

Arendt's account of the experience of statelessness is problematical as a description of the contemporary phenomenon. Unlike the focus of Arendt's attention – the victims of mass denationalization in inter-war Europe – most stateless people today have not been expelled from their homes; the problem they face is lack of recognition and citizenship in the country where they live, and sometimes have always lived. Moreover, the stateless often do not lack all government protection. The development of international human rights law over the last fifty years provides a range of protections (enforced to various degrees) available to individuals on the basis of their personhood.

Rather, to get an accurate picture of why statelessness may be a problem for individuals, it is necessary to understand the key benefits tied to citizenship, or formal membership in the state. In most countries, citizenship is a passport to some key social, economic and political goods that have a huge impact on the well-being of individuals and social groups. The key benefits of citizenship can generally be categorized in terms of access to three goods: privileges, security and voice.

The *privileges* associated with citizenship may involve favoured or exclusive access to public goods (such as housing, welfare, state-provided healthcare, education, etc.); government (public service) positions and membership of the military, and thus access to key elevators for social advancement; and the right to own land, other forms of property and businesses. The good of *security*, on the other hand, is evident primarily in the fact that the possession of citizenship offers a unique level of security of residence in the state. Citizens, unlike non-citizens, typically cannot be deported or expelled, making their access to other rights and privileges in the state uniquely robust. Moreover, they may leave or enter the state at will and claim diplomatic protection when abroad.

By contrast, being stateless deprives one of any equivalent unconditional right to reside in and to re-enter the state. In this respect, the stateless can be considered 'deportable', to use De Genova's term.[17] They are individuals whose daily lives are lived under the shadow of possible expulsion from the state. To be sure, any state wishing to expel a stateless person needs to find another state willing to accept them (as noted above).

---

[16] Arendt, *The Origins of Totalitarianism*, 296.
[17] N. De Genova, 'Migrant "Illegality" and Deportability in Everyday Life', *Annual Review of Anthropology*, 31 (2002) 419–47.

Yet even this constraint is not without a sting in the tail. As observers from Arendt to Agamben have noted, the lack of options for deportation have often provided the impetus for the development of new forms of exclusion within state territory. Some of these forms of exclusion – the detention centre, the off-shore island and even mass extermination camp – can make deportation look civilized.[18]

The final relevant good of citizenship is that of *voice*:[19] the right to air in public fora views about the use and abuse of government power and the direction of society, specifically by participating in (or being elected to) the political institutions that fashion law and policy. The *sine qua non* of citizenship is thus often seen as embodied in key rights associated with voice, namely 'rights to vote, hold elected and appointed government offices, to sit on various sorts of juries, and generally to participate in debates as equal community members'.[20]

This idea of voice, particularly the aspect of participating in debates as equal community members, comes close to what Arendt meant when she described the stateless as lacking a place in the world where their actions were effective and opinions significant.[21] A key consequence of statelessness is the loss of the very right to have rights because, Arendt argued, rights are created through shared political action. This lack of standing has made the stateless targets of racism and other forms of hostile objectification. For when people are deprived of 'a framework' within which they are judged by their 'actions and opinions',[22] they are more susceptible to being judged by ascriptive characteristics: *what* they are (their race, immigration status, ethnicity, etc.) rather than *who* they are (the product of their own words and deeds). A lack of voice thus makes the stateless particularly vulnerable to dehumanization.

2.3.   The political uses of statelessness

From the account of the problem of statelessness I have outlined, it is unclear why statelessness exists for any length of time at all. After all, the

---

[18] See A. R. Zolberg, A. Suhrke and S. Aguayo, *Escape from Violence: Conflict and the Refugee Crisis in the Developing World* (USA: Oxford University Press, 1989), 16.

[19] A. Shachar, *The Birthright Lottery: Citizenship and Global Inequality* (Harvard University Press, 2009).

[20] R. M. Smith, 'Modern Citizenship' in Engin F. Isin and Bryan S. Turner (eds.), *Handbook of Citizenship Studies* (New York: Sage, 2002), 105.

[21] R. Bernstein, *Hannah Arendt and the Jewish Question* (Cambridge, MA: MIT Press, 1996), 83.

[22] *Ibid.*

existence of people without state membership creates difficulties for the state system in terms of maintaining international order, undermines the ability of individual states to rule effectively and denies individual stateless people many basic rights and protections. These difficulties alone would seem to give states sufficient motivation to act to eliminate the phenomenon.

Statelessness is often generated by the unintentional actions of states. Conflicts of citizenship laws, state dissolution, gendered nationality laws and bureaucratic incompetence can lead to people without membership. In fact, statelessness in some shape or form may be an inevitable part of the international system of states. But even if the creation of stateless-ness is unintentional or even inevitable, it is still important to ask: why did some groups of people, such as the Rohingya of Burma or the Estate Tamils of Sri Lanka,[23] remain stateless over long periods of time, excluded from societies in which they lived? This is the question to which I will now turn.

One answer may lie in the weakness and ineffectiveness of some states. Poor or fragile states – particularly those with weak infrastructures or in the throes of conflict or dissolution – may simply fail to register people born on their territory or otherwise eligible for citizenship, and have a cumbersome or inefficient process for rectifying this failure. Yet this is only part of the reason. Contemporary statelessness is as much a symp-tom of state *intention* as it is of state *incompetence*. If statelessness can cause problems, it can also have its uses. There are four major types of reason why it may be in the interests of particular states to keep people stateless.

The first is what I will call 'gain'. To be stateless is, as we have seen, typ-ically to be disempowered. The stateless are vulnerable to state power in part because they lack the rights and institutional representation neces-sary to effect changes in state policy and in part because of their lack of political and social rights. This vulnerability may be useful to social and political elites because it facilitates the exploitation of the group in ques-tion. Groups that lack rights and institutional modes for the expression of grievances lack the ability to act back against economic and other forms of exploitation. For example, workers of Haitian ancestry and their

---

[23] Note that in 2003, Sri Lanka passed a law that allowed the majority of its stateless Estate Tamils to gain citizenship. P. Sivapragasam, 'From Statelessness to Citizenship: Up-Country Tamils in Sri Lanka' in B. Blitz and M. Lynch (eds.) *Statelessness and Citizenship. A Comparative Study of the Benefits of Nationality* (Cheltenham: Edward Elgar, 2011).

children in the Dominican Republic have provided a valuable source of 'live in' labour for economically central activities like harvesting sugar cane and work in building trades.[24] Citizenship laws that exclude them from membership capture such workers in precarious labour, preventing social mobility and facilitating a situation of low wages and poor living standards.

A second set of reasons can be categorized as those stemming from 'fear and distrust'. Statelessness may be reproduced because of a perception that it would be socially or politically dangerous to convert a particular group of people into citizens. The group concerned may be characterized (rightly or wrongly) as possessing foreign loyalties or allegiances that make them threatening to the state. Some countries strip citizenship from terrorists or others deemed grossly disloyal, even if statelessness is the result.[25] For example, in 2012 the United Arab Emirates withdrew the citizenship of five of its nationals (thus making them stateless) because they jeopardized 'the national security of the UAE through their connection with suspicious regional and international organisations and personalities'.[26] But exclusion based on concerns about disloyalty can involve far larger groups as well, crossing over ethnic or culture lines. The Bihari in Bangladesh were, until very recently, excluded from citizenship largely because they were seen as an ethnic group whose real loyalty lay with Pakistan rather than Bangladesh;[27] the situation of those of Russian descent who became stateless after the Baltic States adopted their own nationality laws in the early 1990s reflected similar concerns about distrust and lack of loyalty.[28]

The patterns of fear and distrust that justify exclusion often reflect and reinforce anxieties that some groups are intrinsically 'unworthy' of citizenship. Conceptions of unworthiness themselves tend to track invidious ethnic and racial judgments about groups considered incapable of fulfilling the demands of citizenship or integrating into the national community. While the obvious case here is the racial construction of Jews

---

[24] Amnesty International, 'A Life in Transit: The Plight of Haitian Migrants and Dominicans of Haitian Descent' (2007), available at: www.unhcr.org/refworld/country,,AMNESTY,, HTI,4562d94e2,461224362,0.html, last accessed 9 May 2014.

[25] M. J. Gibney, 'Should Citizenship Be Conditional?' *Journal of Politics* 75 (03 (2013) 646–58.

[26] 'UAE Detains Six Militants', *The Nation*, 11 April 2012.

[27] L. van Waas, *Nationality Matters: Statelessness under International Law* (Antwerp/ Oxford/Portland, OR: Intersentia, 2008), 128.

[28] P. Järve and V. Poleshchuk, *Country Report: Estonia* (EUDO Citizenship Observatory, 2013), available at: http://eudo-citizenship.eu/docs/CountryReports/Estonia.pdf, last accessed 9 May 2014.

under the Nazi regime, other groups before them, such as blacks in the United States and aboriginal groups in Australia, were considered at best less than full citizens and offered diminished versions of its entitlements. A more recent example of the connection between racial and ethnic construction and statelessness can be found in the treatment of Roma in various European countries reforming their citizenship laws in the aftermath of the Soviet Union's demise in 1989. After the division of Czechoslovakia in the early 1990s, for instance, some in the Roma population – long victims of racial discrimination, harassment and negative stereotyping – were left stateless.[29]

A final reason for the persistence of statelessness is that exclusion from membership is often congruent with national processes of 'people building'. While I noted above that statelessness can create difficulties for effective governance, these difficulties may be outweighed by the benefits elites reap in reinforcing or creating national bonds amongst the dominant community. It is no coincidence that statelessness is often a result of state formation or war. Exclusion can be a way of affirming the boundaries of the nation when loyalty or unity is most needed by political elites. The creation of a collective identity is achieved by contrasting the included community with the excluded ones (the Roma, the Jews, the Ugandan Asians) and, in so doing, formulating the distinctive character of the national community (we are not lazy, Muslim, greedy, imperialistic, etc.). Exclusion based on people-building is a timeless feature of political rule. As Freud noted in *Civilization and its Discontents*, 'it is always possible to bind together a considerable number of people in love, so long as there are other people left over to receive the manifestations of their aggressiveness ... In this respect, the Jewish people, scattered everywhere, have rendered most useful services to the civilizations of the countries that have been their hosts.'[30] Statelessness, like refugee generation, may not be an inevitable product of people-building, but they often go hand in hand.

While I have separated out the various political uses of statelessness for analytical reasons here, they are usually intermingled in practice. Ethnic, social or racial groups viewed as unworthy of citizenship, like those of Haitian descent in the Dominican Republic, are obviously plausible candidates for exploitation, and may (justifiably given their maltreatment)

---

[29] S. Swimelar, 'The Making of Minority Rights Norms in the Context of EU Enlargement: The Czech Republic and the Roma' *The International Journal of Human Rights*, 12(4) (2008), 505–27.

[30] S. Freud, *Civilization and its Discontents* (New York: WW Norton & Company Incorporated, 2005), Chapter 5.

often be considered untrustworthy, too. Equally, groups considered untrustworthy, like Jews in Nazi Germany, are scapegoated in order to affirm a common national identity in times of war or social upheaval.

2.4. The moral responsibilities of states

I have now shown that while statelessness may be widely viewed as an undesirable feature of the modern international order of states, there are still reasons why a particular state might have an interest in keeping some groups of people stateless. States have been able to act upon these interests in exclusion, it is important to note, because of a long-held presumption in international law (and, to some extent, common morality) that states have the prerogative to determine the boundaries of their own member- ship, offering and withholding citizenship as they please. Hence, when Alexander Downer, Australia's Foreign Affairs Minister, was asked in the 1960s to defend his government's racially restrictive immigration policy, he stated, 'We seek to create a homogeneous nation... Can anyone reason- ably object to that? Is this not the elementary right of every government to decide the composition of the nation?'[31] More recently, the German immi- gration law scholar, Kai Hailbronner, claimed that 'there are no moral and therefore generally applicable criteria in judging a nation's citizen- ship policy... Naturalisation policy cannot be determined by questions of what is good or bad, moral or immoral. It has to be determined by balanc- ing divergent political interests'.[32] Of course, both of these proponents of state discretion would have accepted that the state's right to decide mem- bership is constrained by the need to avoid conflicts with other states (the requirement of international order) and to respect international law. But should state discretion not also be constrained by a right of stateless peo- ple to citizenship?

In the remainder of this chapter, I want to consider the question of the responsibilities of states to admit stateless people into membership. My concern is not with the *legal* obligations of states (others in this volume will consider this question)[33] but rather with the question of states' *moral* duties. The advantage of this perspective is that it gives us a basis on which

---

[31] Quoted in M. Walzer, *Spheres of Justice* (New York: Basic Books, 1983), 46.

[32] K. Hailbronner, 'Citizenship and Nationhood in Germany', in R. Brubaker (ed.), *Immigration and the Politics of Citizenship in Europe and North America* (New York: University of America Press, 1989), 74–5.

[33] See also Spiro, 'A New International Law of Citizenship'.

to appraise critically the practices of states, regardless of whether they are lawful or not.

There are two main ways in which we might conceptualize the injustice experienced by stateless people, each of which has different implications for state responsibilities. One way is to see the stateless as victims of 'statelessness per se', where the duty-holder is the international society of states; the other way is to conceptualize the stateless as 'unrecognized members', where the duty-holder is the particular state in which the stateless person currently resides (or to which he or she has deep connections). I will now discuss each of these conceptualizations in turn.

Probably the most common way of conceptualizing the stateless is as victims of an injustice inflicted upon them by international society. This conceptualization is implicit in the Universal Declaration of Human Rights, which stipulates that every individual has the right to a nationality. It is present also in Arendt's description of the stateless as the 'scum of the earth', as people rendered superfluous by the fact that no state anywhere would accept them for membership.[34] In this view, statelessness is wrong because it represents the violation of the individual's right to live under the protection of a state, even while it forces them to live in a system of states. Statelessness challenges the state system's very legitimacy because if that system is to be defensible, it should accommodate all of the world's denizens.

Denial of the right to possess citizenship somewhere is a very plausible way of conceptualizing the problem of statelessness but it creates a problem. The entity with the responsibility to rectify the injustice of lack of citizenship (the international society of states) is not the same as the entity that controls the good that needs to be distributed (citizenship). Control over the distribution of membership is still, as we noted above, largely the prerogative of individual states. Therefore, to speak of a right to citizenship (or nationality) begs the question: where? Which *particular* state has a duty to provide citizenship to the stateless person? If an individual's right to a state is not to be empty, a principle for determining the responsibilities of individual states must be found.

There are a number of possible ways that duties might be distributed amongst states to reflect the fact that statelessness is a collective responsibility. One way is through a principle of numerical equality where each of the world's states takes a proportion of the world's stateless people (e.g. Australia must accept into citizenship 10,000; the United States, 10,000

---

[34] Arendt, *The Origins of Totalitarianism*.

and Tunisia, 10,000). The number of people allocated to each state could be adjusted to reflect the relative capabilities and costs to particular states, taking into account, for example, demographic density and GDP. A different way of allocating responsibilities would be to make states responsible for stateless people who are on (or who come to) their territory. This might be called distribution on the basis of proximity and is analogous to the principle of *non-refoulement* in refugee law, whereby persecuted individuals can (subject to some limitations) claim protection in any state at which they arrive. Another possible principle distributes responsibility on the basis of birth, making states responsible for any children born stateless on their territory. This would be a kind of *jus soli* principle for stateless people and, while it would not solve all problems of statelessness (e.g. it would not help those who have *lost* their citizenship, such as through state dissolution), it would significantly reduce them.

Each of these ways of conceiving of state responsibilities would, if enacted, go some way to giving all individuals the right to citizenship somewhere. Yet there is something disturbing about simply distributing stateless people amongst states on the basis of principles of global international justice. The stateless are not, in practice, simply deracinated, homeless people, wandering the globe in search of any state that will have them. They are typically, though not exclusively, people settled in particular societies, lacking legal recognition of and appropriate protection for their status as residents. The primary injustice they experience, then, is not that they cannot find *any* state to grant them citizenship but that the state that really should grant them citizenship will not, for various reasons, do so. As their claim is less to citizenship somewhere than to recognition of their moral claim to membership in the state where they are already making their lives, they are most accurately conceptualized as 'unrecognized citizens'.

Paradoxically, one gets a clearer picture of the injustice of unrecognized citizenship by considering an example of an individual who lost his 'membership' but did *not* become stateless. In 2004, the Australian government deported Robert Jovicic to Serbia, the country in which he held citizenship. Jovicic was a non-citizen permanent resident of Australia who had over many years been repeatedly convicted of crimes related to drug use. In many respects, he was an exemplar for the government's policy of deporting foreign citizens convicted of criminal offences. But his deportation caused a huge public outcry, ultimately forcing the government to facilitate his return. What lay behind this response? Jovicic had lived in Australia for some thirty-six years prior to his deportation.

He had arrived in Australia with his parents when he was two years old; he did not speak or understand Serbian or have any social network in Serbia. In the words of the opposition immigration spokesperson, 'Even though ... [Jovicic] has not been a good member of our community, he is undeniably Australia's responsibility.'[35] The Jovicic case shows that public conceptions of who is a member – and who is thus entitled to the protections of membership – are not exhausted by legal categories of citizenship. Jovicic was widely conceptualized as a member of Australian society (and thus eligible for protection from deportation) despite his lack of formal citizenship. His status grew out of his extended presence in Australian society.

The idea that a society might possess unrecognized citizens – individuals with a compelling moral case to be accepted as citizens – has been explored in recent political thought. Rainer Bauböck, for example, has argued that a morally defensible account of citizenship in a particular political community should include all individuals who have a 'stake' in the future of the society in question.[36] To have a 'stake', in his terms, is to be dependent on the political community for the protection of one's rights and to be reliant on how the state develops over time.[37] According to Bauböck, 'self-governing political communities should include as citizens those individuals who circumstances of life link their individual autonomy or well-being to the common good of the political community'.[38] The legal scholar Ayelet Shachar conceptualizes the moral boundaries of membership only slightly differently. She argues that they should include all those who have a genuine 'link' to the state in question. Her principle of *jus nexi* privileges an idea of membership based on 'social attachment' and 'community ties'. The moral community is, according to Shachar, defined not merely by domicile in the state, but by 'factual membership and affected interests'.[39]

Despite their differences, both of these accounts of who is morally a member of the state draw their power in part from their ability to speak

---

[35] B. Evans, 'Jovicic Awaits Residency Decision', Australian Broadcasting Corporation, 9 March 2006.

[36] R. Bauböck, '*Stakeholder Citizenship: An Idea Whose Time Has Come?*' (Washington, D.C.: Migration Policy Institute, 2008).

[37] R. Yusar, 'Exploring Normative Theories of Democratic Citizenship', MA Thesis, Central European University, Hungary (2012).

[38] R. Bauböck, 'Expansive Citizenship – Voting Beyond Territory and Membership', *PS: Political Science & Politics*, 38(04) (2005) 683–7, at 686.

[39] Shachar, The Birthright Lottery.

to both communitarian and liberal moral sentiments.[40] Consistent with communitarian ideals, each acknowledges the way people's identity is shaped by their social context and thus that extended residence in a society creates moral claims. Consistent with liberal principles, they recognize that if someone is to live under the coercive institutions of a particular society, they are entitled to the protections and rights necessary to act as a political agent in that society.

Both the 'stake' and the 'link' approaches seem highly congenial to the integration of stateless people into membership in the societies in which they are living. For it can hardly be denied that the stateless are dependent on the evolution of the society in which they live, or have interests 'affected' by that society and its political institutions. Indeed, their statelessness situation makes them particularly vulnerable to capricious state power. If Jovicic had a strong claim to be considered a member of Australian society based on extended residence (and he did), the claims to citizenship of those like the stateless Kurds who have lived in Syria for decades seem at least as strong.

Is it best to conceptualize the stateless as unrecognized citizens or as stateless people per se? My feeling is that the most compelling of these approaches is the former. This is partly because the idea of unrecognized membership enables one to bypass the difficulties of determining how responsibility should be divided amongst (in principle) similarly situated agents (states), but also because the claim of stateless people often seems to be to citizenship where they are living, not to citizenship *tout court*.

If this is right, then, paradoxically, the best account of the duties of states to stateless people (and the injustice they are subject to) may be one that does not emphasize their experience of statelessness as such, but simply recognizes their right to be included in a particular state. Indeed, herein lies another advantage of the unrecognized members conceptualization: it avoids the issue of *de jure* versus *de facto* statelessness. The question of a right to membership is not decided by the existence of some other state that may formally claim one as a member but is dependent primarily on one's relationship to the state in which one is actually making one's life.

---

[40] M. J. Gibney, 'The Rights of Non-citizens to Membership' in C. Sawyer and B. Blitz (eds.), *Statelessness in the European Union: Displaced, Undocumented, Unwanted* (Cambridge University Press, 2011), 41–68.

2.5.   A duty to join a state?

If one accepts my argument, states have a duty to offer citizenship to state-less people either directly because they are stateless (subject to a principle of just distribution between states) or indirectly through the obligation states have to any stateless resident on their territory for an extended period. But these conceptualizations of state responsibilities give rise to a question: do stateless people have a corresponding duty to *accept* any offer of citizenship? Let me briefly discuss this question before concluding this piece.

One reason why states have a duty to the stateless is because states exist only to protect the security and welfare of the people over whom they rule, and citizenship is an important marker of the boundaries of a state's rule. By contrast, individual people – stateless or otherwise – do not exist *for* the state in the same way, and they thus have no analogous duty. However, one might argue that those already in receipt of the goods of citizenship (including security) have a duty to formalize their membership in the state (this is what some philosophers call 'a duty of gratitude'). But this position seems unlikely to apply to stateless people because their very need to join a state derives from the fact that they are *not* already receiving the protec-tion of the state. The stateless can have no duty of gratitude for goods they have never received.

Of course, it is likely the case there are still good reasons (short of moral obligation) why stateless persons *should* for their own sake join any state that offers them membership, reasons spelt out earlier in this piece and by a panoply of writers on statelessness. That said, it is sober-ing to remember that citizenship does not only involve 'goods', it also involves burdens, in some cases onerous ones: citizens undertake cer-tain roles, including national service, and may even have to make them-selves available to risk their life for the state at a time of war. Moreover, the 'goods' of citizenship on offer in some states are rather slim indeed. It makes a world of difference whether one has a right to citizenship in Chad or Sweden.

Even if one believes that the duties one assumes represent a fair trade in return for the benefits of citizenship, it is surely a relevant consid-eration that many of the world's citizens are poorly placed to ensure that the citizen–state contract remains mutually advantageous over time. As Joseph Carens has noted, for most of the world's denizens, citi-zenship has no opt-out clause, it is like a 'feudal status that chains one to a particular territory'.[41] Without proper avenues for exit – or even expressing discontent – citizenship cannot be the kind of morally valid association that the stateless (or any other individual) would be obliged to join.[42] The duty of states to offer citizenship to stateless people in their territory thus should create no correlative duty on the part of the stateless to accept the offer.

2.6. Conclusion

I began this chapter by establishing the case for taking statelessness seriously against Joseph Carens' description of citizenship in the modern world as a feudal status. Yet I have now returned to Carens' observation to question the case for a duty on the part of stateless people to join those states that offer them citizenship. Herein lies the key paradox at the heart of attempts to resolve the problem of statelessness in the contemporary world: at its best, the possession of citizenship provides individuals with a particularly secure grounding for rights and protections, yet it also ties people to particular territories and reinforces egregious patterns of global inequality. Indeed, in many countries citizenship does not even offer the security of basic rights or insulate people from humiliating and harmful forms of social exclusion.

Possession of citizenship is almost always a necessary condition for securely holding fundamental rights in the contemporary world, but it is nowhere near a sufficient one. This is no reason to tolerate statelessness or to ignore the legal and moral duties states have to offer citizenship to stateless people. But it *is* a powerful reason not to exaggerate the protections and virtues of modern citizenship for most of the world's denizens: *where* one is born into citizenship is almost as important as *whether* one is born into citizenship. For the time being, statelessness is likely to remain a devastating and precarious plight that we have good reason to strive to eliminate. But, ironically, it might be that the very same principles of equality and security that impel us to put an end to statelessness also require us to start imagining a world beyond states.

---

[41] Carens, 'Migration and Morality'.

[42] Cf. R. M. Smith, *Stories of Peoplehood: The Politics and Morals of Political Membership* (Cambridge University Press, 2003), 136–41.

Questions to guide discussion

1. From the political science – rather than the legal – perspective, is the distinction between *de facto* and *de jure* stateless helpful in normative or descriptive terms?[43]
2. Why is statelessness commonly conceived of as a 'bad'? What are the consequences of a lack of nationality in the contemporary world order of states?
3. How has statelessness been 'used' by governing elites to control and maintain power? What are some of the political motives for creating or maintaining stateless residents?
4. What are the moral – as opposed to legal – imperatives to eradicating statelessness and to granting citizenship to stateless persons?
5. What do you think of Gibney's moral imperative based on 'fair distribution of stateless persons' among states, versus obligations to those already within a state's territory?
6. If one accepts a moral duty on states to admit stateless persons into its circle of membership, is there a correlative duty to accept that membership by the stateless?

---

[43] For the legal distinction and discussion questions, see the contribution by van Waas in this volume at Chapter 3.

3

The UN statelessness conventions

LAURA VAN WAAS

During the early years of the United Nations, statelessness featured prominently on its agenda. In March 1948, the Economic and Social Council (ECOSOC) requested the Secretary-General to undertake a study of 'the existing situation in regard to the protection of stateless persons',[1] to explore the need for further standard setting at the international level to address their vulnerable position. Just a few months later, on 10 December 1948, the Universal Declaration of Human Rights (UDHR) proclaimed that 'everyone has the right to a nationality' and 'no one shall be arbitrarily deprived of his nationality' – an expression of the international community's parallel interest in preventing new cases of statelessness from arising.[2]

Over the course of the years that followed, the UN proceeded to determine how and where international law could play a part in addressing statelessness in accordance with two identified objectives: 1) protecting people who are in need of attention and assistance because they are currently stateless; and 2) avoiding the creation of statelessness (eventually rendering the measures for the protection of stateless people obsolete over time). Thus, two separate instruments came into being: the 1954 Convention relating to the Status of Stateless Persons[3] and the 1961 Convention on the Reduction of Statelessness.[4]

While operating independently of one another – and clearly distinct in their aims and approach – these conventions share a common root in the *Study of Statelessness.*[5] Together the instruments form the core of the

---

[1] Resolution 116 (VI) D, Resolutions adopted by the Economic and Social Council during its sixth session (2 February to 11 March 1948), p. 18.
[2] Universal Declaration of Human Rights, Paris, 10 December 1948, GA Res. 217A(III), UN Doc. A/810 at 71, Art. 15.
[3] Convention relating to the Status of Stateless Persons, New York, 28 September 1954, in force 6 June 1960, 360 UNTS 117.
[4] Convention on the Reduction of Statelessness, New York, 30 August 1961, in force 13 December 1975, 989 UNTS 175.
[5] United Nations, *A Study of Statelessness*, UN Doc. E/1112 (August 1949).

international community's response to statelessness, as the only universal conventions to have a specific, dedicated and comprehensive focus on the issue. This chapter introduces the two United Nations' statelessness conventions and analyses their origins and content in detail, before offering some reflections on their impact and enduring relevance in light of contemporary developments.

3.1. The birth of a dedicated statelessness regime

In its *Study of Statelessness,* the United Nations concluded that 'statelessness is a phenomenon as old as the concept of nationality'.[6] Its existence was perceived to be an inevitable by-product of the freedom of states to set the rules for acquisition and loss of nationality, which at times leads to a conflict of laws situation that leave a person stateless. Such isolated cases, the study suggested, 'did not greatly disturb international life'[7] but, in the post-war era, 'statelessness assumed unprecedented proportions'.[8] This prompted the inclusion of statelessness in the work of the newly formed United Nations, eventually leading to the adoption of the 1954 and 1961 statelessness conventions, as set out below.

3.1.1 Protecting stateless people: the history of the 1954 Convention

The large-scale displacement and denationalization that accompanied the Second World War left hundreds of thousands of people without the protection of any government. Even though the UDHR proclaimed that 'all human beings are born free and equal in dignity and rights' and elaborated a catalogue of rights and freedoms to which everyone is entitled, regardless of their status, these 'unprotected persons' were still considered to be in a highly precarious situation. Given their circumstances, how exactly were their fundamental rights to be guaranteed and who, indeed, was responsible for their protection now that they were cast adrift from their state of origin?

During the drafting of the UDHR, the representative of the International Refugee Organisation[9] suggested that where *national* protection was

---

[6] *Ibid.*   [7] *Ibid.*, p. 4.   [8] *Ibid.*

[9] This is the United Nations' specialized agency established in 1946 to provide assistance to and, where appropriate, facilitate the repatriation of displaced persons and refugees following the Second World War.

lacking, *international* protection must be offered and that this was a role for the United Nations itself.[10] In a similar vein, a concrete proposal submitted during the drafting of the UDHR was to include in Article 15 – after the affirmation that 'everyone has the right to a nationality' – the following text: 'All persons who do not enjoy the protection of any Government shall be placed under the protection of the United Nations.'[11] However, the idea of incorporating a direct reference to international or UN protection in the UDHR did not garner enough support and was dropped in favour of leaving this matter to be dealt with separately by ECOSOC – which had already called for a more detailed study of the question.[12]

The publication, in 1949, of the UN's *Study of Statelessness*, therefore, marked the first real step towards the creation of an international regime for protecting the 'unprotected'. The study concluded that the 'improvement of the position of stateless persons requires their integration in the framework of international law'.[13] In other words, guaranteeing protection for stateless people necessitates the adoption of a 'general convention [as] a lasting international structure' as well as the creation of 'an independent organ which would to some extent make up for the absence of national protection and render them certain services which the authorities of a country of origin render to their nationals resident abroad'.[14]

It should be noted that in these sections of the study, as in the study's title, the term 'stateless' is deemed to refer to all those lacking the protection of a national government.[15] However, the study also draws a distinction between those among the 'unprotected' who are *refugees* and those who are *stateless persons*.[16] Moreover, the study distinguishes between

---

[10] He pointed out that: 'The principle of international protection for stateless people was accepted by the United Nations when it created the International Refugee Organisation, and [that] therefore the Declaration on Human Rights should contain a statement recognising the fundamental need of protection of thousands of people who were stateless either in law or in fact.' Statement by Oliver Stone, as cited in J. Morsink, *The Universal Declaration of Human Rights. Origins, Drafting and Intent* (Philadelphia, PA: University of Pennsylvania Press, 1999), 81.

[11] This was to be followed by a proviso reading 'This protection shall not be accorded to criminals, nor to those whose acts are contrary to the principles and aims of the United Nations.' See the Draft International Declaration on Human Rights in Annex A, Part I of the Report of the Commission on Human Rights, 6th Session, E/600, 17 December 1947.

[12] Resolution 116 (VI) D.

[13] United Nations, *A Study of Statelessness*, 43.   [14] *Ibid.*, 51 and 56.

[15] See also the 'Report of the Commission on Human Rights, 6th Session', E/600 (December 1947) para. 46 ('Miscellaneous Resolutions – Stateless Persons').

[16] For more on this, see A. Edwards and L. van Waas, 'Statelessness' in *The Oxford Handbook of Refugee and Forced Migration Studies* (Oxford University Press, in 2014).

two categories of *stateless person,* namely the *de jure* stateless 'who are not nationals of any state' and the *de facto* stateless 'who, having left the country of which they are nationals, no longer enjoy the protection and assistance of their national authorities'.[17] The latter scenario – that of *de facto* statelessness – was seen to be closely aligned with the situation of refugees since, elsewhere, 'the study identified two causes of *de facto* statelessness, both of them refugee-related: taking refuge abroad as a result of racial, religious or political persecution; or mass emigration caused by changes in a country's political or social system'.[18] Most *de facto* stateless people would therefore be considered refugees. Refugees could meanwhile also be stateless *de jure* 'if they have been deprived of their nationality by their country of origin'.[19]

Although pointing out their distinct circumstances, both refugees and stateless persons were seen by the *Study of Statelessness* as requiring international assistance and so they remained grouped together when the study recommended the drafting of a convention to improve their status. The subsequently convened Ad Hoc Committee on Statelessness and Related Problems quickly agreed that an international treaty should be prepared for the protection of these two categories of 'unprotected person'. The majority of the committee members felt, however, that the two groups should be distinguished within this process.[20] The committee thus compiled the text of a Draft Convention Relating to the Status of Refugees and a Draft Protocol thereto Relating to the Status of Stateless Persons. This set the refugee and the stateless person, who had until then been cast together in the eyes of the international community, on diverging paths – a move which has had far-reaching consequences for the protection of the stateless to this day.

In 1951, the Convention relating to the Status of Refugees (Refugee Convention) was adopted and with it the international legal definition of a refugee was established. In essence, a refugee came to be defined as someone who is 'unprotected' because they have fled their country

---

[17] 'Report of the Commission on Human Rights, 6th Session', p. 7. Note that with regard to the category of *de facto* stateless, the study proceeds to reference the Annex to the Constitution of the International Refugee Organisation, which 'uses this formula: "a person... who... is unable or unwilling to avail himself of the protection of the Government of his country of nationality or former nationality"'.

[18] UNHCR, 'UNHCR and de facto statelessness' LPPR/2010/01 (April 2010), p. 6.

[19] United Nations, *A Study of Statelessness*, 8.

[20] G. Goodwin-Gill, 'Introduction to the 1954 Convention relating to the Status of Stateless Persons, from the United Nations Audiovisual Library of International Law', available at: http://untreaty.un.org/cod/avl/ha/cssp/cssp.html, last accessed 2 January 2013.

and cannot invoke the protection of their government, on account of a well-founded fear of persecution.[21] The refugee may or may not hold a nationality, but this is not the crux of the matter – what is paramount is whether they have a fear of persecution. With the adoption of the Refugee Convention, those stateless people who also met the definition of a refugee could benefit from international protection,[22] while the non-refugee stateless were left unprotected by either a national government or by international law. This was to be remedied by the aforementioned Draft Protocol to the Refugee Convention on the Status of Stateless Persons, but discussion of this text was deferred to a later date because of time pressure to adopt the refugee instrument and a sense that refugees were in urgent need of attention.[23]

A second conference of plenipotentiaries was convened in 1954, which set about drafting a new instrument on stateless persons, taking the Refugee Convention and the Draft Protocol as its point of departure to consider what rights to extend to non-refugee stateless people. Indeed, it was 'the prevailing view of the conference [...] that for a practical consideration (time) they should not engage in rewording the text of the Refugee Convention, except when this was justified by the difference between the two groups (refugees vs. stateless persons)'.[24] In the end, it was decided that the instrument should become a convention in its own right and it was adopted as the 1954 United Nations Convention relating to the Status of Stateless Persons (1954 Convention). The purpose of a separate convention – rather than a protocol – was to allow states to become parties to this statelessness instrument without having to first ratify the Refugee Convention. In practice, this possibility has remained virtually unused, since the Refugee Convention quickly drew dozens of states parties, while the 1954 Convention attracted relatively few and continues to lag behind its sister convention in accessions. Regardless, the shared drafting history of the two instruments as set out here has left an indelible mark on the 1954 Convention: it is almost identical to the Refugee

---

[21] Convention relating to the Status of Refugees, Geneva, 28 July 1951, in force 22 April 1954, 189 UNTS 150, Art. 1A(2).

[22] As well as from the assistance of the Office of the United Nations High Commissioner for Refugees, which was established the year before the Refugee Convention was adopted and is directly mandated with a supervisory role under Article 35 of the Convention.

[23] C. Bachelor, 'Stateless Persons: Some Gaps in International Protection', *International Journal of Refugee Law* (1995), 7; Goodwin-Gill, 'Introduction to the 1954 Convention relating to the Status of Stateless Persons'.

[24] N. Robinson, *Convention relating to the Status of Stateless Persons – Its History and Interpretation* (New York: Institute of Jewish Affairs, 1955).

Convention. The significance of this will be explored when the content and impact of the 1954 Convention is discussed later in this chapter, but first I turn to the drafting process of the second dedicated UN instrument on statelessness.

3.1.2 Avoiding statelessness: the history of the 1961 Convention

The history of the international community's interest in statelessness actually predates the developments described above, which unfolded only after the Second World War. Two decades earlier, there were already attempts to agree international rules that would reduce the incidence of statelessness. Indeed, the ultimate goal of the international community's engagement with statelessness was to eliminate past and future cases. The challenge in doing so rests in the ever-present tension between a state's freedom to set the conditions for acquisition and loss of nationality and the need to address anomalies like statelessness that result precisely from that freedom.[25]

The League of Nations' Hague Convention on Certain Questions relating to the Conflict of Nationality Laws of 1930 (1930 Hague Convention) sought to navigate a course between these tensions.[26] For example, the 1930 Hague Convention details how states should deal with certain situations giving rise to statelessness within their respective nationality laws, including voluntary renunciation of nationality (Articles 7 and 12), potential change of nationality as a result of change in civil status or a change in the nationality of a family member (Articles 8, 9, 13, 16 and 17), acquisition of nationality by foundlings (Article 14) and acquisition of nationality by children born to parents who are themselves of unknown nationality or stateless (Article 15).[27] A Protocol relating to a Certain Case

---

[25] Note that historically, regulating access to nationality was seen as part of the *domaine réservé* of states and it was not initially subject to any rules of international law. *Tunis and Morocco Nationality Decrees case*, Permanent Court of International Justice, 1923, p. 24. A detailed exposition of the developing influence of international law on nationality is given in P. Spiro, 'A New International Law of Citizenship', *The American Journal of International Law*, 105 (2011).

[26] See, in this respect, Article 1 of the Convention on Certain Questions Relating to the Conflict of Nationality Law, The Hague, 13 April 1930, in force 1 July 1937, 179 LNTS 89.

[27] It should be noted that this guidance is issued in varying degrees of obligation, using suggestive language in some provisions (such as Article 15 on granting nationality by place of birth to children whose parents are themselves of unknown nationality or stateless) and directive language in others (such as Article 14 on foundlings).

of Statelessness was also adopted, specifically 'with a view to preventing statelessness'.[28] This protocol's only substantive Article obliges state parties to confer nationality to 'a person born in its territory of a mother possessing the nationality of that State and of a father without nationality or of unknown nationality', even if the state does not usually adhere to the *jus soli* system.[29] Thus, without seeking to harmonize nationality regulations more broadly and with minimal interference in states' sovereignty in the area of nationality, the 1930 Hague Convention and Protocol codified the first significant international rules regarding the avoidance of statelessness.

Although successful in laying some early groundwork for the regulation of nationality matters by international agreement, these 1930s standards proved insufficient to secure the avoidance of statelessness. Then, the right to a nationality was included in the 1948 Universal Declaration of Human Rights, recognizing, for the first time, 'the individual's interest in nationality to be a matter of international law'.[30] Subsequently, in 1954, the International Law Commission (ILC) answered the General Assembly's call for the preparation of 'a draft international convention or conventions for the elimination of statelessness',[31] forwarding two proposals for its consideration: a Draft Convention on the Elimination of Future Statelessness and a Draft Convention on the Reduction of Future Statelessness.[32] While not markedly different in terms of their overall style and content, the two drafts differed significantly in their potential to deal with statelessness. The first of these alternatives contained unconditioned safeguards which, if implemented through each state's nationality laws, would guarantee that no new cases of statelessness would arise in the various conflicts of laws scenarios dealt with. The second draft convention addressed the same set of problems and in a broadly similar fashion. However, this version acknowledged that a state could prescribe certain preconditions for individuals who wish to benefit from some of the safeguards against statelessness to meet.

Both drafts prepared by the ILC focused exclusively on providing a solution in the specific circumstance of a threat of statelessness and did

---

[28] Protocol Relating to a Certain Case of Statelessness, The Hague, 12 April 1930, in force 1 July 1937, 179 LNTS 115, Preamble.

[29] *Ibid.*, Art. 1.

[30] Spiro, 'A New International Law of Citizenship', 710.

[31] Resolution 319 (IV): Provisions for the functioning of the High Commissioner's Office for Refugees, UN General Assembly, 11 August 1950.

[32] International Law Commission, 'Report of the International Law Commission covering the work of its Sixth Session' A/CN.4/88 (1954).

not seek to establish international rules on nationality more generally. Nevertheless, by phrasing the proposed safeguards in absolute terms, the Draft Convention on the Elimination of Future Statelessness was deemed a step too far when government representatives met in 1959 to discuss the texts. Therefore, it was quickly discarded in favour of a detailed consideration of the alternative draft, that on the *reduction* of future statelessness. This version was seen to strike a better balance between states' sovereign interests in the realm of nationality and the common interest of agreeing some restrictions on this discretion with a view to avoiding statelessness.[33] After some further painstaking negotiations, a text was finally agreed and adopted at a second meeting convened in 1961 as the United Nations Convention on the Reduction of Statelessness (1961 Convention).[34]

3.2. The content of the statelessness conventions

Twelve years after publishing its *Study of Statelessness,* the United Nations' international statelessness regime was finally in place. As the drafting history demonstrates, the first instrument adopted, the 1954 Convention, aims to guarantee the enjoyment by stateless people of a minimum set of rights. The second, the 1961 Convention, houses a set of safeguards for the avoidance of statelessness. Details of the approach taken by the conventions to meet these respective aims are set out in the following paragraphs.

3.2.1 *Protecting stateless people: the approach of the 1954 Convention*

A core provision of the 1954 Convention and one that was the subject of intense discussion both during the drafting process and again in recent years, is Article 1(1).[35] This sets out the definition of a stateless person as follows:

> The term 'stateless person' means a person who is not considered as a national by any State under the operation of its law.

---

[33] C. Batchelor, 'Stateless Persons: Some Gaps in International Protection', *International Journal of Refugee Law,* 7 (1995), 250; UNHCR and IPU, 'Nationality and Statelessness. A Handbook for Parliamentarians' (2005), 12.

[34] See further L. E. van Waas, *Nationality Matters. Statelessness under International Law* (Antwerp/Oxford/Portland, OR: Intersentia, 2008), 45.

[35] See, for instance, Robinson, *Convention relating to the Status of Stateless Persons;* UNHCR, 'Expert Meeting – The Concept of Stateless Persons under International Law ("Prato Conclusions")' (May 2010).

What underlies the stateless person's 'unprotected' status and what renders him or her in need of international protection, is simply the absence of a nationality.[36] It is neither relevant how the individual came to be without nationality nor where the person subsequently finds him or herself.[37] Once stateless – and bar some limited exclusion clauses[38] – a person is entitled to the benefits of the 1954 Convention.

Before looking at what these benefits are, it is worthwhile pointing out that several other international instruments also refer to statelessness – including, of course, the 1961 Convention – and it is a term in common use within the UN framework, as well as at the level of both national and regional legal systems.[39] Yet, this opening provision of the 1954 Convention is the only place where international law defines the term. As such, the definition of statelessness provided by this instrument is widely recognized as the basis for interpreting any reference to statelessness found elsewhere in treaty, legislation or soft law texts. It has also been described by the ILC as having attained the status of customary international law, meaning that the definition housed in the 1954 Convention should be adhered to by all states when dealing with the question of statelessness, even if they have not acceded to the convention.[40]

---

[36] The corresponding article of the Refugee Convention defines a refugee as 'unprotected' and in need of international protection due to a well-founded fear of persecution on one of a number of particular grounds.

[37] As the UNHCR Handbook on Protection of Stateless Persons explains, 'the question of free choice is not relevant when determining eligibility for recognition as stateless under article 1(1)'. Moreover, 'article 1(1) applies in both migration and non-migration contexts'. UNHCR, 'Handbook on Protection of Stateless Persons under the 1954 Convention relating to the Status of Stateless Persons'(Geneva, 2014), paras. 51 and 15 respectively.

[38] These can be found in Article 1(2) of the 1954 Convention and are, in effect, also the same as those encountered in the 1951 refugee convention. They detail who is considered to either not need or not deserve this international protection, including: persons who are already receiving assistance from another United Nations agency (primarily excluding Palestinians assisted under UNRWA's mandate) and persons with respect of whom there is serious reason for considering that they have committed a crime against peace or a serious non-political crime. Note that someone who falls within one of these exclusion clauses is still 'stateless' and must be treated as such where international law provides other benefits on the basis of that status, but they fall beyond the specific scope of protection of the 1954 Convention.

[39] Other examples of international and regional instruments that refer explicitly to statelessness include Article 7 of the Convention on the Rights of the Child, Article 9 of the Convention on the Elimination of All Forms of Discrimination Against Women and several Articles of the European Convention on Nationality.

[40] The International Law Commission states in its commentary to the Draft Articles on Diplomatic Protection, which also refers to statelessness without defining it, that the 1954 Convention definition 'can no doubt be considered as having acquired a customary

The benefits accruing to the status of 'stateless person' under the 1954 Convention come in the form of a set of civil, economic, social and cultural rights for which a minimum standard of treatment is guaranteed. The topics covered are the same as those dealt with in the Refugee Convention, upon which this instrument was modelled. They are: religious freedom, access to courts, (moveable, immoveable and intellectual) property, education, employment and labour rights, freedom of association, social security, housing, rationing, free movement and legal personhood. Significantly, although the 1954 Convention does not require states parties to grant their nationality to stateless persons, it does call on states to facilitate the naturalization of stateless people, with a view to helping them to resolve their situation by acquiring a nationality as quickly and easily as possible.[41]

The actual standard of treatment to be enjoyed by a stateless person differs from one right to another, again mimicking the Refugee Convention in this regard. The base level of rights enjoyment is that 'accorded to aliens generally in the same circumstances' and effectively amounts to a non-discrimination clause for stateless persons vis-à-vis other non-nationals.[42] However, most of the provisions ask contracting states to offer 'treatment as favourable as possible' and some demand the same treatment as nationals. There are also a number of absolute rights, to be accorded to stateless people regardless of whether these are available for the country's own nationals.[43] The 1954 Convention also copied another technique of the Refugee Convention: extending these benefits of the convention on a gradual scale, according to the degree of attachment between the person and the state. Thus, only a few of the rights housed in the 1954 Convention can immediately be invoked by anyone within a state's jurisdiction who satisfies the definition of a stateless person. Many of the entitlements are only offered to those who are lawfully present, lawfully staying or even habitually resident in the territory of the contracting state.[44]

---

nature'. However, no further reasoning is provided. ILC, 'Draft Articles on Diplomatic Protection with Commentaries', *Yearbook of the International Law Commission*, 2 (2006) 49.

[41] Art. 32, 1954 Convention.   [42] *Ibid.*, Art. 7(1).

[43] The rights included are: access to courts (Art. 16(1)) and protection from expulsion (Art. 31).

[44] Examples of rights applicable for stateless persons lawfully staying include the right to wage-earning employment, artistic and intellectual property rights and the right to public relief.

The prescription of different standards of treatment, to be enjoyed in accordance with different levels of attachment to the state, creates a complex picture in terms of the exact benefits stateless people are entitled to enjoy under the 1954 Convention.[45] The operation of the convention has also been complicated by the lack of instruction on how the definition of a stateless person is to be applied in practice – the instrument itself is silent on this. The manner in which the 1954 Convention came into being and the core characteristics of the text as described here have conspired to cause problems in its implementation, as will be explored in Part 3.3.1 below. Moreover, the 1954 Convention failed to include any kind of oversight mechanism. Its sister instrument, the Refugee Convention, establishes in contrast a clear role for the Office of the United Nations High Commissioner for Refugees with regards to the interpretation and supervision of its implementation by states.[46] When the 1954 Convention became a stand-alone instrument, rather than a protocol to the Refugee Convention as originally envisaged, it also became divorced from this supervisory machinery.

3.2.2   Avoiding statelessness: the approach of the 1961 Convention

It is time to turn to the content of the 'other' statelessness convention: the 1961 Convention on the Reduction of Statelessness. At first sight, this instrument appears difficult to digest. The first Article alone takes up more than a full page in the official UN version available online, thanks to its various paragraphs and sub-paragraphs.[47] Despite this, the 1961 Convention is actually relatively straightforward. In its ten substantive Articles, it sets out safeguards for the avoidance of statelessness in three broad contexts: acquisition of an original nationality at birth, including by foundlings (Articles 1 to 4);[48] loss, deprivation or renunciation of

---

[45] See the 'Schematic Overview of Rights in the 1954 Statelessness Convention' in Annex 3 of L. van Waas, *Nationality Matters. Statelessness under International Law*, 455.

[46] According to Article 35 of the 1951 Refugee Convention, 'Contracting States undertake to cooperate with the Office of the United Nations High Commissioner for Refugees … in the exercise of its functions, and shall in particular facilitate its duty of supervising the application of the provisions of this Convention.' As such, states have a duty to report to UNHCR on the implementation of the convention. Moreover, under its own Statute UNHCR is also mandated to promote ratification of relevant instruments and implementation of appropriate measures for the protection of refugees. See Article 8 of the Statute of the Office of the United Nations High Commissioner for Refugees, as adopted by the General Assembly on 14 December 1950 (Annex to Resolution 428 (V)).

[47] Available at http://untreaty.un.org/ilc/texts/instruments/english/conventions/6_1_1961. pdf, last accessed 2 January 2013.

[48] See Chapter 6 by de Groot in this volume.

nationality in later life (Articles 5 to 9);[49] and in respect of succession of states (Article 10).[50] In each case, the provision indicates which state is responsible for allowing a person to acquire or retain nationality if they would otherwise be stateless.

The 1961 Convention offers a far more comprehensive framework in this respect than the earlier 1930 Hague Convention and Protocol.[51] At the same time, the 1961 Convention holds true to the approach adopted by its League of Nations' forerunners; it respects the overall freedom of states to legislate as they see fit in the area of nationality and does not attempt to create an international law on nationality. Instead, all bar one of its provisions only enter into effect when the outcome would 'otherwise' be statelessness. The only Article to proclaim a broader obligation for states to adhere to when rendering any decision on nationality is Article 9, which prohibits the deprivation of nationality on 'racial, ethnic, religious or political grounds'. This is a general standard that echoes and reinforces Article 15(2) of the UDHR, which prohibits the arbitrary deprivation of nationality.

Overall, the 1961 Convention thus offers a clear and concrete set of guarantees for the avoidance of statelessness in each of these potential conflict of laws situations that can be readily transposed into domestic law. Nevertheless, the early decision to proceed with a text that prescribes only the *reduction* and not the *elimination* of statelessness means that some cases may still slip through. The text displays the unfortunate hallmarks of an international compromise shaped by the previously discussed tension between states' sovereign interests in the field of nationality and the shared interest of avoiding statelessness – it stops short of prescribing obligations that will decisively eliminate statelessness in all circumstances. Herein lies the explanation for the length and complexity of the 1961 Convention Articles. Had the draft text on the *elimination* of statelessness been adopted, Article 1 would have simply read as follows:

> A person who would otherwise be stateless shall acquire at birth the nationality of the Party in whose territory he is born.[52]

---

[49] See Chapter 8 by Brandvoll in this volume.

[50] See Chapter 9 by Ziemele in this volume.

[51] For instance, the 1961 Convention provides for acquisition of nationality by any child born on a contracting state's territory who would otherwise be stateless (Article 1). This is a more effective guarantee than that offered in either the 1930 Hague Convention or the Protocol Relating to a Certain Case of Statelessness which both focus on securing a nationality for a child, one or both of whose parents are stateless. This latter approach does not address the situation in which the parents do hold a nationality, but are, for whatever reason, unable to transmit this nationality to their child.

[52] 'Draft Convention on the Elimination of Future Statelessness', *Yearbook of the International Law Commission* (1954), 2.

Article 1 in the 1961 Convention on the Reduction of Statelessness, as adopted, comprises five lengthy paragraphs with further sub-paragraphs. In fact, the ten substantive provisions of the Draft Convention on the Elimination of Future Statelessness amounted to just 477 words in total, while the word count for the same ten Articles in the 1961 Convention comes to four times that: 1,855 words.

Sticking with Article 1, the reluctance of states to surrender too much of their freedom to regulate access to nationality can be demonstrated through closer inspection of the various paragraphs and sub-paragraphs, which effectively operate as provisos to the main rule elaborated in the opening sentence: 'A Contracting State shall grant its nationality to a person born in its territory who would otherwise be stateless.'[53] A state may choose the path of automatic conferral of nationality in these circumstances, which would meet the standard envisaged in the Draft Convention on the Elimination of Future Statelessness by ensuring the immediate and unconditional avoidance of childhood statelessness. However, in accordance with paragraph 1(b) of Article 1, a state may also elect to establish an application procedure for the grant of nationality at a later date to a child who is stateless from birth. The state may also make such an application subject to one or more of four conditions detailed in paragraph 2 of the same Article.[54] Recognizing that this system may leave some persons stateless, paragraph 4 offers a further safeguard to help those who fail to acquire a nationality because they missed the application deadline or did not fulfil the residence requirements set – in such circumstances by descent from a parent who is a national. However, there too, access to nationality may be offered through an application procedure and again subject to certain conditions. Thus, although the text asserts the general rule that nationality may not be lost or deprived where it would leave an individual stateless, it also accepts that states may nevertheless render a person stateless in this manner, in a limited set of exceptional circumstances.[55] In all, by giving states

---

[53] Art. 1(1), 1961 Convention.

[54] This exhaustive list of further conditions is as follows: 'a fixed period for lodging an application immediately following the age of majority (Article 1(2)(a)); habitual residence in the Contracting State for a fixed period, not exceeding five years immediately preceding an application nor ten years in all (Article 1(2)(b)); restrictions on criminal history (Article 1(2)(c)); and the condition that an individual has always been stateless (Article 1(2)(d))'. UNHCR, 'Guidelines on Statelessness No. 4: Ensuring Every Child's Right to Acquire a Nationality through Articles 1–4 of the 1961 Convention on the Reduction of Statelessness' HRC/GS/12/04 (21 December 2012), para. 36.

[55] The exceptions concern the following situations: loss or deprivation of nationality where a naturalized person has spent an extended period of residence abroad (Article 7(4)); loss

some freedom with regard to the manner in which certain safeguards are effectuated, the 1961 Convention is realistic in its ambitions and offers flexibility, but it also undercuts its primary objective by admitting that some people will be rendered or left stateless without this amounting to a violation of the Convention's terms.

Given the aforementioned exceptions that states are permitted to maintain under the 1961 Convention to the general rule that statelessness is to be avoided, it is of great importance to ensure that states do not overreach this margin of discretion by interpreting the various exceptions too expansively or upholding conditions that are not prescribed by the 1961 Convention. In this regard, the question of a supervisory mechanism is central. Article 11 of the 1961 Convention aims to address this matter. A person who believes that they are entitled to invoke one of the instrument's safeguards can, if such assistance is required, receive help from an appointed international 'body' to present their claim to the requisite state authority. Since the entry into force of the 1961 Convention, UNHCR has held the mandate to carry out this role.[56] However, this advisory function lacks the power of a true supervisory mechanism and has, in practice, seldom been invoked.[57] This will necessarily have an impact on the level of implementation of the convention's safeguards.

3.3.   Assessing the impact and relevance of the statelessness conventions today

For the first four decades after their adoption, the statelessness conventions drew very little interest. State parties were unforthcoming and the instruments were relatively slow to enter into force.[58] The international

---

or deprivation of nationality for a person who acquired nationality by descent (while born abroad) and failed to take the steps prescribed by law to retain this nationality upon attaining the age of majority (Article 7(5)); deprivation of nationality acquired by fraud (Article 8(2)(b)); and deprivation of nationality as a consequence of the person committing particular acts which are inconsistent with his or her duty of loyalty to the State (Article 8(3)).

[56]   Resolution 3274 (XXIV), UN General Assembly, 10 December 1974.

[57]   Note that both the 1954 and 1961 UN statelessness conventions grant jurisdiction to the International Court of Justice to settle any disputes arising over the interpretation and application of the instruments' terms, but no such referrals have been made under either convention to date. Moreover, it can be questioned whether it is appropriate to rely on a state to initiate proceedings before the ICJ on behalf of a stateless person, given that their lack of national protection is what underlies their situation. See also L. van Waas, *Nationality Matters. Statelessness under International Law*, 46.

[58]   A chart mapping the rate of accessions to both statelessness conventions is available at: www.unhcr.org/4ff2e4b39.html, last accessed 9 May 2014.

community scarcely devoted any attention to promoting the conventions, with calls for ratification – for instance, from the UN General Assembly – only starting to pick up from the late 1990s.[59] UNHCR's involvement was initially also very limited. Although tasked by the General Assembly in the 1970s as the body to which an individual could turn to receive assistance in presenting a claim under the 1961 Convention to the relevant authority, the agency did not actively pursue this element of its mandate, as refugee work continued to monopolize its time and resources. The more expansive, global mandate that UNHCR holds today also only developed later.[60] Nor did the statelessness conventions attract much in the way of analysis or academic writing – only a handful of publications devoted more than a cursory reference to the issue during this period.[61] It was with no false modesty then, that the conventions' own 'Information and Accession Package' – released at the turn of the century to expound their merits to potential state parties – described them as 'orphan conventions'.[62] Yet the question as to the impact and enduring relevance of the UN statelessness conventions is complex and requires a deeper exploration of their value in light of contemporary developments.

3.3.1   Protecting stateless people: challenges and opportunities under the 1954 Convention

One of the most significant consequences of this period of neglect of the statelessness conventions is that certain questions relating to

---

[59] See the UNHCR compilation of 'Extracts of international documents encouraging states to accede to the 1954 Convention relating to the Status of Stateless Persons and the 1961 Convention on the Reduction of Statelessness', available at: www.unhcr.org/refworld/pdfid/4c21c6822.pdf, last accessed 9 May 2014.

[60] See Chapter 4 by Manly in this volume.

[61] These include two works by Paul Weis: Paul Weis, 'The United Nations Convention on the Reduction of Statelessness, 1961', *International and Comparative Law Quarterly*, 2 (1962), 4; and Paul Weis, *Nationality and Statelessness in International Law* (Dordrecht: Kluwer Academic Publishers Group, 1979); as well as a number of articles written by Carol Batchelor from 1995 onwards, including: Carol Batchelor, 'Statelessness and the Problem of Resolving Nationality Status', *International Journal of Refugee Law*, 10 (1998) and Carol Batchelor, 'Developments in International law: The Avoidance of Statelessness Through Positive Application of the Right to a Nationality', Council of Europe's First Conference on Nationality, Strasbourg, 2001.

[62] UNHCR, 'Information and Accession Package: The 1954 Convention relating to the status of stateless persons and the 1961 Convention on the reduction of statelessness', Geneva (January 1999).

the interpretation and application of the 1954 Convention standards remained unaddressed. This is particularly evident with regard to the fundamental issue of what is understood by the term 'stateless'. Although the 1954 Convention sets out a definition of – and legal regime for – the 'stateless person', this did not entirely quell debate about who ought to benefit from international protection. In principal, with the adoption of the 1951 Convention on refugees and, three years later, the 1954 Convention, states had defined the circumstances in which they would be willing to extend such protection to otherwise 'unprotected persons'. This lack of protection warranting international protection must either manifest itself as a fear of persecution or as the absence of nationality. Yet there was a nagging sense among many that the *quality* not just the *possession* of nationality is crucial. Thus, some commentators argued that 'persons with no effective nationality are, for all practical purposes, stateless, and should be labelled and treated as such'.[63] The drafters of the 1954 Convention themselves acknowledged this conundrum in the instrument's Final Act, as previously mentioned, when they recommended that a state party also consider extending the benefits of the convention to others 'when it recognizes as valid the reasons for which a person has renounced the protection of the State of which he is a national'.[64] This recommendation was included as a nod towards the protection of the so-called '*de facto* stateless'.[65]

The notion of '*de facto* statelessness' has more recently attracted considerable attention and has been the subject of varying and at times extremely broad interpretations, usually centring on the basic idea of holding a nationality that is somehow ineffective.[66] What little debate there was on statelessness in international affairs was often distracted by a preoccupation with this broader group, for whom no dedicated international legal framework had been developed and with regard to whom states' obligations of *international* protection were therefore

---

[63] D. Weissbrodt and C. Collins, 'The Human Rights of Stateless Persons', *Human Rights Quarterly*, 28 (2006), 251.

[64] Art. 1, Final Act of the 1954 Convention.

[65] This, in contrast to the '*de jure* stateless' which is the term commonly used to describe those who meet the international legal definition of a stateless person, as contained in Article 1 of the 1954 Convention relating to the Status of Stateless Persons. See also the discussion of the distinction between *de jure* and *de facto* statelessness made within the original United Nations, *A Study of Statelessness*.

[66] A detailed discussion of the history of the concept of *de facto* statelessness and an overview of some of its different usages can be found in H. Massey 'UNHCR and de facto Statelessness' UNHCR Legal and Protection Policy Series, Geneva, April 2010.

highly ambiguous.[67] In contrast, there was scant investment in improving the understanding of the parameters and practical application of the definition of a 'stateless person' as prescribed in Article 1 of the 1954 Convention. For instance, dedicated Stateless Status Determination mechanisms – a logical equivalent to the common Refugee Status Determination procedures – are few and far between.[68] Similarly, while the definition of a refugee was debated and the concept of refugee protection underwent progressive interpretation through doctrinal guidance and jurisprudence, the international statelessness regime has not yet undergone the same kind of organic development, although this is slowly changing.

There has recently been a concerted effort by the international community to make up for lost time in terms of its commitment to the 1954 Convention. The relative enforcement gap pointed out earlier in this chapter has already been closed by the expansion of UNHCR's statelessness mandate to include the protection of stateless persons, in part by acting as a guardian of the 1954 Convention.[69] UNHCR has subsequently taken a leading role in helping to settle the ambiguity surrounding state parties' obligations towards stateless people and the manner in which the determination of statelessness should be conducted, by encouraging doctrinal debate and developing authoritative guidance on these issues, including on the definition.[70]

This is helping to finally put to rest some of the debate surrounding '*de facto* statelessness'. The criticism that the 1954 Convention's definition of a 'stateless person' is too narrow and will only offer a pathway to protection for a select few has been demonstrated as ungrounded. Many situations

---

[67] This is notwithstanding the obligations of states towards all persons within their jurisdiction on the basis of human rights law and the specific obligations relating to the protection of the rights of their citizens.

[68] See Chapter 5 by Gyulai in this volume.

[69] See, for instance, General Assembly Resolution No. 61/37, Office of the United Nations High Commissioner for Refugees, A/RES/61/137, 25 January 2007. See Chapter 4 by Manly in this volume.

[70] UNHCR, 'Guidelines on Statelessness No. 1: The Definition of "Stateless Person" in Article 1(1) of the 1954 Convention relating to the Status of Stateless Persons' HCR/GS/12/01 (20 February 2012); UNHCR, 'Guidelines on Statelessness No. 2: Procedures for Determining whether an Individual is a Stateless Person' HCR/GS/12/02 (5 April 2012); UNHCR, 'Guidelines on Statelessness No. 3: The Status of Stateless Persons at the National Level' HRC/GS/12/03 (17 July 2012). These guidelines have been consolidated into UNHCR, "Handbook on Protection of Stateless Persons under the 1954 Convention relating to the Status of Stateless Persons' (Geneva, 2014).

that have long been described as '*de facto* statelessness' should properly be understood as falling within the scope of the 1954 Convention definition of a stateless person, because the individuals in question are 'not *considered as* a national *under the operation of* [any state's] law'.[71] The assessment of who is a 'stateless person' must take into account not only the letter of the law, but also the manner in which the state interprets and applies this law. As such, even if an objective third party would determine that a certain person enjoys nationality on the basis of their reasoned reading of the legislation in force, if the state reaches the opposite conclusion, this latter viewpoint is decisive. On the other hand, if the state evidently does deem the person to be a citizen but he or she is experiencing problems exercising particular rights in that state – such as voting or owning property – there is a clear violation of human rights norms, which needs to be tackled as such, but it is not a problem of statelessness. There is only a small grey area remaining, where the notion of '*de facto* statelessness' lingers, namely with respect to a person who is *outside* their country of nationality and cannot invoke its diplomatic or consular protection.[72] As shown earlier in this chapter, the original United Nations *Study of Statelessness* coined the term '*de facto* statelessness' in relation to such circumstances, but in most cases such individuals will fall within the scope of the international refugee protection framework. Now that the 1954 Convention's protection scope has been clarified and states are exploring how best to implement this in their national systems, the international community will be better placed to have a focused and informed discussion on the extent to which the UN framework needs to be supplemented. In the few remaining incidences where a person is neither stateless, nor a refugee, but is abroad and without *national* protection, it remains to be seen whether states are willing to go beyond their present obligations and nevertheless extend *international* protection.

The push to make up lost ground and settle the various outstanding questions is an acknowledgement that the protection of stateless people warrants more attention, and that the 1954 Convention – regardless of any intrinsic shortcomings – provides useful tools for this purpose that cannot readily be found elsewhere in international law. Indeed, although human rights law now offers a broader framework for the protection of individual rights, there is no other instrument that is specifically geared

---

[71] Emphasis added, Art. 1(1), 1954 Convention.
[72] On diplomatic protection and consular assistance, see Chapter 1 by Edwards in this volume.

towards the situation and particular needs of the stateless. In particular, the special measures prescribed by the 1954 Convention, such as travel and identity documents, administrative assistance and an appeal for facilitated naturalization, continue to form a vital complement to human rights standards.

3.3.2   Avoiding statelessness: challenges and opportunities under the 1961 Convention

It is interesting to note that, despite its cautious and flexible approach, the 1961 Convention on the Reduction of Statelessness was especially slow to attract support following its adoption – even compared to the 1954 Convention.[73] Nevertheless, upon closer inspection, the influence of the standards housed in the 1961 Convention may, in fact, belie its 'orphan' status. In reality, states continued to face the very same challenges that had paved the way for the negotiation of this international agreement to begin with. They were confronted with conflicts of nationality laws that had the potential to leave people stateless and this was still considered to be a fundamentally undesirable anomaly. The 1961 Convention provides practical solutions for the most common problems encountered by states, including for the avoidance of statelessness among children upon a change of civil status and resulting from renunciation, loss or deprivation of nationality. In elaborating these safeguards, the 1961 Convention takes its cue from the fundamental principles upon which all states' nationality policy is ultimately based: family ties (*jus sanguinis*) and a territorial connection (*jus soli* and *jus domicilli*).[74] By adopting a balanced and pragmatic approach, grounded in existing nationality doctrine, the 1961 Convention actually reflects how states have sought to address the aforementioned problems of statelessness even in the absence of formal ratification of the convention, and thus have wider relevance beyond the circle of states parties.

A comprehensive global review of nationality laws' compliance with the 1961 Convention has yet to be carried out.[75] However, various basic surveys and regional studies provide some sense of the extent to which the 1961 Convention standards have spread. In Africa, for example, a region-wide

---

[73] In the end, it took until December 1975 for the 1961 Convention to enter into force, having finally accrued the six state parties required two years previously.

[74] See Chapter 1 by Edwards in this volume.

[75] UNHCR, the EUDO Citizenship Observatory, the Statelessness Programme of Tilburg Law School and other partners are currently cooperating with a view to establishing a

audit of citizenship laws completed in 2009 indicated that at least nine countries provide some form of explicit protection against statelessness in the context of loss or deprivation of nationality, incorporating all or part of the safeguards set out in Articles 7 and 8 of the 1961 Convention, even though only two of those included in this list are state parties.[76] The same audit uncovered at least thirty-nine African countries with a provision in their nationality laws allowing a child of unknown parentage (i.e., a foundling) to acquire citizenship, concurring with Article 2 of the 1961 Convention – as well as Article 14 of the even more poorly ratified 1930 Hague Convention – despite a very low number of state parties to this instrument in Africa.[77] Similar trends are visible, for instance, in Europe and the ASEAN region.[78] This demonstrates that the lack of interest in formally acceding to the 1961 Convention is not matched by an equal disinterest in the overall avoidance of statelessness. On the contrary, many states have put in place one or more of the safeguards against statelessness which have been codified in this instrument. Moreover, even taking into account developments in the field of international law since the convention was adopted, this statelessness-specific instrument has retained its value and is being given renewed consideration since statelessness started to climb back up the international agenda as an issue of concern from the late 1990s onwards.[79] There is no other universal treaty with such detailed, comprehensive and readily implementable safeguards for the avoidance of statelessness, which helps to explain the recent

---

Global Nationality Law Analytical Database. The aim is to assess each country's nationality law and its compliance with major international standards, including key provisions of the 1961 Convention on the Reduction of Statelessness. Once this data becomes available, the exact reach of the 1961 Convention standards will become more visible.

[76] B. Manby, *Citizenship Law in Africa. A Comparative Study* (New York: Open Society Institute, 2009) at table 6. Status of accessions in all cases cited here as of 9 May 2014.

[77] Thirty-one of the countries in which a foundling provision was traced were not parties to the 1961 Convention at the time of the citizenship audit. Manby, *Citizenship Law in Africa*, at table 1.

[78] L. van Waas, 'Good Practices for the Identification, Prevention and Reduction of Statelessness and the Protection of Stateless Persons in South East Asia', Human Rights in Southeast Asia, Series 1: Breaking the Silence, South East Asia Human Rights Network, (2011). Assessment tables compiled by the European Union Democracy Observatory on Citizenship, available at: http://eudo-citizenship.eu, last accessed 4 January 2013.

[79] The right to a nationality is now widely recognized as a fundamental human right. It has been included in almost every major human rights instrument since the 1948 Universal Declaration – both at the global and at the regional level. Consider, for instance, Article 24 of the International Covenant on Civil and Political Rights; Article 7 of the Convention on the Rights of the Child; Article 29 of the International Convention on the Protection of the Rights of All Migrant Workers and Members of Their Families; Article 9 of the Convention on the Elimination of All Forms of Discrimination Against Women;

increase in accessions.[80] Moreover, it offers a concrete platform from which UNHCR – as the United Nations' agency mandated to assist states to implement the convention – can provide valuable technical advice on the reform and application of nationality laws to prevent and reduce statelessness.[81]

At the same time, certain challenges inherent in the approach of the 1961 Convention must be acknowledged. First, there are the limitations described earlier in this chapter with regard to the sub-clauses that may allow a person to become or remain stateless even when the safeguards are fully implemented. In particular where this has the effect of allowing someone to be stateless from birth into adulthood or even beyond, it can be questioned whether this benchmark is not inappropriately low given the widespread recognition of a *child's* right to a nationality.[82] Second, the 1961 Convention does not deal in any real depth with the problem of statelessness when arising from state succession. Article 10, which addresses this issue, offers neither the required depth nor detail to address the problem decisively. The ILC, which previously undertook the preparatory drafting of the 1961 Convention, has since identified this gap and elaborated the Articles on Nationality of Natural Persons in Relation to the Succession of States. This separate set of standards, however, has yet to attain the status of an international convention and remains a soft law instrument.[83] Third, the 1961 Convention shows its age where it fails to tackle some of the contemporary challenges with regard to the prevention of statelessness. In debating the draft text half a century ago, states could not have foreseen that modern reproductive technology, resulting, for

---

Article 5 of the Convention on the Elimination of All Forms of Racial Discrimination; Article 18 of the Convention on the Rights of Persons with Disabilities; Article 6 of the African Charter on the Rights and Welfare of the Child; Article 20 of the American Convention on Human Rights; Article 7 of the Covenant on the Rights of the Child in Islam; Article 6 of the UN Declaration on the Rights of Indigenous Peoples. However, the formulation of this right tends to be in largely aspirational terms and it is not immediately clear which state would be responsible for attributing nationality in any given circumstances.

[80] Only in the European context has a similar effort to elaborate more concrete safeguards been pursued, resulting in the 1997 European Convention on Nationality – and later also the 2006 Council of Europe Convention on the Avoidance of Statelessness in relation to State Succession.

[81] See, for instance, UNHCR, 'Note on International Protection. Addendum – Note on Statelessness' A/AC/96/1098/Add.1 (28 June 2011).

[82] See Chapter 6 by de Groot in this volume.

[83] Articles on Nationality in relation to the succession of States, as contained in *Yearbook of the International Law Commission*, 1999, vol. II, Part Two. See Chapter 9 by Ziemele in this volume.

instance, in complex international surrogacy arrangements, would manifest itself down the line as a new source of potential conflicts of nationality laws and statelessness. The 1961 Convention is understandably,
yet regrettably, silent on such questions. Finally, there are some areas in
which the 1961 Convention appears to actually stand at odds with subsequent developments in international law. For example, it fails to prescribe
gender equality in the enjoyment of nationality rights and even makes a
distinction within its own safeguards between children born in and out
of wedlock.[84] Furthermore, there is an emerging view among scholars
that any deprivation of nationality resulting in statelessness is, by definition, arbitrary and thereby prohibited under international human rights
law.[85] The 1961 Convention, however, allows for the loss or deprivation of
nationality in several different circumstances, even if this would lead to
statelessness.[86]

3.4.   Conclusion

Since the turn of the century, statelessness has resurfaced onto the international agenda, after a period of relative neglect and with a fresh sense
of urgency. There is evident concern about what is now understood to be
the impact of statelessness on human security and communal stability.[87]
Indeed, whether it be in the (online) media, in multilateral government
meetings, in academic literature or in civil society programming, interest in statelessness is arguably keener today than ever before. What is of
great interest is the position of the statelessness conventions within this
renaissance. In October 2012, as UNHCR welcomed the newest state
parties to the 1954 and 1961 conventions, High Commissioner Guterres
pronounced:

> We are at a turning point. Fifteen states have become parties to the
> Conventions in the past 18 months and we know that many more are

---

[84] Gender is missing from the list of grounds elaborated in Article 9 of the 1961 Convention
on which deprivation of nationality is prohibited. See Chapter 7 by Govil and Edwards in
this volume.

[85] See Chapter 8 by Brandvoll in this volume.

[86] Compare, for instance, Articles 7 and 8 of the 1961 Convention to Article 7 of the
European Convention on Nationality (adopted by the Council of Europe in 1997).

[87] See, for instance, L. van Waas and M. Manly, 'The Value of the Human Security
Framework in Addressing Statelessness' in Edwards and Ferstman (eds.), *Human
Security and Non-Citizens: Law, Policy and International Affairs*, (Cambridge University
Press, 2010) 49–81.

preparing to do so – in the Americas, Africa, Asia, Europe and the Middle East. This is unprecedented.[88]

In fact, by the end of 2012, a new record had been set for attracting the greatest number of new states parties to the two UN statelessness conventions in any year since their adoption. Thus, rather than being cast out as irrelevant in content, inadequate in approach or invalidated by time, the instruments are being widely embraced.

Today, the 1954 and 1961 Statelessness Conventions can best be seen as legitimate and key components of a broader international framework for tackling statelessness – and their provisions should also be interpreted, wherever relevant, in light of subsequent developments, in particular in the field of human rights.[89] Some of the shortcomings discussed in this chapter are likely to remedy themselves in time, with a concerted commitment to the implementation of the standards housed in the two instruments. In fact, the assessment of the 1954 and 1961 Statelessness Conventions provided in this chapter is perhaps premature. In some ways, in spite of the physical age of the instruments, there is a sense that the work starts now and a true evaluation of their effectiveness in offering solutions for statelessness can reasonably be conducted only once some of the most recent developments in terms of accessions, doctrinal debate and the issuance of guidance have had the chance to take hold and any remaining gaps can be properly identified.

Questions to guide discussion

1. Identify the two UN Statelessness Conventions. What were the aims of each convention?
2. What are the limitations of the 1961 Convention? What reasons are there for these limitations?

---

[88] UNHCR 'Ecuador, Honduras and Portugal accede to Statelessness Conventions', News Story (2 October 2011), available at www.unhcr.org/506adfc95.html, last accessed 11 November 2012.

[89] The 1961 Convention on the Reduction of Statelessness should, for instance, be interpreted in accordance with the principle of the best interests of the child, the recommendations of the Committee on the Rights of the Child, and emerging human rights jurisprudence including: Series C, Case 130, *Yean and Bosico* v. *Dominican Republic*, Inter-American Court of Human Rights, 8 September 2005; Case C-135/08 *Janko Rottmann* v. *Freistaat Bayern* [2 March 2010] CJEU; *Nubian Children in Kenya* v. *Kenya*, No. 002/Com/002/209, 22 March 2011; *Genovese* v. *Malta* (App. no. 53124/09), ECHR, 11 October 2011.

3. The 1961 Statelessness Convention has been described as having a 'cautious and flexible approach'. Yet it has still been slow to gather signatures. Would another approach have been better?
4. Describe the debate around the concept of *de facto* statelessness. How would you construct an argument that some cases that have been described as *de facto* statelessness actually fall within the definition of statelessness in the 1954 Convention? Do you agree?
5. Establish whether your country is a signatory to both the 1954 and 1961 Statelessness Conventions. What arguments would you make in favour of the conventions to a government that was considering whether or not to become a signatory?

4

UNHCR's mandate and activities to address statelessness

MARK MANLY

For most of the past sixty years, statelessness has been regarded as a problem for international governance. After a flurry of activity focused on the development of international legal standards from the end of World War II until the early 1960s, the issue essentially disappeared from the global agenda.[1] UNHCR has had some responsibility for stateless persons since its establishment in 1950, but it was only in the mid-1990s that its mandate significantly expanded as a result of resolutions of the United Nations General Assembly. The authority to act did not immediately lead to global action on statelessness by UNHCR, in large part because of significant gaps in the understanding of the scope and nature of statelessness problems around the world. Nevertheless, in recent years this has changed dramatically, as UNHCR's Executive Committee, or ExCom, has provided some flesh to the bare bones of the mandate entrusted to the office by the General Assembly.

This chapter explores the content and scope of that mandate. It begins with a general overview of the basis for the mandate and looks in turn at activities undertaken by the office to promote and clarify the content and scope of existing standards, develop complementary standards, generally raise awareness of the problem and build partnerships to improve responses to statelessness around the world. The chapter then looks at what have become the four key components of the mandate: identification, prevention and reduction of statelessness and the protection of

---

This chapter reflects the views of the author and not necessarily those of UNHCR or of the United Nations. The author gratefully acknowledges comments provided on earlier versions of this chapter by Janice L. Marshall and Laura van Waas.

[1] There were of course references in UN human rights treaties (discussed below) and some activity at the country and regional level such as the recommendations adopted by the Council of Europe and the International Commission on Civil Status (ICCS), Convention No. 13 to Reduce the Number of Cases of Statelessness, 13 September 1973, available at: www.unhcr.org/refworld/docid/3decd5ce4.html, last accessed 21 May 2014.

stateless persons. It does so by looking at some of the key activities under-taken with regard to each of these areas in turn, and ends with a brief ana-lysis of where things stand today.

4.1. The mandate in a nutshell

UNHCR was originally mandated in its 1950 Statute to address the situ-ation of stateless persons, but this was limited to stateless persons who were refugees pursuant to paragraph 6(A)(II) of the UNHCR Statute and Article 1(A)(2) of the 1951 Convention relating to the Status of Refugees. Following the emergence of mass statelessness linked to the dissolu-tion of the USSR, Czechoslovakia and the Federal Socialist Republic of Yugoslavia, in 1995 UNHCR's Executive Committee adopted a conclu-sion on the Prevention and Reduction of Statelessness and the Protection of Stateless Persons.[2] The United Nations General Assembly then took up the issue in its 'omnibus' resolution on UNHCR of the same year.[3] This resolution established a truly global mandate for UNHCR on statelessness.

The General Assembly identified statelessness as a cause of forced displacement and then indicated that 'the prevention and reduction of statelessness and the protection of stateless persons are important also in the prevention of potential refugee situations'. The resolution then endorsed the activities already being undertaken and linked them to the office's protection and solutions mandate. The General Assembly '[e]ncourages the High Commissioner to continue her activities on behalf of stateless persons, as part of her statutory function of providing international protection and of seeking preventive action'.[4] The General Assembly specifically requested that UNHCR focus on promotion of accession to the two statelessness conventions and 'to provide rele-vant technical and advisory services pertaining to the preparation and implementation of nationality legislation'.[5] The focus on accessions to the conventions and technical advice on nationality legislation became a central part of UNHCR's activities over the following decade. Much of

---

[2] Executive Committee of the UN High Commissioner for Refugee's Program, 'Prevention and Reduction of Statelessness and the Protection of Stateless Persons', Conclusion No. 78 (XLVI) 1995.

[3] UN General Assembly resolution A/RES/50/152, on 'Office of the High Commissioner for Refugees', 9 February 1996.

[4] *Ibid.*, para. 14.   [5] *Ibid.*, para. 15.

this work was focused on Europe and related to efforts to mitigate the impact of state succession.

The year 2006 marked a turning point. The Executive Committee adopted a detailed conclusion on the identification, prevention and reduction of statelessness and the protection of stateless persons.[6] Comprising twenty-four operative paragraphs, it provided a great deal more guidance on how the office was to implement the mandate. Much of the conclusion is focused on operational responses to statelessness such as studies to identify statelessness in regions where there are information gaps,[7] support to states in undertaking citizenship campaigns[8], support for states to disseminate information on nationality procedures[9] and establishing programmes to protect and assist stateless persons including through legal aid.[10] As in 1995, the General Assembly's resolution on UNHCR adopted later the same year endorsed the conclusion and the work already being undertaken by the office and specifically referred to the four distinct areas of activity. The General Assembly:

> notes the work of the High Commissioner in regard to identifying stateless persons, preventing and reducing statelessness, and protecting stateless persons, and urges the Office of the High Commissioner to continue to work in this area in accordance with relevant General Assembly resolutions and Executive Committee conclusions.[11]

UNHCR's global mandate is supplemented by a specific role under the 1961 UN Convention on the Reduction of Statelessness ('1961 Convention'). When the sixth instrument of ratification/accession to the 1961 Convention was deposited in 1974, the General Assembly designated UNHCR as the body referred to in Article 11 of the Convention 'to which a person claiming the benefit of this Convention may apply for the examination of his claim and for assistance in presenting it to the appropriate authority.'[12] This was initially on an interim basis but was confirmed by the General Assembly in 1976 and in more recent resolutions.[13] As set out

---

[6] ExCom, 'Conclusion on Identification, Prevention and Reduction of Statelessness and Protection of Stateless Persons, No. 106 (LVII) – 2006'.

[7] *Ibid.*, para. (c).   [8] *Ibid.*, para. (q).

[9] *Ibid.*, para. (r).   [10] *Ibid.*, para. (v).

[11] UN General Assembly resolution 61/137, on 'Office of the High Commissioner for Refugees', 25 January 2006, para. 4.

[12] UN General Assembly resolution 3274 (XXIV) of 10 December 1974.

[13] See UNHCR, 'United Nations General Assembly Resolutions of particular relevance to statelessness and nationality', 25 March 2013, available at: www.unhcr.org/refworld/docid/4c49a02c2.html, last accessed 21 May 2014.

in UNHCR's 2010 global statelessness strategy,[14] relevant activities under Article 11 include:

- Publicizing UNHCR's role, including through contacts with relevant state authorities, NGOs and lawyers' networks;
- Reaching out to individuals who Field Offices believe may have valid claims under the terms of the 1961 Convention;
- Assessing the compatibility of the state's legislation with its obligations under the 1961 Convention with relevance to the case;
- Assessing whether the individual falls under the scope of a relevant provision, e.g. whether or not a child would otherwise be stateless if not granted the nationality of the state in question;
- Presenting findings to the individual concerned, the authorities or in court proceedings where necessary through *amicus curiae* briefs.

The 1954 UN Convention relating to the Status of Stateless Persons ('1954 Convention') has only a minimalist supervisory regime, setting out in Article 33 that '[t]he Contracting States shall communicate to the Secretary-General of the United Nations the laws and regulations which they may adopt to ensure the application of this Convention'. In practice UNHCR has performed this function. This is complemented by the request of the Executive Committee that UNHCR 'provide technical advice to States Parties on the implementation of the 1954 Convention so as to ensure consistent implementation of its provisions'.[15]

For the most part, states have accepted, at least tacitly, that UNHCR has responsibility to address statelessness in their territory. In the limited number of situations in which UNHCR has been requested by governments not to act, they have tended to indicate that the issue was not one of statelessness, as opposed to denying that UNHCR has a mandate to address it. The following sections set out in greater detail how this mandate has been implemented in recent years.

The issue of mandate inevitably leads to questions of scope: where does UNHCR's responsibility end and that of another agency begin? The question of institutional responsibilities within the UN system was addressed

---

[14] UNHCR, 'UNHCR Action to Address Statelessness: A Strategy Note', March 2010, para. 69, available at: www.unhcr.org/refworld/docid/4b9e0c3d2.html, last accessed 21 May 2014.

[15] ExCom, 'Conclusion on Identification, Prevention and Reduction of Statelessness and Protection of Stateless Persons, No. 106 (LVII) – 2006', para. (x).

in the UN Secretary-General's Guidance Note on The United Nations and Statelessness, which states:

> The UN General Assembly has entrusted the Office of the United Nations High Commissioner for Refugees (UNHCR) with a mandate relating to the identification, prevention and reduction of statelessness and protection of stateless persons. However, this Guidance Note affirms that all UN entities system-wide must increase their efforts to address statelessness. The UN should tackle both the causes and consequences of statelessness as a key priority within the Organization's broader efforts to strengthen the rule of law.[16]

Nonetheless, there may be overlap between mandates and competencies of different agencies, something that is a particular concern in the context of humanitarian action in conflict and internal displacement settings, where rapid responses, and hence clear delineation of responsibilities and good coordination, are essential. The Guidance Note therefore specifies that 'At the country level, the UN Country Teams provide the appropriate framework for coordination between UN entities dealing with statelessness with a lead responsibility exercised by UNHCR under its mandate.'[17]

4.2. Implementation – setting the agenda at the international level

There has been uneven and sometimes halting progress towards implementation of the mandate for most of the period since 1995. In a litter of two offspring, statelessness was the metaphorical runt. It was overlooked and unloved while the refugee mandate received all of the attention. Statelessness was dramatically overshadowed by UNHCR's work on internal displacement, an area where mandate responsibility is not as strongly rooted. Increasingly, though, UNHCR has been successful in improving implementation of the mandate in terms of both 'breadth' and 'depth'. As will be seen, it has achieved some success in putting statelessness on the international agenda.

As will be clear from the remainder of this chapter, 'breadth' has increased dramatically in terms of the range of issues addressed since 1995, moving beyond a focus principally on accessions to the conventions

---

[16] UN Secretary-General, 'Guidance Note of the Secretary-General: The United Nations and Statelessness', June 2011, p. 3, available at: www.unhcr.org/refworld/docid/4e11d5092. html, last accessed 21 May 2014.
[17] *Ibid.*, p. 15.

and reform of nationality laws to a range of technical, operational and awareness-raising responses. Breadth has also increased in geographic terms, measured both in terms of the number and location of states in which UNHCR operates. In the period 2009–13,[18] the number of UNHCR offices that set objectives on statelessness more than doubled. Whereas in the 1990s most activities were in Europe, in 2011–13 the largest country budgets were elsewhere, in particular in Africa[19], the Americas[20] and Asia.[21]

Implementation is now far 'deeper' than it was previously, in particular as a result of more detailed guidance on treaty standards and a growing body of expertise relating to operational responses. As a result, UNHCR has provided more effective technical advice to governments on appropriate operational responses, specific aspects of nationality legislation and determination procedures under the 1954 Convention. These trends are set to continue, not least as a result of the creation of dedicated country and regional statelessness posts in 2011–13 in Asia, the Middle East and North Africa, Europe, the Americas and West Africa.

4.3. Promotion of existing standards of international law

The 1954 Convention and the 1961 Convention are the only modern-day, global treaties designed specifically to address aspects of the problem of statelessness.[22] As at 20 July 2014, the 1954 Convention had eighty-two states parties, with the majority in Africa (17), the Americas (18) and Europe (37). There are only six states parties in Asia and four in the Middle East and North Africa (MENA). The 1961 Convention had fifty-nine states parties including twelve in Africa, twelve in the Americas, five in Asia and the Pacific, twenty-nine in Europe and two in MENA.

These two treaties cannot be applied in isolation and should be viewed as forming part of a much wider web of international standards relating to prevention and reduction of statelessness and protection of stateless persons, in particular in UN human rights conventions and regional treaties. Looked at in this way, the international legal framework addresses many, but not all, of the issues relating to statelessness.

---

[18] There is no data prior to this time because the budget structure did not separate statelessness activities from those oriented towards refugees, returnees and internally displaced persons.
[19] Sudan, South Sudan and Côte d'Ivoire.
[20] The Caribbean.   [21] Myanmar, Central Asia.
[22] See also Chapter 3 by van Waas in this volume.

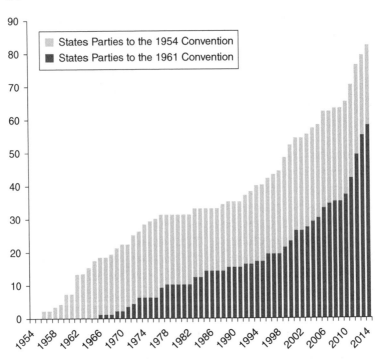

Figure 4.1 The number of states parties to the 1954 and 1961 Conventions since their adoption

UNHCR has undertaken a number of activities to promote existing standards. Since the mid-1990s, it has advocated for accession[23] to the 1954 and 1961 Conventions. Previously, no UN entity actively promoted accession. The impact of UNHCR's efforts in this area are evidenced by the upturn in the rate of accessions beginning in 1995 and in particular in 2011–14 as a result of the campaign linked to the fiftieth anniversary of the 1961 Convention,[24] which led to seventeen accessions to the 1954 Convention and twenty-two to the 1961 Convention between mid-2011 and July 2014.

[23] Note that because the 1954 Convention closed for signature on 31 December 1955, states that did not sign can only become parties by accession (see Art. 35). The same holds for the 1961 Convention, which closed for signature on 31 May 1962 (see Art. 16).

[24] See the range of tools developed for this campaign, available at: www.unhcr.org/refworld/statelessness.html, last accessed 21 May 2014, including 'Protecting the Rights of Stateless Persons: The 1954 Convention relating to the Status of Stateless Persons', September 2010 and 'Preventing and Reducing Statelessness: The 1961 Convention on the Reduction of Statelessness', September 2010.

Documents produced by UNHCR also systematically refer to standards of international human rights law, in particular those relating to the right to a nationality.[25] Faced with a series of instances of state succession, UNHCR has also referred on multiple occasions to the ILC Articles on the Nationality of Natural Persons in Relation to Succession of States. [26]

4.4.   Clarification of the content and scope of existing standards

Statelessness has often been viewed as a highly specialized but obscure area of international law. This is no doubt explained in part by the complexities of and wide divergences in approach between nationality laws of different states. The sheer range of issues and standards involved also provides part of the explanation. For example, prevention and reduction of statelessness are rather different from protection of stateless persons.

Another challenge, though, is the manner in which key elements of the 1954 and 1961 Conventions are worded. For example, the definition of a stateless person in the 1954 Convention is more complex than it appears at first glance and has been interpreted in wildly diverging manners. The 1961 Convention has several provisions which are lengthy and highly technical. The Executive Committee therefore requested UNHCR to provide technical advice to states on the adoption and implementation of safeguards to prevent statelessness[27] and also on the implementation of the 1954 Convention.[28]

The Division of International Protection of UNHCR responded by developing authoritative guidance on key doctrinal issues through a process the starting point of which is consultation with external experts[29] and UNHCR field staff. The first of the issues addressed was the definition

---

[25] Just two of many examples are UNHCR, 'Guidelines on Statelessness No. 4: Ensuring Every Child's Right to Acquire a Nationality through Articles 1–4 of the 1961 Convention on the Reduction of Statelessness', 21 December 2012, HCR/GS/12/04, available at: www.unhcr.org/refworld/docid/50d460c72.html and UNHCR, 'UNHCR Action to Address Statelessness: A Strategy Note', March 2010, available at: www.unhcr.org/refworld/docid/4b9e0c3d2.html, last accessed 21 May 2014.

[26] See, for example, UNHCR, 'Sudan Citizenship Symposium – Keynote Address by Ms. Erika Feller, Assistant High Commissioner – Protection, UNHCR', 6 November 2010, available at: www.unhcr.org/refworld/docid/4cf384662.html, last accessed 21 May 2014.

[27] ExCom, 'Conclusion on Identification, Prevention and Reduction of Statelessness and Protection of Stateless Persons, No. 106 (LVII) – 2006', para. (s).

[28] *Ibid.*, para. (x).

[29] Meetings were attended by a mix of government officials, members of the judiciary, NGO representatives, legal practitioners, academics, members of human rights supervisory bodies and UNHCR staff.

of a stateless person in international law. UNHCR organized an expert meeting in Prato, Italy in 2010[30] and published guidelines[31] in February 2012. The conclusions of this meeting were groundbreaking. They analysed the definition in far more detail than had been done previously in any UNHCR document, making it clear that in many instances it had been interpreted too restrictively in the past.

The conclusions also helped clarify the limits of the notion of '*de facto*' statelessness, a term which had often been employed as a catch-all category for people who were deemed to have some nationality 'problem'.[32] The very idea of '*de facto*' statelessness has been questioned, not least because it is not defined, nor does it give rise to specific standards of treatment in an international treaty.[33] Yet there is also some consensus that the 'traditional' (read: 1940s and 1950s) usage of the term describes individuals who are 'unprotected' and who continue to fall into a protection gap. A perennial debate has therefore arisen: Should the notion of '*de facto*' statelessness be discarded altogether or is there any advantage in terms of promoting the protection of specific individuals in continuing to employ it? UNHCR has opted to note the limitations inherent in the concept while attempting to salvage what it can to address the situation of those people who possess a nationality but are denied the protection of their state.[34]

Expert consultations held subsequently went on to examine procedures to determine who is stateless and the status to be granted to stateless persons at the national level.[35] Guidelines on these two topics were also issued in 2012.[36] The final meeting in the series focused on the prevention

---

[30] UNHCR, 'Expert Meeting – The Concept of Stateless Persons under International Law (Summary Conclusions)', Prato, May 2010 ('Prato Conclusions').

[31] UNHCR, 'Guidelines on Statelessness No. 1: The definition of "Stateless Person" in Article 1(1) of the 1954 Convention relating to the Status of Stateless Persons', HCR/GS/12/01, 20 February 2012.

[32] This issue is explored in some detail in the background paper prepared for the meeting by Hugh Massey, 'UNHCR and De Facto Statelessness', April 2010, Legal and Protection Policy Research Series, LPPR/2010/01.

[33] Guy S. Goodwin-Gill, 'Definitions, Statelessness, and Stateless Persons. Some notes on some of the issues', prepared for UNHCR's 2010 Expert Meeting held in Prato, Italy; Alison Harvey, 'Statelessness: The "de facto" Statelessness Debate', *Immigration, Asylum and Nationality Law*, 24 (2010), 257, 258.

[34] UNHCR, 'Handbook on Protection of Stateless Persons under the 1954 Convention relating to the Status of Stateless Persons' (Geneva, 2014), paras. 123 and 124.

[35] UNHCR, 'Expert Meeting – Statelessness Determination Procedures and the Status of Stateless Persons (Summary Conclusions)' Geneva, December 2010.

[36] UNHCR, 'Guidelines on Statelessness No. 2: Procedures for Determining whether an Individual is a Stateless Person', HCR/GS/12/02, 5 April 2012; and UNHCR, 'Guidelines

of statelessness under the 1961 Convention amongst children born in the territory of a state party or to a national abroad.[37] Guidelines on this issue were issued in December 2012.[38] In 2014, UNHCR consolidated the first two guidelines relating to the protection of stateless persons into a handbook.[39]

Given the importance of international human rights standards, UNHCR has provided significant input to human rights supervisory bodies. For example, in coordination with UN country teams, it has provided background information during the review of each UN member state in the context of the Human Rights Council's Universal Periodic Review. It has also advocated for and provided input to general comments on specific treaty standards.[40]

4.5.   Standard setting

Development of complementary global and regional treaty and non-treaty standards has been a key priority given the relatively low number of states parties to the two statelessness conventions as well as gaps in the standards they contain.

UNHCR's role in the development of treaty standards has a long history and includes participation in the drafting of the 1961 Convention

on Statelessness No. 3: The Status of Stateless Persons at the National Level', HRC/GS/12/03, 17 July 2012.

[37] UNHCR, 'Expert Meeting – Interpreting the 1961 Statelessness Convention and Preventing Statelessness among Children: Summary Conclusions', Dakar, Senegal, September 2011 ('Dakar Conclusions').

[38] UNHCR, 'Guidelines on Statelessness No. 4: Ensuring Every Child's Right to Acquire a Nationality through Articles 1–4 of the 1961 Convention on the Reduction of Statelessness', 21 December 2012, HCR/GS/12/04.

[39] UNHCR, 'Handbook on Protection of Stateless Persons under the 1954 Convention relating to the Status of Stateless Persons' (Geneva, 2014).

[40] See, for example, 'General Recommendation XXX of the Committee for the Elimination of Racial Discrimination (CERD)', 'CRC General Comment No. 6 (2005) on Treatment of Unaccompanied and Separated Children Outside their Country of Origin, of the Committee on the Rights of the Child (CRC)' and the 'General Comment on Undocumented Children of the Committee on the Rights of Migrant Workers and their Families'. For an example of advocacy aimed at adoption of a general comment, see Alice Edwards, 'Displacement, Statelessness and Questions of Gender Equality under the Convention on the Elimination of All Forms of Discrimination against Women', August 2009, PPLAS/2009/02, available at: www.unhcr.org/refworld/docid/4a8aa8bd2.html, last accessed 21 May 2014, produced for a joint CEDAW/UNHCR seminar in 2009.

itself.[41] At the regional level, UNHCR has worked with other actors to further develop international standards in the field of nationality, in particular to address emerging issues and gaps under the 1961 Convention. It has maintained a long and productive collaboration with the Council of Europe in this area. UNHCR participated actively in the drafting of the 1997 European Convention on Nationality.[42] Moreover, given that the 1961 Convention contains only a limited provision on state succession, UNHCR provided input to the drafting of the International Law Commission's Articles on the Nationality of Natural Persons in Relation to Succession of States, as well as to the 2006 Council of Europe Convention on the avoidance of statelessness in relation to state succession.

Thus far, UNHCR involvement in standard setting in other regions has been limited to declarations, resolutions and other non-binding documents, notably of the Organization of American States[43] and the Asian-African Legal Consultative Organization.[44] Going forward, UNHCR will support adoption of additional treaty standards, for example as recommended for Africa by an African Union symposium in 2012.[45]

UNHCR has played an active role in negotiation of a number of resolutions of the UN Human Rights Council and the former Commission of Human Rights,[46] notably the series of resolutions on arbitrary deprivation of nationality and the resolution on nationality of women and children, adopted for the first time in 2012.

---

[41] See the historical overview provided in the United Nations Audiovisual Library of International Law, 'Convention on the Reduction of Statelessness, 1961: Introductory note' by Guy S. Goodwin-Gill, available at: http://legal.un.org/avl/ha/crs/crs.html, last accessed 21 May 2014.

[42] UNHCR played a significant role also in the drafting of the 1999 'Recommendation on the Avoidance and Reduction of Statelessness' and the 2009 'Recommendation on the Nationality of Children'. See also Chapter 6 by de Groot in this volume.

[43] See Resolutions 2599 (XL-O/10) and 2665 (XLI-O/11) on 'Prevention and Reduction of Statelessness and Protection of Stateless Persons in the Americas'.

[44] See Asian-African Legal Consultative Organization (AALCO), Resolution on the Half-Day Special Meeting on 'Legal Identity and Statelessness', 8 April 2006, RES/45/SP.l, available at: www.unhcr.org/refworld/docid/44eaddc54.html, last accessed 21 May 2014.

[45] See African Union, Recommendations of the African Union Symposium on 'Citizenship in Africa: Preventing Statelessness, Preventing Conflicts', 24 October 2012, available at: www.unhcr.org/refworld/docid/510139472.html, last accessed 21 May 2014.

[46] Relevant resolutions of both the Council and the former Commission are available at: www.unhcr.org/refworld/statelessness.html, last accessed 21 May 2014.

4.6. Awareness raising

Much of the foregoing reflects one of the traditional weaknesses of the discourse surrounding statelessness: it focuses on the legal and technical aspects of the problem. Often, however, what is most needed is more general information, highlighting the terrible impact of statelessness in human terms, and straightforward explanations of what can be done to address it. Thus, UNHCR has published a range of documents,[47] media stories[48] as well as photo[49] and video resources[50] that target a wider audience, in particular policy and opinion makers.

Thus far, the high-water mark of these efforts was the fiftieth anniversary of the 1961 Convention on the Reduction of Statelessness. The year 2011 was marked by unprecedented activity. The broad range of activities undertaken succeeded in placing statelessness on the international agenda. Over the course of the year, UNHCR intensified bilateral contact with governments to raise a series of priority issues: accessions and withdrawal of reservations, establishment of determination procedures, reform of nationality laws, measures to reduce statelessness and resolving obstacles to civil registration and issuance of proof of nationality. Field offices organized a series of activities including workshops and round-tables with government authorities and civil society in a broad range of countries,[51] including states where there had never been discussion of statelessness between government authorities and the United Nations. Country-level meetings were complemented by regional meetings, including in South-East Asia, Southern Africa, West Africa, Central Asia and the European Union.[52] These discussions served to underline and to

---

[47] See, for example, Chapter 4 of UNHCR, 'State of the World's Refugees: In Search of Solidarity', 2012. Available in abridged form at: www.refworld.org/docid/5100fec32.html, last accessed 21 May 2014.

[48] See UNHCR news archive at: www.unhcr.org/statelessness, last accessed 21 May 2014.

[49] The photo exhibition 'Nowhere People' by Greg Constantine has been shown in a wide range of venues including UN Headquarters during the high-level segment of the General Assembly and during meetings of UNHCR's ExCom and the Human Rights Council at the Palais des Nations in Geneva as well a range of world capitals.

[50] See, for example, the 'storytelling' videos 'Zeinab and Manal' from Lebanon and 'I am stateless' from France at www.unhcr.org/pages/49c3646c161.html, last accessed 21 May 2014.

[51] Locations included Georgia, Lebanon, Mexico, Namibia, Spain, South Sudan and Turkmenistan.

[52] Preparatory and outcomes documents for a number of these meetings are available on the statelessness page of UNHCR's Refworld site at: www.unhcr.org/refworld/statelessness.html, last accessed 21 May 2014.

better understand the gravity of the problem but also to discuss possible solutions. The most effective advocates for action to address statelessness proved to be representatives of governments which had already taken steps themselves.

A media campaign on the occasion of the anniversary of the 1961 Convention led to hundreds of reports in television, radio, print and electronic media on all continents.[53] These activities helped set the stage for a ministerial-level conference organized by UNHCR in Geneva in December 2011, which proved to be a turning point for international efforts on statelessness.

The ministerial meeting was undoubtedly the highest-level discussion of statelessness ever. More than 150 states participated and over 70 did so at the ministerial level. Many states expressed concern at the magnitude and impact of statelessness around the world. A number referred to action they had already taken and it was clear that many states wished to be able to show they were taking the problem seriously and leading by example. Perhaps most important of all were the outcomes of the pledging process. Sixty-one states made pledges on statelessness. These included thirty-three pledges on accession (some of which refer to accession to both treaties), twelve to reform nationality laws to prevent statelessness, eleven on the establishment or improvement of determination procedures, twelve on improvements to civil registration to prevent statelessness and twelve on studies and surveys of stateless populations. These pledges ensure that there will be continued progress in the short and medium term. UNHCR's biennial Note on Statelessness covering the period 2011–13 provides details on implementation.[54]

Overall, the anniversary of the 1961 Convention helped to demystify issues of statelessness and to slowly put paid to the idea that they are taboo and best left to states to address as they see fit.

4.7.   Partnerships

The low level of awareness of statelessness and lack of interest in addressing it at the international level can be explained in large part by the absence of any kind of global coalition to address the problem – until

---

[53] See UNHCR, 'Media Backgrounder: Millions Are Stateless, Living in Legal Limbo', August 2011, at www.unhcr.org/statelessness, last accessed 21 May 2014.

[54] See UNHCR, 'Note on Statelessness', June 2013, EC/64/SC/CRP.11, at: www.refworld. org/docid/51d2a8884.html, last accessed 21 May 2014.

recently at least. Other major human rights and humanitarian problems such as landmines, child soldiers, human trafficking or refugee protection have given rise to concerted action by government 'champions', NGOs, faith-based organizations and academics, together with the UN and regional organizations. For a very long time, there was nothing of the sort to address statelessness, despite its massive impact around the world. UNHCR has attempted to change this, promoting action by a range of actors. A particular focus has been on NGOs, through training, partnerships in mapping and operational responses, participation in regional meetings with governments, expert meetings on the standards contained in the 1954 and 1961 Conventions and discussion of statelessness at the annual UNHCR consultations with NGOs, held in Geneva.

4.8.   Identification of statelessness: beyond numbers

Refugees are often highly visible because by definition they have crossed an international border. Most stateless people, on the other hand, remain in the country of their birth (or a successor state), and are mixed in with the general population. As a result, stateless persons are often difficult to identify and generally they are not identified as such in national statistics. In statistical terms they are often, to use the cliché, 'invisible'. UNHCR's Executive Committee has requested that the office address this through a number of actions, including the undertaking and sharing of research 'with relevant academic institutions or experts, and governments, so as to promote increased understanding of the nature and scope of the problem of statelessness' and 'to establish a more formal, systematic methodology for information gathering, updating, and sharing'.[55] Identification of statelessness goes beyond 'counting', though. It also includes understanding causes of statelessness, looking at the profile of the population (including age, gender and diversity elements), their human rights situation and avenues (and obstacles) to acquisition of a nationality.

While some states have detailed data on stateless persons in their territory, many do not. At the end of 2013, UNHCR possessed up-to-date population data on seventy-five states.[56] This is close to double the data

---

[55] ExCom 'Conclusion on Identification, Prevention and Reduction of Statelessness and Protection of Stateless Persons, No. 106 (LVII) – 2006', paras. (c) and (d) available at: www.unhcr.org/refworld/docid/453497302.html, last accessed 21 May 2014.

[56] Note that when stateless persons are also recognized as refugees, they are reported by UNHCR in its refugee statistics. They are not reported in statelessness statistics to avoid double-counting. In any event, statistical information on stateless refugees is incomplete

coverage of 2004, when population figures were only reported for thirty states.[57] Most population figures are from registration systems, although for some countries data is from censuses or surveys. Some of the figures derived from registration systems are problematic. This occurs for a variety of reasons, for example because they do not provide a full account of the population as there is no fully functioning individual statelessness determination procedure[58] or other identification mechanism, or because the criteria applied for registration are not consistent with the international definition of a stateless person.[59] In some situations UNHCR has worked with governments to register specific populations as a first step towards solutions, as in Turkmenistan with regard to undocumented former Soviet citizens[60] and in Burundi with the population of Omani origin.

The absence of population figures and information on the profiles and protection needs of stateless persons makes it difficult to design effective responses. UNHCR has used various approaches to address these data gaps. It has promoted the use of population censuses as one means of gathering population data and made specific recommendations to this effect at a Joint UNECE/Eurostat Meeting on Population and Housing Censuses in 2008.[61] The impact of the 2010 round of population censuses has yet to be felt but is expected to lead to improved statistical reporting in a number of countries.

Field offices and partners have also intensified efforts to identify stateless populations through survey methodologies and other quantitative

because many national statistical databases do not correctly report them as stateless, in many cases referring to refugees only on the basis of country of origin. For the most recent statistics available at the time of writing see UNHCR, 'UNHCR Global Trends 2013', June 2014 available at: www.unhcr.org, last accessed 12 July 2014.

[57] UNHCR, 'Statistical Yearbook', 2004, 59.

[58] These procedures are designed to determine whether individuals are stateless for the purpose of establishing the standards of treatment to which they are entitled. For more information see UNHCR, 'Handbook on Protection of Stateless Persons under the 1954 Convention relating to the Status of Stateless Persons'(Geneva, 2014), Part Two. See also Chapter 5 by Gyulai in this volume.

[59] See, for example, UNHCR, 'Mapping Statelessness in the Netherlands', November 2011, section 3.2.

[60] See UNHCR, 'Statelessness: More than 3,000 Stateless People Given Turkmen Nationality', 7 December 2011, available at: www.unhcr.org/4edf81ce6.html, last accessed 21 May 2014.

[61] UNHCR, 'Measuring Statelessness through Population Census. Note by the Secretariat of the United Nations High Commissioner for Refugees', 13 May 2008.

methods as in Bangladesh,[62] Kyrgyzstan[63] and Serbia.[64] Studies in industrialized countries such as the United States,[65] Japan,[66] the United Kingdom,[67] the Netherlands[68] and Belgium[69] have tended to take a different approach in large part because the stateless are generally a much smaller proportion of the overall population. In several of these, the research included a review of existing administrative databases to verify whether any information they contained would serve to identify the size of the stateless population in the country. Qualitative methodologies were then used to better understand the profile of the stateless populations in each country.

4.9. Prevention: why wait for people to become stateless?

The mandate responsibility to take preventive action sets UNHCR's work on statelessness apart from its activities with regard to refugees. UNHCR generally reacts to refugee situations only with respect to those individuals who have crossed an international border.[70] With respect to statelessness, however, UNHCR has a responsibility to take preventive action. A broad range of interventions may be undertaken to prevent statelessness. These are often low profile and technical in nature but arguably the most cost-effective means of addressing statelessness. Four areas of activity will be highlighted here. The first two are inter-related: promotion of accession to the 1961 Convention and reform of nationality laws. The third is action in the context of state succession, which generally includes an element of law

[62] A survey of settlements of the Urdu speakers (or 'Biharis'), which was used as a basis for statistical reporting in 2006–7.

[63] UNHCR, 'A Place to Call Home: The Situation of Stateless Persons in the Kyrgyz Republic', 2009, available at: www.unhcr.org/4b71246c9.html, last accessed 21 May 2014.

[64] A survey of the Roma, Ashkali and Egyptian (RAE) households was conducted, which used census data as a sampling frame. The survey confirmed that 6.8 per cent of the population (up to 30,000 persons) face a risk of statelessness. Of these individuals, 21 per cent are children and 26 per cent are displaced from Kosovo.

[65] UNHCR, 'Citizens of Nowhere: Solutions for the Stateless in the US', December 2012, available at: www.unhcr.org/refworld/docid/50c620f62.html, last accessed 21 May 2014.

[66] UNHCR, 'Overview of Statelessness: International and Japanese Context', April 2010, available at: www.unhcr.org/refworld/docid/4c344c252.html, last accessed 21 May 2014.

[67] UNHCR, 'Mapping Statelessness in The United Kingdom', 22 November 2011, available at: www.unhcr.org/refworld/docid/4ecb6a192.html, last accessed 21 May 2014.

[68] UNHCR, 'Mapping Statelessness in the Netherlands', November 2011, available at: www. unhcr.org/refworld/docid/4eef65da2.html, last accessed 21 May 2014.

[69] UNHCR, 'Mapping Statelessness in Belgium', October 2012, available at: www.unhcr. org/refworld/docid/5100f4b22.html, last accessed 21 May 2014.

[70] Increasingly, UNHCR has alerted populations within countries of origin to the dangers of smuggling and perilous sea and overland journeys.

reform. The fourth area is civil registration. Largely because of increased migration, conflicts of law resulting in statelessness continue to occur – with devastating consequences for the people concerned. Therefore, it is in the interest of individuals and of states to ensure that common standards are adopted and applied. The rules set out in an international treaty such as the 1961 Convention give an important degree of certainty to states and to individuals.

Prevention requires, first and foremost, UNHCR to work with states to ensure that nationality laws have in place adequate safeguards to avoid statelessness in accordance with international standards. UNHCR emphasizes the question of safeguards in order to avoid any misunderstandings on the part of states or other actors that the Office is promoting the general application of either *jus soli* or *jus sanguinis*, or recommending that states allow dual nationality in all instances. UNHCR emphasizes that states continue to have a degree of freedom to regulate acquisition, renunciation, loss and deprivation of nationality, but must design their laws to prevent statelessness at birth and later in life.

The global treaty which sets out these safeguards is the 1961 Convention. Fifty years on, the number of accessions to the 1961 Convention was not something to celebrate. At the time of writing, only fifty-one states are party to the 1961 Convention – far less than to any major human rights treaty adopted in the 1960s. Nevertheless, the 1961 Convention is more influential than the number of states parties would appear to indicate. In particular, the convention has influenced subsequent developments in international human rights law such as the Convention on the Rights of the Child and regional treaties such as the American Convention on Human Rights (ACHR), the African Charter on the Rights and Welfare of the Child (ACRWC) and the European Convention on Nationality (ECN). Various safeguards found in the 1961 Convention to prevent statelessness at birth are now found in regional treaties, including the ECN. All told, more than 100 states worldwide now have an explicit obligation to grant nationality to children born in their territory who would otherwise be stateless.[71]

---

[71] Such an obligation can also be derived from the International Covenant on Civil and Political Rights and the Convention on the Rights of the Child but it is not explicitly set out therein. A list (albeit one which is not completely up to date), of the states referred to here is available in Annex V, UNHCR, 'UNHCR Action to Address Statelessness: A Strategy Note', March 2010, available at www.unhcr.org/refworld/docid/4b9e0c3d2.html, last accessed 21 May 2014.

Moreover, the standards set out in the 1961 Convention (which in some instances reflect pre-existing standards such as those set out in the 1930 Hague Convention on Certain Questions relating to the Conflict of Nationality Laws), are now reflected in the nationality laws of numerous states, including many which are not states parties. As noted above, the 1961 Convention is complemented by the ACHR, ACRWC and the ECN. But it should be stressed that the regional standards do not replace the global standards – in particular, because common rules are necessary not only within each region, but also globally, in particular between those regions sending or receiving migrants. It is therefore in the interest of all states to not only become parties to the 1961 Convention, but also to encourage states in other regions to do so as well.[72] If states do not wish to become parties to the 1961 Convention immediately, they should take into account the standards set out in the treaty.

The comparative analysis done thus far by UNHCR and partners to analyse nationality laws shows a trend among states to gradually incorporate some of the key safeguards against statelessness into their nationality laws. On the other hand, there are many states with nationality laws that have significant elements dating back many decades, often to independence, and which are not consistent with the international standards adopted in the past five decades. For example, at least twenty-seven states retain provisions that discriminate against women with regard to conferral of nationality on children.[73] Over 100 states have an explicit obligation to grant nationality to children born in the territory who would otherwise be stateless.[74] A number of these states have no such safeguard or only one that is inadequate. This is worrisome, given that this safeguard is the cornerstone of international efforts to prevent statelessness.

---

[72] Additional information on the importance of accession to the 1961 Convention is set out in UNHCR, 'Preventing and Reducing Statelessness: The 1961 Convention on the Reduction of Statelessness', September 2010, available at: www.unhcr.org/refworld/docid/4cad866e2.html, last accessed 21 May 2014.

[73] See UNHCR, 'Revised Background Note on Gender Equality, Nationality Laws and Statelessness', 8 March 2014, available at: www.unhcr.org/4f5886306.html, last accessed 21 July 2014.

[74] See the list found in Annex V in 'UNHCR Action to Address Statelessness: A Strategy Note', March 2010, available at: www.unhcr.org/refworld/docid/4b9e0c3d2.html, last accessed 21 May 2014. At least seven additional states are bound by this standard as a result of accession to the 1961 Convention since 2010.

Nonetheless, there continues to be steady, if slow, progress towards improved nationality legislation. UNHCR has often been involved through the provision of technical advice on reform of nationality legislation. One set of examples is from Latin America where there is a trend to eliminate conditions on *jus sanguinis* transmission of nationality to children born abroad. Most significantly, a 2007 amendment to the Brazilian Constitution eliminated the requirement that children born to nationals abroad must take up residence in Brazil in order to acquire nationality. Thenceforth, only a consular registration was required. This prevented future cases of statelessness among the large expatriate population and also served to resolve the situation of some 280,000 children born abroad to Brazilian parents. In 2010, Georgia (which is not yet party to the 1961 Convention) introduced reforms to prevent individuals from voluntarily renouncing their nationality if it would leave them stateless and in 2011 Austria eliminated a provision whereby nationality was lost on account of foreign military service, even where this results in statelessness. There are numerous other examples from around the world. All told, at least fourteen states reformed nationality legislation to prevent statelessness from mid-2011 to mid-2013.[75] Recent accessions to the 1961 Convention coupled with pledges at the UNHCR ministerial meeting to accede (or work towards accession)[76] or to amend nationality laws will lead to additional reforms.[77]

Even where nationality laws appear on their face to be consistent with international standards, there may continue to be problems with implementation. Perhaps the highest profile demonstration of this with regard to the 1961 Convention was the failure by Denmark to implement Article 1 of the convention over a number of years.[78]

---

[75] UNHCR, 'Note on Statelessness', 4 June 2013, EC/64/SC/CRP.11, available at: www.refworld.org/docid/51d2a8884.html, last accessed 21 May 2014.

[76] Pledges were made by thirty-two states, though several of these already have nationality laws that are fully compliant with the Convention. Belgium, Benin, Bulgaria, Côte d'Ivoire, Ecuador, Gambia, Honduras, Moldova, Paraguay, Portugal, Ukraine had fulfilled their pledges to accede to the 1961 Convention at the time of writing. Although they did not make pledges, Jamaica (in 2013) and Turkmenistan (in 2012) both acceded following the Ministerial Meeting.

[77] For a full list of pledges, see page 34 of UNHCR, 'Pledges 2011: Ministerial Intergovernmental Event on Refugees and Stateless Persons (Geneva, Palais des Nations, 7–8 December 2011)'.

[78] Denmark had an application procedure in place pursuant to Article 1 of the 1961 Convention for individuals born in the territory. A number of applications from stateless persons who satisfied the conditions for nationality were not resolved. See 'European Commission Against Racism and Intolerance, ECRI Report on Denmark (Fourth Monitoring Cycle)', 22 May 2012, para. 13. Among many other media articles, see BBC

In view of gaps in nationality laws and gaps in implementation, exercise by UNHCR of its responsibilities under Article 11 of the 1961 Convention has become increasingly important and will require stepped-up technical advice to states on nationality laws and their implementation, support to individuals (often through partners where high numbers of individuals so require) and court interventions.[79] In addition, to establish better base-line data, UNHCR has entered into a series of partnerships to develop a comprehensive analytical database of nationality laws.

Given the massive human suffering produced by statelessness follow-ing state succession[80] in the 1990s, UNHCR has increasingly sought to anticipate and mitigate the risks of statelessness in situations of state suc-cession. Most recently it has worked intensively to prevent statelessness as a result of the independence of South Sudan by promoting applica-tion of the principles set out in the Articles on the Nationality of Natural Persons in relation to the Succession of States,[81] advising South Sudan on the drafting of its nationality law and supporting training and deploy-ment of nationality officers to issue documentation to citizens of the new state.

A fourth area of activity where continued efforts are needed is in rela-tion to civil registration and issuance of documents proving identity and nationality. Lack of birth registration is not sufficient to render a person stateless. However, as set out in UNHCR in 2010:

> [b]irth registration establishes in legal terms the place of birth and paren-tal affiliation, which in turn serves as documentary proof underpinning acquisition of the parents' nationality (jus sanguinis), or the nationality of the State based on where the child is born (jus soli). Thus, while nation-ality is normally acquired independently and birth registration in and

---

'Danish immigration minister Hornbech fired over scandal', available at: www.bbc.co.uk/news/world-europe-12674360, last accessed 21 May 2014.

[79] See also the efforts to develop authoritative guidance on the 1961 Convention, referred to above, including a 2011 expert meeting (UNHCR, 'Interpreting the 1961 Statelessness Convention and Preventing Statelessness among Children: Summary Conclusions', ('Dakar Conclusions'), September 2011, available at: www.refworld.org/docid/4e8423a72.html) and UNHCR, 'Guidelines on Statelessness No. 4: Ensuring Every Child's Right to Acquire a Nationality through Articles 1–4 of the 1961 Convention on the Reduction of Statelessness', 21 December 2012, HCR/GS/12/04.

[80] 'State succession' is defined by the International Law Commission in its Articles on Nationality of Natural Persons in Relation to the Succession of States as 'the replacement of one State by another in the responsibility for the international relations of territory'.

[81] UNHCR, 'Sudan Citizenship Symposium – Keynote Address by Ms. Erika Feller, Assistant High Commissioner – Protection, UNHCR', 6 November 2010, available at: www.unhcr.org/refworld/docid/4cf384662.html, last accessed 21 May 2014.

of itself does not normally confer nationality upon the child concerned, birth registration does constitute a key form of proof of the link between an individual and a State and thereby serves to prevent statelessness.[82]

Given the massive deficits in birth registration, a key challenge is to set a threshold at which a problem of birth registration becomes something that needs to be tackled under the prevention component of UNHCR's mandate. In guidance for field offices, a strategy note issued in 2010 identifies the following categories of persons, which are not mutually exclusive, as being at particular risk of statelessness due to absence of birth registration:

- persons living in border areas where lack of birth registration may lead to confusion as to whether they are nationals of one state or another;
- minorities and persons who have perceived or actual ties with foreign states;
- nomadic or semi-nomadic populations whose territories cross international borders;
- migrant populations where difficulties to prove nationality of the country of origin may occur when one or more generations of children are born abroad (a risk that increases with each successive generation). [83]

The combination of a series of such factors is what has led UNHCR offices in Bosnia, Croatia, Kosovo, Macedonia, Montenegro and Serbia to undertake a wide range of activities with civil society partners to address deficits in birth registration and identity documentation. This has included a series of surveys to document the extent of the problem,[84] provision of free legal aid to over 28,000 direct beneficiaries and some 81,000 indirect beneficiaries (family members), support for technical improvements to some civil registries and advocacy for legal and administrative reform.

In Côte d'Ivoire, for a number of years UNHCR has worked to assist individuals with late birth registration, the first step towards documentation of nationality in many cases. Statelessness in Southern Africa, caused by conflicts between nationality laws and migration, has been compounded by lack of birth registration. Together with partner Lawyers

---

[82] UNHCR, 'Birth Registration: A Topic Proposed for an Executive Committee Conclusion on International Protection', EC/61/SC/CRP.5, 9 February 2010, para. 3.

[83] 'UNHCR, Action to Address Statelessness: A Strategy Note', March 2010, para. 35, available at: www.unhcr.org/refworld/docid/4b9e0c3d2.html, last accessed 21 May 2014.

[84] See, for example, UNHCR, May 2009, 'Civil Registration and the Prevention of Statelessness: a Survey of Roma, Ashkaelia and Egyptians in Montenegro', Mary 2009, available at www.unhcr.org/4b71228e9.html; UNHCR, August 2011, 'UNHCR Urges the

for Human Rights in South Africa, UNHCR has focused on assisting individuals to complete late birth registration as a first step to untangling their nationality status.[85]

4.10.   Reduction: a different way of saying 'durable solutions'

The third component of UNHCR's mandate is the reduction of statelessness. The principal concern in this area is the halting progress to resolve protracted problems.

UNHCR has promoted two approaches to resolve the situation of stateless populations.[86] The first involves changing the law and/or policy defining who belongs in the body of citizens. In a number of situations around the world, additional or amended criteria have been introduced in nationality laws or as policy to recognize specific categories of individuals as nationals based on strong links to the state such as residence or birth in the territory.[87] These changes generally operate automatically and may be accompanied by simplified procedures for acquisition of documentation proving nationality. They are therefore effective for addressing the situation of large stateless populations, and at relatively low cost.

UNHCR played a central role in supporting the implementation of this type of reform in Sri Lanka in 2003. Following a progressive law reform, UNHCR and the Ceylon Workers Congress conducted a citizenship documentation campaign in coordination with local officials that ensured individuals who had automatically acquired nationality were able to acquire documentary proof that they were Sri Lankan nationals.[88] More recently, in Kyrgyzstan, UNHCR has worked with the government and NGOs to bolster capacity to process the cases of individuals who fall under the provisions of the 2007 Law on Citizenship designed to

---

Government to Amend Legislation', available at http://rs.one.un.org/news.php?id=203, last accessed 21 May 2014.

[85] Despite these efforts, many of the individuals concerned are ultimately found to be stateless.

[86] This is outlined in UNHCR, 'UNHCR Action to Address Statelessness: A Strategy Note', March 2010, paras. 41–6, available at: www.unhcr.org/refworld/docid/4b9e0c3d2.html, last accessed 21 May 2014.

[87] Examples are Sri Lanka (2003) with respect to residence in the territory and the *sui generis* approach adopted by Nepal (2006) with respect to birth in the territory.

[88] A smaller group of individuals who possessed expired Indian passports were able to acquire nationality upon application. See UNHCR, 'Sri Lanka makes citizens out of stateless tea pickers', 7 October 2004, www.unhcr.org/416564cd4.html, last accessed 21 May 2014.

reduce statelessness.[89] UNHCR advocated quietly for a change in policy regarding the Urdu-speaking minority (the so-called Biharis), who were not considered nationals following independence in 1971.[90] This subsequently changed following a judgment of the High Court of Dhaka,[91] which ordered registration of the entire population as nationals and issuance of identity cards – something that occurred for those Urdu speakers who wished to acquire identity cards and to vote in the December 2008 elections.

Many industrialized states, in Europe in particular, have tended to adopt a second approach, which is facilitated naturalization for stateless persons. This is particularly suited to address the situation of individuals, but has in a number of instances been applied so as to resolve the situation of larger populations. One example of this is the impact of the 2002 Law on Citizenship of the Russian Federation which established a simplified procedure for naturalization of stateless former citizens of the USSR, with over 630,000 reported to have acquired nationality in the nine years following adoption of the law.

Although some provisions of the 1961 Convention are of use for the resolution of existing cases of statelessness (e.g. Article 12 in relation to Articles 1 and 4), the principal standard at the global level is Article 32 of the 1954 Convention, which sets out that states parties 'shall as far as possible facilitate the assimilation and naturalization of stateless persons. They shall in particular make every effort to expedite naturalization proceedings and to reduce as far as possible the charges and costs of such proceedings.' Apart from these standards, general provisions of human rights law and provisions of the ECN, however, there is little by way of treaty law regulating reduction of statelessness.[92]

Perhaps not surprisingly, almost none of the existing protracted statelessness issues are in states that are party to the treaties referred to. As a

---

[89] In essence, this law provides that former USSR citizens who are stateless are considered nationals provided that they have legally resided in the country for five years. However, each case must be processed by state bodies called 'conflict commissions'.

[90] Eric Paulsen, 'The Citizenship Status of the Urdu-speakers/Biharis in Bangladesh', *Refugee Survey Quarterly*, 25 (2006), available at: http://rsq.oxfordjournals.org/cgi/reprint/25/3/54.pdf, last accessed 21 May 2014.

[91] *Md. Sadaqat Khan (Fakku) and Others* v. *Chief Election Commissioner, Bangladesh Election Commission*, Writ Petition No. 10129 of 2007, Bangladesh: Supreme Court, 18 May 2008, available at: www.unhcr.org/refworld/docid/4a7c0c352.html, last accessed 21 May 2014.

[92] See Art. 6(4)(g), ECN and the maximum residence period that may be required of applicants for naturalization in Art. 6(3).

consequence, the steps taken thus far to resolve major statelessness situations have generally not followed a detailed prescription laid out in an international treaty. Rather, solutions have been tailored to the situation at hand and have tended to follow the first approach outlined above, changing the basic rule of nationality.

Overall, progress to resolve existing situations of statelessness has slowed in recent years. Data available to UNHCR showed that approximately 348,000 stateless people acquired, re-acquired or confirmed a nationality in 2010–12. In his speech to the Executive Committee in 2012, High Commissioner António Guterres underlined that this was not sufficient, stating that '[t]hese protracted statelessness situations are not a problem to be addressed at some future date. Solutions are needed now, and I call on all States to make a firm commitment to ending statelessness within the next decade.'[93]

4.11. Protection: the value of an overlooked treaty

UNHCR's mandate also requires that it provide technical advice to states to identify and protect stateless persons in accordance with the 1954 Convention relating to the Status of Stateless Persons and human rights law.

Most of the world's stateless persons remain in their countries of residence, but some do travel and seek protection elsewhere. Many are refugees, but most are not. Non-refugee stateless persons are entitled to protection under international human rights law but the 1954 Convention relating to the Status of Stateless Persons specifically regulates the treatment of stateless persons and provides a framework to prevent non-refugee stateless persons from ending up in a situation of legal limbo. The 1954 Convention:

- defines a 'stateless person' as someone who is not considered as a national by any state under the operation of its law;
- establishes an internationally recognized status for stateless persons;
- sets out specific rights which are to be enjoyed by stateless persons including rights requiring treatment at the level of foreigners generally and may require that persons be lawfully present or residing in the country.

---

[93] See the speech at www.unhcr.org/506987c99.html, last accessed 21 May 2014.

It has been asserted that the 1954 Convention is now of limited value because of developments in international human rights law. Indeed, stateless persons are also covered by a range of international human rights standards. These complement the 1954 Convention through application in states that are not parties to the 1954 Convention, by addressing issues not referred to therein (such as detention and conditions of detention), or by providing for higher standards with regard to some specific rights. UNHCR has emphasized, however, that similar to the 1961 Convention, the 1954 Convention must be viewed as part of a wider web of international legal standards. The convention contains a number of standards which are not contained in any other treaty. These include: Article 25, which sets out obligations for provision of administrative assistance such as issuance of documents and certificates to which the individual would not otherwise have access on account of being stateless;[94] and Article 28, which provides for issuance of an internationally recognized Convention Travel Document to permit international travel. The 1954 Convention does not have any direct equivalent at the regional level.

As of July 2014, the 1954 Convention has eighty-two states parties. Twenty-two states pledged at the UNHCR ministerial meeting to accede (or to take steps towards accession).[95] When advocating for accession, UNHCR has sometimes been confronted with concerns from governments that upon becoming party to the convention, the state will face a flood of stateless persons seeking protection. The experience of states parties demonstrates that these fears are unfounded. Those that are parties and have determination procedures in place show two clear tendencies: first, low numbers of people seek recognition as stateless persons relative to the number who seek refugee status and second, the number of persons granted protection has not risen dramatically over time. Implementation of the 1954 Convention by states parties has been a problem and UNHCR has worked with governments for roughly a decade to

---

[94] The practical value of this provision is explained in detail in Nehemiah Robinson, 'Convention relating to the Status of Stateless Persons. Its History and Interpretation', 1997, available at www.unhcr.org/refworld/docid/4785f03d2.html, last accessed 21 May 2014.

[95] For a full list of pledges, see page 34 of UNHCR, 'Pledges 2011: Ministerial Intergovernmental Event on Refugees and Stateless Persons (Geneva, Palais des Nations, 7–8 December 2011)'. Benin, Bulgaria, Côte d'Ivoire, Gambia, Georgia, Honduras, Moldova, Paraguay, Peru, Portugal and Ukraine had all acceded to the convention at the time of writing. Although they did not makes pledges, Burkina Faso, Nicaragua and Turkmenistan both acceded in 2012, following the Ministerial Meeting.

develop determination procedures and adequate protection regimes for stateless persons.[96] With the issuance of guidelines on key aspects of the 1954 Convention, these efforts will be given a significant boost. Eleven states pledged to develop or improve status determination procedures during UNHCR's ministerial meeting in 2011[97] and three have at the time of writing passed the relevant legislation (Georgia, Moldova and Philippines).

A broader problem of implementation relates to the steps that need to be taken by states that have 'in situ' populations, generally people who have been stateless for decades or generations. Is it appropriate to channel individuals through determination procedures and grant them a status as stateless persons? This was addressed in one of UNHCR's expert meetings and the clear answer, later set out in the 2012 Guidelines and 2014 Handbook, was a clear 'no':

> 'For these groups, determination procedures for the purpose of obtaining status as stateless persons are not appropriate because of their long-established ties to these countries. Based on existing international standards and state practice in the area of reduction of statelessness, such ties include long-term habitual residence or residence at the time of state succession. Depending on the circumstances of the populations under consideration, states might be advised to undertake targeted nationality campaigns or nationality verification efforts rather than statelessness determination procedures.[98]

4.12.   Moving forward: a global movement to address statelessness

UNHCR's activities to address statelessness have expanded significantly in recent years and the anniversary of the 1961 Convention in 2011 provided new momentum. UNHCR is only one of a series of stakeholders, however,

---

[96] See, for example, UNHCR, October 2003, 'The 1954 Convention relating to the Status of Stateless Persons: Implementation within the European Union Member States and Recommendations for Harmonisation', October 2003, available at: www.unhcr.org/refworld/docid/415c3cfb4.html, last accessed 21 May 2014. For more recent examples, see the Netherlands and UK mapping studies cited previously.

[97] For full list of pledges, see page 34 of UNHCR, 'Pledges 2011: Ministerial Intergovernmental Event on Refugees and Stateless Persons (Geneva, Palais des Nations, 7–8 December 2011)'.

[98] UNHCR, 'Guidelines on Statelessness No. 2: Procedures for Determining whether an Individual is a Stateless Person', 5 April 2012, HCR/GS/12/02, para. 6 and UNHCR, 'Handbook on Protection of Stateless Persons', para. 58.

and additional progress will depend to some degree on its ability to convince others to take action. There are a growing range of actors involved including NGOs, academic institutions and individual researchers and teachers and interested journalists. However, there is nothing even closely resembling an international movement of the kind which currently exists to address child soldiers, landmines, or even refugee rights. There is relatively little academic research being undertaken and teaching on the issue is relatively new. Yet statelessness has numerous dimensions and complexities that mean that it relates to the work of a broad range of civil society work and academic disciplines. UNHCR seeks to use these inter-linkages to 'mainstream' issues of statelessness within the areas of child rights, gender equality and migration, among others.

Needless to say, states are the central actors as they determine the criteria for acquisition and loss of nationality and establish (or not) policies relevant to the protection of stateless persons. States can also play a key role through international diplomacy. Some progress has been achieved in this area, too, with a number of states playing the role of champions in efforts to address statelessness, including by highlighting statelessness concerns in UNHCR's Executive Committee or making recommendations to states with large stateless populations in the Universal Periodic Review of the United Nations Human Rights Council.[99]

In summary, UNHCR's mandate has continued to evolve and activities to address statelessness have now become a central part of what it does around the world. There is also increasing recognition that statelessness is a concern of the international community as a whole. This reflects, at least in part, the increasing effectiveness of action undertaken by UNHCR under its mandate. Yet, the magnitude of the problem is such that even this much-increased level of activity has left many problems untouched or inadequately addressed. It is essential to build on the smattering of recent success stories and increased international concern by achieving the breakthroughs necessary to resolve the major protracted situations which affect millions across the globe.[100] UNHCR is well positioned to play a major role in achieving this.

---

[99] The number of recommendations relating to nationality and statelessness made by states during the Universal Periodic Review has risen dramatically, going from a mere one recommendation during the first session in 2008 to an average of eighteen recommendations during the eleventh to fifteenth sessions (2011–13). States have expressed particular concern regarding a number or protracted situations.

[100] High Commissioner António Guterres set this out in bold terms in his address to the Executive Committee in 2012: 'These protracted statelessness situations are not a

Questions to guide discussion

1. How does UNHCR's work on statelessness complement its refugee protection and solutions mandate? What is unique to its statelessness mandate?
2. What can UNHCR do to ensure a more effective international response?
3. What role can be played by other UN agencies, regional organizations and by UN and regional human rights supervisory bodies to identify, prevent and reduce statelessness and protect stateless persons?

problem to be addressed at some future date. Solutions are needed now, and I call on all States to make a firm commitment to ending statelessness within the next decade.' See the speech at www.unhcr.org/506987c99.html, last accessed 21 May 2014.

5

The determination of statelessness and the establishment of a statelessness-specific protection regime

GÁBOR GYULAI

The 1954 Convention relating to the Status of Stateless Persons (1954 Convention) obliges states parties to provide protection to those who are not considered as a national by any state under the operation of its law.[1] An effective statelessness determination mechanism is an indispensable pre-condition of any effort aimed at the protection of stateless persons, or to put it simply: in order to implement protection measures in favour of a certain population, one has to know who the people concerned are. It is, therefore, striking to learn that at the time of writing only a handful of countries (representing less than 10 per cent of all states parties to the 1954 Convention) have established a specific legal mechanism dedicated to both the identification and protection of stateless persons.

In recent decades, the already rather limited public and professional debate on statelessness has tended to focus on the avoidance and reduction of this phenomenon, keeping the protection aspect of statelessness in the shadows. This is an area that deserves far greater attention. Thus, drawing in particular on empirical examples, this chapter outlines the main features and challenges of statelessness-specific protection mechanisms, with an emphasis on the determination of statelessness.[2] In addition, the chapter proposes a structured framework for understanding and classifying national 'protection environments' stateless persons presently face in different countries.

---

[1] Convention relating to the Status of Stateless Persons, New York, 28 September 1954, in force 6 June 1960, 360 UNTS 117, Art. 1.
[2] Most empirical experiences are, at the time of writing, related to European states. The dominance of European examples of state practice in the present chapter is due to this fact and does not, by any means, indicate disregard of relevant developments in other parts of the world.

Even in the context of what van Waas calls the 'progressive denationalization of human rights', or in other words the gradual transformation of the 'rights of citizens' to the 'rights of all human beings', the international community deemed it necessary to create a specific instrument to protect stateless persons' rights, confirming their position as a vulnerable group.[3] The 1954 Convention outlines states' protection obligations vis-à-vis stateless persons, as well as the set of rights states parties shall guarantee to this group.[4] However, this crucial instrument remains silent about the manner in which beneficiaries of such protection shall be identified, or how such protection shall be provided in practice.[5]

Together with the examination of the guidelines and Handbook issued by the Office of the United Nations High Commissioner for Refugees (UNHCR), and using insights gained from years of closely following state practice in a number of countries, this chapter will put forward a number of definitions and concepts in order to increase the clarity and consistency of the nascent international framework for the protection of stateless persons.

5.1.   The content and the limits of protection

Protection, in its broadest sense, means that a stateless person has access to and can enjoy the rights embedded in the 1954 Convention and in other relevant international human rights instruments. Protection also means, in a narrower sense, official recognition as a stateless person and being granted a legal status that ensures the proper enjoyment of the above-mentioned rights. In either event, protection differs from reduction or elimination of statelessness, as it stops short of offering a nationality to the person concerned (who remains stateless).[6]

It is important to recall that statelessness can surface in a wide range of situations, from purely individual cases where gaps in legislation or administrative practice render a person stateless, through to massive populations who have been deprived of their nationality on discriminatory

---

[3] L. van Waas, 'Nationality and Rights' in B. Blitz and M. Lynch (eds.), *Statelessness and the Benefits of Citizenship: A Comparative Study* (Oxford Brookes University, 2009), 26.

[4] See also Chapter 3 by van Waas in this volume.

[5] Molnár states that part of the problem is the non-self-executing nature of convention obligations: T. Molnár, 'Stateless Persons under International Law and EU Law: A Comparative Analysis Concerning their Legal Status, with Particular Attention to the Added Value of the EU Legal Order', *Acta Juridica Hungarica*, 51 (2010), 293–304, at 296.

[6] Note that reduction does have a role in the protection machinery, see details later in this chapter. On the content of protection more generally, see Chapter 3 by van Waas in this volume on the statelessness conventions.

grounds, such as ethnic affiliation. The Summary Conclusions from UNHCR's Geneva roundtable held in 2011 ('Geneva Conclusions') summarize the 'two different contexts, [as] the first consisting of countries – many industrialized – that host stateless persons who are predominantly, if not exclusively, migrants or of migrant background; and the second consisting of countries that have *in situ* stateless populations (i.e. those that consider themselves to already be "in their own" country)'.[7] The response to statelessness will need to vary, depending on these circumstances.

However important it is, international protection is not always the appropriate response to the statelessness of a certain population. Many people who are currently living without a nationality have strong ties to a certain country, many in fact having lived there since birth, the nationality of which they have reasonable and well-founded grounds to claim. In such situations the most suitable resolution of their statelessness is to move towards naturalization or recognition of the nationality of the population concerned, instead of creating a specific 'stateless person' protection status, which would maintain their situation of statelessness.[8] Examples of where recognition of nationality is the most appropriate response would include stateless Rohingyas in Myanmar, the stateless Kurds in Syria and stateless Nubians in Kenya.

Other stateless populations may not, or may not yet, have sufficiently strong ties with the country where they live (or with any other country).[9] This is commonly the case in a migration context. For example, a number of migrants originating from the former Soviet Union or Yugoslavia remained stateless after the dissolution of these states in the 1990s, but were not able to apply for a new nationality in their country of residence. In such circumstances a meaningful and rights-based protection mechanism may be advisable where the state in question refuses to naturalize its residents to avoid statelessness. Such a mechanism could lay a pathway to a durable solution (i.e. the elimination of statelessness) later on.

---

[7] UNHCR, 'Expert Meeting – Statelessness Determination Procedures and the Status of Stateless Persons (Summary Conclusions)' (Geneva, December 2010) – hereinafter referred to as the 'Geneva Conclusions', p. 2.

[8] Geneva Conclusions, para. 24 ('For stateless individuals within their own country, as opposed to those who are in a migration context, the appropriate status would be one which reflects the degree of attachment to that country, namely, nationality.'), see also UNHCR, 'Handbook on Protection of Stateless Persons under the 1954 Convention relating to the Status of Stateless Persons' (Geneva, 2014), para. 58.

[9] Consider that different states may have highly diverging views of what can be considered as 'sufficiently strong ties'.

Instead of relying exclusively on the 1954 Convention in these two afore-mentioned group situations, human rights law may offer some answers. In particular, the legal concept of one's 'own country' and the rights attached thereto may prove to be useful.[10] Article 12 of the International Covenant on Civil and Political Rights, for example, grants individuals the right to freedom of movement including the right to leave and to return to one's 'own country'. The UN Human Rights Committee (HRC) has held that this concept of 'own country' applies not only to nationals but also embraces any non-national who due to their 'special ties to or claims in relation to a given country, cannot be considered to be a mere alien'. The examples provided by the HRC by way of illustration include individuals who have been stripped of their nationality in violation of international law; whose country of nationality has been incorporated in or transferred to another national entity, whose nationality is being denied them; state-less persons arbitrarily deprived of the right to acquire the nationality of the country they reside in; as well as long-term residents. It is important to underline that the HRC left this concept open and explicitly recognized that 'other factors may in certain circumstances result in the establish-ment of close and enduring connections between a person and a coun-try',[11] giving rise to rights.

Even with this guidance, establishing whether a certain stateless popu-lation is residing in its 'own country' may prove to be challenging in prac-tice. In any event, states should apply an inclusive approach in this respect and move towards the reduction of statelessness wherever possible. This approach gains firm support from international law, in particular based on the universally recognized objective of reducing statelessness[12] on the one hand, and the right to a nationality,[13] including every child's right to acquire a nationality,[14] on the other, as embedded in international instruments.

---

[10] See also Geneva Conclusions, p. 2.

[11] HRC, 'CCPR General Comment No. 27: Article 12 (Freedom of Movement)', CCPR/C/21/Rev.1/Add.9 (2 November 1999), para. 20.

[12] Convention on the Reduction of Statelessness, New York, 30 August 1961, in force 13 December 1975, 989 UNTS 175, preamble; Council of Europe, European Convention on Nationality, Strasbourg, 6 November 1997, in force 1 March 2000, ETS 166, Art. 4(b).

[13] Universal Declaration of Human Rights, 10 December 1948, GA Res. 217A(III), UN Doc. A/810 at 71, Art. 15(1); American Convention on Human Rights (ACHR), San Jose, 22 November 1969, 18 July 1978, OAS Treaty Series No. 36, Art. 20; European Convention on Nationality, Art. 4(a).

[14] Convention on the Rights of the Child (CRC), New York, 20 November 1989, in force 2 September 1990, 1577 UNTS 3, Art. 7(1).

In addition to the protection versus reduction dilemma, the boundaries between the protection of stateless persons and refugee protection should also be designated. Many stateless persons are forced migrants. Statelessness often constitutes (or at least is an element of) the 'push factor', while in other cases forced migration results in statelessness.[15] Stateless refugees are explicitly protected under Article 1A(2) of the 1951 Refugee Convention. Regional instruments extending the application of the refugee definition or creating regional complementary protection mechanisms also make explicit or implicit reference to stateless persons.[16] Because of this, and the different protections needed by stateless refugees outside their 'own countries', regimes envisaging protection for stateless persons should concentrate on those who do not qualify for refugee status (or subsidiary protection in the EU). Notwithstanding the numerous shortcomings in the international refugee protection system, it is at least an existing and functioning protection framework in many countries, whilst currently the same cannot be said of the statelessness protection regime. Much more could be said about the interface between statelessness and refugee law. However, this chapter will concentrate on the protection and identification of non-refugee stateless persons.[17]

Outside these particular scenarios – stateless populations living in their own countries in particular – the 1954 Convention still remains very relevant to individual stateless persons, and the remainder of the chapter deals with these situations.

5.2. Classifying the protection environment

If statelessness has remained in the cupboard for several decades, the protection of stateless persons has been kept right at the back, on its dustiest

---

[15] See Chapter 10 by Nonnenmacher and Cholewinski in this volume.

[16] See Convention Governing the Specific Aspects of Refugee Problems in Africa, Addis Ababa, 10 September 1969, in force 20 June 1974, 1001 UNTS 45, Art. 1(2); Cartagena Declaration on Refugees, Colloquium on the International Protection of Refugees in Central America, Mexico and Panama, Cartagena, 22 November 1984, para. 3; Council Directive 2004/83/EC of 29 April 2004 on Minimum Standards for the Qualification and Status of Third Country Nationals or Stateless Persons as Refugees or as Persons Who Otherwise Need International Protection and the Content of the Protection Granted, Luxembourg, 19 May 2004, 2004/83/EC, Art. 2(e).

[17] For more on the inter-relationship between refugee protection and stateless protection, see A. Edwards and L. Van Waas, 'Statelessness' in *Oxford Handbook on Refugee and Forced Migration Studies* (Oxford University Press, 2014) and G. Gyulai, 'Statelessness in the EU Framework for International Protection', *European Journal of Migration and Law*, 14 (2012), 279–95.

shelf. Nearly six decades after the adoption of the 1954 Convention, stateless individuals still lack an opportunity to claim and enjoy protection in most countries, and existing protection regimes are far from ideal. In recent years, this issue has started to attract greater international attention, yet the analytical literature available is extremely limited. A fundamental paradigm shift seems necessary in order to improve this state of play. Therefore, this chapter introduces new terminology and a simple classification method in the hope of stimulating and providing a conceptual foundation for future debates and research initiatives.

In the process of establishing a functioning international protection system for people without a nationality, introducing the concept of a 'statelessness-specific protection mechanism' can be of great utility. This label indicates that statelessness per se provides a ground for protection. One does not need to establish a statelessness-*plus* ground for protection, that is, there is no need to be stateless *and* a refugee, to be stateless *and* a legal resident, or to be stateless *and* present compelling humanitarian grounds for non-returnability. In such a system, an individual is able to claim protection based on her or his statelessness, and if this fact is objectively confirmed, she or he will receive a legal status on this ground alone. The 1954 Convention and international human rights law provide a firm basis for the creation of a statelessness-specific protection regime. Nevertheless, as already noted, most states parties still ignore this obligation.

Some countries do offer some kind of protection status to stateless persons, but not on the ground of their statelessness. The relevant protection ground is rather something commonly related to statelessness, or a phenomenon thereof. In a migratory context, for example, this usually means that legal and/or practical obstacles to expulsion give an entitlement to residence (at least after a certain amount of time). While this 'non-statelessness-specific' protection helps to avoid an enduring situation of legal limbo, it still raises a number of concerns. Rights attached to such statuses regularly remain below the standards set by the 1954 Convention, while this 'half-way' solution maintains the invisibility of statelessness.

Most countries at the time of writing fail to provide any sort of protection machinery at all for stateless people. The negative consequences can be numerous: unjustifiable lengthy immigration detention, enduring legal limbo, social exclusion and destitution – to mention just a few examples.[18]

---

[18]   See, for example, UNHCR, 'Mapping Statelessness in The United Kingdom' (22 November 2011), Chapter 5; UNHCR, 'Mapping Statelessness in the Netherlands' (November 2011), Chapter 3.4.

Based on research into state practice, the following five categories can be used to describe the protection environments and determination machineries that currently exist:

1. A statelessness-specific protection mechanism, based on clear procedural rules established in law (Spain, Hungary, Moldova, Georgia and the Philippines);
2. A statelessness-specific protection mechanism, without clear procedural rules established in law, but with a general 'consensus' on procedural modalities (France);
3. A statelessness-specific protection mechanism, without clear procedural rules established in law and with no general 'consensus' on procedural modalities (Italy);
4. A non-statelessness-specific protection mechanism, where for instance legal and/or practical obstacles to expulsion provide a ground for residence rights (Germany and Poland);
5. Neither a statelessness-specific protection status, nor alternative (non-statelessness-specific) protection is available (the majority of states).

At the time of writing, a positive shift towards categories 1 and 2 can be witnessed. For example, a recent judgment of the Italian Supreme Court of Appeal *(Corte Suprema di Cassazione)* put an end to a decades-long debate concerning the procedural modalities to be applied in judicial statelessness determination, clearly indicating that a centralized procedure be followed.[19] Slovakia has adopted a legislative basis for a statelessness-specific protection regime, the procedural modalities of which will hopefully be elaborated and codified in due course.[20] The same is expected in Mexico, where only a limited set of procedural rules exists in soft law (official guidance) at the time of writing.[21] Two (unfortunately unsuccessful) bills have attempted to establish a statelessness-specific protection framework in the United States of America.[22] Furthermore, a number of other states

[19] Judgment no. 7614 of 4 April 2011 of the Supreme Court of Appeal – the actual consequences of this judgment are yet to be analyzed at the time of writing.
[20] Act no. 404/2011 coll. on the stay of aliens and on the amendment of some other acts of 21 October 2011 (Zákon 404/2011 Z. z. o pobyte cudzincov a o zmene a doplnení niektorých zákonov), s. 46.
[21] Manual of Migration Criteria and Procedures of the National Institute of Migration, 29 January 2010 (Manual de Criterios y Trámites Migratorios del Instituto Nacional de Migración, 29 de enero de 2010), s. L.
[22] Bill no. S.3113, 111th Congress, 2nd Session, s. 24; Bill no. S.1202, 112nd Congress, 1st Session, s. 17.

pledged in December 2011 to establish a statelessness-specific protection mechanism in the near future – or at least to consider this possibility.[23] The forthcoming decade is therefore likely to bring an unprecedented shift towards statelessness-specific protection regimes in different parts of the world. Against this background, the need to better understand how protection systems function becomes all the more evident and this will be turned to next.

5.3.   The building blocks of a statelessness protection mechanism

After clarifying the conceptual framework of statelessness-specific protection, it is essential to determine its main building blocks. Practice shows that statelessness has some specific features that should play a crucial role in shaping related protection measures. First of all, statelessness is often a hidden characteristic, and the awareness about this issue, or the relevant protection obligations, appears to be rather weak globally. The lack of visibility and awareness can be particularly striking in countries with very small stateless populations. Secondly, statelessness is usually an enduring phenomenon (for example, once lost, nationality is often unlikely to be recovered within a short period of time); therefore stateless persons in relevant situations (described below) have long-term protection needs. Finally, statelessness usually renders those affected vulnerable in various ways, thus it requires the creation of a sensitive and protection-oriented framework. All nascent protection frameworks should address these specific challenges, for which concrete examples will be offered below.

As stated earlier, due to the lack of practical experience and widely accepted, authoritative procedural norms, government officials or advocates will be in need of a certain level of creativity if they want to establish a national protection mechanism for stateless persons. However, creativity will fortunately not be their only tool. The following can all serve as sources of inspiration.

A handful of countries already have specific identification and protection mechanisms for stateless persons in place (including France, Georgia, Hungary, Italy, Latvia, Mexico, Moldova, the Philippines, Spain and the United Kingdom). While none of these regimes can be presented

---

[23] Australia, Austria, Belgium, Brazil, Costa Rica, Peru, the United States of America and Uruguay – UNHCR, 'Pledges 2011 – Ministerial Intergovernmental Event on Refugees and Stateless Persons', Geneva, Palais des Nations, 7–8 December 2011.

as ideal, these countries' experiences definitely serve as a source of reflection and guidance. Unfortunately, not many of these systems have been subject to in-depth, practice-focused analysis so far.[24] A limited body of national jurisprudence (in particular from French, Hungarian, Italian and Spanish courts) may also provide useful guidance in some particular aspects.

Meanwhile, the protection of stateless persons shares a number of common characteristics with refugees, including a very similar international legal basis and joint drafting history, as well as the lack of proper protection by one's 'own state' in both cases. This means that in countries where statelessness arises primarily in a migratory context (as in most industrialized states), much can be learned from asylum procedures and regulations.

A further source of guidance is UNHCR's 'guidelines on statelessness', which so far have dealt with the meaning of 'stateless person', the status of stateless persons at the national level, and status determination procedures, which have been consolidated into a Handbook on the Protection of Stateless Persons, in 2014.[25] UNHCR's Executive Committee has also produced a number of relevant conclusions, even though they are of a rather general nature.[26]

Last but not least, general due process safeguards should also be observed and applied to the maximum extent. The prohibition of discrimination,[27] the right to an effective remedy[28] and respect for the child's best interests[29] deserve special reference in this context.

---

[24] See, for example, G. Gyulai, 'Statelessness in Hungary: The Protection of Stateless Persons and the Prevention and Reduction of Statelessness' (December 2010) Hungarian Helsinki Committee.

[25] UNHCR, 'Handbook on Protection of Stateless Persons', para. 58.

[26] See, in particular, UNHCR Executive Committee, 'Conclusion on Identification, Prevention and Reduction of Statelessness and Protection of Stateless Persons' No. 106 (LVII) (6 October 2006); and also UNHCR 'Executive Committee Conclusions No. 50 (XXXIX) – 1988, No. 90 (LII) – 2001 and No. 96 (LIV) – 2003.

[27] See, for example, International Covenant on Civil and Political Rights (ICCPR), New York, 16 December 1966, in force 23 March 1976, 999 UNTS 171, Art. 26; European Convention for the Protection of Human Rights and Fundamental Freedoms (ECHR), Rome, 4 November 1950, Art. 13; American Convention on Human Rights (ACHR), 22 November 1969, in force 1 June 2010, Art. 14; American Convention on Human Rights, Art. 1(1).

[28] See, for example, (ICCPR), Art. 2(3); ECHR, Art. 13; ACHR, Art. 25.

[29] CRC, Art. 3.

Based on the above-presented general features and sources of guidance, this chapter puts forward a five-step protection model[30] to ensure that all stateless persons have effective access to the protection they are entitled to under international law:

1. *Ratification and due observance of relevant international instruments.* Practice shows that mere accession to the 1954 Convention and other relevant treaties does not, of itself, ensure the establishment or implementation of a national protection framework. Most states parties to the convention do not, at the time of writing, operate any identification and protection mechanism. Nevertheless, accession is key to raising awareness about protection obligations both at the national and international level (for example, reaching a 'critical mass' of states adhering to the convention globally). In addition, it creates a direct legal basis for requiring states to develop a proper identification and protection mechanism.[31]

2. *Ensuring visibility of the issue of statelessness and stateless populations.* To reach any improvement in protection standards, the 'legal ghosts' should be brought to light. Legislators, politicians and advocates should understand the phenomenon of statelessness, the relevant international obligations and who the populations concerned are. Improved and targeted statistical data collection can be pivotal in this respect. Another area for enhanced visibility is legislation. It is preferable that states enact a separate legal Act,[32] or at least a particular chapter in a relevant law,[33] to enable all parties to know where to turn to for legal guidance. Of course, non-legislative measures such as training are also fundamental.

---

[30] These steps indicate a 'roadmap' for states wishing to establish a statelessness-specific protection mechanism and civil society actors advocating to this end, rather than describing different scales through which a stateless person can access protection.

[31] Cf. Geneva Conclusions, para. 1; UNHCR, 'Handbook on Protection of Stateless Persons', para. 8.

[32] As in the Spanish legislation, see Royal Decree 865/2001 of 20 July approving the Regulation for the Recognition of the Status of Stateless Persons (Real Decreto No 865/2001, de 20 de julio, por el que se aprueba el Reglamento de Reconocimiento del Estatuto de Apátrida).

[33] As in the Hungarian and Moldovan legislation. See Act II of 2007 on the Admission and Right of Residence of Third-Country Nationals (2007. évi II. törvény a harmadik országbeli állampolgárok beutazásáról és tartózkodásáról), Chapter VIII, and Act 200 of 16 July 2010, on the Regime of Foreigners in the Republic of Moldova (Legea Nr. 200 din 16.07.2010 privind regimul străinilor în Republica Moldova), Chapter X[1] (respectively).

3. *Effective determination of statelessness.* Any protection measure requires the proper identification of those entitled to it.[34] Below I set out a broader overview of challenges and responses with regard to this process.

4. *Providing for a proper protection status.* Stateless persons are entitled to a set of rights under the 1954 Convention and international human rights instruments. The most effective way to ensure these rights for those identified as stateless is the creation of a specific protection status, which can also be crucial in enhancing visibility as mentioned in point 2 above. At the same time, alternative solutions are also possible (where stateless persons gain an entitlement to an already existing, broader or more generous legal status, e.g. permanent residence permit).[35] In any case, the status granted should be protection-oriented, should reflect the enduring protection needs of stateless persons and, as such, should provide meaningful possibilities for economic and social integration.

5. *Offering a route to a durable solution.* Stateless persons, like refugees, require a durable solution, beyond their immediate or medium-term protection needs. UNHCR distinguishes three durable solutions for refugees, namely: voluntary repatriation, local integration in the country of first asylum and resettlement in a third country. These solutions are deemed durable, as they put an end to the 'refugee cycle'[36] and thus the need for international protection. Applying this thinking to statelessness, one can only identify a single durable solution: the acquisition of a nationality. A protection status designed for stateless persons may offer a broad set of rights and a number of social entitlements, yet it will never provide a veritable exit from the 'statelessness cycle'. Besides the likely disadvantages of this status vis-à-vis holding the nationality of the country of residence, one should also not underestimate the

---

[34] Cf. Geneva Conclusions, para. 1; UNHCR, 'Handbook on Protection of Stateless Persons', para. 8.

[35] The line between these two scenarios may sometimes be blurred and mixed solutions are also possible. In Hungary, for instance, stateless persons are issued a humanitarian residence permit, which determines the majority of the rights they enjoy (e.g. legal residence, restricted access to the labour market or right to family reunification). However, statelessness – as a legal ground – is specified on the residence permit and entails some entitlements that are specific to stateless status (e.g. the maximum validity of the permit upon first issuance is longer than in other cases).

[36] See inter alia R. Black and K. Koser, 'The End of the Refugee Cycle?' in R. Black and K. Koser (eds.), *The End of the Refugee Cycle? Refugee Repatriation and Reconstruction* (Oxford: Berghahn Books, 1999), 2–17.

psychological factor of belonging to, or being excluded from, a political, national and cultural community. Therefore, stateless persons' access to nationality should be facilitated in various ways, such as reducing the minimum waiting period, fees and other administrative obstacles.[37]

The same five-step model can – with some adaptations – be used in situations where stateless persons reside in their 'own country'. The main necessary modification will be that identification would be followed immediately by naturalization or recognition of nationality, instead of the granting of a protection status.

5.4.   Statelessness determination

Determining statelessness is somewhat similar to proving the existence of an 'invisible' particle in physics. Its 'presence' as such may be impossible to demonstrate – as one needs to prove a negative ('not considered a national of any State under the operation of law')[38] – but identifying the interaction it has with the environment can fulfil the same purpose. Literally speaking, establishing statelessness means proving that someone is not a national of any of the world's nearly two hundred states. This would be an incredibly lengthy and cumbersome (or largely impossible) endeavour. Yet statelessness determination remains an indispensable cornerstone of any statelessness protection mechanism, as already described, and it also plays a crucial role in prevention and reduction measures. Luckily, practice demonstrates that statelessness can be realistically identified through its impact on certain aspects of the person's life, and there are simple methods to reduce the scope of examination to a realistic level. The following parts outline the framework for statelessness determination and the main challenges related thereto.

5.4.1   Access to statelessness determination

Protection mechanisms have no actual impact if those in need of protection are prevented from accessing them. Practice shows that protection-oriented asylum regulations, facilitated naturalization mechanisms and progressive frameworks offering protection to victims of domestic

---

[37]   See 1954 Convention, Art. 32.
[38]   1954 Convention, Art. 1(1). See Chapter 3 in this volume by van Waas on the UN statelessness conventions.

violence too often remain promises on paper, as the machinery that would give access to them is ineffective. These protection mechanisms are like a fancy and perfectly equipped concert hall where no concert ever takes place. They are still good for impressing foreign delegations or the press, but they will never reach the objective for which they have been built.

The first question to answer, therefore, relates to the initiation of the procedure. In most cases, if a person seeks the recognition of a certain legal status or residence entitlement, it is required that she or he – as the interested person – initiates the procedure that would establish this entitlement (e.g. through submitting an application for asylum, a work visa or naturalization). An important argument against simply applying this general principle to statelessness determination is that even the persons concerned may often have difficulties recognizing or accepting that they are stateless, which may significantly delay their access to a proper legal status.[39] This particularly concerns vulnerable groups, such as unaccompanied minors. Another reason for opting for a different approach to immigration procedures is the declaratory character of the recognition of statelessness (i.e. the recognition and the consequent grant of a protection status does not create statelessness, it only recognizes this condition).[40] It is thus unsurprising that UNHCR argues that 'Given that individuals are sometimes unaware of statelessness determination procedures or hesitant to apply for statelessness status, procedures can usefully contain safeguards permitting State authorities to initiate a procedure.'[41]

Nevertheless, there appears to be some general reticence about an *ex officio*-initiated statelessness determination procedure, the main argument being that a state authority cannot 'force someone to be stateless'. At the time of writing, only Spain and Moldova provide for such a possibility in their legislation.[42] Several avenues are available for states seeking

---

[39] See the general characteristics of statelessness (hidden phenomenon, lack of awareness, vulnerability of the population concerned, etc.) as described earlier.

[40] See UNHCR, 'Handbook on Protection of Stateless Persons', para. 16. The same approach is applied with respect to refugee status: see UNHCR, 'Handbook on Procedures and Criteria for Determining Refugee Status under the 1951 Convention relating to the Status of Refugees (1979, re-issued 1992 and 2011), para. 28.

[41] Ibid., para. 68.

[42] Royal Decree 865/2001 of 20 July approving the Regulation for the Recognition of the Status of Stateless Persons, s. 2(1); Act 200 of 16 July 2010, on the Regime of Foreigners in the Republic of Moldova (Legea Nr. 200 din 16.07.2010 privind regimul străinilor în Republica Moldova), s. 87(1).

a balance between the two options. For instance, *ex officio* initiation can be allowed, but the explicit consent of those found to be stateless shall be obtained before recognition. Another option is to limit *ex officio* initiation to unaccompanied minors, or other groups or individuals lacking full legal capacity or particular difficulties.[43] A third option only allows the person concerned to initiate the procedure, while placing an obligation on immigration, asylum and/or naturalization authorities to provide information about the system, the possibility of applying for stateless status and the rights that can be acquired in this way to any person whose potential statelessness arises in any of these procedures.[44]

Beyond the 'who', the 'how' question is also essential. Bureaucratic difficulties (such as complicated applications that can only be completed in written form, in the country's official language) can encumber, or even impede access to determination mechanisms. The protection-oriented framework requires a flexible interpretation of such rules, as in the case of Hungary, where claims for stateless status can be submitted both in written and oral form and in any language.[45] Moreover, claims submitted to any state authority should be forwarded to the competent regional directorate of the immigration authority.[46] Similarly in Spain, claims can be entered at immigration offices, police stations or the asylum authority.[47] The reverse is true in the French practice, where such claims are only received if written in the French language and only at one single place in the country (the headquarters of the French Office for the Protection of Refugees and Stateless Persons, *Office français de protection des réfugiés et apatrides* – OFPRA).[48] Beyond the evident difficulties regarding communication and distance one should not forget that the circle of advisors

---

[43] See, for example, *Report of the Hungarian Parliamentary Commissioner for Civil Rights on cases no. AJB 2629/2010 and AJB 4196/2010*, September 2010, as well as Gyulai, 'Statelessness in Hungary', 43–5.

[44] Hungary applies this approach, see Government Decree 114/2007. (V. 24) on the execution of Act II of 2007 on the Admission and Right of Residence of Third-Country Nationals (170/2001. (IX. 26.) Korm. rendelet a külföldiek beutazásáról és tartózkodásáról szóló 2001. évi XXXIX. törvény végrehajtásáról), s. 160(1).

[45] Government Decree 114/2007. (V. 24) on the execution of Act II of 2007 on the Admission and Right of Residence of Third-Country Nationals, s. 159(1).

[46] Act CXL of 2004 on the general rules of administrative procedures and services (2004. évi CXL. törvény a közigazgatási hatósági eljárás és szolgáltatás általános szabályairól), s. 22(2).

[47] Royal Decree 865/2001 of 20 July approving the Regulation for the Recognition of the Status of Stateless Persons, s. 2(3).

[48] While, for example, asylum claims can be submitted at any *préfecture* (local representation of the national government) all over the country.

(NGOs, lawyers, etc.) trained on statelessness and active in supporting stateless people is still extremely limited, even in the industrialized
world (as compared in particular to the fields of asylum, immigration or
naturalization). This means that such a restrictive approach can significantly hinder access to procedures and protection.

A further challenging issue is whether states are allowed to set any
specific admissibility conditions. In Hungary, for example, only lawfully
staying foreigners can claim stateless status.[49] This restriction – besides
being evidently absurd[50] – is in breach of the 1954 Convention. The latter
sets forth an exhaustive list of exclusion grounds and does not allow for
further ones. As the Metropolitan Court *(Fővárosi Bíróság)* in Hungary
correctly observed:

> it is the Convention that sets the material conditions of the recognition
> of stateless status, according to which a stateless person is a person who
> is not recognised as a citizen by any country under its national law. As
> compared to the Convention, the Aliens Act [...] cannot establish further
> material conditions for the recognition of statelessness.[51]

Another such limitation can be found in the Spanish legislation, which
sets a time limit for applications. Claims for stateless status are only
admitted within one month after entry into Spain or following the expiration of a residence entitlement.[52] In any other case, the application will
be automatically rejected as manifestly unfounded.[53] This approach is
again contrary to the 1954 Convention, in addition to being conceptually
erroneous. Statelessness is an objective condition, which does not need to
be underpinned by a subjective fear or other specific conditions.[54] While
having an effective opportunity and still not applying for refugee status
for a long period may, in certain cases, cast doubt on the credibility of
the asylum claim, no parallel principle exists in statelessness determination. For example, it is more than realistic that a stateless person only

---

[49] Act II of 2007 on the Admission and Right of Residence of Third-Country Nationals, s.
76(1).
[50] Since statelessness in Hungary arises mainly in a migratory context, this rule requires
a stateless person to obtain a valid travel document and fulfil a set of difficult material
conditions (such as accommodation, livelihood and health insurance) before even being
able to claim protection as a stateless person.
[51] Judgment no. 24.K.31.412/2009/6.
[52] An exception is made only for *sur place* cases, in which the one month deadline is counted
from the day when the applicant (who already resides in Spain) becomes stateless.
[53] Royal Decree 865/2001 of 20 July approving the Regulation for the Recognition of the
Status of Stateless Persons, s. 4.
[54] See Geneva Conclusions, para. 21.

realizes her or his condition as such after numerous unsuccessful (yet time-consuming) attempts to renew her or his passport. Or to put it simply: under the 1954 Convention's definition, a stateless individual is still stateless even if she or he has already stayed in the 'host country' illegally for more than a year. UNHCR overtly rejects both limitations, declaring that neither a condition of lawful stay, nor a time limit for application has any legal foundation in the 1954 Convention.[55]

5.4.2   The legal status of applicants

A closely related and similarly challenging question is that of the legal status that should be given to those who apply for stateless status while the determination process is ongoing. The Geneva Conclusions suggest that 'States should afford applicants for statelessness determination a minimum set of rights (including work, education, healthcare and housing rights), subject to this being consistent with the requirements of the 1954 Convention and the norms on non-discrimination contained in international human rights law.'[56] UNHCR guidance advises against the removal of applicants from the territory pending their statelessness determination, as well as calling on states to provide applicants with an identity document, the right to self-employment and freedom of movement. As a practical solution, UNHCR recommends that 'individuals awaiting a determination of statelessness receive the same standards of treatment as asylum-seekers'.[57] Yet, this question sheds light on one of the most significant shortcomings in the formalized determination mechanisms that exist at the time of writing. Currently, no national legislation applies a clear and meaningful legal concept of 'applicant for stateless status' or 'applicant for statelessness determination'.

Research has shown that applicants *may* be provided with a temporary residence permit in other national systems as well, but this only happens as a matter of discretion (in Spain) or on an ad hoc basis, without any clear legal foundation (as in the Italian judicial determination procedure). In France, alien-policing authorities may refrain from expelling applicants for stateless status in practice, but there is no legal obligation to do so. This means that such applicants may be subject to expulsion measures, lengthy administrative detention or destitution during the

---

[55] UNHCR, 'Handbook on Protection of Stateless Persons', paras. 69–70.
[56] Geneva Conclusions, para. 23.
[57] UNHCR, 'Handbook on Protection of Stateless Persons', para. 145.

determination procedure, even if their claim is well founded. It is therefore especially promising that the three statelessness-specific protection
regimes created in 2012 all make important steps towards a proper solution for this *lacuna*. The law of Moldova stipulates that 'the applicant has
the right to stay on the territory of the Republic of Moldova during the
examination of his/her claim and may only be removed from the territory for reasons of national security and public order'. Moreover, it fore-
sees the issuance of a temporary residence permit for the duration of the
determination process.[58] Georgian legislation also prohibits the expulsion of applicants until a decision is made, as well as explicitly stipu-
lating that the applicant's stay shall be considered lawful, even if she or
he was staying in the country unlawfully upon the submission of the
claim.[59] The Philippines have also adopted rules ordering the suspen-
sion of deportation measures during status determination and offering a
(non-mandatory) possibility to release the applicant from immigration
detention, if relevant.[60]

Whilst the problem is apparent, it is difficult to argue for a fully fledged
applicant status solely on the basis of the 1954 Convention, mostly because
this instrument remains entirely silent about determination issues.
Relevant UNHCR guidance does, however, offer support: 'An individual
is a stateless person from the moment that the conditions in Article 1(1) of
the 1954 Convention are met. Thus, any finding by a State or UNHCR that
an individual satisfies the test in Article 1(1) is declaratory, rather than
constitutive, in nature.'[61] This means that a stateless individual does not
become a stateless person through the status determination procedure,
but is rather recognized as being a stateless person. As a matter of principle, therefore, she or he is already entitled to the rights defined in the
1954 Convention.[62] Meanwhile, as van Waas concludes, the convention's
formulation of rights seriously endangers the actual enjoyment of these
rights. The precondition of entitlement is usually, at least, lawful presence
(if not an even more substantial connection with the state), and instead of

---

[58] Act 200 of 16 July 2010, on the Regime of Foreigners in the Republic of Moldova, ss. 87³
(1)–(2).
[59] Decree of the President of Georgia No. 515 of 27 June 2012, s.7(2).
[60] Department Circular No. 058 – Establishing the Refugees and Stateless Status
Determination Procedure, Department of Justice, 18 October 2012, s. 7.
[61] UNHCR, 'Handbook on Protection of Stateless Persons', para. 16.
[62] The same line of argumentation is usually followed when interpreting the 1951 Refugee
Convention: See UNHCR, 'Handbook on Criteria and Procedures for Determining
Refugee Status', para. 28.

an absolute standard, most mandatory provisions prescribe a treatment only on a par with 'aliens generally'.[63] So even if we accept that applicants for stateless status should be considered as entitled to the rights defined by the convention until the contrary is proved, this will only have a limited impact. Practical considerations may then have the final say on this issue: it is not difficult to accept that the lack of a proper legal condition for the applicant renders the entire identification (and protection) framework meaningless. States should aim for efficient and well-regulated procedures that can assist in determining, in a realistic time frame, who is entitled to protection and who is not.

5.4.3 The institutional framework

As previously mentioned, when establishing the procedural machinery of statelessness determination, a number of models and sources of guidance can be consulted. The primary institutional question is which authority (immigration, nationality, asylum or other) ought to be in charge of identifying, and determining the status of, stateless persons. The answer can only be context specific. In situations where the population concerned is predominantly in its 'own country' authorities in charge of nationality issues and naturalization appear to be the most appropriate bodies for statelessness determination (given the fact that the likely solution for statelessness will be reduction, instead of protection, by implementing the country's own nationality legislation).[64] In an international protection context – the primary focus of this chapter – the response may be more complex. Populations concerned may be rather limited in countries where most stateless persons are from a migratory background; therefore states are likely to favour the integration of statelessness determination into already existing structures. Existing protection mechanisms tend to delegate this task either to asylum authorities (France, Spain, the Philippines) or immigration authorities (Hungary, Moldova).

The typical procedural acts of statelessness determination are alien to asylum procedures where some of these are even prohibited (e.g. contact with the country of origin). Nonetheless, delegating the task of statelessness determination to asylum authorities may be the preferred option for

---

[63] L. E. van Waas, *Nationality Matters. Statelessness under International Law* (Antwerp/ Oxford/Portland, OR: Intersentia, 2008), 391.
[64] See Geneva Conclusions, para. 5.

a number of reasons. Asylum and statelessness share the same characteristic of being based on international protection obligations. Asylum authorities or judges specialized in this field may prove to be better able to accept and effectively deal with the specific procedural features resulting from the protection-oriented character of the procedure, such as a lowered standard of proof or the scarcity of documentary evidence. An immigration officer, who usually operates in a stricter procedural framework, may have adaptation difficulties, especially if only rarely confronted with statelessness cases. A centralized structure and the specialization of officers dealing with statelessness determination should be supported for the same reason.[65] Such merged procedures could also deal with 'stateless refugees', and ensure that they are processed through the most appropriate procedure.[66]

A further interesting question is whether statelessness determination can be performed in a purely judicial context. At the time of writing, such a system – in the framework of a functional protection apparatus – can only be found in Italy, where it exists in parallel with a largely dysfunctional administrative determination mechanism.[67] Electing for the judicial determination of statelessness may raise a number of concerns, including usually lengthy delays, difficult data collection and diverging decision-making practices. At the same time, the Italian experience shows that such a framework can eventually also provide more space for a progressive, inclusive and human-rights-focused approach and facilitates a continuous and fruitful professional debate on (re-)interpreting statelessness.[68]

---

[65] See UNHCR, 'Handbook on Protection of Stateless Persons', para. 63. Note that a centralized decision-making structure should not mean a centralized access mechanism (e.g. only one or a very limited number of physical 'points of entry').

[66] The definition of a refugee in the 1951 Refugee Convention includes refugees who have lost their nationality and are stateless: Art. 1A(2), second paragraph.

[67] The administrative procedure is seldom used, as it requires the applicant to be lawfully present in Italy (see concerns regarding the similar regulation in Hungary earlier) and to present a wide range of documentary evidence. In addition it has unrealistic deadlines and the regulation does not create a clear protection obligation for the proceeding Ministry of the Interior, it just offers the possibility. See: Presidential Decree no. 572 of 12 October 1993, executive regulation of Act no. 91 of 5 February 1992 on new citizenship rules, s. 17.

[68] This conclusion is partly based on discussions with Paolo Farci, attorney-at-law, on statelessness in Italy; Budapest, 8 December 2011.

5.4.4   The procedural framework

In addition to the above structural issues, a number of procedural guarantees also need to be observed.[69] First, the right to a personal hearing, which provides the most adequate opportunity to collect oral evidence. Here, national practices vary: the applicant's personal hearing is mandatory in Hungary, usual in France and optional in Spain and Italy. Second, given the evident vulnerability of stateless persons, access to state-funded legal aid (a right guaranteed — at least in principle — in Hungary and Italy, but not in France) would be crucial in most cases. Third, access by UNHCR to proceedings, governed by its mandate to protect stateless people's rights, would be important.[70] This may include access to files and overall data, a possibility to intervene in individual cases with expert opinions and assistance in establishing facts and information from the country of origin. At the time of writing, Hungarian regulation shows an exemplary practice in this respect.[71]

Fourth, effective judicial review also constitutes an indispensable procedural safeguard in statelessness determination (regardless of whether the first-instance determination is administrative or judicial).[72] Besides evident due process and quality considerations, practice demonstrates that judicial guidance is crucial in shaping protection mechanisms – particularly in such a 'new' area of protection, where only limited international experience, soft law and academic literature is available. Rules and frameworks for judicial review differ greatly, even within the small group of countries operating a statelessness-specific protection mechanism. A personal hearing is mandatory in Hungary, while Spanish and French courts usually decide *sur dossier*. Spanish, Hungarian and Italian judges can grant stateless status themselves, while their French colleagues can only quash lower-instance decisions. Regardless, the increasing involvement of the judiciary in statelessness-related work (training, research, etc.) seems

---

[69] See also UNHCR, 'Handbook on Protection of Stateless Persons', paras. 71–3.

[70] See in particular UN General Assembly, 'Office of the United Nations High Commissioner for Refugees: Resolution adopted by the General Assembly' A/RES/49/169 (24 February 1995); UN General Assembly, 'Office of the United Nations High Commissioner for Refugees: resolution adopted by the General Assembly, 9' A/RES/50/152 (February 1996); UN General Assembly, 'Resolution 61/137 Adopted by the UN General Assembly: Office of the United Nations High Commissioner for Refugees' A/RES/61/137 (25 January 2007).

[71] Act II of 2007 on the Admission and Right of Residence of Third-Country Nationals, s. 81.

[72] See UNHCR, 'Handbook on Protection of Stateless Persons', paras. 76–7.

a crucial objective, as the number of protection mechanisms is likely to multiply in forthcoming years.

The fifth procedural safeguard of relevance to statelessness determination is setting the proper time frame for decision making and establishing deadlines. However, this is not straightforward either. Statelessness determination often requires several months in order to be completed (as in most cases it requires obtaining information from foreign authorities). Unreasonably short procedural deadlines can therefore result in serious difficulties and a failure to meet the aim of effective determination. At the same time, irrationally long deadlines can also render the procedure void, by – among other issues – reducing the authority's motivation to conduct the determination process with due diligence. A striking example is the largely unused Italian administrative procedure, for which the law sets a 350-day deadline, or 895 days if the intervention of the Ministry of Foreign Affairs is required (which seems to be a regular necessity). On the other hand, administrative procedures are usually (even if not always) closed within a couple of months in France and Hungary. UNHCR suggests six months as a realistic time frame for statelessness determination, enabling an extension to twelve months, if official responses are required from foreign states regarding the applicant's nationality.[73]

A sixth issue that has arisen in some countries is the unfortunate codification mistake that states should avoid. This mistake is the use of non-binding language in respect of the granting of status. Both the Italian rules on administrative statelessness determination and the Slovak regulation stipulate that the competent authority *can* grant protection to a stateless individual (instead of *shall*).[74] This language creates legal uncertainty by delegating unreasonable discretion to the officer in charge, and as such, it raises serious concerns regarding compliance with the 1954 Convention.

Finally, failure to regulate the relationship between statelessness determination and asylum procedures may also cause difficulties. Stateless persons can be refugees at the same time, and many may seek protection through the asylum procedure as well. Given that the most common procedural act in statelessness determination (contact with and information gathering from foreign authorities) is strictly prohibited in asylum procedures, the regulatory framework ought to clarify

---

[73] See also UNHCR, 'Handbook on Protection of Stateless Persons', para. 75.
[74] Presidential Decree no. 572 of 12 October 1993, executive regulation of Act no. 91 of 5 February 1992 on new citizenship rules, s. 17(1); Act 404/2011 Coll. on aliens and the amendment of some laws (Zákon č. 404/2011 Z.z. o pobyte cudzincov a o zmene a doplnení niektorých zákonov), s. 46(2)(b).

the relationship between these two. In most functioning protection regimes, no legal rule has been created to this end. However, in the event of parallel claims, the general practice is to prioritize the asylum application and suspend statelessness determination until a final decision is reached on that question. This approach is correct, in particular because contact with authorities in the country of origin (a usual procedural step in statelessness determination) is strictly forbidden until the validity of the asylum claim is rejected by a final decision. The Philippines was the first country to properly codify this rule in its regulatory framework adopted in 2012, which stipulates that where during statelessness determination 'a refugee claim appears to exist, the stateless status determination shall, with the consent of the Applicant, be suspended and the application shall be considered first for refugee status determination. If the claim to refugee status is denied with finality, the stateless status determination shall recommence automatically.'[75] On the other hand, a rather unreasonable approach has been taken in Mexico, where *all* applicants for stateless status shall first go through the asylum channel, even if they do not refer to any asylum-related protection ground. Such an inflexible obligation causes unnecessary delays, costs and a waste of resources.

5.4.5   The evidentiary framework

Establishing statelessness is often a cumbersome exercise and if the evidentiary rules are too strict, this can easily undermine the protection objective of the 1954 Convention. The Geneva Conclusions therefore rightly point out that 'determination procedures should adopt an approach to evidence which takes into account the challenges inherent in establishing whether a person is stateless'.[76] There appears to be a general perception among states and other actors that in order to be qualified as stateless an individual does not need to prove that she or he is not the citizen of any single country of the world. Nevertheless, more concrete principles are still in the making.

The first pivotal issue is the burden of proof, meaning the question of who bears the burden of establishing whether or not the applicant is stateless. The Geneva Conclusions and UNHCR guidance both suggest a shared

---

[75] Department Circular No. 058 – 'Establishing the Refugees and Stateless Status Determination Procedure', Department of Justice, 18 October 2012, s. 8.
[76] Geneva Conclusions, para. 14.

onus, with the applicant being obliged to cooperate with the determining authority.[77] From a practical standpoint, it would be difficult to argue
against this approach: stateless persons often face insurmountable difficulties in demonstrating their lack of nationality, and if they were left alone in
this task, most of them would never have access to protection. Moreover,
foreign authorities have diverging attitudes towards claims for the confirm-
ation of citizenship coming from individuals and state offices. Research
from Hungary,[78] for instance, indicates that some foreign authorities will
only respond to such a query if submitted by the person concerned (for
reasons of data protection, for example). Others may disregard individual information requests (especially if coming from an individual not perceived as a citizen) and would attach more importance to 'official' claims
submitted by a foreign state authority. Sometimes the very same state may
apply either of these approaches, depending on the case (or the officer who
receives the information request). As such, flexibility and 'labour-division'
can seriously enhance the efficiency of the determination procedure.

It is comprehensible, therefore, that most states resort to some sort of
burden sharing. In France and Spain, the asylum authority, which processes statelessness claims, has the responsibility to establish whether or
not the applicant is stateless, while the applicant solely has the obligation
to cooperate in this process (by, for example, submitting all relevant evidence at her or his disposal). In Hungary, the principal burden of proof is
incumbent on the claimant, but the competent authority is obliged to provide administrative assistance on request and has the general obligation
to establish all relevant facts of the case.

Another key issue in this context is the applicable standard of proof.
The difficulty of proving statelessness has been mentioned repeatedly in
this chapter. As with the issue of the burden of proof, flexibility and a
protection-oriented approach is required in this respect, too. It is important to note that legislators and judges in civil law jurisdictions – unlike
their counterparts in the common law context – usually refrain from
a formalistic interpretation of the standard of proof.[79] Nevertheless, a
growing body of legislation and jurisprudence indicates that 'proving'
should be understood flexibly and a high, for example 'beyond all reasonable doubt', standard cannot be expected. Hungarian legislation uses

---

[77] Geneva Conclusions, para. 13. See also UNHCR, 'Handbook on Protection of Stateless
Persons', para. 89.
[78] Gyulai, 'Statelessness in Hungary', 26.
[79] Most states operating a statelessness-specific determination and protection mechanism
at the time of writing follow a civil law tradition.

the verb 'substantiate' (*valószínűsít*) instead of 'prove', a term borrowed from national asylum legislation and international refugee law, indicating a lower and more flexibly interpreted standard of proof.[80] Some Italian court decisions also argue for a lowered standard: for instance, the Court of Appeal of Florence (*Corte di Appello di Firenze*) ruled in 2009 that in certain situations, in particular when the applicant has never had any nationality, circumstantial or indicative evidence (*un quadro indiziario*) can be sufficient for the recognition of statelessness.[81]

A more practical question related to evidence assessment is the circle of countries with regard to which a potential nationality tie should be tested. Evidently, this group should be limited and should only reflect realistic possibilities of nationality. To put it simply: if a woman was born in Bangladesh and lived most of her life in the United Kingdom, where she married a Pakistani national, there is no need to check whether she is a national of Ecuador or Cape Verde. Hungarian and Slovak legislation provide, for example, that statelessness shall be tested in particular with regard to the country of birth, the country or countries of former residence and the country of nationality of parents and family members.[82] In the practice of Hungary, this meant a maximum of two or three countries in every case presented in 2007–9. Italian jurisprudence has also adopted a similar approach: since the 1970s, a number of court decisions have ruled that the nationality link should be tested with regard to the country of origin and that of residence (Italy and, if relevant, the last place of residence), if there are significant ties.

The general requirement of flexibility also applies to the types of evidence accepted in statelessness determination, the following types being the most frequently used:

- *Information provided by foreign authorities (consular authorities, civil registry offices, etc.).* The main challenge linked to this type of evidence is that the authorities approached may often fail to respond within a reasonable time frame. Enduring silence could indicate a negative answer, yet it is difficult to set concrete benchmarks for how much time and how many unsuccessful attempts the determining authority should be allotted before arriving at this conclusion. Certainly, no

---

[80] Act II of 2007 on the Admission and Right of Residence of Third-Country Nationals, s. 79(1).

[81] Judgment no. 1654 of 17 November 2009 of the Court of Appeal of Florence.

[82] Act II of 2007 on the Admission and Right of Residence of Third-Country Nationals, s. 79(1); Act 404/2011 Coll. on aliens and the amendment of some laws, s. 46(3).

reaction for a month after the first official request is sent does not, per se, substantiate the lack of nationality. On the other hand, the refusal to answer for eight months and after five official letters is likely to indicate that the person in question does not have a legal bond with the given state.[83]

- *Country information.* Reliable, accurate and up-to-date information about nationality legislation and related practices in foreign countries can provide significant assistance in statelessness determination. Quality standards can be entirely borrowed from the field of asylum, with particular emphasis on individualization and the examination of actual legal practices (instead of the 'law in the books').[84]

- *Information provided by UNHCR.* Through its global presence and relevant mandate, UNHCR may be helpful in obtaining evidence, even in cases where the competent foreign authorities remain silent.

- *Documentary evidence.* Some applicants may be able to submit proof regarding the loss of a previous nationality or a travel document, which indicates that its holder is stateless (e.g. a specific document issued to stateless Palestinians in Kuwait or Lebanon). Other documents may help in establishing the place of birth or previous residence, such that the possible country or countries of nationality can be identified.

- *The applicant's own submissions.* Coherent and relevant statements made by the applicant should be accepted as evidence and should play a central (even if not necessarily self-sufficient) role in decision making.

National practices indicate a mixed use of all these types of evidence, with a clear emphasis on the first two.

Beyond these various considerations of a general scope, national courts have occasionally provided useful guidance on particular issues of interpretation. For example, the Metropolitan Court (*Fővárosi Bíróság*) in Hungary ruled in 2009 that an applicant's previous rejected asylum

---

[83] A state's usual 'attitude' in dealing with such queries should also be observed: no response after several attempts from a country that is usually diligent in providing such information can be quite indicative. On the other hand, the silence of a small, badly resourced state in the middle of a grave political and economic crisis may simply be due to a general incapacity to react on *any* such request.

[84] See, for example, G. Gyulai, *Country Information in Asylum Procedures – Quality as a Legal Requirement in the EU* (Budapest: Hungarian Helsinki Committee, 2011); Hungarian Helsinki Committee and International Association of Refugee Law Judges, 'Judicial Criteria for Assessing Country of Origin Information (COI): A Checklist', Paper for the 7th Biennial IARLJ World Conference, Mexico City (6–9 November 2006).

claims, expulsion and criminal conviction are all irrelevant facts when deciding upon his application for stateless status[85] (i.e., there is no 'good conduct' requirement in statelessness determination, except for particularly serious cases covered by the exclusion clauses of Article 1(2) of the 1954 Convention). The Italian Supreme Court of Appeal *(Corte Suprema di Cassazione)* held in 2007 that it is not necessary to prove the loss of a former nationality by an official state declaration. The loss of nationality can also be shown through the demonstration of acts by which the state denies protection to the individual concerned.[86] The French Council of State *(Conseil d'État)* ruled in 2000 that the mere legal possibility of recovering one's previously lost nationality does not exclude her or him from stateless status.[87] Overall, it is evident that clear guidance on evidentiary burden, standards and guidance in law or regulations can make the process of determination more fair and efficient, as well as helping to avoid excessively lengthy procedures.

5.5.   Conclusion

The current decade is, without a doubt, a crucial one in the struggle against statelessness and for the protection of those affected by this undesirable phenomenon. After half a century of unjustifiable neglect, states, international organizations, the academic world and the civil sector seem to realize the severity of the problem and efforts to find suitable solutions are multiplying. This growing interest is particularly significant in the case of identification and protection of stateless persons, which has so far been *terra incognita* for most states and other actors (while, at least, the issues of avoidance and reduction of statelessness have received some limited attention).

Yet the road to be travelled before stateless persons around the globe receive the support and protection they are entitled to on the basis of the 1954 Convention and international human rights law looks to be long and dusty. To start with, states and other actors must first understand the concept and necessity of statelessness-specific protection, while also becoming familiar with what building blocks are indispensable for the construction of such a regime. As indicated in this chapter, however, to help ensure the effective identification of stateless

---

[85] Judgment no. 24.K.31.412/2009/6 of the Metropolitan Court.
[86] Judgment no. 14918 of 20 March 2007 of the Supreme Court of Appeal.
[87] Judgment no. 216121 of 29 December 2000 of the Council of State.

persons (a cornerstone of any protection mechanism), states and other stakeholders finally have a growing body of soft law guidance, academic literature and some good state practice to look at.[88] Nevertheless, additional mapping, research and legal analysis remain pivotal in this quickly evolving field. Of particular relevance will be the assessment of newly created identification and protection mechanisms, together with the comprehensive compilation and analysis of national jurisprudence on this matter.

In this process, one fundamental principle should never be overlooked. According to international human rights law, everybody has the right to a nationality, and consequently, statelessness constitutes a grave violation of a basic human right (usually with multiple negative impacts on the enjoyment of other human rights). Therefore, identification and protection mechanisms should always be constructed in an inclusive and rights-based manner. Moreover, for this very same reason, they should never simply aim for a 'practical solution' by offering a quick remedy to the most striking problems (such as lengthy detention or hopeless destitution). In the true spirit of the 1954 Convention and human rights law, these regimes should always promote, sooner or later, an effective way out from the anomalous condition of statelessness and provide a pathway to nationality. This chapter cannot but conclude with expressing hope that the years to come will witness the much-needed shift towards statelessness-specific protection regimes all over the world, and that this issue will find its well-deserved place on the map of international protection.

Questions to guide discussion

1. Is international protection the answer to the problem of statelessness? In what situations are other options more appropriate?
2. What are some of the key challenges to establishing statelessness determination procedures, for states and for individual stateless persons?
3. Outline the five-step protection model proposed by the author. What is your view of this? Are there any suggestions to complete this scenario (e.g. in a specific national context)?
4. What are the seven procedural safeguards the author sees as fundamental requirements in statelessness determination procedures, and

---

[88] See also: European Network on Statelessness, 'Statelessness Determination and the Protection Status of Stateless Persons', 2013.

what are some of the peculiarities compared with other determination systems?

5. What are some of the procedural differences between refugee status and statelessness determination procedures mentioned in this chapter?

6

Children, their right to a nationality and child statelessness

GERARD-RENÉ DE GROOT

6.1. Introduction

The pivotal juncture in guaranteeing a person's right to a nationality is the moment of birth. If a child does not secure a nationality at birth, he or she may be left stateless for many years, or even a lifetime – with severe consequences. Childhood statelessness threatens access to education, an adequate standard of living, social assistance, health care and other specific forms of protection to which children are entitled. This is why a child's right to acquire a nationality is laid down in numerous international instruments, including the almost universally ratified 1989 Convention on the Rights of the Child (CRC).[1] Yet new cases of childhood statelessness surface around the world every day, raising the issue to what extent states' international obligations are being effective implemented. A second issue is whether the international standards themselves are adequate or are in need of further clarification. Guided by such questions, this chapter looks at the scope and implementation of the right to a nationality generally, and from the specific perspective of the avoidance of childhood statelessness. In this latter regard, it asks: When is a child considered to be 'otherwise stateless' for the purposes of invoking the standards to acquire a nationality under relevant instruments? How are nationality norms to be applied in the context of complex situations in order to avoid statelessness, such as those involving abandoned children, international adoption or surrogacy arrangements, or foundlings? These questions are explored through an analysis of core universal and regional human rights instruments, as well as the specific rules on the avoidance of statelessness among children

---

[1] Convention on the Rights of the Child, New York, 20 November 1989, in force 2 September 1990, 1577 UNTS 3.

found in the 1961 Convention on the Reduction of Statelessness[2] (1961 Convention) and those developed within the framework of the Council of Europe, which offers the most detailed and comprehensive set of regional standards elaborated on this issue to date.

6.2. The right of children to a nationality under international human rights law

Article 15 of the 1948 Universal Declaration of Human Rights[3] (UDHR) guarantees 'nationality' as a human right by prescribing that 'Everyone has the right to a nationality' and 'No one shall be arbitrarily deprived of his nationality nor denied the right to change his nationality'. The obvious weakness of Article 15(1) is that it does not indicate which nationality a person may have a right to, nor which state has the obligation to grant it. This principle elaborated in Article 15 is repeated in several binding international treaties. As will be seen below, the formulation of this right in successive universal and regional human rights treaties shows a particular interest in ensuring that children have access to a nationality.

Article 24(3) of the International Covenant on Civil and Political Rights (ICCPR)[4] guarantees, for example, that '[e]very *child* has the right to acquire a nationality' [emphasis added]. Like the UDHR, this provision does not indicate to which state a child may claim his or her right to nationality. Additionally, Article 24(3) only guarantees a right to *acquire* a nationality, without any specification by which time this right has to be implemented. Nevertheless, a positive element of the ICCPR is that it articulates the right of a *child* to acquire a nationality.[5] This imposes an obligation to implement the provision in a way that gives a child a meaningful opportunity to exercise their right to acquire a nationality before (s)he reaches the age of majority. Read in conjunction with Article 24(2), which requires children to be registered immediately after birth, early conferral of nationality is expected. This implies that it is not acceptable to

---

[2] Convention on the Reduction of Statelessness, New York, 30 August 1961, in force 13 December 1975, 989 UNTS 175.

[3] Resolution 217 A (III), UN General Assembly, 10 December 1948.

[4] International Covenant on Civil and Political Rights, New York, 16 December 1966, in force 23 March 1976, 999 UNTS 171.

[5] This term should be interpreted as 'every human being below the age of 18 years unless, under domestic law applicable, majority is attained earlier'. See Article 1 CRC.

postpone the right to acquire a nationality until a person reaches the age of eighteen years. Nor it is acceptable that children be denied access to the right to nationality on discriminatory grounds. In fact, sub-paragraph (1) of the same Article specifically provides that 'Every child shall have, without any discrimination as to race, colour, sex, language, religion, national or social origin, property or birth, the right to such measures of protection as are required by his status as a minor, on the part of his family, society and the State.' The United Nations Human Rights Committee (HRC) has explicitly recognized that discrimination in respect of the acquisition, deprivation or loss of nationality is prohibited.[6] In that light the HRC stressed in General Comment No. 17 on Article 24:

> While the purpose of [Article 24] is to prevent a child from being afforded less protection by society and the State because he is stateless, it does not necessarily make it an obligation for States to give their nationality to every child born in their territory. However, States are required to adopt every appropriate measure, both internally and in cooperation with other States, to ensure that every child has a nationality when he is born. In this connection, no discrimination with regard to the acquisition of nationality should be admissible under internal law as between legitimate children and children born out of wedlock or of stateless parents or based on the nationality status of one or both of the parents.[7]

Article 7 of the CRC renders the obligations set forth in Article 24(3) of the ICCPR slightly more concrete. It provides:

> 1. The child shall be registered immediately after birth and shall have the right from birth to a name, the right to acquire a nationality and, as far as possible, the right to know and be cared for by his or her parents.
> 2. States parties shall ensure the implementation of these rights in accordance with their national law and their obligations under the relevant international instruments in this field, in particular where the child would otherwise be stateless.

Neither the ICCPR nor the CRC indicate which nationality a child may have a right to, nor do they guarantee that the nationality is acquired at birth.[8] Former Chairperson of the UN Committee on the Rights of the Child (CRC Committee), Jaap Doek has observed that 'the drafters of

---

[6] Human Rights Committee, 'General Comment No. 17: Rights of the Child (Art. 24)', 7 April 1989, para. 4, referring to Articles 2 and 26 of the ICCPR.

[7] Ibid., para. 8.

[8] In contrast, Principle 3 of the UN Declaration of the Rights of the Child, UNGA res. 1386 (XIV) adopted in 1959, provided that 'the child shall be entitled *from his birth* ... to a nationality' (emphasis added), meaning that a child should be spared even temporary statelessness by acquiring a nationality immediately at birth.

the ICCPR felt that a State could not accept an unqualified obligation to accord its nationality to every child born on its territory regardless the circumstances'.[9] He also emphasized that the CRC Committee does not suggest that state parties should introduce 'the *jus soli* approach', but rather that 'all necessary measures are taken to prevent the child from having no nationality'.[10] His views are similar to the approach adopted by the HRC.[11] As such, those measures to be taken to prevent a child having no nationality fall not only on the country of birth of the child, but also on the country of the nationality of the parent(s). The obligations imposed on states by Article 7(2) of the CRC are not exclusively directed to the country of birth of a child, but to all countries with which the child has a link by way of parentage, residence or place of birth.[12]

Furthermore, where nationality is attributed on the basis of descent, human rights law demands that states not discriminate on the basis of gender. In other words, a child should have equal access to the state's nationality whether it is the mother or father who holds it. This obligation is explicit in Article 9(2) of the Convention on the Elimination of All Forms of Discrimination Against Women, but also flows from the non-discrimination clauses of the ICCPR and CRC.[13] Ensuring that women have an equal opportunity to pass on their nationality to their children plays an important part in preventing childhood statelessness, since any of a variety of reasons may preclude access to the father's nationality.[14]

In addition to the global instruments, several regional instruments also contain provisions on the nationality rights of children. The American Convention on Human Rights (ACHR) was the first regional instrument to reaffirm Article 15 of the UDHR's universal promise of the right to nationality.[15] An interesting divergence is that Article 20(2) of the ACHR guarantees the acquisition of nationality of the country of birth (*jus soli*) if

---

[9] Jaap Doek, 'The CRC and the Right to Acquire and Preserve a Nationality', *Refugee Survey Quarterly* 25 (2006) 26–32, at 26.

[10] *Ibid.*, at 28.

[11] See Human Rights Committee, 'General Comment 17'.

[12] See also Laura van Waas, *Nationality Matters. Statelessness under International Law* (Antwerp/Oxford/Portland, OR: Intersentia 2008), 63–4.

[13] See further on gender discrimination in nationality laws and the response of international law to this phenomenon Chapter 7 by Govil and Edwards in this volume.

[14] UNHCR, 'Background note on gender equality, nationality laws and statelessness' (2014).

[15] Article 20 of the American Convention on Human Rights, 22 November 1969, in force 18 July 1978, OAS Treaty Series No. 36 reads as follows: '1. Every person has the right to a nationality. 2. Every person has the right to the nationality of the State in whose territory he was born if he does not have the right to any other nationality. 3. No one shall be arbitrarily deprived of his nationality or of the right to change it.'

a person does not have the right to another nationality.[16] This clear choice for a default *jus soli* rule can be explained by the strong preference for *jus soli* for the acquisition of nationality at birth in the Americas.[17]

The African Charter on the Rights and Welfare of the Child enshrines the right to a nationality for children in its Article 6(3) and (4).[18] Like the ACHR, Article 6(4) contains a clear default to *jus soli* acquisition of nationality for otherwise stateless children. Of particular note is that the African Children's Charter provision requires 'constitutional recognition' of the principles for the granting of nationality by states where children who would otherwise be stateless are born.[19]

The foregoing shows that, within the realm of human rights law, there is broad recognition of the child's right to acquire a nationality, but some variation in the manner in which this right is formulated. There is also limited guidance on how the right is to be exercised. The next sections study how the right to acquire a nationality has inspired the elaboration of more concrete norms in other treaties, in particular the UN's 1961 Convention and the detailed regional standards developed by the Council of Europe.

6.3. Access of children to a nationality under the 1961 Statelessness Convention

The 1961 Statelessness Convention[20] obliges contracting states to grant nationality to persons born in their territory who without such nationality

---

[16] See for an application of Article 20 by the Inter-American Court of Human Rights the decision on the enjoyment of nationality by children of Haitian descent in the Dominican Republic Inter-American Court of Human Rights, *Yean and Bosico* v. *Dominican Republic,* Series C, Case 130, 8 September 2005.

[17] van Waas, *Nationality Matters,* 60, 61.

[18] African Charter on the Rights and Welfare of the Child, 11 July 1990, in force 29 November 1999, OAU DOC. CAB/LEG/24.9.49; Article 63(3) and (4) provides: '3. Every child has the right to acquire a nationality. 4. States Parties to the present Charter shall undertake to ensure that their Constitutional legislation recognise the principles according to which a child shall acquire the nationality of the State in the territory of which he has been born if, at the time of the child's birth, he is not granted nationality by any other State in accordance with its laws.'

[19] See for an application of Article 6(3) and (4) African Committee of Experts on the Rights and Welfare of the Child, *Institute for Human Rights and Development in Africa and Open Society Justice Initiative on behalf of Children of Nubian Descent in Kenya* v. *The Government of Kenya ('Nubian Children case'),* Communication No. Com/002/2009, 22 March 2011.

[20] This paragraph is based on a considerably more detailed description of and comments on Articles 1–4 of the 1961 Statelessness Convention in Gerard-René de Groot, 'Preventing Statelessness Among Children: Interpreting Articles 1–4 Convention on the

would not be recognized by any state as a national, and would thus be stateless ('otherwise stateless'). In obliging states to grant nationality to these otherwise stateless children, Article 1 of the 1961 Convention gives contracting states several alternatives in implementing this requirement. The state of birth of an otherwise stateless person can either provide for an automatic (*ex lege*) acquisition of its nationality upon birth in its territory or provide for acquisition on application. Article 1 also allows contracting states to provide for automatic (*ex lege*) acquisition of nationality at an age determined by domestic law, if certain conditions are fulfilled. It is important to underscore that the reference to persons 'who would otherwise be stateless' refers to the status of the child born on the territory and not that of the parents of the child. Children of parents who have nationality are also covered by the convention if they are stateless because the parents cannot transmit their nationality to them.[21]

States that do not provide for an *ex lege* acquisition of their nationality for otherwise stateless children at birth may require the fulfilment of one or more of the conditions exhaustively listed in Article 1(2) of the 1961 Convention (acquisition by application). Imposing any other conditions than those elaborated would violate the terms of the 1961 Convention. Moreover, the exhaustive character of the list implies that the state does not have any discretionary power to deny nationality if the conditions mentioned under domestic law in conformity with Article 1(2) are met. To provide for a discretionary naturalization procedure for otherwise stateless children is thus not in conformity with the 1961 Convention.[22]

The first permissible condition for acquiring nationality through application is that a state can require an individual to lodge an application during a period of time beginning not later than after the applicant reaches the age of eighteen years and ending not earlier than the age of twenty-one years. Moreover, the person concerned shall be allowed at least one year during which to make the application without having to obtain

---

Reduction of Statelessness and relevant international human rights norms', Background paper, UNHCR: Geneva (March 2012), 70. See also: UNHCR, 'Interpreting the 1961 Statelessness Convention and Preventing Statelessness among Children', Expert meeting, ("Dakar Conclusions")', September 2011; and UNHCR, 'Guidelines on Statelessness No. 4: Ensuring Every Child's Right to Acquire a Nationality through Articles 1–4 of the 1961 Convention on the Reduction of Statelessness', HRC/GS/12/04, 21 December 2012 (Guidelines No. 4).

[21] A further exploration of how the notion of 'otherwise stateless' should be interpreted and applied is offered in section 6.4.1 of this chapter.

[22] See 'Summary Record of the 3rd Meeting of Committee 1' A/CONF.9/C.1/SR.3 (2–4–1959), p. 7. See also No. 4, para. 37.

authorization of the parent or guardian to do so. In light of provisions of several more recent treaties already mentioned above,[23] which oblige states to facilitate the acquisition of a nationality by *children* who otherwise would remain stateless, it is no longer acceptable to leave children stateless for a significant period by fixing a late start date for the application period, e.g. at reaching the age of eighteen years. Indeed, the almost universal ratification of the CRC suggests that an otherwise stateless child should acquire the nationality of the country of birth immediately at birth or as soon as possible after birth.

A second permissible condition is that a state can require an applicant to establish habitual residence in a country for a period not exceeding five years immediately preceding the lodging of the application nor ten years in all. The notion 'habitual residence' has to be distinguished from 'residence' or 'domicile' as regulated in domestic law. 'Habitual residence' is very much fact oriented: it indicates 'a stable factual residence'[24] and does not imply a legal or formal qualification. The expression 'habitual residence' refers to an autonomous, international concept and, for example, is also used in The Hague Conventions on Private International Law.[25] Thus, it is important to stress that it is only permitted to require a period of 'habitual residence' and the 1961 Convention does not allow a state to make a successful application conditional on *lawful* residence. It also follows from Article 1(2)(b) that a state may *not* require a certain period of uninterrupted habitual residence *since birth*. A stateless person born on the territory of a certain contracting state who did not acquire the nationality of this state at birth may later lodge an application for the acquisition of this nationality, even if (s)he was living for a considerable period of time in another country.[26]

The text of Article 1(2)(b) of the 1961 Convention can be interpreted in two different ways:

1) A continuous habitual residence of five years directly preceding the application may be required, but an application must also be allowed if

---

[23] In particular Article 24(3) of the ICCPR, Article 7(1) of the CRC, Article 6(3) of the African Charter on the Rights and Welfare of the Child.

[24] See Article 1 of the Council of Europe Convention on the Avoidance of Statelessness in relation to State Succession 19 May 2006, ETS No. 200. Compare also No. 10 of the Explanatory Report to that Convention.

[25] See also Resolution (72)1 of the Council of Ministers of the Council of Europe on the standardization of the legal concepts of 'domicile' and 'residence', 18 January 1972, in particular at no. 7: 'The residence of a person is determined solely by factual criteria; it does not depend upon the legal entitlement to reside'; and several Regulations of the European Union, e.g. Regulation EU 2201/2003 (the so-called Brussels Ibis regulation).

[26] See 'Summary Record of the 9th Plenary Meeting' A/CONF.9/SR.9 (15 April 1959), p. 2.

the total duration of shorter periods of habitual residence exceeds ten years;[27] or

2) A habitual residence of ten years may be required, of which a period not exceeding five years directly precedes the lodging of the declaration.

The drafting history of the convention provides no clear view on the intention of the drafters. It only becomes clear that the maximum term of five years' residence immediately before the application was inserted because the drafters realized that young people may go abroad for a period for the purposes of education. States should therefore avoid requiring too long a period of uninterrupted residence immediately preceding the application.[28] Again, it should be underlined that a period of ten years, and even a period of five years, could be considered long in light of the principles contained in more recent human rights treaties and the overall objective of the treaty to reduce the cases of statelessness. States that apply an application procedure requiring a certain period of habitual residence are, therefore, encouraged to provide for a period as short as possible.[29]

The third permissible condition that can be imposed upon otherwise stateless persons who apply to acquire citizenship of the country of birth is a criminal conviction test. States can require that an individual has neither been convicted of an offence against national security nor sentenced to imprisonment for a term of five years or more on a criminal charge. Article 1(2)(c) refers to the criminal history of an otherwise stateless person and not to acts of his or her parents.

Finally, Article 1(2)(d) of the 1961 Convention allows states to require that an applicant 'has always been stateless'. It follows from the exhaustive character of the permissible grounds for rejection that there should be a presumption that the applicant has always been stateless and the burden of proof rests with the state to prove the contrary.[30] If a state does not explicitly require that a person has always been stateless, they might then allow a person born on their territory the right to acquire their nationality if, for example, a person was not born stateless or was born stateless, acquired a nationality but lost this nationality again with statelessness the consequence.[31]

---

[27] van Waas, *Nationality Matters*, 62 seems to interpret the provision in this way.
[28] 'Summary Record of the 3rd Meeting of Committee 1' A/CONF.9/C.1/SR.3 (2 April 1959), p. 6.
[29] This also applies for the period of habitual residence which may be imposed under Articles 1(5) and 4(2), 1961 Convention.
[30] See 'Guidelines No. 4', para. 48.
[31] See 'Summary Record of the 3rd Meeting of Committee 1', p. 6.

As already noted, providing that nationality can be acquired upon application – rather than automatically at birth – can leave a child stateless for a considerable number of years, with all of the negative consequences for the enjoyment of other rights that this may entail in the interim. Alternatively, states could provide for the loss of the nationality acquired by birth on the territory in order to avoid statelessness if it is later discovered that the child actually does hold, or has acquired, another nationality.[32] It is therefore preferable to provide for children born on the territory of a state who would otherwise be stateless to be able to acquire the nationality of that state at birth or shortly after birth with retroactivity. However, the 1961 Convention allows for states to provide for the acquisition of nationality without retroactive effect.[33]

Automatic acquisition of nationality by otherwise stateless children under Article 1 of the 1961 Convention may have as a consequence that the mere 'accidental' birth on the territory would also give the right to acquire the nationality of the state of birth. Even though the number of such cases is small, some states are afraid that such a rule could be abused. To avoid this, a state makes the *ex lege* acquisition of its nationality by potentially stateless children conditional on the lawful and habitual residence of a parent on its territory. However, if states do so, they will – in order to meet the standards of Article 1 of the 1961 Convention – also have to provide for the grant of nationality by application for those children who do not acquire the nationality of the country of birth immediately, due to the fact that their parent did not reside lawfully and habitually in that country. Contracting states must then also observe the fact that the 1961 Convention does not allow the requirement of *lawful* residence of the applicant as a condition for a successful application.

A special rule is given in Article 1(3) of the 1961 Convention. The approach taken to the avoidance of statelessness of the 1961 Convention was a compromise between *jus soli* and *jus sanguinis* countries. An essential element of this compromise was Article 1(3). At the time of negotiating the text, most *jus sanguinis* countries applied *jus sanguinis a patre*. In those countries, in principle only male nationals could transmit their nationality to their children. Female nationals could transmit their nationality to children born out of wedlock, often only if paternity could not be

---

[32] See e.g. Article 7(1)(f) European Convention on Nationality (ECN), 6 November 1997, ETS No. 166, see 6.4 of this chapter.

[33] Compare Principle 2 of 'Recommendation 2009/13 of the Committee of Ministers of the Council of Europe on the nationality of children', CM/Res(2009)13, 9 December 2009 and the Explanatory Memorandum on the Recommendation, at Nr. 11.

established or recognized. Consequently, in these states the children of a mother who is a national and a stateless father, or a father who could not transmit his nationality, would be born stateless. Inspired by the earlier League of Nations' Protocol on a Certain Case of Statelessness[34] to the 1930 Hague Convention on Certain Questions Relating to the Conflicts of Nationality Laws.[35] Article 1(3) of the 1961 Convention prescribes the acquisition of the nationality of the country of birth for children born on the territory of a state of which their mother is a national, if they otherwise would be stateless.[36]

Attention should also be devoted to the obligations that arise under Article 1(4)–(5) and Article 4 of the 1961 Convention. Article 1(4)–(5) addresses the nationality position of a stateless person who was not able to acquire the nationality of the contracting state of birth due to the age or residence conditions of Article 1(2).[37] In principle, their acquisition of a nationality is no longer facilitated by the convention unless a parent is a national of another contracting state. In the latter case, the country of nationality of this parent has to grant its nationality, *ex lege* or upon application. An application may only be rejected on the grounds exhaustively mentioned in Article 1(5). These grounds have strong similarities with those of Article 1(2), but differ in some details.[38] Article 1(4) also addresses cases where a stateless person is the child of two parents who are nationals of two different contracting states by allowing states to determine whether the child can acquire the nationality of the father or of the mother under national law.

The obligations of the state of nationality of a parent are stronger under the 1961 Convention if the otherwise stateless child is born in the territory of a non-contracting state, but has a parent who possesses the nationality of a contracting state at the time of birth of his or her child. In that case the state of nationality of a parent may have an immediate obligation to grant its nationality to the child, because the 1961 Convention

---

[34] League of Nations, Protocol Relating to a Certain Case of Statelessness, 12 April 1930, No. 4138, 179 LNTS 115.

[35] League of Nations, Convention on Certain Questions Relating to the Conflict of Nationality Law, 13 April 1930, 179 LNTS 89.

[36] See further on gender discrimination in nationality laws and the response of international law to this phenomenon Chapter 7 by Govil and Edwards in this volume.

[37] The obligations of the country of birth under the 1961 Convention take precedence over the obligations of the country of citizenship of a parent.

[38] For a comparative table regarding the grounds for rejection of an application under Article 1(2), Article 1(4)–(5) and Article 4 of the 1961 Convention, see de Groot, 'Preventing Statelessness Among Children'.

cannot force the non-contracting state of birth to confer its nationality. According to Article 4, acquisition of nationality by an otherwise stateless person may occur *ex lege* at birth or subsequently on application. If the state opts for the application route it may make this subject to one or more of the conditions listed in Article 4(2). These conditions are similar to those of Article 1(4).

Lastly, it should be noted that Article 2 of the 1961 Convention deals specifically with the acquisition of nationality by foundlings. A detailed discussion of this provision can be found under section 6.4.2 below.

6.4.   Access of children to a nationality under Council of Europe standards

Regional standard setting in relation to children's rights to a nationality has progressed the furthest in the Council of Europe by means of the European Convention on Nationality 1997 (ECN) and a significant body of soft law instruments. Some jurisprudence of the European Court of Human Rights (ECtHR) is also relevant to this issue. As such, the Council of Europe framework for the nationality rights of children makes an interesting comparator for the international standards discussed.

The 1961 Convention had considerable influence on the provisions of the ECN and several of its provisions address the avoidance of cases of statelessness among children. First of all, Article 4(a)–(c) of the ECN repeats the message of Article 15 UDHR, i.e. that everyone has the right to a nationality and no one may be arbitrarily deprived of nationality. Article 6(1)(b) of the ECN prescribes the acquisition of nationality to foundlings found in its territory, which is dealt with later in this chapter. Article 6(2) regulates access to nationality for otherwise stateless children and will be looked at here.

Article 6(2) ECN, dealing with access to the nationality of the country of birth for otherwise stateless children born in the territory of that state has many similarities with the regime of the 1961 Convention, but there are some important differences. The 1961 Convention allows a state to postpone access to their nationality to the moment the stateless person concerned reaches the age of eighteen, whereas according to the ECN access has to be given after five years of lawful and habitual residence, while a child is still a minor. The 1961 Convention also allows states to reject an application because of a sentence for a crime which constitutes a threat to national security, or more than five years' imprisonment. The ECN does not allow this ground for a rejection of the application. As such, the obligations of the ECN are stricter than those under the 1961

Convention, reflecting developments in the prohibition of statelessness under international law.

However, the 1961 Convention guarantees that a person born stateless has – in principle – at least one year after attaining the age of majority to take a decision on the acquisition of the nationality of his country of birth.[39] Furthermore, the ECN allows states to require a period of *lawful* and habitual residence, whereas the 1961 Convention only allows states to require *habitual* residence during the relevant period. The drafters of the 1961 Convention sought to guarantee a right to nationality and were concerned that by allowing states to require a *lawful* residence, a state could avoid obligations by refusing a stateless person a residence permit.

Article 6(1)(a) ECN is also of importance to the avoidance of statelessness, where it prescribes that a child of a national should acquire the nationality of the parent (*jus sanguinis*), subject to exceptions made for children born abroad. Furthermore, it requires that states:

> provide that children whose parentage is established by recognition, by court order or similar procedures acquire the nationality of the parent concerned, subject only to a procedure determined by their internal law.

It must be stressed that only procedural requirements may be imposed and not any substantive conditions. In addition, since the decision of the ECtHR in *Genovese* v. *Malta*,[40] it is clear that a different treatment of children born out of wedlock in respect of their access to the nationality of their father violates Article 14 in conjunction with Article 8 of the ECHR. Although the ECHR does not expressly guarantee access to a nationality, the ECtHR states that the non-acquisition of, in this case, Maltese nationality (the court speaks of 'the denial of citizenship') had an impact on the applicant's social identity. Discriminatory rules regarding access to nationality, therefore, affect a person's private life as safeguarded by Article 8 ECHR.

It is worthwhile noting that the ECtHR presumed that states are under no obligation to provide for acquisition of nationality *jus sanguinis* by children born abroad to one of their nationals. This becomes clear from the fact that the court stated that Malta 'has gone beyond its obligations under Article 8'. Yet, if a country provides for such a mode of acquisition, it should be applied in a non-discriminatory manner. The statement by the ECtHR that (non-)access to a nationality has an impact on the social identity of a person and thereby on his or her private life, is also highly

---

[39] See on this difference van Waas, *Nationality Matters*, 61, 62 (in particular footnote 55).
[40] European Court of Human Rights, *Genovese* v. *Malta*, Application 53124/09, 11 October 2011.

relevant for the formulation and application of rules for the avoidance of statelessness, that is, those rules have to be non-discriminatory.

In addition to the ECN and the ruling of the EctHR in *Genovese* v. *Malta*, another tool for tackling statelessness among children in the Council of Europe is Recommendation 2009/13, adopted by the Committee of Ministers on 9 December 2009.[41] This was drafted by a Committee of Experts, appointed by the Secretary-General in April 2008[42] to further develop the Council of Europe's work on nationality issues. The committee was asked to pay special attention to statelessness issues and to the access of children to the nationality of their parents and of their country of birth and residence. Furthermore, the committee had to draft rules to improve the nationality position of adopted children.

Recommendation 2009/13 contains twenty-three principles, the first ten of which deal with the avoidance of statelessness. Principle 1 prescribes that states should 'provide for the acquisition of nationality by right of blood (*jus sanguinis*) by children without any restriction which would result in statelessness'. According to Article 6(1) ECN each state party shall provide in its internal law for its nationality to be acquired automatically by a child, one of whose parents possesses, at the time of the child's birth, the nationality of that state. However, states are allowed to make exceptions, first for children born abroad and second, to provide for special procedural rules for the acquisition of nationality *jus sanguinis* for children whose parenthood is established by recognition, court order or similar procedures. In several countries, a child of a national born abroad does not automatically acquire the nationality of the parent, but has the right to acquire this nationality either by registration or by option.[43] Principle 1 already underpinned that such a construction should be drafted in a way which does not cause statelessness. Principle 3 recommends that the state of birth or residence should provide the child 'with any necessary assistance' to exercise their right to acquire the nationality

---

[41] Council of Europe, *Recommendation CM/Rec(2009)13 of the Committee of Ministers to member States on the nationality of children*, 9 December 2009, CM/Rec(2009)13 Recommendation CM/Re (2009). This type of recommendation is an important soft law instrument within the Council of Europe, adopted through a consensus procedure and directed towards all Council of Europe member states.

[42] Chairman of the Committee was Frans van der Velden, whereas Gerard-René de Groot was appointed as expert-consultant.

[43] M. Vink and G. de Groot, 'Birthright Citizenship: Trends and regulations in Europe', Comparative Report, RSCAS/ EUDO-CIT-COMP. 2010/5, paras 2 and 3; Table 1. See also on the nationality position of children born out of wedlock also nn. 63–4 below.

of the parent. The obligation to document the existence of the child and his parentage in a birth certificate is of paramount importance in this context and is laid down in the Recommendation's principle 23. But the Explanatory Memorandum also mentions that it may be necessary to appoint a special guardian *ad litem*, who can inter alia apply for registration or lodge a declaration of option as representative of the child.

Principle 2 recommends states to 'provide that children born on their territory who otherwise would be stateless acquire their nationality subject to no other condition than the lawful and habitual residence of a parent'. This principle is supplementary to the obligations already existing in Article 6(2) ECN and the corresponding provisions of the 1961 Convention. A clear majority of member states of the Council of Europe grant their nationality to otherwise stateless children born on their territory automatically at birth. Some states do so with the additional condition that the parents have lawful and habitual residence in the state at the time of the birth of the child.[44] Most other states provide for a right of registration as a national or acquisition of nationality via the lodging of a declaration of option after a certain period of lawful and habitual residence. The Recommendation's Explanatory Memorandum indicates that acquisition of nationality by a child born in the territory who is otherwise stateless should ideally occur at birth or shortly after birth, with retroactivity, but the principle allows for the acquisition of nationality without retroactive effect.

Even if states implement all of the aforementioned principles and the obligations derived from both the 1961 Convention and the ECN, some children will still not possess any nationality. The ECN does not include a provision on the individual naturalization of children. Many European states do not permit children to acquire their nationality individually.[45] Consequently, stateless children often have to wait until they reach the age of majority before they can apply for naturalization in the state of residence. Such a long period of statelessness is contrary to the best interests of the children concerned. Principle 5 of the Recommendation therefore underlines: 'stateless children have the right to apply for their nationality after lawful and habitual residence on their territory for a period not exceeding five years immediately preceding the lodging of the applica-

---

[44] *Ibid.*, para. 5 and Table 4.
[45] S. Wallace Goodman, 'Naturalisation Policies in Europe: Exploring patterns of inclusion and exclusion, Comparative Report', EUDO Citizenship Observatory, 2010.

tion'. A state may require that they must be represented by their legal representative.[46]

A striking difference between the Council of Europe Recommendation 2009/13 on the one hand and the 1961 Convention on the other has to do with the relationship between Article 1 and Article 4 of the 1961 Convention: the *jus soli*-inspired obligations of Article 1 of the 1961 Convention have precedence over the *jus sanguinis*-inspired rules of Article 4. In Recommendation 2009/13 the opposite can be observed: the default *jus sanguinis* rule of principle 1 has precedence above the default *jus soli* rule of principle 2. This difference may be explained by the fact that within the Council of Europe the *jus sanguinis* tradition is stronger than that of *jus soli*.

The principles of Recommendation 2009/13 are a welcome supplement to the rules enshrined in the ECN. Ideally, they should constitute the basis for the drafting of a Protocol to the ECN. The principles are also a source of inspiration for other international and regional debates on the improvement of rules avoiding and reducing cases of statelessness. One such debate took place during an expert meeting on the interpretation of Articles 1–4 of the 1961 Convention, convened by the UNHCR in 2011 in Dakar, Senegal. In the conclusions of the Dakar Meeting and in the guidelines that followed, the influence of Recommendation 2009/13 is obvious.[47]

6.5.   Specific challenges in relation to children's access to a nationality

In the sections above, the general standards developed under international law for the avoidance of statelessness among children have been outlined in some detail. Already, a number of challenges inherent in the application of these standards has been highlighted. In the following paragraphs, some further questions are considered, including those relating to the specific difficulty of implementing safeguards that rely on states identifying 'otherwise stateless' children and how to deal with particular categories of children who find themselves more acutely at risk of statelessness.

---

[46] Compare the Principles 19–22 of Recommendation CM/Rec(2009)13.
[47] UNHCR, 'Interpreting the 1961 Statelessness Convention and Preventing Statelessness among Children: ("Dakar Conclusions")', September 2011; and UNHCR, 'Guideline No. 4'.

6.5.1   Establishing that a child is 'otherwise stateless'

A general difficulty with the application of every statelessness avoidance rule is the determination of potential statelessness – that is, the identification of a child as 'otherwise stateless'. Article 1 of the 1954 Convention on the Status of Stateless Persons[48] defines a stateless person as a person 'who is not considered as a national by any State under the operation of its law'. This definition is also used for the determination of the scope of application of the statelessness avoiding rules in the 1961 Convention and the ECN, thus available guidance on the determination of statelessness under the 1954 Convention is also relevant here.[49] In addition, to deal with particular questions surrounding the determination that a child is – or was, at birth – otherwise stateless, the Council of Europe's 2009 Recommendation provides a number of helpful insights.

Firstly, in order to determine whether rules concerning the avoidance of statelessness are applicable, authorities often need detailed information, in particular on the acquisition or non-acquisition of a certain foreign nationality. Not providing information could under the circumstances cause or prolong statelessness of the child involved. Of course, states have to observe data protection rules, but they should provide relevant data to another state if this is required in the best interests of the child. Therefore, principle 6 calls on states to 'co-operate closely on issues of statelessness of children, including exchanging information on nationality legislation and public policies, as well as on nationality details in individual cases, subject to applicable laws on personal data protection'.

Some states are keen to avoid the acquisition of nationality by *jus soli* or any other preferential access to the nationality of their state of birth by children who could easily acquire the nationality of one of their parents and will expressly exclude children who could acquire the nationality of a parent by registration.[50] The Explanatory Memorandum of Recommendation 2009/13 has the following to say about such constructions:

> This is in line with the object and purpose of rules for avoiding state-lessness in international instruments, like the 1961 United Nations Convention on the Reduction of Statelessness and the ECN. The rules of these conventions can clearly not lead to an obligation for the contracting

---

[48] Convention relating to the Status of Stateless Persons, New York, 28 September 1954, in force 6 June 1960, 360 UNTS 117.

[49] See further Chapter 5 by Gyulai in this volume.

[50] See for details Vink and de Groot, 'Birthright Citizenship, para. 5, Table 4.

States to grant their nationality to a person who decided for strict personal convenience not to exercise a right to acquire the nationality of another state.[51]

However, the non-use of the right to register a child as a national of the country of a parent is not in all cases unacceptable, for instance where the parent has disappeared or has 'good reasons that his or her child will not be registered (not even through a representative) as a national of this parent's State of origin [as] is e.g. the case if the parent left that State as a refugee'.[52] With such cases in mind, principle 4 of the Recommendation asks states to 'provide that children who, at birth, have the right to acquire the nationality of another state, but who could not reasonably be expected to acquire that nationality, are not excluded from the scope of principles [allowing for acquisition of nationality for the avoidance of statelessness]'.

In light of the difficulty involved in establishing a child's exact nationality entitlement, authorities sometimes register a person as being of unknown or undetermined nationality or classify the nationality of a person as being 'under investigation'. Such classification is quite often necessary, but only reasonable as a transitory measure during a brief period of time. Again, the Council of Europe Recommendation 2009/13 is helpful here:

Register children as being of unknown or undetermined nationality, or classify children's nationality as being 'under investigation' only for as short a period as possible.

The Explanatory Memorandum also refers to Article 8 of the Council of Europe Convention on the Avoidance of Statelessness in relation to State Succession, requesting states to lower the burden of proof for statelessness.[53] It urges states to implement their obligations under international

---

[51] Recommendation CM/Rec(2009)13 and explanatory memorandum of the Committee of Ministers to member States on the nationality of children, pp. 18–19.

[52] Compare the facts in European Court of Justice, *Gerardo Ruiz Zambrano* v. *Office national de l'emploi*, C-34/09, 8 March 2011. See on *Zambrano* S. C. G. Van den Bogaert, G. R. de Groot and A. P. van der Mei., 'De arresten Ruiz Zambrano en McCarthy: Het Hof van Justitie en het effectieve genot van EU burgerschapsrechten', *Nederlands tijdschrift voor Europees Recht* (2011), 188–99.

[53] Article 8 (1) reads: 'A successor State shall not insist on its standard requirements of proof necessary for the granting of its nationality in the case of persons who have or would become stateless as a result of State succession and where it is not reasonable for such persons to meet the standard requirements.'

law by not indefinitely leaving the nationality status of an individual as undetermined.[54]

6.5.2 Foundlings and their access to a nationality

Foundlings present a particular challenge to states in terms of guaranteeing access to nationality since key facts about their origin are unknown. Article 2 of the 1961 Convention provides as follows:

> A foundling found in the territory of a Contracting State shall, in the absence of proof to the contrary, be considered to have been born within that territory of parents possessing the nationality of that State.

The rule established in Article 2 reflects that of Article 14 of the 1930 Hague Convention.[55] However, an important difference is that Article 2 of the 1961 Convention only mentions 'foundlings' and not, as Article 14 of the 1930 Hague Convention, also 'children of unknown parentage'. Article 6(1)(b) ECN also prescribes a state to grant nationality to a foundling found on its territory. Three questions arise from these provisions: 1) When is a child a 'foundling'? 2) What happens if evidence demonstrates that the child was born abroad or that the child has non-national parents? 3) What is the position of children of unknown parentage?

The term 'foundling' in itself requires clarification on whether it refers only to new-born babies or whether it also can include children. The English term 'foundling' seems to point in the direction of very young children. The Oxford English Dictionary defines this word as 'an infant that has been abandoned by its parents and is discovered and cared for by others'.[56] The word 'infant' is defined as 'a very young child or baby'.[57] Also in the light of the majority of the language versions of the 1961 Convention it could be argued that a restriction of the foundling rule to new-born children is not contrary to the obligations of the convention.[58]

Nevertheless this leaves a gap with regard to the avoidance of statelessness of children found abandoned if it is obvious that the child concerned

---

[54] Compare the 'Explanatory Report, Nr. 32–37'. See also De Groot 'Preventing statelessness', at 26, 27. See 'Guidelines No. 4', para. 22.
[55] League of Nations, Convention on Certain Questions Relating to the Conflict of Nationality Law, 13 April 1930, 179 LNTS 89.
[56] Oxford English Dictionary, Oxford University Press, 1989.
[57] *Ibid.*   [58] The same would apply for Article 6 ECN.

is not a new-born baby.[59] Therefore, in light of the object and purpose of Article 2 of the 1961 Convention, Article 6(2) ECN and Article 7 CRC, states should be encouraged to treat children found abandoned on their territory with no known parentage, as far as possible, as foundlings with respect to the acquisition of nationality. At a minimum, the safeguard for contracting states to grant nationality to foundlings should apply to all young children who are not yet able to communicate accurate information pertaining to the identity of their parents or their place of birth. A contrary interpretation would leave some children stateless.

A state could decide to extend the provision on foundlings to all minors found abandoned on their territory, as some states already do,[60] but a state could also determine an age limit. It has to be underscored that in all cases where a state sets an age limit for foundlings to acquire nationality, the age of the child at the date the child was found should be decisive and not the date when a child came to the attention of the authorities.[61]

The 1961 Convention does not expressly regulate the situation in which evidence is subsequently found of the parents or place of birth of the foundling. However, the interpretation given during the preparatory negotiations was that 'the child would possess the nationality of the country in which he had been found until shown to be entitled to another nationality'.[62] As a general rule, and in keeping with the object and purpose to reduce statelessness, one could argue that the discovery of parents who hold another nationality or birth abroad does not lead to loss of the nationality acquired on the basis of the Article 2 safeguard for foundlings if statelessness would be the consequence.[63]

Notwithstanding the question of the age of the child, as discussed above, if the parentage of the child is factually unknown, the child is of course a foundling. But under the family law of several countries it is

[59] This gap is also identified by Recommendation CM/Rec 2009/13. See Principle 9 of that Recommendation.

[60] See e.g. Article 3(2) of the Kingdom Act on Netherlands Nationality. EUDO Citizenship, 'Comparing Citizenship Laws: Acquisition of Citizenship', online database, available at http://eudo-citizenship.eu/databases/modes-of-acquisition?p=&application=&search=1&modeby=idmode&idmode=A03a, last accessed 10 April 2013.

[61] See 'Guidelines No. 4', para. 59.

[62] 'Summary Record of the 5th Meeting of Committee 1' A/CONF.9/C.1/SR.5 (3 April 1959), p. 10.

[63] Compare Article 7(1)(f) ECN: If later the child's parents or the place of birth are discovered, and the child derives a citizenship from (one of) these parents or acquired a citizenship because of his place of birth, the citizenship acquired because of the foundling provision may be lost. However, according to Article 7(3) such discovery may never cause statelessness.

also possible that a child has no *legal* parent, although a biological parent may be known. This is, for example, the case with the so-called 'delivery under X' (*'accouchement sous X'*) in France.[64] French law allows a woman who gives birth to a child out of wedlock to ask not to be mentioned as the mother on the birth certificate of the child. Consequently, the child will not have a family relationship with that woman.[65] Such children are legally in a similar vulnerable position as foundlings, and should enjoy the benefit of the relevant statelessness avoiding rules.[66] This is also the case if there are strong indications that the woman who gave birth to the child is a foreigner.

6.5.3   Adopted children and their nationality

Through adoption, a family relationship is created between the adopted child and his or her adopted parent(s). Consequently, the adopted child's legal position in nationality law should be, as far as possible, identical to the position of a biological child. This is inter alia prescribed by the Hague Convention on Protection of Children and Cooperation in respect of Inter country Adoption of 29 May 1993[67] as well as the European Convention on the Adoption of Children (revised).[68] The latter states that: 'Upon adoption a child shall become a full member of the family of the adopter(s) and shall have in regard to the adopter(s) and his, her or their family the same rights and obligations as a child of the adopter(s) whose parentage is legally established'.[69]

It is nevertheless unfortunate that few international treaties deal with the nationality position of adopted children. Those treaties that contain a provision on adopted children provide exclusively that the loss of

---

[64] Article 326 French Code civil: 'Lors de l'accouchement, la mère peut demander que le secret de son admission et de son identité soit préservé.' [During childbirth, the mother may request that her admission and identity is not disclosed.]

[65] The same applies for legal systems which still require that a mother has to recognize her child born out of wedlock in order to establish a family relationship. The ECtHR concluded that such requirement of recognition violates Article 8 ECHR. European Court of Human Rights, *Marckx* v. *Belgium*, C-6833/74, 13 June 1979. As a consequence of that decision, this requirement was abolished in the member states of the Council of Europe.

[66] Compare also Article 7(3) of the 2005 Organization of the Islamic Conference, Covenant on the Rights of the Child in Islam, June 2005, OIC/9-IGGE/HRI/2004/Rep. Final, adopted by the 32nd Conference of Foreign Ministers, Sana'a, Yemen.

[67] Hague Convention on Protection of Children and Cooperation in respect of Intercounty Adoption (Hague Convention), 1870 UNTS 167, in force 1 May 1995.

[68] European Convention on the Adoption of Children (revised), 24 April 1967, in force 26 April 1968, CETS No. 058.

[69] *Ibid.*, Article 11(1).

nationality as the result of adoption shall be conditional on the possession or acquisition of another nationality.[70] An exception is the ECN, which prescribes the facilitation of the acquisition of the nationality of a state for children adopted by one of their nationals (Article 6(4)(d)), as well as stating that the adoption of a child should not lead to statelessness (Article 7(1) (g) *juncto* (2)). The same rules are also included in Article 12 of the 2008 European Convention on the Adoption of Children (revised). However, neither convention prescribes concrete rules for this to take place, which are needed.[71]

Given this gap, the principles enshrined in Recommendation 2009/13 deserve attention: in no other international instrument can more concrete guidelines improving the nationality position of adopted children be found. Some of the core principles found in the Recommendation that could helpfully be used as a basis for specific rules to be included in a Protocol to the ECN or a Protocol to the 1961 Convention are discussed here. Principle 13 of Recommendation 2009/13 underlines that states should:

> Subject the granting of their nationality to children adopted by a national to no other exceptions than those generally applicable to the acquisition of their nationality by right of blood, if as a consequence of the adoption the family relationship between the child and the parent(s) of origin is completely replaced by the family relationship between the child and the adopter(s).[72]

The Explanatory Memorandum stresses, too, that it should be irrelevant whether the adoption decree was issued in the state of the adopting parents or abroad. In the latter case, the mere fact of the recognition of the foreign adoption by the state of the nationality of the adoptive parents should have nationality consequences.

Another issue relevant to inter-country adoption is what happens in the event of the revocation or annulment of an adoption. Principle 10 of Recommendation 2009/13 deals with the avoidance of statelessness in the case of a revocation or annulment of an adoption. Such revocation or annulment of an adoption should not cause the loss of the nationality acquired by this adoption, if statelessness would be the consequence. It

---

[70] Article 17, 1930 Hague Convention; Article 5(1) 1961 Convention.

[71] On current state practice see Vink and de Groot, 'Birthright Citizenship', para. 4 and Table 3.

[72] Recommendation CM/Rec(2009)13 and explanatory memorandum of the Committee of Ministers to member States on the nationality of children, p. 10.

should not matter whether or not the revocation or annulment operates with retroactivity.

Principle 15 makes an additional step by providing that 'revocation or annulment of an adoption will not cause the permanent loss of the nationality acquired by the adoption, if the child is lawfully and habitually resident on their territory for a period of more than five years'. In the exceptional and tragic circumstances of a child taking up residence in a country with a view to being adopted, but the adoption never being finalized, the child should be entitled to apply for the acquisition of the nationality of the state of residence. Principle 16 recommends: 'States should not in this case require a period of more than five years of habitual residence on their territory.' Here, the Explanatory Memorandum mentions: 'As a result of the child's residence on this territory he or she acquires a genuine link with the State involved, whereas insufficient ties are developed with his or her country of origin. Furthermore, due to the residence of the child on its territory the State has a special responsibility for the future of this particularly vulnerable child.'[73]

6.5.4   Avoiding statelessness of children born through surrogate mothers

Most births of children conceived through medically assisted reproductive techniques do not cause special problems in the field of nationality law. Births resulting from medically assisted reproductive techniques involving only the biological parents will result in a *jus sanguinis* acquisition of the nationality of the parents, subject to the normal exceptions the state involved makes on this principle. However, problems may arise if a third person is involved who does not share the nationality of the biological parents, in particular in the growing number of cases of children being born through surrogacy arrangements. In those cases, there is a serious risk of statelessness for a child if the state of the surrogate mother's nationality does not attribute her nationality to the child and the state of the commissioning mother does not attribute its nationality because the commissioning mother did not give birth to the child and is thus not considered by that state as the child's mother.[74]

---

[73] Recommendation CM/Rec(2009)13 and explanatory memorandum of the Committee of Ministers to member States on the nationality of children, p. 28.

[74] Compare Royal Courts of Justice, *Re X and Y (Foreign Surrogacy)* London [2009] 1 FLR 733 and Supreme Court of India, *Baby Manji Yamada* v. *Union of India* JT 2008 (11) SC 150.

To date, no treaty provisions deal with the nationality position of children born through surrogate mothers with a different nationality to the commissioning parents. Instead, it is possible to turn to Council of Europe Recommendation 2009/13 for some much-needed guidance. Principle 12 is concerned with children conceived through medically assisted reproductive techniques, in particular children born by a surrogate mother. It requests member states to apply to children their provisions on acquisition of nationality by right of blood if, as a result of a birth conceived through medically assisted reproductive techniques, a child–parent family relationship is established or recognized by law. Recommendation 2009/13 does not oblige states to recognize the child–parent relationship between the child and the commissioning parent(s) as an automatic consequence of the use of surrogacy. Whether such recognition takes place depends on private international law and – if applicable – the domestic law of the country of the commissioning parents.[75] However, Principle 12 underlines that *if* recognition takes place this should also have consequences in nationality law.[76]

More generally one could argue that the state of nationality of the commissioning parents has a strong obligation to give access to the nationality of that state if the child involved already has habitual residence on the territory of that state. A recent decision of the Austrian Constitutional Court ('Verfassungsgerichtshof') of 14 December 2011 illustrates this very well.[77] An Austrian couple concluded a surrogacy contract with an American woman who gave birth, in the United States of America, to two children. The Austrian spouses were the genetic parents of these children. By birth in the US, the children were American citizens, but American courts recognized the Austrian couple as their parents. They were brought to Austria and were registered as Austrian citizens by the city of Vienna. When the mother claimed child benefits, however, the Ministry

---

[75] Compare K. Saarloos and J. van Berkel, 'From Russia with love: ouderschap na draagmoederschap en de Wet conflictenrecht afstamming', *Nederlands Internationaal Privaatrecht* (2008) 117–24.

[76] Recommendation CM/Rec(2009)13 and explanatory memorandum of the Committee of Ministers to member States on the nationality of children, 9 May 2009, CM/Rec(2009)13 at p. 25.

[77] Case B 13/11–10 of 14 December 2011 of the Austrian Constitutional Court, available at www.eudo-citizenship.eu. See also the summary of this case by Rainer Bauböck on EUDO Citizenship Observatory of 25 January 2012, available at http://eudo-citizenship. eu/news/citizenship-news/565-constitutional-court-confirms-austrian-citizenship-for-children-born-by-american-surrogate-mother (both sites last accessed 10 April 2013).

of Interior determined that the children did not possess Austrian nationality because surrogate motherhood was illegal under Austrian law and the Austrian mother could not be recognized as the legal parent of the child.

The Constitutional Court rejected the arguments raised by the Ministry. After some preliminary observations on the application of conflicts of laws rules, the court stated that it would be against the best interests of the child to force the American surrogate mother into the position of the legal mother against her will through the application of Austrian law, given that she was neither the biological mother nor, according to US law, the legal mother, nor did she ever establish family life with the children. If Austria did not respect the US courts' decision to recognize the Austrian couple as the children's parents, the children would lose all their rights against their genetic mother, who is also their 'factual mother' due to their family life. The court held that such far-reaching negative consequences cannot be viewed as in the best interest of the child.

This decision of the Austrian Constitutional Court has to be welcomed as a 'best practice' which should be followed by courts in other countries. Certainly, we have to admit that the Austrian case was special, in so far as the children were genetically the children of the Austrian couple, had family life with them and had their residence in Austria. But the main line is clear: the best interest of the child has to be the guiding principle in answering the question of whether the family relationship established abroad had to be recognized, with all the attendant consequences for nationality law.

6.6. Conclusion

From the foregoing the following general propositions are supported by Recommendation 2009/13 and/or UNHCR's Guideline No. 4:

a) States should always attribute their nationality to the child of a national, if this child would otherwise be stateless (see Recommendation 2009/13 and Guidelines No. 4);

b) States have to offer access to their nationality to otherwise stateless children born on their territory, at birth or as soon as possible after birth (preferably with retroactivity) (see Recommendation 2009/13 and Guidelines No. 4);

c) Foundlings and small children left abandoned on the territory of a state should be presumed to be born on the territory of that state as children of parents with the nationality of that state; they should only lose the nationality acquired on the basis of this presumption if it is proven that they possess another nationality (see Recommendation 2009/13 and Guidelines No. 4);

d) Children with legally unknown parentage should be treated as foundlings (see Guidelines No. 4);

e) Rules on the nationality position of adopted children should follow the principles enshrined in Recommendation 2009/13;

f) Children born as a result of a surrogacy arrangement should acquire the nationality of a commissioning parent under the same conditions as a child born to a parent outside such a context, if the family relationship between the child and this parent is recognized. The answer to the question of whether the family relationship is recognized or not should be given in light of the best interests of the child and should be certainly affirmative if the child is genetically the daughter or son of the commissioning parent or there is family life between the child and the commissioning parent (see Recommendation 2009/13).

Questions to guide discussion

1. In which international and regional human rights instruments can the child's right to acquire a nationality be found and what differences are there in the way this norm is formulated?

2. What safeguard is prescribed in Article 1 of the 1961 Convention on the Reduction of Statelessness and what conditions may states require potential beneficiaries to meet?

3. When is a child deemed to be 'otherwise stateless' for the purposes of international law standards that guarantee a child's right to a nationality?

4. Describe three considerations or challenges in the context of guaranteeing the right to a nationality for foundlings.

5. The European Convention on Human Rights does not protect the child's right to acquire a nationality, yet the Council of Europe can be considered at the forefront of standard setting in relation to the avoidance of childhood statelessness. Use examples to explain why this is the case.

6. How can international adoption and surrogacy arrangements create problems for a child's right to acquire a nationality and what solutions does international law prescribe in such cases?

7

Women, nationality and statelessness

The problem of unequal rights

RADHA GOVIL AND ALICE EDWARDS

7.1.   Introduction

In October 2011, the United Nations High Commissioner for Refugees
(UNHCR) convened a regional roundtable in Beirut, Lebanon, to discuss
with women from the Middle East and North Africa their experiences
of discrimination in the nationality laws of their countries. This is the
story of a Lebanese mother, Um Ali. Her children, now adults, are stateless
because as a woman, Um Ali is prevented by law from being able to confer
her nationality to them.

> Um Ali's husband, an Egyptian man, died before completing procedures
> to have his seven children registered as Egyptian citizens. Following her
> husband's death, when Um Ali tried to complete the registration proce-
> dures, she learned that her husband's brother in Egypt sent a letter order-
> ing that the children be sent to Egypt for him to take custody of them.
> Refusing to leave her home country and give up custody of her children,
> Um Ali stopped pursuing contacts with the Egyptian authorities, resign-
> ing herself to struggle to support her family through her individual means
> in Lebanon. Her children have birth certificates and 'maktoum al kayd'
> identity cards (cards that specify that the individuals are not registered
> and do not have Lebanese citizenship).
>
> Um Ali's oldest daughter married a Lebanese man. While this daughter
> is listed on her husband's family's civil record, she is unable to acquire
> Lebanese citizenship through her husband. In Lebanon, an individual
> must have at least one nationality in order to be granted Lebanese citi-
> zenship. One of Um Ali's sons married a Lebanese woman and has two
> children. His family also faces problems as his Lebanese wife can nei-
> ther transfer her citizenship to him nor confer her citizenship on their

The views contained in this chapter are those of the authors and do not necessarily reflect
those of the United Nations or the United Nations High Commissioner for Refugees
(UNHCR).

children. This son owns a car, but it is registered in UmAli's name. UmAli also signs all official documents for her children, even those who are adults.

UmAli sent two of her daughters to an Evangelical Christian orphanage where they could be educated. Her daughter Zeynab was particularly bright and rose to the top of her class. In fact, Zeynab won a scholarship to travel to Canada for a summer school program, but could not go because she did not have a nationality. Zeynab attended a private technical college and has specialized in marketing and sales. She now works for a cosmetics retailer, but because she does not have a nationality and no identity papers, she is paid informally in cash and earns almost half of what she would earn if she were Lebanese.

Zeynab says: 'Sometimes I hate myself. I feel like I am not a human being. I can't handle it. My friends can live a natural life. I can't. My dream to own a car, I can't have it. Even if I have the money to buy it, it would never be registered in my own name. I dream of getting married, but one man has turned me down because I don't have a citizenship. I feel like a prisoner. Lebanese papers are worth more than gold, you can pay millions but still not get them. It's hard for me to see Lebanese girls who have nationality and their papers, especially when they're not taking advantage of their status as they could – studying, working, fulfilling the dreams I wish I could achieve, but can't.'[1]

UmAli's story illustrates how gender-based discrimination in nationality laws can cause and perpetuate a cycle of statelessness, from one generation to the next, as well as the debilitating and disempowering consequences of not being a national of any country. Gender-based discrimination in nationality laws manifests itself in various ways. For example, nationality laws may discriminate against women when it comes to the ability of women to acquire, change or retain their nationality (typically upon marriage to a foreigner) or in relation to conferral of their nationality upon their children. Although there is a distinct lack of sex disaggregated data in this area, nationality laws that grant, change, withdraw or confer nationality on a gender-discriminatory basis are likely to lead to a higher rate of statelessness, of both women and their children.[2]

---

[1] UNHCR and Collective for Research and Training Development – Action, 'A Regional Dialogue on Gender Equality, Nationality and Statelessness: Overview and Key Findings', January 2012, available at: www.unhcr.org/refworld/docid/4f267ec72.html, last accessed 22 May 2014.

[2] Alice Edwards, 'Displacement, Statelessness and Questions of Gender Equality under the Convention on the Elimination of All Forms of Discrimination against Women' (UNHCR, Protection Policy and Legal Advice Research Series) August 2009, 39.

Despite the many international and regional human rights protections against discrimination, including in respect of nationality laws,[3] up to as many as sixty countries still maintain gender-discriminatory provisions in their nationality laws.[4] These countries can be found in most regions of the world: Africa, Asia, the Caribbean and the Middle East.

While the evolution of international standards on women's nationality rights reflects changes in family relations norms that had prevented women from enjoying equal rights to citizenship, until recently there has been relatively little focus placed on the issue of the links between unequal nationality laws and statelessness. Specifically, there has been limited examination of the two statelessness conventions – the 1954 Convention relating to the Status of Stateless Persons[5] (1954 Convention) and the 1961 Convention on the Reduction of Statelessness[6] (1961 Convention) – and how they deal with the question of the discriminatory treatment of women in nationality matters, especially where the consequence is statelessness.

Unequal rights, when it comes to acquisition and loss of nationality, affect women and their families in various ways. In particular, statelessness amongst women and their children is of growing concern. This can be linked to globalization, the increasingly free movement of persons and the 'feminization' of migration, resulting in more mixed marriages, and precipitating complex issues around the modification of women's nationality upon marriage or divorce and the passage of nationality to children.[7]

This chapter reflects on the problem of unequal nationality rights for women in general and its link with statelessness in particular. Section 7.2 summarizes the historical origins of gender discrimination in nationality laws, followed in sections 7.3 and 7.4 by an outline of the various

---

[3] See, for example, Articles 1(3), 55 and 56 of the United Nations Charter 1945; Article 2 of the Universal Declaration of Human Rights 1948; Article 2 of the International Covenant on Civil and Political Rights (ICCPR) 1966; Article 2 of the Convention on the Rights of the Child 1984, Article 1 of the Convention on the Elimination of Discrimination Against Women (CEDWA) 1979; Article 5 of the European Convention on Nationality (ECN) 1997; Article 1(1) of the American Convention on Human Rights 1969; Article 3 of the African Charter on the Rights and Welfare of the Child, 1990; Article 2 of the African Charter on Human and Peoples' Rights 1981 (Banjul Charter).

[4] UNHCR, *State of the World's Refugees* (Oxford University Press, 2012), 106.

[5] Convention relating to the Status of Stateless Persons, 28 September 1954, in force 6 June 1960, 360 UNTS 117.

[6] Convention on the Reduction of Statelessness, 30 August 1961, in force 13 December 1975, 989 UNTS 175.

[7] K. Rubenstein and D. Adler, 'International Citizenship: The Future of Nationality in a Globalised World', *Indiana Journal of Global Legal Studies*, 7 (2000), 519–48.

bases upon which nationality is acquired and lost and the ways in which gender discrimination can create and sustain situations of statelessness. Section 7.5 analyses the current international and regional legal frameworks applicable to the prevention and reduction of statelessness and how they address gender inequality in nationality laws, as well as their shortcomings. The chapter concludes by responding to the question of how the international community should address the impact of gendered nationality laws on the creation and perpetuation of statelessness.

7.2. Historical origins of gender discrimination in nationality matters

Historically, gender-based discrimination in nationality matters stemmed from the 'principle of unity of nationality of the family' according to which every member of the family should have the same nationality – that of the husband or father. Further, it was believed that a family's allegiance should be to only one state, because of the demands, for example, made on citizens in terms of military service. It was perceived that permitting only a single (and shared) nationality would avoid any conflicts of loyalty.[8]

Patriarchal legal values derived from both the English common law and civil law systems also had a strong influence over family relations. The common law concept of a married woman's 'coverture' or coming under what the English jurist Blackstone described as the husband's 'wing of protection', meant that a woman had no separate personal identity.[9] Lack of personal identity and the dominant concept of the male breadwinner/head of family consolidated the norm of a married woman's 'dependent nationality'. Consequently, women often automatically lost their nationality upon marriage to a foreigner, and they automatically acquired, or enjoyed facilitated procedures to acquire, the nationality of their husbands. It also followed that a child's nationality was derived from the married man. Only in the case of birth out of marriage would a mother's nationality determine the legal status of a child.[10]

---

[8] Savitri W. E. Goonesekere, 'Article 9' in Marsha Freeman, Christine Chinkin and Beate Rudolph (eds.), *The UN Convention on the Elimination of All Forms of Discrimination against Women: A Commentary* (hereinafter *CEDAW: A Commentary*) (Oxford University Press, 2012) at 234.

[9] W. Blackstone, *Commentaries on the Laws of England*, 16th edn (1825) 366, 454–9, referred to in Freeman *et al.* (eds.), *CEDAW: A Commentary*.

[10] On nationality laws that had a discriminatory element in the 1940s, 1952 as well as more recently, see Brief of Amicus Curiae, Scholars of Statelessness in Support of the Petitioner, in the Supreme Court of the United States of America, *Ruben Flores-Villar* v. *United States of America*, 24 June 2010, in which Alice Edwards was lead amicus.

Under the civil law tradition, the Roman law on *patria potestas* (power of the father), the husband's preferred guardianship rights, and the illegality of non-marital relationships, created similar norms to the common law system.[11] Unsurprisingly, many domestic legal systems, influenced by these legal concepts, recognized the principle of a married woman's 'dependent nationality' and her general incapacity to pass on her nationality to her children. Under colonialism, these gender-discriminatory approaches from common and civil law systems also took root in places far from where they were developed.[12]

After decolonization, although women had joined men in freedom struggles to achieve independence from colonial rule, women, for the most part, did not gain independent rights to nationality. The failure of newly independent states to recognize women's rights to equality, including in relation to nationality matters, was sometimes a restatement of what new elites perceived to be 'traditional' family values, and at other times, the automatic continuation of colonial legal values and codes without criticism or review.[13] This was particularly the case in those states which cited religious values, such as those based on Shar'ia law, to justify discrimination against women in the area of nationality. These systems generally reflected the post-colonial impact of their civil or common law predecessors as well as customary patriarchal traditions.[14]

The feminist campaign for equality and non-discrimination on the grounds of sex also put gender discrimination in nationality laws under

---

[11] Freeman *et al.*, *CEDAW: A Commentary*.

[12] See various concluding observations by the Committee on the Elimination of Discrimination Against Women, which demonstrate how colonialism influenced the legal systems of colonized nations to entrench English common law and civil law approaches, including in relation to nationality laws (e.g. CO Nigeria, A/63/38, 41st session (2008) para. 316; CO Lebanon, A 63/38, 40th Session (2008) para. 202; CO Pakistan, A/62/38, 38th Session (2007) paras 254, 265 and 266).

[13] CEDAW, General Recommendation 21: Equality in Marriage and Family Relations (13th Session, 1994), as well as the Committee's concluding observations on various countries, highlight the necessity of amending laws on family relations in countries with a received colonial legal tradition to create a context for reforms that reject the norm of dependent nationality.

[14] S. Sarder Ali (ed.), *Conceptualising Islamic Law, CEDAW and Women's Human Rights in Plural Legal Settings* (New Delhi: UNIFEM South Asia Regional Office, 2006); A. E. Mayer, 'Reform of Personal Status Laws in North Africa: A Problem of Islamic or Mediterranean Laws?' *Middle East Journal* 49 (1995) 432; P. Kasemsup, 'Reception of Law in Thailand – A Buddhist Society' in M. Chiba (ed.), *Asian Indigenous Law in Interaction with Received Law* (London and New York: KPI, 1986), 267; E. S. Yassin, 'Development of Plural Structures of Law in Egypt' in Chiba (ed.), *Asian Indigenous Law*, 13.

the spotlight.[15] Nationality matters came to be recognized as essential to the agenda on gender equality. In recognition of women as full members of a state, women's rights to equal political participation and enjoyment of rights in both the public and private spheres became a focus.[16] In fact, international law on women's nationality rights began to develop from the 1930s.[17]

The issue was first highlighted at the Hague Codification Conference in 1930 and was followed by a campaign at the League of Nations for a separate treaty eliminating discrimination in nationality law. The 1933 Montevideo Convention on the Nationality of Married Women (Montevideo Convention), adopted by the Pan-American Conference, was the first regional treaty to express this aspect of civil and political equality of women. This was followed in 1957, by the United Nations Convention on the Nationality of Married Women, which established independent nationality of married women,[18] and finally in 1979, the Convention on the Elimination of All Forms of Discrimination against Women (CEDAW), which dedicates a specific provision to nationality and statelessness issues (discussed in section 7.4).[19]

7.3.   Discrimination against women in the conferral of nationality to their children

There are two main modes for the acquisition of nationality at birth, *jus soli* ('law of the soil') provides for the acquisition of nationality based on birth in the territory of a state and *jus sanguinis* ('law of the blood'), which provides for acquisition of the nationality of one or both parents based on descent. Most states have adopted a combination of both of these systems as the basis for granting nationality at birth, albeit with variances in the relevant prerequisites.[20] Of the two systems, *jus soli* is a more gender-

---

[15] K. Knop and C. Chinkin, 'Remembering Chrystal Macmillan: Women's Equality and Nationality in International Law', *Michigan Journal of International Law*, 22 (2001) 523, 524.

[16] *Ibid.*; A. Shachar, 'The Worth of Citizenship in an Unequal World', *Theoretical Inquiries in Law*, 8 (2007) 367.

[17] Freeman *et al.* (eds.), *CEDAW: A Commentary*.

[18] Convention on the Nationality of Married Women 1957, 29 January 1957, in force 11 August 1958, GA res. 1040 (XI).

[19] Convention on the Elimination of All Forms of Discrimination Against Women, 18 December 1979, in force 3 September 1981, 1249 UNTS 13.

[20] On general rules relating to nationality acquisition, including naturalization, see Chapter 1 by Edwards in this volume. See also ECOSOC, United Nations Division for the

neutral approach to nationality conferral, based on birth in the territory regardless of the nationality of one's parents. National systems that operate on the basis of a combination of *jus soli* and *jus sanguinis* principles or *jus sanguinis* alone, however, present particular risks for statelessness in women and their children.

Many countries continue to maintain *jus sanguinis* nationality laws, which grant citizenship primarily through *paternal* descent. A recent study by UNHCR notes that twenty-seven countries do not give mothers the ability to confer their nationality on their children on an equal basis with fathers.[21] These nationality laws can be charted along a spectrum depending on the severity of the discrimination. At one end are laws which allow only fathers to confer nationality on their children in all circumstances. This is the practice, for example, in Kuwait. If a Kuwaiti mother has a child with a father who is unknown or whose paternity has not been established, the only way she is able to pass on her nationality to the child is if the child might be considered eligible for Kuwaiti citizenship at majority by decree based on the recommendation of the Minister of Interior.[22] However, this is an extraordinary measure that occurs rarely in practice.

Other national laws require a combination of birth on the territory and descent. Following reform in 2006, the laws of Sierra Leone, for example, provide that a child born in Sierra Leone after 1971 acquires Sierra Leonean citizenship by birth if their father, mother or any grandparent was born in Sierra Leone.[23] Children born abroad, however, only acquire Sierra Leonean citizenship by descent if their father is a Sierra Leonean citizen.[24] Nevertheless, the Sierra Leone nationality law contains a safeguard granting Sierra Leonean citizenship to any child born to a Sierra Leonean mother who has not acquired another nationality, thereby avoiding statelessness resulting from the residual discriminatory elements of the law.[25]

In countries where gender-biased laws prevail, a mother's inability to pass on her nationality to her children may cause problems of residency,

---

Advancement of Women, *Women 2000 and Beyond: Women, Nationality and Citizenship* 3 (2003).

[21] UNHCR, Background Note on Gender Equality, Nationality Laws and Statelessness 2014, 8 March 2014, available at: www.refworld.org/docid/532075964.html, last accessed 22 May 2014.

[22] Article 3 of the Kuwaiti Nationality Law 1959.

[23] Section 3 of the Sierra Leone Citizenship (Amendment) Act 2006.

[24] Section 5 of the Sierra Leone Citizenship Act 1973.

[25] Section 6 of the Sierra Leone Citizenship Act 1973.

mobility and access to state benefits for her and her children, particularly when the children reside in the mother's country of nationality and the father is a non-national of that country.[26]

More seriously, gender inequality in nationality laws can result in statelessness where children can neither acquire the nationality of the father nor that of the country of their birth. Set out below is a typology of situations where the inability of children to acquire their father's citizenship, coupled with the impact of gender discrimination in nationality laws against women, could give rise to statelessness.

i) **Marriage to a stateless man**
   Marrying a stateless man can risk statelessness for the wife and her children, and perpetuate statelessness from one generation to the next. For instance, the laws in Brunei Darussalam, Burundi, Iran, Nepal, Qatar, Somalia, Sudan and Swaziland do not provide any exceptions that would allow mothers married to stateless men to confer their nationality on their children, even if this would result in their children being stateless.

ii) **Birth out of marriage**
   The application of the *jus sanguinis* principle based on paternal lineage as the sole basis for grant of nationality at birth can also create situations of statelessness for children born out of marriage.[27] In circumstances where the father is unknown, unless the law of the state allows women giving birth out of marriage to pass their nationality onto their children, the child will be stateless. Administrative laws and policies may also lead to statelessness. For example, even where children who are abandoned by a national father prior to their birth out of marriage are entitled to his nationality, they may not be able to prove paternity. The same scenario would prevail where a child born out of marriage is abandoned *after* birth and prior to the initiation of relevant administrative processes needed to confer nationality.[28]

iii) **Marriage to a foreign national**
   Statelessness may also ensue in cases where conferral of nationality through the paternal line is the only option and the laws of the

---

[26] See *Unity Dow* v. *Attorney General of Botswana* (1992) L.R. Commonwealth (Const.) 623; 103 International Law Reports 128 (Boswana C.A.).

[27] Including as a consequence of rape.

[28] An exception to this situation would be a case where nationality is automatically conferred at the time of birth, or birth certification is provided at the point of birth and such documentation is accepted as adequate proof for the conferral of nationality.

father's country do not permit him to confer nationality in certain circumstances.

For instance, if the father's state places limits on the father's ability to confer his nationality on a child born abroad, and the child is born on the territory of the mother's state (or the territory of a third state that only permits transmission of nationality by descent), the combined effect of the nationality laws in the mother and father's states will lead to statelessness of any child born outside the territory of the father's state.

In contrast, if the father's state grants nationality on the basis of the *jus sanguinis* principle, a child born on the territory of the mother's state could receive the nationality of the father, subject to overcoming the necessary administrative hurdles (see paragraph iv below on administrative and other problems). However, if the child were to remain in the mother's state, and in time marry a national woman of that state, statelessness could be created in their children if the father's state limits conferral of nationality to the first generation born abroad, as is the case in Canada and the United Kingdom.

iv) **Administrative barriers to nationality acquisition**

As noted above, if the father's state permits acquisition of nationality by a child based on the *jus sanguinis* principle, a child born in the territory of the mother's state could acquire the father's nationality. However, if the father is unable to fulfil the requisite administrative steps to confer his nationality, or acquire proof of nationality for his children, the risk that the children will be left stateless again arises. Typical reasons why fathers do not complete administrative requirements include where they have died or where they have abandoned the family. Other reasons include obstacles to registering children as foreign nationals, where, for example, there is an absence of consular services.[29] Absence of proof of birth and paternity can be additional evidentiary challenges.

---

[29] Centre for Research and Training on Development – Action, Gender, Citizenship and Nationality Programme, 'Denial of Nationality: The Case of Arab Women: Summary of Regional Research', February 2004. This report studied the implementation of nationality laws in the Middle East, specifically Lebanon, Syria, Jordan, Palestine, Yemen, Tunisia, Morocco and Egypt. The study indicated many consequences for Arab women married to non-national men. Specifically, it revealed that in cases of the absence of consular services from the country of the husband in the wife's country, there were difficulties associated with registering their children as foreign nationals. In particular, difficulties exist where there is no diplomatic representation between countries or where there has been a severing of diplomatic ties, for example following conflict.

v) **Children born using reproductive technology**
Grant of nationality at birth, based solely on paternal descent, also presents problems for families who rely on reproductive technology. Single women and lesbian couples who seek to have children through non-traditional means such as artificial insemination could find that their children are rendered stateless if they are nationals of countries which do not recognize maternal descent for the grant of nationality at birth.

7.4.   Discrimination against women in the acquisition, loss and retention of nationality by marriage and naturalization

7.4.1   Marriage

As noted earlier, 'dependent nationality' is a concept linking the nationality of a married women to that of her husband and makes her nationality contingent on that of her husband's.[30] In some cases, states automatically alter a woman's nationality status when she marries a non-national. In the absence of legislative or administrative safeguards to prevent statelessness, or ineffective implementation of such safeguards, strict application of the principle of dependent nationality could render a woman married to a non-national stateless upon the death of, or divorce from, her husband. This is because the wife's only link to a nationality, that of her citizenship-bearing husband, has been severed.

In addition, if a woman's nationality is automatically withdrawn through operation of a state's laws at the time of her marriage to a foreign national, or she is required to renounce her nationality in order to acquire her husband's nationality (because the state subscribes to the concept of dependent nationality) the woman's vulnerability to statelessness depends on the naturalization laws applicable in her husband's country. Unless naturalization laws automatically confer nationality on foreign female spouses upon marriage, such women will be rendered stateless (even if only for a temporary period). This stateless status will persist until they are able to comply with the legal and administrative conditions necessary to acquire nationality from their husband's country. In this regard, the immigration or nationality laws applicable in the husband's state may contribute to the prolongation of statelessness. Moreover, death of, or divorce from, the husband, prior to obtaining citizenship could lead to women being

---

[30] Knop and Chinkin, 'Remembering Chrystal Macmillan', 544–6.

suspended in a state of statelessness where their own country of national-ity does not permit them to reacquire their original nationality.

Notwithstanding the ultimate grant of nationality to a foreign spouse, due to the application of the principle of dependent nationality, women may continue to be vulnerable to statelessness. For example, if the hus-band were to be deprived of his nationality because of fraud or misrep-resentation in his original acquisition of nationality or through an act of disloyalty to the state, or where the husband renounced his nation-ality or acquired another, the wife could automatically become stateless unless legislative safeguards were in place to allow her to retain her new nationality, to automatically reacquire her original nationality, or in the case where her husband were to acquire a new nationality, for her to also acquire the same. Where a woman loses her nationality based on loss or change of her husband's nationality status, she may be refused the right to return to her country of original nationality on the grounds that she is not a national.[31]

Gaps in ostensibly gender-neutral nationality laws can also have a disproportionate impact on women and render them stateless. A clear illustration is found in the cases of thousands of Vietnamese women who, prior to 2008, had renounced their nationality in order to acquire that of their foreign husbands, mostly poor workers from Taiwan, South Korea, Hong Kong and Singapore who were unable to attract a woman or afford the cost of an expensive wedding in their home countries. These women were left stateless when their marriages ended before they acquired the nationality of their husbands. Children of these women born outside Vietnam were unable to acquire nationality from their stateless mothers, and could not always acquire the nationality of their foreign fathers, for example, if the marriage was not registered, ended in divorce, or if the husband had died or abandoned the family before the child was born. For those who returned to Vietnam, many found that they had lost the 'right to have rights' – to work legally or to be eligible for social assistance. To alleviate the 'stateless Vietnamese brides' syn-drome, in 2008 the Vietnamese Government reformed its nationality law to allow for the restoration of Vietnamese citizenship to women in such situations.[32]

---

[31] This is despite the right to return to 'one's own country', guaranteed in Article 12(4) of the ICCPR and a range of other international and regional instruments.

[32] Kitty McKinsey, 'Lose a Husband, Lose a Country', *Refugees Magazine* 147(3) (2007) 26–7.

However, it is not only women who may be rendered stateless. Adherence to the principle of dependent nationality also has the capacity to foster statelessness in subsequent generations. Take the case of a woman who marries a foreign national, has children with him but, along with her children, subsequently loses her husband's nationality when her husband loses or is deprived of his nationality. If the woman returns to her former country of nationality with her children and reacquires her original nationality she may still find that her children are unable to acquire her nationality as her state applies the *jus sanguinis* principle based purely on paternal descent. In such a case, unless the children retain their father's nationality, they will be stateless.

7.4.2   Naturalization

Naturalization laws that restrict the ability of women to transfer their nationality to their spouses discriminate in situations where men are permitted to transfer their nationality to their wives. Such laws can also prolong situations of statelessness where women marry stateless men. This is the case, for example, in Jordan and Oman, where laws prevent married women from transferring their nationality to their husbands. Even if women are able to transfer their nationality to their spouses, some states impose more stringent requirements on men seeking to acquire the nationality of their wife compared to women who seek to acquire the nationality of their husbands.

Another aspect of naturalization procedures tending to have a discriminatory impact on women is the practice of 'citizenship testing'. An increasing number of states demand language or cultural knowledge testing of the country of proposed nationality as prerequisites to the grant of nationality. Such requirements may be especially burdensome on women who may not have had the same educational opportunities as men. This tends to be the case where women have remained within the home or have been prevented from working whilst on dependency visas. In contrast, men are often more likely to have worked outside the home and to have had greater exposure to local languages and customs to enable them to pass such citizenship tests.[33] Other naturalization prerequisites such as proof of economic self-sufficiency or adequate housing may also be more

---

[33] For example, Paragraph 3 of the Council of Europe Parliamentary Assembly Recommendation No. 1261 on the situation of immigrant women in Europe (1995)

difficult for women to meet, especially if they are female-headed house-holds with little income, financially dependent on their spouse or if they are stateless or refugees.[34] Where there is no facilitation of naturalization through, for example, waiver of certain naturalization prerequisites, stateless women may find it especially difficult to naturalize.

7.5.   International and regional legal framework

As outlined above, there are various ways in which gender-biased laws generate or perpetuate statelessness and entrench its impacts from generation to generation. The following section provides an overview of the international and regional legal frameworks for the regulation of nationality laws, and the limitations of this framework when it comes to addressing the impacts of gendered nationality laws.

As noted earlier in this book, the exclusive right of states in nationality matters is not an unfettered power and is in fact tempered by international treaties, international custom and general principles of international law.[35] Traditional notions of state sovereignty,[36] which have also served to allow states to discriminate in nationality on the basis of gender, have been eroded by a number of key international legal principles. These are dealt with in turn below, and include: (a) the recognition in treaty law of every individual's right to a nationality; (b) the prohibition of discrimination on the basis of sex including in nationality matters; (c) the principle of the prevention of statelessness; and (d) the prohibition of arbitrary deprivation of nationality, including on grounds of gender.

---

[34] Edwards, 'Displacement, Statelessness and Questions of Gender Equality', 44.

[35] See Chapter 1 by Edwards in this volume.

[36] Johannes M. N. Chan, 'The Right to Nationality as a Human Right: The Current Trend Towards Recognition', *Human Rights Law Journal* 12(1) (1991), 1; see also OSI, Citizenship and Equality in Practice: Guaranteeing Non-Discriminatory Access to Nationality, Protecting the Right to be Free from Arbitrary Deprivation of Nationality, and Combating Statelessness 3 (2005). For example, Article 1 of the 1930 Hague Convention on Certain Questions Relating to the Conflict of Nationality Laws states that '[i]t is for each State to determine under its own law who are its nationals'. Article 2 further buttresses this broad discretion by stating that '[a]ny question as to whether a person possesses the nationality of a particular State shall be determined in accordance with the law of that State': Convention on Certain Questions Relating to the Conflict of Nationality Laws, 13 April 1930, 179 LNTS 89 (1930 Hague Convention).

7.5.1   Everyone has the right to a nationality

International interest in recognizing a right to nationality occurred as early as the 1930s. Recognition of statelessness during the first half of the twentieth century influenced the adoption of the Hague Convention[37] and its protocol: the Protocol Relating to a Certain Case of Statelessness ('Hague Protocol').[38] These instruments were intended to address a range of conflicts in nationality laws leading to statelessness including, primarily, those relating to women and children.[39] They were also the first attempt to ensure every person a nationality.[40] The preamble to the Hague Convention pronounced that 'it is in the general interest of the international community to secure that *all* its members should recognise that *every* person should have a nationality' (emphasis added).

The atrocities of the Second World War and the displacement and mass denationalizations which occurred during that time led to further development and formal recognition of a right to a nationality. In adopting the Universal Declaration of Human Rights (UDHR), the international community declared its commitment to human rights and acknowledged the critical link between nationality and access to, and enjoyment of, other human rights.[41] Equality language permeates the UDHR, and was also intended to apply to the right to a nationality.

In the following decades, the right to a nationality has been firmly accepted through explicit inclusion in international and regional legal instruments.[42] A child's right to acquire a nationality has received widespread recognition due to its inclusion in the Convention on the Rights of the Child (CRC),[43] which enjoys almost universal ratification.[44] Although the International Covenant on Civil and Political

---

[37] 1930 Hague Convention.

[38] League of Nations, Protocol Relating to a Certain Case of Statelessness, The Hague, 12 April 1930, in force 1 July 1937, 179 LNTS 115.

[39] Laura van Waas, *Nationality Matters: Statelessness under International Law* (Antwerp/ Oxford/Portland, OR: Intersentia, 2008), 119.

[40] Chan, 'The Right to Nationality as a Human Right', 3.

[41] Article 15 of the UDHR.

[42] See, for example, Article 18(1) of the Convention on the Rights of Persons with Disabilities, 24 January 2007, in force 3 May 2008, 2515 UNTS 3.

[43] Convention on the Rights of the Child, 20 November 1989, in force 2 September 1990, 1577 UNTS 3. Article 7(1) of the CRC states that '[t]he child shall be registered immediately after birth and shall have the right from birth to a name, *the right to a nationality* and, as far as possible, the right to know and be cared for by his or her parents' (our emphasis). See also Articles 7(2) and 8(1) of the CRC.

[44] The CRC has been ratified by all states with the exception of the USA and Somalia.

Rights (ICCPR)[45] does not incorporate a broad right to a nationality as enunciated in the UDHR, it reinforces the right to acquire a nationality for children.[46] The International Convention on the Protection of Rights of All Migrant Workers (ICMW)[47] guarantees the right to a nationality for children of migrant workers,[48] whilst the African Charter on the Rights and Welfare of the Child (ACRWC)[49] guarantees the right to a nationality for children.[50]

The American Convention on Human Rights (ACHR)[51] articulates the clearest right to a nationality for all persons at the regional level. The Inter-American Court has declared, for example, that '[i]t is generally accepted today that nationality is an inherent right of *all* human beings' (emphasis added).[52] Although neither the European Convention on Human Rights and Fundamental Freedoms (ECHR)[53] nor the European Convention on Nationality (ECN)[54] explicitly espouses a right to a nationality, the ECN notes the right of states parties to determine nationality

---

[45] International Covenant on Civil and Political Rights, 19 December 1966, in force 23 March 1976, 999 UNTS 171.

[46] Article 24(3) of the ICCPR states that '[e]very child shall have, without any discrimination as to race, colour, sex, language, religion, national or social origin, property or birth, the right to such measures of protection as are required by his status as a minor, on the part of his family, society and the State', and that '[e]very child shall be registered immediately after birth and shall have a name' and '[e]very child has the right to acquire a nationality'.

[47] International Convention on the Protection of Rights of All Migrant Workers and Members of their Families, 18 December 1990, in force 1 July 2003, 2220 UNTS 3.

[48] Article 29 of the ICMW states that '[e]ach child of a migrant worker shall have the right to a name, to registration of birth and to a nationality' (ICMW).

[49] African Charter on the Rights and Welfare of the Child, 11 July 1990, in force 29 November 1999, CAB/LEG/24.9/49 (1990).

[50] Article 6 African Charter on Human and Peoples' Rights 1981, 27 June 1981, in force 21 October 1986, CAB/LEG/67/3 rev. 5, 21 I.L.M. 58 (1982) states that '[e]very child has the right to acquire a nationality'.

[51] American Convention on Human Rights, 'Pact of San Jose', Costa Rica, 22 November 1969, in force 18 July 1978. Article 20 provides: '1. Every person has the right to a nationality; 2. Every person has the right to the nationality of the State in whose territory he was born if he does not have the right to any other nationality; 3. No one shall be arbitrarily deprived of his nationality or his right to change it.'

[52] *Re Amendments to the Naturalisation Provisions of the Constitution of Costa Rica*, Advisory Opinion of OC-4/84, Inter-American Court of Human Rights (IACrtHR), 19 January 1984, paragraph 34 reported in (1984) 5 HRLJ 161.

[53] Council of Europe, European Convention for the Protection of Human Rights and Fundamental Freedoms, as amended by Protocols Nos. 11 and 14, 4 November 1950, ETS 5, in force 3 September 1953.

[54] Council of Europe, European Convention on Nationality, 6 November 1997, in force 1 March 2000, ETS No. 166.

while concomitantly requiring states to ensure that rules on nationality are based on the principle that everyone has the right to a nationality.[55] It thereby acknowledges the existence of such a right.

The right to a nationality, with its strong foundation in treaty law, means that gender-discriminatory nationality laws, which perpetuate or create situations of statelessness, run contrary to this important principle of international law. In particular, given the near universal endorsement by states of the right of every child to a nationality,[56] there are strong grounds for challenging domestic laws that discriminate against mothers in their ability to pass their nationality to their children and the risk of rendering these children stateless.

7.5.2   Prohibition against discrimination on the basis of sex in nationality laws and equality before the law

As early as 1933 with the adoption of the Montevideo Convention, the question of the rights of women to nationality on an equal basis as men was on the international agenda. The Montevideo Convention explicitly called on states to end distinctions based on sex in nationality laws and practices.[57] By 1957, the United Nations Convention on the Nationality of Married Women (1957 Convention)[58] had been adopted, entering into force in 1958, and became the first global pronouncement of the principle of the independent nationality of married women, and split with the previously accepted 'dependence' principle.

The 1957 Convention was the precursor to Article 9 of CEDAW, which provides:

1. States Parties shall grant women equal rights with men to acquire, change or retain their nationality. They shall ensure in particular that neither marriage to an alien nor change of nationality by the husband during marriage shall automatically change the nationality of the wife, render her stateless or force upon her the nationality of the husband.
2. States Parties shall grant women equal rights with men with respect to the nationality of their children.

---

[55] Article 4 of the ECN.   [56] See n 43.
[57] Article 1, Montevideo Convention.
[58] Convention on the Nationality of Married Women, 29 January 1957, 309 UNTS 65, entered into force 11 August 1958.

Apart from granting women equal rights with men to acquire, change or retain their nationality, and in particular proscribing practices which automatically change the nationality of the wife upon marriage, there is also an explicit reference to statelessness. This aspect of Article 9(1) aimed to cover the possibility of a woman losing her original nationality upon marriage and becoming stateless if she is unable to acquire her husband's nationality, or if she acquires the husband's nationality upon marriage and subsequently loses it upon dissolution of that marriage. In interpreting Article 9(1), the Committee on the Elimination of Discrimination Against Women's General Recommendation 21 ('General Recommendation 21') has emphasized this risk of statelessness and that nationality should not be arbitrarily removed because of marriage or dissolution of marriage or because the husband or father changes his nationality.[59] Article 9(1) therefore complements the international instruments that support the reduction of statelessness.

In addition to the Montevideo Convention, regional instruments have contained a variety of provisions, albeit some in conflict with global standards. The Protocol to the African Charter on Human and Peoples' Rights on the Rights of Women in Africa[60] contains an entire section on equality of rights in marriage, which provides that 'a woman shall have the right to retain her nationality or to acquire the nationality of her husband' and equal rights in respect of the nationality of their children.[61] The latter, however, is qualified and allows states to ignore it if such equality is not allowed by national laws or if contrary to national security interests. Meanwhile, the Arab Charter on Human Rights,[62] in force since 2008, copies the UDHR general statements on right to nationality,[63] while diverging from the CEDAW standards. In particular, Article 29(2) provides: 'States parties shall take such measures as they deem appropriate, in accordance with their domestic laws on nationality, to allow a child to acquire the mother's nationality, having due regard, in all cases, to the best interests of the child.' There are surprisingly no explicit standards

---

[59] General Recommendation 21: Equality in Marriage and Family Relations (13th Session, 1994), para. 6.
[60] African Union, Protocol to the African Charter on Human and Peoples' Rights on the Rights of Women in Africa, 11 July 2003.
[61] Article 6(g) and (h), respectively, Protocol to the African Charter on Human and Peoples' Rights on the Rights of Women in Africa.
[62] League of Arab States, Arab Charter on Human Rights, 15 September 1994.
[63] Article 29(1), Arab Charter on Human Rights provides: 'Everyone has the right to nationality. No one shall be arbitrarily or unlawfully deprived of his nationality.'

contained expressly in any European instruments, although national practice has now consistently eradicated such discrimination.

The second major achievement of Article 9 of CEDAW is the recognition that women have equal rights to men with respect to the nationality of their children. As recounted above, this has long been a problem in *jus sanguinis* countries in particular, where parentage and thus nationality is traced through the male line. The famous case of *Unity Dow* v. *Attorney General of Botswana* put this issue squarely on the global map, highlighting the discrimination faced by women when the link between women's nationality and children's nationality is not recognized.[64]

The plain language of Article 9(2), alongside the Committee's General Recommendation 21 and the jurisprudence which has emerged in national and regional courts reinforces the equal rights of women in relation to the transmission of nationality.[65] The CEDAW Committee has noted that dual nationality of children is supported by CEDAW's equality norm, rather than being viewed as a problem that should be avoided, and that the prospect of dual nationality cannot justify a state party's determination of a child's nationality only according to the father's nationality. The committee has also confirmed that failure to amend discriminatory laws in this area on the basis of culture or religion is not justified.[66]

Further, the imperative to prevent statelessness in women is explicitly referred to in Article 9(1) of the CEDAW, and as a corollary, this is clearly a risk that Article 9(2) also sought to avoid, and should be read alongside Article 7(1) of the CRC on the child's right to acquire a nationality.[67]

Despite the clear language of Article 9 of the CEDAW, coupled with the fact that the convention has garnered a significant number of states

---

[64] *Unity Dow* v. *Attorney General of Botswana* (1992) LRC Const 623 (CA, Botswana). The case highlighted how a range of women's human rights with regard to child custody, personal travel and freedom of movement, as well as the child's rights relating to health, education and child support in the country of the mother's nationality, can be undermined when a woman holds a nationality but cannot transmit her nationality to her children because of the nationality of their father. Please see Freeman *et al.* (eds.) *CEDAW: A Commentary*, 241.

[65] Cf. the *travaux préparatoires* of the CEDAW, which show that the drafters selected the language in Article 9(2) to avoid recognizing an equal right *to transmit* nationality based on the argument that this could result in a child acquiring dual nationality or a risk of statelessness where there was parental disagreement.

[66] Freeman *et al.* (eds.) *CEDAW; A Commentary*, 244.

[67] See Chapter 6 by De Groot in this volume.

parties,[68] it has also gained notoriety for receiving a high number of reservations, including against Article 9,[69] which has been widely documented and critiqued.[70] Nonetheless, it is arguable that the combined effect of the rights to nationality and non-discrimination contained in many other international instruments form part of a body of international norms that reinforce the equal right of women in relation to nationality matters and that strengthen the content of Article 9 of CEDAW, notwithstanding the many reservations to this Article.

Even in situations where states parties have entered blanket reservations to Article 9, the legitimacy of these reservations must be questioned, insofar as they conflict with the object and purpose of the treaty, not least its core non-discrimination goal.[71] In some cases, reservations made by certain states to Article 9 are inconsistent with obligations they have assumed under other international instruments relating to non-discrimination and right to a nationality, particularly a child's right to a nationality, which is threatened by gender-discriminatory nationality laws. Examples include obligations assumed without reservation by states under Article 24 of the ICCPR and Article 7 of the CRC.[72] In this regard, states are obliged to comply with the obligations they have undertaken pursuant to other treaties.

7.5.3   Prohibition against statelessness

As noted in section 7.3, women and their children are at heightened risk of statelessness in countries that operate discriminatory nationality laws. The 1930 Hague Convention and Protocol[73] acknowledged this fact and

---

[68] As at the date of writing, there were 188 states parties.

[69] At least seventeen states have reserved in some fashion against Article 9 of CEDAW.

[70] For example, see S. Mullally, *Gender, Culture and Human Rights: Reclaiming Universalism* (Oxford and Portland, OR: Hart Publishing, 2006) at Chapter 6; J. Minor, 'An Analysis of Structural Weaknesses in Convention on the Elimination of All Forms of Discrimination Against Women', *Va. J. Int'l L.* 3 (1990) 643; B. Clark, 'The Vienna Convention Reservations Regime and the Convention on Discrimination Against Women', *Amer. J. Int'l K.* 85 (1991) 281.

[71] CEDAW, General Recommendation No 4: Reservations (1987); CEDAW, General Recommendation No. 20: Reservations (1992).

[72] Of the seventeen states that have entered reservations to Article 9 CEDAW as at 28 February 2013, only three have entered reservations to Article 7 of the CRC and none to Article 24 of the ICCPR.

[73] The 1930 Conference for the Codification of International Law, which was convened at The Hague, was intended to resolve emerging issues of dual nationality and statelessness as states moved away from the concept of dependent nationality to independent

sought to remedy it explicitly. Article 8 of the Hague Convention provides that, 'if the national law of the wife causes her to lose her nationality on marriage with a foreigner, this consequence shall be conditional on her acquiring the nationality of the husband'. Similarly, the Hague Protocol gives a mother a right to pass on her nationality to her child where the child would otherwise be stateless.[74] While the effectiveness of these early treaties was curtailed by low numbers of ratifications, these instruments were the forerunners to the formal duty to avoid statelessness under United Nations' treaty law.[75]

In 1948, because of the uncertain nationality of the displaced throughout Europe, and upon request of the Economic and Social Council of the United Nations,[76] the Secretary-General prepared a study on statelessness.[77] This study addressed improvements to the status of persons who were stateless and put forward the idea of the elimination of statelessness.[78] In particular, the study acknowledged the specific situation of the effect of marriage on the nationality of married women and the risks of statelessness.[79] This crucial report was the precursor to the creation of an ad hoc Committee on Refugees and Stateless Persons, the subsequent adoption of the 1954 Convention as well as the 1961 Convention.[80]

As the 1954 Convention is primarily concerned with the protection of persons who are already stateless, it is the 1961 Convention which first articulated a positive legal duty on states to prevent and reduce statelessness in nationality laws and practices. From the outset, Article 1 of the 1961 Statelessness Convention provides that contracting states have a duty to grant nationality to persons born on their territory who would otherwise be stateless. The same convention explicitly provides that a 'child

---

nationality, which resulted in conflict of nationality laws and statelessness. See Tang Yay Lee, *Statelessness, Human Rights and Gender: Irregular Migrant Workers from Burma* (Leiden: Martinus Nijhoff Publishers, 2003) 25–7.

[74] Article 1 of the Hague Protocol.

[75] Lee, *Statelessness, Human Rights and Gender*, 20. Only nineteen states have ratified the Hague Convention and only twenty-one states are parties to the Hague Protocol.

[76] ECOSOC Res, 116D (VI), 1 and 2 March 1948.

[77] The United Nations Department of Social Affairs, *A Study of Statelessness* (1949) 9 UN Doc E/1112 and UN Doc E/1112/Add.1.

[78] For example, the study recommended two principles in relation to the elimination of statelessness: first, that every child must receive a nationality at birth, and second, that no person should lose his nationality until he has acquired a new one.

[79] See, in particular, under Part Two The Elimination of Statelessness, Chapter 1, a section dedicated to 'The Effect of Marriage on the Nationality of Married Women', *A Study of Statelessness*, 136–8.

[80] See Chapter 3 by van Waas in this volume.

born in wedlock, in the territory of a Contracting State, whose mother has the nationality of that State, shall acquire at birth that nationality, if it otherwise would be stateless'.[81]

While these provisions go a long way to preventing statelessness, they *do not* prohibit discriminatory nationality laws that prevent a woman in normal circumstances from passing on her nationality to her child. Rather, they only require states to permit the passage of nationality from mother to child in circumstances where the child would *otherwise* be stateless. The provisions accept that nationality laws may be based on patrilineal descent, and that conferral of nationality based on maternal descent is the exception. Moreover, Article 1(3) only applies to children born 'in wedlock' and does not extend to the many children born out of marriage, who may also be stateless.

Another shortcoming is that the 1961 Convention defers to national laws in the case of persons who would *otherwise* be stateless because they cannot fulfil the requirements of application (such as residence or age). Article 1(4) provides: 'If his parents did not possess the same nationality at the time of his birth, the question whether the nationality of the person concerned should follow that of the father or that of the mother shall be determined by the national law of such Contracting State.' Similarly, Article 4 of the 1961 Convention defers to national laws of states whether to grant nationality to a child born outside the territory of the state who would otherwise be stateless. It is within the relevant state's discretion whether to make provision in its nationality law to grant the nationality of the father, mother or either parent in such circumstances.

That said, even though the 1961 Convention does not expressly address all aspects of the question of the discriminatory treatment of women in nationality matters, it is complemented by, and must be read in light of, subsequent developments in international human rights law,[82] which, as shown above, provide a robust basis upon which to argue the illegality of such discrimination and the ensuing statelessness.[83]

Importantly, the 1961 Convention is not entirely silent as to the situation of women. In fact, the 1961 Convention includes a general principle that if, as a consequence of any change in the personal status of a person

---

[81] Article 1(3), 1961 Statelessness Convention.

[82] Article 31(3)(c), Vienna Convention on the Law of Treaties.

[83] See paragraphs 13–15 of UNHCR, 'Guidelines on Statelessness No. 4: Ensuring Every Child's Right to Acquire a Nationality through Articles 1–4 of the 1961 Convention on the Reduction of Statelessness', 21 December 2012, HCR/GS/12/04.

(i.e. marriage, divorce), the law of the contracting state leads to loss of nationality, such loss must be conditional upon the possession or acquisition of another nationality. Article 6 explicitly extends the application of this principle to spouses and children of a person who loses, or is deprived of, their nationality. Similarly to Article 1, Article 8 aims to strike at another root cause of statelessness by imposing a clear duty on states not to create statelessness through deprivation of nationality.[84] These general principles, read together with developments in international law relating to women's rights to equality, support the argument that there is a duty on states to reform their nationality laws to ensure that (a) they do not discriminate against women (or their children); and (b) they do not create or perpetuate situations of statelessness.

7.5.4   Prohibition against arbitrary deprivation of nationality

An additional constraint on state discretion regarding regulation of nationality matters is the prohibition against the arbitrary deprivation of nationality, which was identified in parallel with the right to nationality in the UDHR.[85] Although there are some permissible grounds for the deprivation of nationality under international law, for example, where nationality has been obtained through fraud or misrepresentation,[86] nowhere is discrimination a permitted ground to deprive someone of their nationality, and in fact, it is clearly prohibited as a general principle of international law.[87]

By extension, the combined effect of Article 15(2) (the prohibition against arbitrary deprivation of nationality) and Article 2 (the prohibition against discrimination including on the basis of sex) of the UDHR, supports the proposition that depriving someone of their nationality on the basis of gender discrimination is arbitrary. Endorsing this view, the UN Commission on Human Rights stated that 'arbitrary deprivation of nationality on … gender grounds, is a violation of human rights and fundamental freedoms'[88] and calls 'all States to refrain from taking discriminatory measures and from enacting or maintaining legislation that would arbitrarily deprive such persons of their nationality

---

[84] Although there are limited exceptions. See Chapter 8 by Brandvoll in this volume.
[85] Article 15 of the UDHR.
[86] Article 8 of the 1961 Statelessness Convention.
[87] See analysis on this in Chapter 1 by Edwards in this volume.
[88] Paragraph 2, Human Rights Council, Human Rights and Arbitrary Deprivation of Nationality, 27 March 2008, A/HRC/RES/7/10 (2008).

on grounds of … gender … especially if such measures and legislation would render a person stateless'.[89]

On this basis, there is firm ground for contending that instances in which women are deprived of their nationality based on adherence to the principle of dependent nationality are arbitrary.

7.6. Conclusion

One of the most profound and far-reaching consequences of gender discrimination in nationality matters is that women, their children and occasionally their spouses may be left stateless. Preventing statelessness can be complex because of the myriad technical grounds upon which nationality can be lost or removed. While there are many positive features of the 1961 Convention, it provides only partial answers to the many issues facing women when it comes to their rights to acquire, confer, change and retain their nationality on an equal basis with men. Although there are textual differences in the way in which the right to nationality is expressed in various international and regional human rights instruments, as well as in relation to how gender equality principles inform that right, it is not possible to treat the right to acquire a nationality as distinct from the right to equality.

International human rights law pushes states to do more than just reduce or prevent statelessness, regardless of whether the methods employed to do so reinforce the unequal position of women in society. The principle of non-discrimination and the right to equality underpin the United Nations' system and, as such, international human rights law prohibits the arbitrary deprivation of nationality by discriminatory nationality laws.

A more direct and vigorous application of an equality lens to the statelessness problem would in the authors' view accelerate the reduction in and prevention of statelessness in women and their children. The historically preferred approaches of states to issues of statelessness that centre on 'conflict of laws' or ideas of 'dependent nationality' gloss over many of the complexities of statelessness amongst women and their children, and related rights deprivations.

While gender discrimination might be a root cause of statelessness in some countries, it is also helpful to use human rights principles that promote the right to a nationality and the prohibition of statelessness to

---

[89] *Ibid.*, paragraph 3.

complement efforts by women's rights actors to combat such laws. Such an approach could be furthered by better coordinating efforts in the fields of women's and children's rights and statelessness. For example, at the international level, UN Women, the Committee on the Elimination of Discrimination Against Women, the Committee on the Rights of the Child and UNHCR, the UN agency mandated to reduce and prevent statelessness,[90] should complement each other so that efforts to achieve gender equality in nationality matters, to ensure that every child enjoys the right to acquire a nationality and initiatives to prevent and reduce statelessness are conducted in tandem.

The outlook for achieving gender equality in nationality matters and thereby eliminating statelessness is a positive one. In the last decade, there has been a marked willingness by states to take action to remove gender discrimination from their nationality laws. Reforms to eliminate gender discrimination from nationality laws have taken place in states as diverse as Sri Lanka (2003), Egypt (2004), Algeria (2005), Indonesia (2006), Sierra Leone (partial reform in 2006), Morocco (2007), Bangladesh (2009), Zimbabwe (2009), Kenya (2010), Tunisia (remaining gaps addressed in 2010) and Monaco (2005, 2011). At a Ministerial Meeting convened by UNHCR in December 2011, Senegal and Liberia also pledged to reform their respective nationality laws to remove elements that discriminate against women, with the specific aim of preventing statelessness.[91] In June 2013, Senegal implemented its pledge, becoming the most recent state to eliminate gender discrimination from its nationality law.

UmAli's story recounted in the introduction to this chapter provides a glimpse into how discriminatory nationality laws reproduce gendered hierarchies and disadvantages in society, and can create situations and cycles of statelessness. These very real consequences need to be kept central in the campaign for women's equality, as it remains true that the way in which states frame their laws tells us a great deal about how they perceive and treat their women. In the remaining pockets of the world where statelessness is still caused by laws that deny women equality in nationality matters, real progress will be witnessed if efforts to achieve rights to equality, non-discrimination and to a nationality are deployed in tandem, with an understanding of the true interdependence and complementarity of these human rights.

[90] On the mandate of UNHCR, see Chapter 4 by Manly in this volume.
[91] UNHCR, Revised Background Note on Gender Equality, Nationality Laws and Statelessness.

Questions to guide discussion

1. What does the principle of 'unity of nationality of the family' mean and how did it contribute to the introduction, historically, of gender-discriminatory nationality laws?
2. On what basis can it be argued that *jus soli* is not a completely gender-neutral approach to conferral of nationality?
3. Explain why laws which restrict the right of women to transmit their nationality to their children increase the risk of childhood statelessness. Give at least three concrete examples of situations in which problems may arise.
4. In what ways may women face disadvantage in the enjoyment of nationality rights in the context of a) marriage or divorce; and b) naturalization?
5. Even though the 1961 Convention on the Reduction of Statelessness prescribes safeguards to prevent childhood statelessness, including as a result of gender discrimination in nationality laws, alone it is insufficient to combat statelessness arising as a result of such discrimination. Why?
6. Imagine that you have been asked to put together a policy paper to convince the government of a state that still discriminates against women in its nationality law to reform those regulations. What are your three most compelling arguments?

8

Deprivation of nationality

Limitations on rendering persons stateless under international law

JORUNN BRANDVOLL

8.1. Introduction

On 2 May 2010, a car bomb was discovered in Times Square in New York. The next day, a suspect was arrested. The man turned out to be a naturalized United States citizen who had links with Pakistan's Taliban.[1] A domestic debate arose around Faisal Shahzad's citizenship: Did not the foiled bomb plot prove his disloyalty to the Constitution and that he no longer deserved to be a citizen?[2] A bill was introduced in the US Congress, proposing revocation of US citizenship for persons who join terrorist organizations or who engage in or support hostilities against the USA or its allies.[3] The proposed measure had no regard for whether the person concerned, like Faisal Shahzad, also possessed a foreign citizenship and could therefore have opened a new route to statelessness. However, the bill did not receive sufficient backing.[4] Faisal Shahzad was sentenced to life imprisonment but preserved his US citizenship.[5]

Had the bill been adopted, would it have been consistent with principles for the avoidance of statelessness under international law? Article 15 of the Universal Declaration of Human Rights (UDHR) establishes that everyone has the right to a nationality and that that 'no one shall be arbitrarily deprived of his nationality nor denied the right to change

---

[1] 'Suspect in Failed Times Sq Bomb Attempt is Indicted', *New York Times*, 17 June 2010.
[2] 'Bombing Suspect's Route to Citizenship Reveals Limitations', *New York Times*, 7 May 2010.
[3] Terrorist Expatriation Act, available on the website of Senator Joseph Lieberman: http://lieberman.senate.gov/assets/pdf/TEA_full.pdf, last accessed on 19 June 2012.
[4] 'Bill Targets Citizenship of Terrorists' Allies', *New York Times*, 7 May 2010. By 22 June, the Bill had only gathered the support of one congressman in addition to the three sponsoring it, see 'Brown Renews Call for Terrorist Expatriation Act', *Boston Globe*, 22 June 2010.
[5] 'Profile: Faisal Shahzad', *BBC News US & Canada*, 5 October 2010.

his nationality'.[6] An explicit prohibition against arbitrary deprivation of nationality has also been included in some subsequent human rights treaties,[7] in particular at the regional level.[8]

But what does it mean that no one shall be 'arbitrarily deprived of citizenship'? And to what extent does it translate into a limitation on the opportunity states have to use deprivation of nationality as a punishment or administrative measure? Considering the human cost of being stateless, it is particularly worth asking whether deprivation of citizenship is ever justifiable if it results in statelessness. These questions will all be explored in this chapter.

8.2.   When does deprivation of nationality become arbitrary?

International law prohibits any deprivation of nationality that is arbitrary, but what does this mean? The Oxford Dictionary defines the word 'arbitrary' as acts that are based on random choice or personal whims rather than on any reason or system.[9] Such a 'system' may, for instance, be a country's laws, which means that deprivation of nationality is arbitrary whenever it is not undertaken in accordance with these laws.

Arbitrariness extends beyond this dictionary definition, however, to certain situations where an act is based on law. 'Arbitrariness' has, for example, been interpreted in relation to particular human rights, more specifically in relation to arbitrary detention[10] and arbitrary interference with privacy.[11] According to the UN Human Rights Committee, arbitrary interference can extend to interference that is provided for by law, but

---

[6] Universal Declaration of Human Rights, Paris, 10 December 1948, GA Res. 217A(III), UN Doc. A/810 at 71, Art. 15.

[7] Convention on the Rights of Persons with Disabilities, 13 December 2006, in force 3 May 2008, 2515 UNTS 3, Art. 18(1)(a). According to this treaty, states parties shall ensure that disabled persons are not deprived of their nationality arbitrarily or on the basis of their disability.

[8] American Convention on Human Rights (ACHR), 22 November 1969, in force 18 July 1978, OAS Treaty Series No. 36, Art. 20; Arab Charter on Human Rights, 22 May 2004, in force 15 March 2008, Art. 29; Commonwealth of Independent States Convention on Human Rights and Fundamental Freedoms, 26 May 1995, in force 11 August 1998, Art. 24. It is worth noting that neither the European Convention on Human Rights nor the African Charter on Human and Peoples' Rights includes the right to a nationality and not to be arbitrarily deprived of it.

[9] 'Arbitrary', Oxford Dictionaries at: http://oxforddictionaries.com/definition/arbitrary?q=arbitrary, last accessed 2 June 2012.

[10] International Covenant on Civil and Political Rights (ICCPR), 16 December 1966, in force 23 March 1976, 999 UNTS 171, Art. 9.

[11] *Ibid.*, Art.17.

which is incompatible with the provisions, aims and objectives of human rights law, and not reasonable in the particular circumstances.[12]

The principle of non-discrimination forms a central part of the aims and objectives of all universal human rights treaties. In numerous past situations, groups or individuals have been deprived of their citizenship on the basis of their race, ethnic belonging or religious or political beliefs.[13] One of the most significant examples is the denationalization of Jews in Germany on the basis of discrimination before and during the Second World War.[14] Following the war, these events motivated the inclusion of a prohibition against arbitrary deprivation of nationality in the UDHR. Later, a prohibition of deprivation of nationality on discriminatory grounds was also included as a separate provision of the 1961 Convention on the Reduction of Statelessness ('the 1961 Convention'). According to Article 9 of this convention, 'A Contracting State may not deprive any person or group of persons of their nationality on racial, ethnic, religious or political grounds.'[15] Over time, the list of discriminatory grounds has grown and today it is considered that any case of deprivation of nationality on the basis of race, colour, sex, language, religion, political or other opinion, national or social origin, property, birth, or other status is arbitrary and thus prohibited under international law.[16]

---

[12] UN Human Rights Committee, 'General Comment No. 16: The right to respect of privacy, family, home and correspondence, and protection of honour and reputation (Article 17)' 04/08/1988 (1988), para. 4.

[13] Examples include the collective deprivation of nationality affecting persons of Eritrean origin in Ethiopia and the black population in Mauritania (see Bronwen Manby, *Struggles for Citizenship in Africa* (London: Zed Books, 2009), 98–108); the refugees from Bhutan in Nepal (see Human Rights Watch, 'Last Hope: The Need for Durable Solutions for Bhutanese Refugees in Nepal and India' (Report) (16 May 2007), Volume 19, No. 7(C)); and the Feili Kurds in Iraq (see UNHCR 'Feili Kurds in Iran Seek Way out of Identity Impasse' (28 May 2008), Geneva). A number of examples may also be cited of individuals who have been deprived of their citizenship on the basis of political opinion or religious belief, such as the Botswanan politician John K. Modise (see *John K. Modise* v. *Botswana* (1997) African Commission on Human and Peoples' Rights, Comm. No 97/93) or the Shiite cleric Ayatollah Hussein al-Najati in Bahrain (see 'Bahrain revokes citizenship of top cleric: report', *Al Arabiya News*, Dubai, 20 September 2010). None of the states mentioned here as examples are parties to the 1961 Convention on the Reduction of Statelessness.

[14] Paul Weis, *Nationality and Statelessness in International Law* (Alphen aan den Rijn: Sijthoff & Noordhoff, 1979), 119–24.

[15] Convention on the Reduction of Statelessness, 30 August 1961, in force 13 December 1975, 989 UNTS 175.

[16] Successive UN Human Rights Council/UN Commission on Human Rights resolutions have expressed concern with arbitrary deprivation of nationality on discriminatory

Any decision to deprive a person of his or her nationality must also follow certain procedural and substantive standards[17] to avoid being arbitrary. Among the procedural standards to be followed are the right to have the reasoned decision issued in writing, open to administrative or judicial review and subject to an effective remedy.[18]

The substantive standards imply that the decision must have a legitimate purpose and follow the principle of proportionality. What may serve as a legitimate purpose for deprivation of nationality will be discussed below when I look further into what international standards exist in relation to deprivation of nationality. In the context of these standards, it will also be discussed in further detail how the proportionality principle limits what actions states can take to deprive people of their citizenship, in particular when the result is statelessness.

8.3. Is deprivation of nationality arbitrary if it results in statelessness?

It has been argued by some in academic circles and civil society that deprivation of nationality is also arbitrary if it results in statelessness. The academic Johannes Chan has, for instance, maintained that any deprivation of nationality which destroys the right to a nationality itself and renders the person stateless would be contrary to the aims and objectives of the Universal Declaration and thus arbitrary.[19] The NGO Open Society Justice Initiative has similarly claimed that deprivation of nationality that results in statelessness must be considered arbitrary,

---

grounds. The latest of these recognized that 'arbitrary deprivation of nationality, especially on discriminatory grounds such as race, colour, sex, language, religion, political or other opinion, national or social origin, property, birth or other status, is a violation of human rights and fundamental freedoms', see United Nations General Assembly (UNGA), A/HRC/20/L.9 (28 June 2012). For previous resolutions, see UNGA, 'Oral Revisions', A/HRC/13.L4 (19 March 2010); UN Human Rights Council (UNHRC), Res 10/13, A/HRC/RES/10/13 (26 March 2009); UNHRC, Res 7/10, A/HRC/RES/7/10 (27 March 2008); UN Commission on Human Rights, Res 2005/45, E/CN.4/RES/2005/45 (19 April 2005).

[17] UNGA, 'Human Rights and Arbitrary Deprivation of Nationality. Report of the Secretary-General', A/HRC/13/34 (14 December 2009), para. 25.

[18] *Ibid.*, paras. 43–6. These principles are for instance set out in Articles 11 and 12 of the European Convention on Nationality 1997 (ECN) 6 November 1997, in force 1 March 2000, ETS, 166. Article 8(4) of the 1961 Convention provides that decisions on deprivation of nationality should provide the person concerned the right to a fair hearing by a court or other independent body.

[19] Johannes M. M. Chan, 'The Right to a Nationality as a Human Right: The Current Trend towards Recognition', *Human Rights Law Journal* 12(1–2) (1991), at 1, 3.

because the right to a nationality is a fundamental human right.[20] The academic Ruth Donner was also of the opinion that the prohibition against arbitrary deprivation in international law would include deprivation as a discriminatory measure or deprivation resulting in statelessness, or both.[21]

Donner recognized that while it is not certain that laws depriving citizens of their nationality are invalid under international law, there appears to be 'some support in the arguments of learned writers for the view that *de lege ferenda* a withdrawal of nationality is invalid unless accompanied by the acquisition of a new nationality'.[22] More recently, the academic Laura van Waas has questioned whether there is sufficient evidence that deprivation of nationality resulting in statelessness per se qualifies as arbitrary deprivation of nationality and has called for a clarification of the matter at the global level.[23]

In the following sections, this chapter will move on to canvassing international and regional treaties, jurisprudence and UN human rights mechanisms to see to what extent there is a basis for claiming that any deprivation of nationality that renders persons stateless is prohibited under international law. It will also look into the degree to which such a prohibition is reflected in the practice of states. The analysis will show that, even though there is not yet sufficient evidence to support the claims cited above that any case of deprivation of nationality that results in statelessness is arbitrary, it is clear that such deprivation will be arbitrary if it fails to comply with specific procedural and substantive standards.[24] Most importantly, where deprivation of nationality leads to statelessness, it needs to serve a legitimate purpose and observe the proportionality principle.

---

[20] Open Society Justice Initiative, 'Citizenship and Equality in Practice: Guaranteeing Non-Discriminatory Access to Nationality, Protecting the Right to be Free from Arbitrary Deprivation of Nationality, and Combating Statelessness' (submission to the UN Commission on Human Rights for consideration at its 62nd session) (November 2005), p. 9; James A. Goldston, 'Holes in the Rights Framework: Racial Discrimination, Citizenship, and the Rights of Noncitizens', *Ethics and International Affairs* 20(3) (2006), at 321, 333.

[21] Ruth Donner, *The Regulation of Nationality in International Law, Second Edition* (Irvington-on-Hudson, NY: Transnational Publishers, Inc., 1994), 245.

[22] *Ibid.*, 181.

[23] Laura van Waas, *Nationality Matters – Statelessness under International Law* (Antwerp/Oxford/Portland, OR: Intersentia, 2008), 86, 88, 95.

[24] UNGA, A/HRC/13/34, paras. 25, 27.

8.4. When is deprivation of nationality legitimate?

The prohibition against arbitrary deprivation of nationality has been set out in the UDHR, the UN Convention on the Rights of Persons with Disabilities and in regional human rights treaties in the Americas and the Arab world.[25] None of these prohibit deprivation of nationality other than in situations when it is 'arbitrary'.

However, treaties have also been developed to deal specifically with questions of nationality and the prevention of statelessness, in particular where it results from conflicts of laws. The most important of these is the 1961 Convention, which establishes common principles states should apply to prevent statelessness from occurring as a result of how nationality is conferred and withdrawn.

The principles governing withdrawal of nationality are set out in Articles 5 to 9 of the 1961 Convention. The convention distinguishes between two types of such withdrawal: loss of nationality, which is when nationality is withdrawn automatically by the operation of law, and deprivation of nationality, which happens by a discretionary act at the initiative of a state authority.[26] The 1961 Convention lists a range of situations where loss and deprivation of nationality typically occur and serve a legitimate purpose. For each type of withdrawal, it also specifies how states should seek to avoid statelessness. Article 5 for instance aims to prevent statelessness resulting from loss of nationality linked to a change in personal status,[27] while Article 6 concerns situations where withdrawal of nationality causes the individual's wife and/or children also to lose their citizenship. Renunciation of nationality at the initiative of the individual is dealt with in Article 7(1) and (2). In all these situations the 1961 Convention prescribes that citizenship shall only be lost when the individual concerned possesses or acquires another nationality.

Articles 7 and 8 of the 1961 Convention contain a general prohibition against loss and deprivation of nationality if it renders a person stateless (Articles 7(6) and 8(1)). However, at the time the convention was drafted,

---

[25] These are the American Convention on Human Rights and the Arab Charter on Human Rights.

[26] This follows the distinction made between the two concepts in the *travaux préparatoires* of the 1961 Convention, see United Nations Conference on the Elimination or Reduction of Future Statelessness (UN Conference), 'Summary Record of the Fifteenth Meeting' A/CONF.9/C.1/SR.15/24 (April 1961), p. 12; UN Conference, 'Summary Record of the Sixteenth Meeting,' A/CONF.9/C.1/SR.16/24 (April 1961), p. 2.

[27] This includes marriage or the termination of marriage, recognition, legitimation and adoption.

states were not yet prepared to completely prohibit loss or deprivation of nationality that would result in statelessness.[28] Most nationality laws at the time permitted withdrawal of nationality on multiple grounds, and did not limit them to situations where the person concerned avoided becoming stateless. A compromise was thus sought between the general principles in Articles 7(6) and 8(1), and state practice, by listing distinct grounds in Articles 7(4), (5), 8(2) and (3) where loss and deprivation of nationality serve a legitimate purpose even when it renders individuals stateless.[29]

As such, Article 7(3) generally prohibits withdrawal of nationality as a result of departure, residence abroad, failure to register or similar. However, the 1961 Convention makes an exception in two cases: when a naturalized citizen resides abroad for seven years or more and fails to declare an intention to retain his/her nationality (Articles 7(4) and 8(2)(a)), and for citizens who are born abroad and fail to comply with a requirement to return to reside in their country of nationality or to register with an appropriate authority within one year of reaching the age of majority (Articles 7(5) and 8(2)(a)).

The 1961 Convention also permits deprivation of nationality to result in statelessness when:

- nationality is acquired on the basis of misrepresentation or fraud (Article 8(2)(b));
- nationals carry out acts contrary to the duty of loyalty to the state. This includes rendering services to or receiving emoluments from another state in disregard of an express prohibition by the country of nationality (Article 8(3)(a)(i)) and conduct which is seriously prejudicial to the vital interests of the state (Article 8(3)(a)(ii)); and
- an oath or formal declaration of allegiance or definitive evidence of determination to repudiate the allegiance to the state of nationality is given to another state (Article 8(3)(b)).

---

[28] The International Law Commission prepared two draft conventions: one on the elimination and the other on the reduction of future statelessness, in case some states would not be ready to commit to completely avoid future statelessness. The UN Conference on the Elimination or Reduction of Future Statelessness, which was convened by the General Assembly to conclude a convention on the topic, subsequently decided to use the draft Convention on the Reduction of Future Statelessness as the basis for its discussions, UN Conference, 'Organization and Work of the Conference During the Period from 24 March to 17 April 1959' A/CONF.9/12/9 (August 1961), pp. 3–4.

[29] UN Conference, 'Summary Record of the Nineteenth Plenary Meeting' A/CONF.9/SR.19/11 (October 1961), p. 2; UN Conference, 'Summary Record of the Twenty-First Plenary Meeting' A/CONF.9/SR.21/11 (October 1961), p. 3.

It is worth noting that the convention distinguishes between the grounds set out in Article 8(2), which may be applied unconditionally, and those listed in Article 8(3), which can only be used to deprive citizens of their nationality if the contracting states have specified their retention of this right at the time of signature, ratification or accession and on the basis of grounds existing in national legislation at that time. The list of grounds set out in the 1961 Convention is exhaustive, which means that any other ground states may use as a basis for loss or deprivation of nationality cannot be considered to serve a legitimate purpose and can for this reason be viewed as arbitrary.

The grounds for loss and deprivation listed in the 1961 Convention are motivated by two different ideas. Articles 7(4), (5), 8(2)(a) and (3)(b) represent the idea that when citizens are born abroad or reside for a long period of time in another country and fail to take measures to retain their nationality, or they take oaths or make declarations of allegiance to foreign states, they tacitly demonstrate a will to sever their ties with the country of nationality.[30] Historically, this was thought to justify the withdrawal of nationality, even when the individual concerned had not yet acquired the nationality of another state and ended up stateless. The grounds set out in Article 8(2)(b), (3)(i) and (ii), on the other hand, represent situations where deprivation of nationality serves as a punishment, for instance for acts contrary to the duty of loyalty to the state, or as an administrative measure, such as when nationality is fraudulently acquired.

Since 1961, one regional treaty has sought to set out general principles for acquisition, loss and deprivation of nationality: the European Convention on Nationality (ECN), which was adopted by the Council of Europe in 1997.[31] This regional treaty reaffirms many of the principles found in the 1961 Convention, whereas in other respects it refines these principles further.

Compared to the 1961 Convention, the ECN restricts the situations where 'loss of nationality *ex lege* or at the initiative of the State Party' may render a person stateless to just one: 'acquisition of the nationality of the State Party by means of fraudulent conduct, false information or concealment of any relevant fact attributable to the applicant'.[32] The ECN also allows loss of nationality on several other grounds that are similar to

---

[30] Weis, *Nationality and Statelessness in International Law*, 117.

[31] European Convention on Nationality, 6 November 1997, in force 1 March 2000, ETS No. 166.

[32] *Ibid.*, Article 7(1)(b).

those stipulated in the 1961 Convention – including lack of a genuine link between the state and a national residing abroad, voluntary service with a foreign military force or conduct seriously prejudicial to the vital interests of the state party. However, it explicitly prohibits such loss resulting in statelessness.[33]

The Explanatory Report to the ECN outlines in rather vague terms that activities directed against the vital interests of the state include 'treason and other activities directed against the vital interests of the State concerned (for example work for a foreign secret service)'. It moreover explicitly mentions that 'conduct seriously prejudicial to the vital interests of the State Party' would not include 'criminal offences of a general nature, however serious they might be'.[34] Another category of acts which is neither referred to in the Report, nor listed as a ground in the 1961 Convention, but which has been increasingly considered as a basis for deprivation of nationality in the past decade, is terrorism.[35] To the extent that terrorist acts are found to be seriously prejudicial to vital state interests, it would seem that they could fall within the application of Article 8(3)(a)(ii) of the 1961 Convention, as well as Article 7 of the ECN, while criminal offences of a general nature would not.

The analysis in this section has shown that while there is a general guarantee against statelessness resulting from loss or deprivation of nationality in the 1961 Convention, the same convention subsequently allows a series of exceptions to this principle. The only more recent treaty which enunciates principles in this area is a regional treaty: the ECN. We have seen that it limits the situations which may result in statelessness to one, which is where nationality was acquired on the basis of fraudulent conduct, false information or concealment of any relevant fact attributable to the applicant.

Below, the chapter will discuss whether it can be said that the ECN is a reflection of state practice and whether such practice extends beyond Europe to the global level. If this is the case, it may suggest that rendering persons stateless through deprivation of nationality is less tolerable now than in 1961 and that some of the grounds for deprivation of nationality listed in the 1961 Convention are no longer acceptable.

---

[33] *Ibid.*, Art. 7.
[34] Council of Europe, 'European Convention on Nationality, Explanatory Report' ETS No. 166 (1997), p. 67.
[35] Harald Waldrauch, 'Loss of Nationality' in Rainer Bauböck, Eva Ersbøll, Kees Groenendijk and Harald Waldrauch (eds.), *Acquisition and Loss of Nationality. Volume 1: Comparative Analysis. Policies and Trends in 15 European Countries* (Amsterdam University Press, 2006), 23, 29.

8.5. The view of regional courts and UN human rights mechanisms

UN and regional organizations and institutions contribute to the development of new standards of international law through judgments and decisions issued by courts; resolutions from the UN Human Rights Council and General Assembly; and general comments, concluding observations to reports by states parties and decisions on individual communications prepared by UN human rights treaty bodies.

Regional courts have a mixed track record in dealing with cases of deprivation of nationality. The American Convention on Human Rights contains an explicit prohibition on arbitrary deprivation of nationality and the Inter-American Court of Human Rights (I-ACtHR) has found a violation of this prohibition in two judgments.[36] In the case of *Baruch Ivcher Bronstein* v. *Peru*, the owner of a Peruvian TV station was accused by the Fujimori regime of having endangered national security by publishing materials that discredited the army.[37] In this case the court found that the state had violated both the right to a nationality and the right not to be arbitrarily deprived of it in the American Convention on Human Rights.[38] Among the recommendations made by the Inter-American Commission of Human Rights was the proposal that the state should reinstate the victim with his Peruvian nationality, which Peru subsequently did.[39]

The second case of *Yean and Bosico* v. *Dominican Republic* concerned two stateless children of Haitian origin born in the Dominican Republic. The girls were denied birth certificates by the Dominican authorities, which also prevented one of them from attending school for one year. The court held that the children were arbitrarily deprived of nationality contrary to domestic law and on the basis of discrimination. Interestingly, in this judgment the court found that the children had been deprived of a citizenship they never had; in other words, it interpreted arbitrary deprivation to also include arbitrary denial of nationality.[40]

---

[36] In a third judgment, the court found that the fact that four Chilean citizens had been convicted of treason in Peru did not constitute a violation of their right to a nationality because their nationality was not in question, see *Castillo Petruzzi et al.* v. *Peru* (judgment), 30 May 1999, para. 102.

[37] *Ivcher Bronstein Case (Baruch Ivcher Bronstein* v. *Peru)* (judgment), Inter-American Court of Human Rights, 6 February 2001, para. 18.

[38] *Ibid.*, paras. 64–5.   [39] *Ibid.*, paras. 4, 179–80.

[40] *Case of the Yean and Bosico Children* v. *The Dominican Republic* (judgment), Inter-American Court of Human Rights, 6 September 2005, paras. 173–4.

The European Court of Human Rights (ECtHR) and the former European Commission on Human Rights (ECmHR) have been far less progressive. For example, in *Sevket Kafkasli contre Turquie*, the commission found that the state acted within its margin of appreciation and did not violate the right to family life when it imposed limitations on the freedom of movement for a stateless person who had been deprived of his Turkish citizenship based on allegations of espionage.[41] The commission did not pronounce on whether the act of depriving Sevket Kafkasli of his citizenship and thereby rendering him stateless had been wrongful.

The difference between the judgments and decisions in the Inter-American and European human rights bodies to date is striking and can probably be attributed to the fact that the American Convention includes the right to a nationality and not to be arbitrarily deprived of it, whereas the European Convention on Human Rights (ECHR) does not. Consequently, the ECtHR and the former Commission have generally been hesitant to address issues relating to nationality, usually citing in its judgments and decisions that the convention does not guarantee the right to acquire a particular nationality.[42]

The issue of statelessness arising as a result of deprivation of nationality has, however, come up in an important recent judgment in the Court of Justice of the European Union (CJEU): *Janko Rottmann* v. *Freistaat Bayern*.[43] The case established that decisions to withdraw naturalization on the basis of deception may be implemented even if they render individuals stateless, since this is permitted under the ECN and the 1961 Convention. Importantly, however, the court established that such decisions need to take into account the principle of proportionality. What this means will be explored in greater detail in section 8.7 of this chapter.

Deprivation of nationality resulting in statelessness has not often been raised as an issue by any of the UN human rights mechanisms. The exception is a series of UN Commission on Human Rights and UN Human Rights Council Resolutions on arbitrary deprivation of nationality,

---

[41] *Sevket Kafkasli contre Turquie* (App no 21106/92), European Commission on Human Rights, 1 July 1997.

[42] See, for example, *Slepcik v. the Netherlands and the Czech Republic* (App no 30913/96), European Commission on Human Rights, 2 September 1996. However, the judgment in *Genovese v. Malta* (App no 53124/09), ECtHR, 11 October 2011, may indicate that the court has become more open to considering issues relating to nationality. Here the court found a violation of Article 8 read together with Article 14 because the child, who was born out of wedlock, according to Maltese law was denied the right to acquire the father's Maltese nationality.

[43] Case C-135/08 *Janko Rottmann* v. *Freistaat Bayern* [2 March 2010] CJEU.

UN General Assembly Resolution 50/152 from 1995, as well as General Comment No. 27 of the UN Human Rights Committee on freedom of movement.[44]

The UN Commission on Human Rights and Human Rights Council Resolutions are – as their title indicates – concerned with arbitrary deprivation of nationality and urge states to adopt and implement nationality legislation with a view to avoiding statelessness.[45] They do not, however, go as far as to say that any deprivation of nationality that results in statelessness is arbitrary and should be avoided. UN General Assembly Resolution 50/152 sets out the most comprehensive road map to date for work on statelessness. It also called upon states 'to adopt nationality legislation with a view to reducing statelessness, ... in particular by preventing arbitrary deprivation of nationality', while recognizing the right of states to establish laws governing the acquisition, renunciation or loss of nationality.[46]

General Comment No. 27 interprets the right to enter 'one's own country' in Article 12, paragraph 4 of the International Covenant on Civil and Political Rights as including persons who have special ties to or claims in relation to a given country without being nationals of the state. The Human Rights Committee offers by way of example persons 'who have been stripped of their nationality in violation of international law'.[47] It does not, though, define what would constitute deprivation of nationality contrary to international law and it is also beyond the scope of the General Comment to define any deprivation of citizenship that results in statelessness as arbitrary.

In other words, compared for instance to the issue of discrimination between men and women in the right to transmit nationality – which is expressly prohibited in the Convention on the Elimination of All Forms of Discrimination against Women (CEDAW) – the issue of loss or deprivation of nationality resulting in statelessness only appears to have received

[44] This analysis does not include a comprehensive examination of recommendations from the Universal Periodical Review process, or of concluding observations resulting from the examination of state reports by UN human rights treaty bodies.

[45] The most recent resolution calls upon all states 'to refrain from taking discriminatory measures and from enacting or maintaining legislation that would arbitrarily deprive persons of their nationality on grounds of race, colour, sex, language, religion, political or other opinion, national or social origin, property, birth or other status, especially if such measures and legislation render a person stateless'. See A/HRC/26/L.25 (23 June 2014), para. 4.

[46] A/RES/50/152 (21 December 1995).

[47] UN Human Rights Committee, 'General Comment No. 27: Freedom of Movement (Article 12)' 02/11/99, CCPR/C/21/Rev.1/Add.9 (1999), para. 20.

limited attention from UN human rights mechanisms and regional courts. Where it is addressed, this is mostly in the context of arbitrary deprivation of nationality.

The discussion above indicates that among the UN and regional human rights mechanisms, the I-ACtHR is the regional court that has gone furthest in establishing standards on deprivation of nationality in its case law. This has been possible through application of the arbitrary deprivation provision of the ACHR, which is the only effective provision of this kind in a regional treaty. More cases would need to be brought to the court, however, to be able to argue that any deprivation of nationality that results in statelessness is arbitrary.

8.6.   Is there a global trend towards limiting the use of deprivation of nationality?

Through an examination of nationality legislation, summarized in this section, it will become evident to what extent states implement the international principles relating to loss and deprivation of nationality that are set out in the 1961 Convention. It will also show whether states have in fact gone further than this convention in prohibiting any withdrawal of nationality that results in statelessness.

It is particularly important to look at the domestic laws setting out rules for acquisition, retention, loss and deprivation of nationality for this purpose. These rules are usually stipulated in the state's constitution and nationality law. No global study exists yet of nationality laws that could establish a comprehensive understanding of state practice in the area of deprivation of nationality. Comparative studies have, however, been undertaken of nationality legislation in the European Union (EU), as well as in Africa. These shed some light on whether there is a global trend towards prohibiting any deprivation of nationality that renders the individual stateless.

In his 1991 article, Chan analyzed state practice in Western Europe and thought that it indicated acceptance of the principle that 'no one shall be deprived of his nationality if this would lead to statelessness'.[48] However, if his statement is compared with a comprehensive study undertaken by Gerard-René de Groot and Maarten P. Vink in 2010 of the laws in thirty-three European states, it is unclear how Chan arrived at his conclusion. In their study, de Groot and Vink found that in twenty-three of

---

[48] Chan, 'The Right to a Nationality as a Human Right', at 8.

twenty-six countries which allow deprivation of nationality for fraud or misrepresentation, this may render an individual stateless.[49] Among fourteen states that allow deprivation of nationality on the basis of conduct seriously prejudicial to the state's vital interests or acts such as disloyalty, treason, terrorism or crimes against the state, only five clearly limit such deprivation to situations where the individual holds dual citizenship. Finally, four of the fifteen states that allow nationals to have their nationality withdrawn due to entry into the service of a foreign state expressly limit such deprivations to situations where the individual does not become stateless.[50]

In a similar study undertaken by Harald Waldrauch four years earlier of laws in fifteen EU member states, he identified a trend towards making it easier for nationals to be deprived of their nationality rather than the contrary. This was particularly the case with deprivation grounds related to fraud and misrepresentation, crimes against the state and military service for a foreign state.[51] This development partly reflects growing uneasiness in Western Europe about immigration, as well as measures some of the states have taken in the 'war on terrorism'.

In Africa, a comparative study carried out in 2010 by the Open Society Institute of nationality laws in fifty-four countries found that only eight laws had safeguards against statelessness resulting from loss or deprivation of nationality. In addition to these, the laws in four states do not make any provision for the deprivation of nationality.[52] In Africa, it is more difficult to tell whether there is a trend towards growing recognition of avoidance of statelessness as a result of loss and deprivation of nationality, due to a lack of past comparative studies of nationality laws in the region.[53] Moreover, none of the regional treaties in Africa contains a guarantee against arbitrary deprivation of nationality, though the

---

[49] Gerard-René de Groot and Maarten P. Vink, *Loss of Citizenship. Trends and Regulations in Europe* (EUDO Citizenship Observatory, Robert Schuman Centre for Advanced Studies in collaboration with Edinburgh University Law School, June 2010, revised October 2010), 16–18.

[50] *Ibid.*, 22–3.   [51] Waldrauch, 'Loss of Nationality', 29.

[52] Bronwen Manby, *Citizenship Law in Africa: A Comparative Study* (New York: AfriMAP & Open Society Justice Initiative, 2009), 84–5.

[53] In five African countries where nationality legislation has been amended since 2009, two countries – Kenya and Zimbabwe – introduced additional safeguards against statelessness in cases of loss and deprivation of citizenship. According to the 2010 Kenyan Constitution and the 2013 Zimbabwean Constitution, residence abroad no longer serves as a ground for depriving naturalized citizens of their citizenship. On the other hand,

African Charter on the Rights and Welfare of the Child includes the right to a nationality.[54]

Although no comparative study has yet been undertaken of nationality laws on the Asian continent, there is reason to believe that the situation in these countries is similar to the one in Africa. On both continents, most nationality laws were influenced by the laws of a former colonial power, predecessor states or another state with strong historical influence in the country.[55] At the time the countries became independent, the laws that were adopted generally permitted deprivation of nationality on multiple grounds, even when it resulted in statelessness. Only in some cases have these laws been significantly reformed since independence[56] to limit the grounds through which persons can become stateless through deprivation of citizenship. However, no trend can be discerned in Asia towards prohibiting all cases of deprivation of nationality resulting in statelessness. A comparative study has also yet to be undertaken of laws on the American continent.

The examination of trends in nationality legislation shows that the great majority of states do not consider that all cases of deprivation of nationality that result in statelessness should be prohibited. However, there does appear to be a global trend towards eliminating certain grounds for deprivation of nationality that are 'out of tune' with other developments in

in Guinea-Bissau and South Africa, the amendments either maintained the existing grounds for deprivation of citizenship or introduced new ones. The latter was the case in South Africa, where the 2010 amendment to the Citizenship Act permits naturalized citizens to be deprived of their South African citizenship if they 'engage, under the flag of another country, in a war that the Republic does not support' (Section 6 of the South African Citizenship Amendment Act 2010, adopted on 3 December 2010).

54   African Charter on the Rights and Welfare of the Child, July 1990, in force 29 November 1999, OAU Doc. CAB/LEG/24.9/49 (1990), Art. 6(3).

55   The latter is the case with Afghanistan, Lao PDR, Mongolia and Vietnam, which were under strong Soviet influence during the cold war and have nationality laws with many similarities to the USSR Citizenship Law.

56   Five notable examples from the past decade are Indonesia, Iraq, Kyrgyzstan, Kazakhstan and Nepal. In Nepal the new Citizenship Act adopted in 2006 removed most of the grounds that had existed for deprivation of citizenship in the 1964 Citizenship Act, leaving fraudulent acquisition of nationality as the only remaining one. In Indonesia, Kyrgyzstan and Kazakhstan, the new or amended Citizenship Laws adopted in 2006, 2007 and 2011, respectively, introduced a safeguard against statelessness in situations where citizens reside abroad and fail to declare their intention to retain their citizenship, but did not otherwise limit the grounds for deprivation of nationality. In Iraq, a new Citizenship Law was also adopted in 2006. It removed foreign service as a reason for withdrawal of nationality but introduced fraud and misrepresentation as new grounds.

international law. Desertion and evasion of military service, for instance, have all but disappeared as grounds for deprivation, perhaps partly as a result of the growing acceptance of conscientious objection.[57] Prolonged residence abroad is similarly becoming less and less considered a legitimate purpose for deprivation of nationality, as exemplified by the recent legal reforms in Indonesia, Kenya, Kazakhstan, Kyrgyzstan, Nepal and Zimbabwe referred to in this section. In Europe, only three of the thirteen states that maintain this ground for deprivation in their laws allow it to result in statelessness.[58] This development may reflect the positive impact of 1961 Convention standards on nationality legislation, even beyond the state parties to the convention.[59]

8.7. Limitations on deprivation of nationality: the question of proportionality

Decisions to deprive a person of his or her nationality must follow certain procedural and substantive standards, which include the principle of proportionality. Proportionality means that the decision should assess the aim of the measure against its impact on the persons affected; there must be 'a reasonable relationship of proportionality between the means deployed and the aim sought to be realised'.[60]

8.7.1 Selecting the 'least intrusive means'

The main significance of the *Rottmann* case, referred to in section 8.5, is that it established that decisions to deprive persons of their citizenship for deception must observe the principle of proportionality. As such, they must take into account, among other things, the gravity of the offence committed compared to the consequences withdrawal of

---

[57] See, for instance, UN Human Rights Committee, 'General Comment No. 22: The Right to Freedom of Thought, Conscience and Religion (Article 18)' 10/11/89 (1993), para. 11; UN Human Rights Council, 'Conscientious objection to military service' A/HRC/24/L.23, 23 September 2013.

[58] de Groot and Vink, *Loss of Citizenship*, 32–3.

[59] Article 7(3) of the 1961 Convention prohibits loss of nationality resulting in statelessness on the basis of departure or residence abroad.

[60] The principle is, for instance, frequently referred to in judgments from the European Court of Human Rights, see D. J. Harris, M. O'Boyle, Colin Warbrick and Ed Bates, *Harris, O'Boyle and Warbrick: Law of the European Convention on Human Rights*, 2nd edn (Oxford University Press, 2009), 10–11.

nationality entails for the person concerned.[61] The link of the persons affected with the state would be one of the factors to consider in these cases,[62] with relevant links being, for example, residence in the territory of the state or marriage to a national. Time is also of relevance to proportionality, both for establishing the profoundness of an individual's link with the state based on residence and to limit the scope for depriving persons of their nationality several years after committing the act on which the deprivation decision is based. It thus becomes important that the means selected be the least intrusive amongst those that might achieve the desired result.[63]

Some of the acts which may lead to deprivation of nationality have traditionally been met with the most serious punishment available to the state: death penalty or life imprisonment. This has typically been the case for persons convicted of treason or espionage. In terms of the consequences for the person concerned, it is clearly preferable to be rendered stateless, as spending life as a stateless person does not compare to spending the rest of one's life in prison, or of course, being deprived of one's life altogether.[64]

For crimes which are typically punished with shorter sentences, it is more questionable what punishment carries worse consequences for the individual: statelessness or imprisonment. While a prison sentence has an exact time limit, statelessness does not and may not even be resolved during a person's lifetime.[65] Most individuals rendered stateless, moreover, face serious problems regularizing their stay and enjoying basic rights in the country where they reside. In many states, the fact that an individual is rendered stateless through deprivation of nationality may also cause nationality to be withdrawn from his or her children[66] and in a few states

---

[61] *Rottmann*, paras. 55–6.

[62] Council of Europe Committee of Ministers, 'Recommendation R (1999) 18 of the Committee of Ministers to Member States on the Avoidance and Reduction of Statelessness' (15 September 1999), para c).

[63] UNHRC, 'General Comment No. 27', para. 14.

[64] This was, for instance, the argument of International Law Commission (ILC) member Scelle during the discussions about the draft Convention on the Elimination of Future Statelessness, which led to the adoption of the 1961 Convention, see United Nations, '214th Meeting' (1953) *I Y.B. Int'l L. Comm'n, Summary records of the fifth session'* (1 June–14 August 1953), at 194.

[65] This difference between deprivation of nationality, which is 'final and irrevocable', and other types of penalties was stressed by Hsu in the same ILC meeting, *ibid.*, at 194.

[66] For instance, in six of the twenty-two European states that allow persons to be rendered stateless as a result of fraud or misrepresentation, deprivation of nationality may also be extended to the persons' children, see 'Modes of Loss Database', European Union

even from the spouse.[67] Because of these consequences for the individuals affected, it has been argued that states should maintain a high standard of proof when decisions are made to deprive individuals of their nationality.[68] They may also resort to other measures to reach their aims.[69] It has, for instance, been suggested that if a primary goal is to prevent individuals from exercising political influence, withholding their voting rights and opportunity to run for office may be equally efficient as withdrawing their nationality.[70]

From the perspective of selecting the less intrusive means to achieve an aim, it would thus seem that deprivation of nationality may be proportional as a punishment in the case of very serious offences, such as treason or espionage. However, deprivation is not proportional in the case of less serious offences when other measures can be taken that have a less detrimental effect on the individual. It was already mentioned above that common crimes do not fall within the scope of Article 8 of the 1961 Convention, which reflects the fact that most states use other types of punishment to address such cases. Proportionality considerations may be part of the explanation for this.

Democracy Observatory on Citizenship, available at: http://eudo-citizenship.eu/data-bases/modes-of-loss?p=&application=modesLoss&search=1&modeby=idmode&idmo de=L11, last accessed 23 May 2014.

[67] In Europe, deprivation of nationality on the basis of fraud affects also the spouse in only one state: Bulgaria, see *ibid.*, http://eudo-citizenship.eu/databases/modes-of-loss?p=& application=modesLoss&search=1&modeby=idmode&idmode=L11. The practice of extending the deprivation to a person's spouse or children is contrary to Article 6 of the 1961 Convention.

[68] Charles H. Hooker, 'Comment: The Past as Prologue: Schneiderman v. United States and Contemporary Questions of Citizenship and Denationalization', *Emory International Law Review* 19 (Spring, 2005), 325. Hooker shows how denationalization decisions in the USA rely on the Supreme Court decision in *Schneiderman v. United States*, which introduced a new and higher standard of proof for such proceedings. The justification for this was that the stakes are so high in such cases and the loss so severe for the individual that the government would need to prove non-allegiance by 'clear, unequivocal, and convincing evidence which does not leave the issue in doubt', Hooker, 325.

[69] This was, for instance, argued by Chief Justice Warren in the US Supreme Court case of *Trop v. Dulles* in 1958. See *Trop v. Dulles, Secretary of State, et al.,* 356 US 86 (1958).

[70] Emmanuel Gross, 'Defensive Democracy: Is it Possible to Revoke the Citizenship, Deport, or Negate the Civil Rights of a Person Instigating Terrorist Action against his own State' *UMKC Law Review,* 72(51) (Fall 2003), 92–4; Shai Lavi, 'Citizenship Revocation as Punishment: On the Modern Duties of Citizens and their Criminal Breach' *University of Toronto Law Journal* 61 (2011), 806.

8.7.2   Selecting the means that best serve the aim sought to be achieved

Another element of the proportionality principle is to what extent deprivation of nationality serves the aim sought to be achieved. T. Alexander Aleinikoff found that denationalization grounds can be grouped into three categories depending on their purpose: those addressing issues of allegiance, those acting as punishment and those aimed at ensuring public order.[71] It should be noted, however, that many situations appear to fall into more than one of these categories. For instance, when service with a foreign army leads to deprivation of nationality, it seems to both act as a punishment and address issues of allegiance or loyalty, whereas in discussions about terrorism and deprivation of nationality, issues of allegiance/loyalty are linked with concerns for public order.

A distinction may also be drawn between deprivation of nationality serving as punishment and deprivation used as an administrative measure. Where deprivation of nationality is used as punishment, it enters among the range of punitive measures available to the state to fulfil the traditional aims of punishment, central among which are retribution, prevention and deterrence.[72] On the issue of prevention, for instance, if the choice is between imprisoning an individual or taking away his or her citizenship, the likelihood that the individual will continue committing offences after release from a prison sentence needs to be compared with the prospect that the individual continues committing crimes after the citizenship has been withdrawn, which may speak in favour of imprisonment.

It needs to be stressed here that deprivation of nationality is only one among several types of punishment available to the state and that they must therefore be wary of using it in addition to another type of punishment, such as a prison sentence, already imposed against an individual at a different time for the same crime. Such 'double punishment' would violate the principle of *ne bis in idem* or double jeopardy. This issue was raised in the 2006 appeal case against the Muslim preacher Abu Hamza in the United Kingdom, where the appellant contended that the fact that the Home Secretary had elected to remove his citizenship in 2003 by way of punishment for the conduct he was subsequently prosecuted for constituted an

---

[71] T. Alexander Aleinikoff, 'Symposium on Law and Community: Theories of Loss of Citizenship' *Michigan Law Review* 84 (June 1986), 1473–6.
[72] Lavi, 'Citizenship Revocation as Punishment', 788–9.

abuse of process. The judge, however, rejected the claim, as the evidence relied on by the Secretary of State was different from the evidence the criminal indictment was based on, plus the decisions were the competence of different officers of state and fell to be made on different principles.[73]

Where deprivation of citizenship is carried out both as a punishment and as an administrative measure, preserving national security and/or public safety and order is often an overriding concern. In such cases, deprivation of nationality may be used to *facilitate subsequent deportation* or to *prevent persons from entering the territory of the state* if they are abroad.[74] In the UK, the scope for depriving citizens of their nationality appears to have been broadened specifically to make it easier to expel individuals from the country for national security reasons.[75]

General Comment No. 27 of the Human Rights Committee interprets the right to enter one's own country as including the principle whereby a state 'must not, by stripping a person of nationality or by expelling an individual to a third country, arbitrarily prevent this person from returning to his/her country'.[76] In line with the explanation of the concept of 'arbitrariness' above, this could, for instance, be the case where the prevention of return is not based on law or where it is discriminatory. At the same time, the Explanatory Report of the Fourth Protocol to the ECHR indicates that although the drafting committee approved the principle that states 'would be forbidden to deprive a national of his nationality for the purpose of expelling him', they elected to leave such a provision out of the ECHR due to the delicate nature of deprivation of nationality.[77] The admissibility decision in *Naumov* v. *Albania,* however, hints to the fact

---

[73] *Regina* v. *Abu Hamza* [2006] ECWA Crim 2918, [2007] Q.B. 659, pp. 14–15, Similarly, the ECtHR has found in *R.T.* v. *Switzerland* that sanctions that were issued at the same time by two different authorities, for instance a criminal and an administrative authority, do not violate the principle of *ne bis in idem,* see *R.T.* v. *Switzerland* (App. no. 31982/96), ECHR, 30 May 2000.

[74] Council of Europe Bureau of the European Committee on Legal Co-operation, 'Nationality Issues and the Denial of Residence in the Context of the Fight against Terrorism – Feasibility Study' (Strasbourg 5 December 2006), CDCJ-BU 22 (2006), 10; Gross, 'Defensive Democracy', 87–9.

[75] Hina Majid, 'Protecting the Right to Have Rights: The Case of Section 56 of the Immigration, Asylum and Nationality Act 2006', *Journal of Immigration Asylum and Nationality Law* 22(1) (2008), 27. See Chapter 11 by Rubenstein and Lenagh-Maguire in this book.

[76] HRC, 'General Comment No. 27', para. 21.

[77] Council of Europe, 'Protocol No. 4 to the European Convention for the Protection of Human Rights and Fundamental Freedoms. Explanatory Report' (1965) (ETS No. 46), para. 23.

that revocation of citizenship followed by expulsion may, in some cases, raise problems under Article 3 of this Protocol.[78]

If an individual is rendered stateless through deprivation of nationality, it is, moreover, generally considered as a violation of the territorial sovereignty of the other state to deny these individuals residence and expel them to that state or to refuse to readmit them, as it pushes the responsibility of the person considered a security threat onto other states.[79] States are likely to refuse to accept these individuals on their territory.[80] It can thus be concluded that deprivation of citizenship which renders a person stateless is not legitimate where the aim is expulsion.

Is the measure proportional to the aim sought to be achieved when the state deprives persons of their nationality for the purpose of increasing internal security but *without subsequently expelling them to another country*? Although statelessness normally makes individuals unable to vote or to be elected, leaving individuals stateless in their former country of nationality would not otherwise remove the threat to national security and public safety and order[81] unless additional measures are taken. On the contrary, the severe impact statelessness has on individuals may make them more inclined to continue acting against the state.

In some situations, preventing travel abroad is part of the purpose of withdrawing the nationality of an individual and indeed statelessness usually creates major obstacles for international travel. In human rights law, states are permitted to restrict the right to enter and leave one's own country on the basis of concerns for, among others, national security and public order. Such restrictions must, however, be provided by law, necessary in a democratic society and consistent with all other rights recognized in human rights treaties.[82] Considering the human cost of deprivation of nationality, states should consider other, less intrusive measures available for restricting travel abroad for particular individuals.

The discussion above has demonstrated that deprivation of nationality is rarely the means that best serves the aim sought to be achieved, in particular if there is a great risk that the persons concerned will

---

[78] *Naumov* v. *Albania* (App no 10513/03), ECHR, 4 January 2005.
[79] Weis, *Nationality and Statelessness in International* Law, 125–6; Gross, 'Defensive Democracy', 90–2; Lavi, 'Citizenship Revocation as Punishment', 808. See Chapter 1 by Edwards in this book.
[80] Council of Europe, 'Nationality Issues and the Denial of Residence', 11.
[81] *Ibid.*, 11.
[82] HRC, 'General Comment No. 27', para. 11.

continue to pose a threat to national security and public safety and order if they are deprived of their nationality but not deprived of their liberty. In cases where states use deprivation of nationality as a measure to enable them to expel persons posing a security threat or to prevent them from re-entering the country, this may violate principles of international law.

8.8. Conclusion

Arbitrary deprivation of nationality includes situations where deprivation takes place contrary to a state's laws, or in line with these laws, but on the basis of discrimination or without following certain procedural and substantive standards. While there is no doubt that deprivation on the basis of race or ethnicity – such as the denationalization of the Jews by the Nazi regime in Germany during the Second World War – is arbitrary, distinguishing in some other situations when such decisions are arbitrary may be more difficult. As an example, the 1961 Convention permits deprivation of nationality resulting in statelessness on the basis of conduct that is prejudicial to the vital interests of the state but what kind of conduct does this refer to? Desertion was, for instance, considered a legitimate ground for deprivation of nationality at the time the 1961 Convention was drafted. Today, such deprivation may be considered arbitrary on the basis of international human rights law. On the other hand, the drafters of the 1961 Convention did not discuss terrorism as a ground for deprivation of nationality, yet in the post 9/11 world it seems plausible that terrorist acts would be considered seriously prejudicial to vital state interests. However, this in turn raises questions as to what acts can be categorized as 'terrorism' – a concept which remains ill-defined in international law. This discussion indicates that the legitimate purposes of deprivation of nationality are evolving as international law also develops.

Moreover, the chapter found that deprivation of nationality rendering persons stateless is considered arbitrary, and thus prohibited, except when it serves a legitimate purpose and follows the principle of proportionality. The legitimate purposes are set out in international and regional treaties, such as the 1961 Convention and the ECN. As for the principle of proportionality, this chapter discussed how the *Rottmann* judgment of the CJEU has helped concretize its relevance for decisions on deprivation of nationality. Further jurisprudence both at the regional and domestic level may over time help to define this further.

As demonstrated in the case of the Times Square bomber, serious acts that threaten national security and public safety tend to provoke discussions about deprivation of nationality. In what situations would such deprivation be proportionate to the aim sought, such as the desire to protect national security, considering the array of other measures available to states? In the concrete case, Faisal Shahzad was sentenced to life imprisonment and was not deprived of his US citizenship. The discussion above sought to bring out some of the considerations that would speak in favour of applying one or the other measure. Considering the great human cost of statelessness, however, there is reason to argue that deprivation of nationality should only be exceptionally applied when the result is statelessness.

Questions to guide discussion

1. When will the deprivation of nationality be arbitrary? Is the deprivation of nationality resulting in statelessness arbitrary per se?
2. According to the 1961 Convention, when can nationals be legitimately deprived of their nationality?
3. In what situations, according to the ECN, can a state legitimately render a person stateless?
4. What arguments can be made for (and against) concluding that there is a global trend towards prohibiting any deprivation of nationality which renders the individual stateless? Are there any current issues that could influence this trend?
5. Describe the proportionality principle as established in *Rottmann*. Should other factors be included or omitted in the test? If so, what factors, and why is this the case?

9

State succession and issues of nationality and statelessness

INETA ZIEMELE

9.1. Introduction

The wave of disappearances or dissolutions of states that took place in the 1990s, especially in Europe, created a vast problem for many of the nationals of these former states, specifically in relation to citizenship status, and left many persons stateless. This is not the first time that world history has witnessed such consequences of state succession. For instance, the period of decolonization in the 1960s and 1970s saw similar problems, with the emergence of many newly independent states.

The international community has shown concern as to the resolution of nationality problems in these situations and 'such concerns have re-emerged in connection with recent cases of succession of States'.[1] Through the work of the International Law Commission (ILC) on the *Articles on Nationality in relation to the Succession of States* ('Articles on Nationality'), an insight can be gained into what, more specifically, these concerns are. First of all, paragraph six of the accompanying commentary refers to the protection of human rights of persons whose nationality may be affected by a succession of states. Secondly, paragraph eight of the commentary points out the need for greater juridical security for states and for individuals. In many ways, the concerns remain classical in that where an individual does not have a nationality or the nationality status is uncertain, he or she is much less protected and more vulnerable to abuse. This reality comes up in different contexts, but can present an especially acute challenge in state succession situations. As such, the response of the international community to nationality in the specific state succession context is the focus of the present chapter.

---

[1] See Articles on Nationality of Natural Persons in relation to the Succession of States with commentaries, 1999, *Yearbook of the International Law Commission*, 1999, vol. II, Part Two, pp. 23–4.

The chapter begins by outlining how the succession of states has historically been viewed under international law and by commentators, presenting some of the major developments in thinking and debate in this field. Thereafter, an overview is provided of international law instruments that contain relevant rules and principles for the regulation of nationality in situations of state succession. I will attempt to highlight the concerns and the aims that international efforts in this area have tried to cater for. I will also look at the role that nationality was considered to play in situations of change of sovereignty and how the emergence of human rights has influenced this. Lastly, I will look more closely at the phenomenon of state succession by exploring the meaning and importance of different types of change of sovereignty over the territory.

For the purposes of this chapter I adopt the following description of the phenomenon of state succession, as provided for in Article 2 of the two Vienna Conventions on State Succession and as followed by all other legislative efforts, i.e., 'Succession of States' means the replacement of one state by another in the responsibility for the international relations of territory and assuming that such replacement generally falls within the framework of international law. I will also touch upon instances of replacement of one state by another, which are often described as transitions from illegal regime and where very special questions arise concerning both the qualification of this transition process and solutions to be adopted in relation to nationality. It is in this respect that the decolonization process is of interest and the way it was approached within the law of state succession.

9.2.   The state succession paradigm

The key question underlying this chapter is whether international law sets forth rules or principles which may obligate the states concerned to solve, in one way or another, the nationality status of those individuals who may be affected by state succession. The views in the classical legal literature of the mid-twentieth century – coinciding with the major wave of decolonization – were divided. In Ian Brownlie's analysis, 'the population follows the change of sovereignty in matters of nationality'.[2] Manley Hudson argued that such a rule did not reflect state practice because nationality

---

[2] See I. Brownlie, 'The Relations of Nationality in Public International Law', *British Yearbook of International Law* 39 (1963), 320.

was not necessarily attributed to all inhabitants in these situations.[3] Daniel O'Connell observed that: 'Undesirable as it may be that any person becomes stateless as a result of a change of sovereignty, it cannot be asserted with any measure of confidence that international law, at least, in its present stage of development, imposes any duty on the successor State to grant nationality'.[4] He qualified this problem as 'one of the most difficult problems in the law of State succession'[5] and called for codification or legislation at an international level.[6]

In fact, the topic of succession of states and governments was one of the topics that the ILC selected as early as its first session, in 1949, with a view to their codification. The question of nationality, which was covered by a broader title, namely, 'Status of the inhabitants', was the first part of the codification efforts under the title 'Succession in respect of matters other than treaties'. However, in view of the breadth and complexity of the topic it was later narrowed down to the economic aspects of succession. Nationality was not included.[7] Subsequently, it took several more decades and one more wave of dissolutions and disappearances of states for the international community to react and adopt several documents containing some rules and principles relevant to the regulation of nationality in cases of succession.

The 1990s wave of dissolutions of states took place within a different legal and political reality, one which can be characterized by denser legal regulation in general and in the field of human rights in particular. Apart from the fact of more legal regulation, the nature of modern international law had seemingly changed. In the decolonization period of the 1960s and 1970s, the manner in which succession issues were addressed represented an attempt to part from international law's colonial past.[8] The vindication of the 'clean slate' principle in the Vienna Conventions on

---

[3] See M. Hudson, 'Nationality, Including Statelessness' *Yearbook of the International Law Commission* 2, Part Three (1952), 7.

[4] See D. P. O'Connell, *State Succession in Municipal and International Law* vol. I (Cambridge University Press, 1967) 499, 503.

[5] *Ibid.*   [6] *Ibid.*

[7] Vaclav Mikulka, Special Rapporteur on Succession of States with respect to Nationality/ Nationality in relation to the succession of States, 'First report on State succession and its impact on the nationality of natural and legal persons', A/CN.4/467, (Mikulka Report) paras. 5–6.

[8] See A. Anghie, 'The Evolution of International Law: Colonial and Postcolonial Realities' *Third World Quarterly* 27(5) (2006), 739.

State Succession,[9] even if recognizing a number of limitations, was seen as a proper functioning of self-determination and the sovereign equality of states, as reflected in the UN Charter.[10] At the same time, international law has always been preoccupied with the search for legal continuity and has disliked the disruption represented by the 'clean slate' principle. It is therefore no surprise that the majority of commentators of the events in the 1990s were engaged in the search for arguments that would support the least possible disruption in legal relations. Mathew Craven notes in this regard that '[a]ll were agreed that the "new events" were profoundly different from the past, and the sense of contestation that had under-pinned discussions during decolonization was almost entirely absent'.[11]

Thus, the ILC, when working on the Articles on Nationality in the 1990s, took the following approach to the practice generated during the decolonization process:

> Notwithstanding the fact that the Commission has duly taken into account the practice of States during the process of decolonization for the purpose of the elaboration of the provisions in Part I, it decided to limit the specific categories of succession dealt with in Part II to the following: transfer of part of the territory, unification of States, dissolution of a State and separation of part of the territory. It did not include in this Part a separate section on 'Newly independent States', as it believed that one of the above four sections would be applicable, mutatis mutandis, in any remaining case of decolonization in the future.[12]

The ILC considered that the general principles within the broad categories of state succession which it identified would apply to any possible newly independent state.

It is important to point out in this context that Article 3 of the Articles on Nationality makes a clarification of the scope of the Articles in that:

> The present draft articles apply only to the effects of a succession of States occurring in conformity with international law and, in particular, with the principles of international law embodied in the Charter of the United Nations.

---

[9] See Vienna Convention on Succession of States in Respect of Treaties, Vienna, 23 August 1978, in force 6 November 1996, 1946 UNTS 3; Vienna Convention on Succession of States in Respect of State Property, Archives and Debts, Vienna, 18 April 1983, not yet in force, 22 ILM 308.

[10] See M. Craven, *The Decolonization of International Law. State Succession and the Law of Treaties* (Oxford University Press, 2007), 263.

[11] *Ibid.*, 264.

[12] See Articles on Nationality, p. 23.

In the commentary to this article the ILC explains that 'it was not incumbent upon it to study questions of nationality which could arise in situations such as illegal annexation of territory'.[13] Nevertheless illegal territorial transfers also generate questions about the status of the populations. I submit that the wave of dissolutions of the 1990s embraced also situations that more properly fall within this category of illegal territorial regimes. However, it is true that since the codification work of the law of state succession has focused on 'normal' situations of state succession, and since the decolonization process received a somewhat separate approach, state practice and debate on cases outside this scope have shown to be rather inconsistent. This chapter will nevertheless make a few remarks in this regard in section 9.4.

Given the foregoing developments, the question arises of what effect the evolution in rules and nature of international law has had with respect to the problem of statelessness and nationality in situations of state succession. The analysis of this question has to be situated within a broader analysis as to whether the traditional paradigm that considered nationality as a matter of state sovereignty and national identity is changing. In other words, is the individual rights paradigm meant to trump the discretionary power of states in this field and in relation to specific claims related to sovereignty, identity and security that successor states have raised in the past and continue to raise today?[14] These questions will be dealt with as the chapter further explores the international law on nationality in the context of state succession.

9.3.   The law of state succession and nationality

The acquisition and loss of nationality has traditionally been a matter for each state to regulate under municipal law and in accordance with its own interests and values. It follows that the main principle and point of departure for any discussion on nationality, is that 'it is for each State to determine under its own laws who are its nationals'.[15] However, over the past century, states have cooperated to agree international rules that would influence the content of these municipal laws, in order to address certain nationality questions (such as dual nationality and statelessness)

---

[13] *Ibid.*, p. 27.   [14] See also Chapter 1 by Edwards in this volume.
[15] Convention on Certain Questions Relating to the Conflict of Nationality Law, The Hague, 13 April 1930, in force 1 July 1937, 179 LNTS 89. See further Chapter 1 by Edwards in this book.

or provide guidance for particular contexts in which the issue of nationality arises (such as the succession of states).

The initial approach to questions relating to nationality in situations of state succession was very much in line with the notion expressed above: that it is for the state concerned to deal with as a matter of sovereign interest. Early instruments did not delineate whose nationality would or should be affected by state succession, or how.[16] Even when the decolonization process of the 1960s and 1970s raised new questions about the nationality and residence status of different groups of inhabitants in these territories, the issue was not legislated at an international level, giving preference to a case-by-case approach and the principle of self-determination in these cases.[17] The 1961 Convention on the Reduction of Statelessness,[18] which sought to limit the incidence of statelessness in various contexts, also takes a rather minimalist approach in relation to the regulation of nationality following state succession. Article 10 called for treaties that provide for the transfer of territory to include provisions 'designed to secure that no person shall become stateless as a result of the transfer' – an obligation of conduct only, rather than result. However, where states have failed to agree such provisions, the second paragraph of Article 10 does establish an explicit obligation for the state to which territory is transferred to 'confer its nationality on such persons as would otherwise become stateless as a result of the transfer or acquisition'.[19] This is one of the first norms laid down in a general instrument of international law for the regulation of nationality in the context of state succession.

Yet, it was only after the last major wave of state successions in the 1990s that international law really made strides in elaborating standards for the regulation of nationality in this context. These state successions affected Europe in particular and, as such, the Council of Europe took an active

---

[16] For instance, the Latin American States' Code of Private International Law adopted in 1928 (known as the Bustamante Code) acknowledged that, while the nationality of a population could be collectively affected by the transfer of sovereignty, it is for the new state to develop rules for determining who its nationals are on a case-by-case basis. See further I. Ziemele, *State Continuity and Nationality: The Baltic States and Russia* (Leiden: Martinus Nijhoff Publishers, 2005), 192–3.

[17] R. Hofmann, 'Denaturalization and Forced Exile', in R. Wolfrum (ed.), *The Max Planck Encyclopedia of Public International Law* vol. III (Oxford University Press, 2012), 33.

[18] Convention on the Reduction of Statelessness, New York, 30 August 1961, in force 13 December 1975, 989 UNTS 175.

[19] See further on the content of the 1961 Statelessness Convention in relation to the avoidance of statelessness following state succession, L. E. van Waas, *Nationality Matters. Statelessness under International Law* (Antwerp/Oxford/Portland, OR: Intersentia, 2008), 130–4.

role in addressing the issues and problems that arose in this context. One of the key questions was that of the status of inhabitants in a number of former federal states.

In the following sections, the development of standards in the Council of Europe will therefore be discussed first, before turning to the work pursued at United Nations level. As the presentation of relevant instruments advances in this chapter, I will pay attention to the inter-play between the principles of the right to a nationality, avoidance of statelessness and the right of option and the criterion of genuine or effective link to the territory. Since the 1990s, normative efforts in the field of nationality and state succession were based on these principles and, most importantly, on the search for a proper balance between them.

9.3.1   Council of Europe

The first step taken in the Council of Europe was the adoption in 1980, by the European Commission for Democracy through Law (the Venice Commission), of a Declaration on the Consequences of State Succession for the Nationality of Natural Persons (hereafter the Venice Declaration).[20] The Venice Declaration does not express any particular view on the meaning of nationality and its function in relation to state succession, but a vision emerges from a set of principles that the Venice Commission identifies as relevant for its work in drafting the Declaration. The Venice Commission thus took the following principles as a backbone for its work:

(a)   the principle that questions of nationality fall within the national jurisdiction of each state;[21]
(b)   the principle that everyone has the right to a nationality, and
(c)   the principle that statelessness must be avoided.

Bearing these principles in mind and keeping in view state practice, the Venice Commission established that all the nationals of the predecessor state, who are genuinely resident in the transferred territory – the condition of attachment to this territory is of paramount importance – lose the

---

[20] See Declaration on the Consequences of State Succession for the Nationality of Natural Persons (and commentary), reproduced in Council of Europe, European Commission for Democracy through Law, 'Consequences of State Succession for Nationality' CDL-INF (97).

[21] *Nationality Decrees issued in Tunis and Morocco*, PCIJ Advisory Opinion of 7 February 1923, Series B, No. 4, p. 24.

nationality of the predecessor state and acquire that of the successor state. It follows that the successor state may choose not to confer its nationality on those nationals of the predecessor state who do not have effective links with the transferred territory, or on those who are resident in the territory for reasons of public service, such as civil servants of the predecessor state, members of the armed forces, etc. The Commission also noted the importance of taking into consideration the wishes of the individuals concerned and thus discerns the importance of the right to opt where possible.

It is interesting to note that the Venice Commission speaks about genuine residence in the territory subject to succession events and specifies that individuals who belonged to the state apparatus of the predecessor state may not have such genuine connection with the territory. This position of the Commission indicates a certain view of nationality. I would submit that the Venice Commission did not abandon the view that generally nationality evidences certain loyalty or some sort of attachment to the political entity concerned. I believe that the genuine attachment to the territory should be seen in this context, which explains the view adopted by the Venice Commission that individuals loyal to the state apparatus of the predecessor state form a separate group and require special consideration when a new state determines its nationals. Here, one can recall one of the main premises that the ILC identified at the early stages of its work on Articles on Nationality. It was pointed out that:

> The problem of nationality is closely linked to the phenomenon of population as one of the constitutive elements of the State, because '[i]f States are territorial entities, they are also aggregates of individuals'.[22]

While statehood is contingent on the existence of at least some permanent population, nationality is contingent on decisions of the state. And, being in fact 'a manifestation of sovereignty, nationality is jealously guarded by States'.[23] It can be argued that the Venice Commission was especially mindful of the particular relationship between nationality and state sovereignty when adopting the Declaration.

In this regard, it is useful to look briefly at the meaning of nationality. Article 2 of the 1997 European Convention on Nationality (ECN) defines

---

[22] See J. Crawford, *The Creation of States in International Law* (Oxford: Clarendon Press, 1979), 40.

[23] See J. M. M. Chan, 'The Right to a Nationality as a Human Right: The Current Trend Towards Recognition', *Human Rights Law Journal* 12 (1991), 1; Mikulka Report, para. 35.

nationality as 'the legal bond between a person and a State that does not indicate the person's ethnic origin'.[24] The Explanatory Report to the ECN states that 'It thus refers to a specific legal relationship between an individual and a State which is recognised by that State.'[25] It should be recalled that the International Court of Justice (ICJ) in the *Nottebohm* case defined nationality as 'a legal bond having as its basis a social fact of attachment, a genuine connection of existence, interests and sentiments, together with the existence of reciprocal rights and duties'.[26] Even if the ECN does not refer to the sense of belonging aspect of nationality, as compared with the ICJ's approach, the fact is that the Explanatory Report to the ECN takes the *Nottebohm* case as its point of departure.[27] It is therefore necessary to understand the meaning of the description attributed by the Explanatory Report to the bond of nationality as being 'specific' and its reference to the *Nottebohm* judgment.

Neither the text of the ECN nor the Report explains directly what is specific about the bond of nationality. It might be suggested that the following elements, as they appear in the ECN and the Report, could be relevant nevertheless. First, it is noted that matters of nationality continue to fall within the domestic jurisdiction of each state. Second, it is admitted that states can give more preferential treatment to nationals of certain states and that this may not automatically lead to discrimination. There is also a reference to the need to set criteria for naturalization which may include the knowledge of a national language and the reflection that long-term immigrants are more likely to integrate into society with greater ease. These elements are sufficient to suggest that even if the ECN does not take up the *Nottebohm* definition word by word, in fact the questions of attachment, integration and belonging are part of the ECN's meaning of nationality. I would also suggest that the European approach, which leaves the choice of the nature of decisions and modalities of procedures for granting nationality in situations of state succession to states (see further on this below), is directly linked to the above-described understanding of nationality.

---

[24] European Convention on Nationality, Strasbourg, 6 November 1997, in force 1 March 2000, CETS No. 166.

[25] Council of Europe 'European Convention on Nationality and Explanatory Report', Council of Europe Doc. DIR/JUR (97)6 (14 May 1997), para. 23.

[26] *Nottebohm Case (Liechtenstein* v. *Guatemala); Second Phase*, International Court of Justice (ICJ), 6 April 1955, ICJ Reports 1955, p. 23.

[27] See ECN Explanatory Report, para. 22.

Article 18 of the ECN specifically addresses nationality in situations of
state succession. The Article lists several criteria which a successor state
has to take into account when either 'granting or retaining' nationality.
These are: (1) the genuine and effective link of a person with the state; (2)
the habitual residence of a person at the time of state succession; (3) the
will of a person; and (4) the territorial origin of a person. The drafters of
the ECN admitted that in their understanding a person having a 'substantial connection' with the successor state should be entitled to acquire the
nationality of that state through the procedures determined by the state.
Their main concern was to develop such guidelines for states that would
enable them to tackle the problem of statelessness, as the case may be, in
situations of state succession.[28] It is true that the ECN does not pronounce
on the character of domestic procedures for granting of nationality, nor
does it explain the use of the term 'grant'. However, it is noted that the rule
of law shall govern any such procedures, with the overall aim in mind of
protecting former nationals of the predecessor state from being placed in
a vulnerable position in view of state succession.[29]

The Council of Europe continued to be seized with this matter and
adopted a new specific Convention on the Avoidance of Statelessness in
relation to State Succession in 2006. The reason for the special focus on
a problem of statelessness following state succession was that the ECN
was considered to be too general, while other international instruments
addressing the issue of statelessness in state succession situations were not
binding and the problem in Europe persisted. The key Articles are 5 and
6, which determine responsibility of a successor state and predecessor
state respectively. Article 5 states:

1. A successor State shall grant its nationality to persons who, at the
    time of the State succession, had the nationality of the predecessor
    State, and who have or would become stateless as a result of the State
    succession if at that time:
    a. they were habitually resident in the territory which has become
        territory of the successor State, or
    b. they were not habitually resident in any State concerned but had
        an appropriate connection with the successor State.
2. For the purpose of paragraph 1, sub-paragraph b, an appropriate
    connection includes *inter alia*:
    a. a legal bond to a territorial unit of a predecessor State which has
        become territory of the successor State;

[28] Ziemele, *State Continuity and Nationality*, 216–18.
[29] Article 18 of the ECN.

   b.   birth on the territory which has become territory of the successor State;

   c.   last habitual residence on the territory of the predecessor State which has become territory of the successor State.

Article 6 provides that 'A predecessor State shall not withdraw its nationality from its nationals who have not acquired the nationality of a successor State and who would otherwise become stateless as a result of the State succession.'

The drafters used the opportunity to explain their choice concerning the term 'grant of nationality' in this context. In relation to Article 5 they explained that:

> It should be noted that the Convention does not prescribe any specific way in which States should grant their nationality since this belongs to the domain of the internal law of the States concerned. Thus, the State can either grant its nationality on the basis of a voluntary act of the person concerned or automatically (*ex lege*).[30]

This is an important clarification since it is now clear that under the European standards, successor states can either pass legislation accepting the population concerned as nationals of the state *ex lege* or provide for registration or naturalization procedures. These choices are left to states with a view to accommodating specific circumstances and the particular historical role that nationality plays in each society. In that sense, state sovereignty in the matter is preserved. It is also true that whatever procedures new states see as more appropriate for their purposes, they should not be such as to render meaningless the right of individuals concerned to have their nationality status determined.

In this context, one should also keep in mind the question of choice and option. Article 7 of the 2006 Convention addresses the situation where the person might have the right to acquire more than one nationality. It is in this situation that the person's wishes should be respected. However, it is hard to imagine that a person's wish to remain stateless should also be respected in view of the fundamental principles on which the two European Conventions rely, that is, the existence of the right to a nationality as linked to the obligation to avoid statelessness and the obligation to prevent persons from becoming stateless in state succession situations. Therefore, it should be concluded that once the state has put

---

[30] See Council of Europe Convention on the Avoidance of Statelessness in relation to State Succession, CETS No. 200, Explanatory report, para.19.

in place reasonable procedures for granting nationality, the persons concerned should make use of them.

Certainly, the development of relevant procedures and their use by the persons concerned is to be seen as part of the identification, or even building, of a genuine link between the individual and the state and as falling within the sovereignty of states. Overall, the European approach seems to be mindful of the role that nationality plays traditionally as a means to determine a particular polity. In other words, citizenship encompasses the formal acknowledgment of membership in a political community and reflects its particular identity. The European rules developed in relation to state succession respect this context.

9.3.2   International Law Commission

While the Council of Europe has been very active in adopting international instruments dealing with the problem of nationality in situations of state succession, the United Nations began its work even earlier. The question was included on the agenda of the ILC in 1993. The General Assembly adopted resolution 55/153 on Nationality of Natural Persons in relation to the Succession of States on 12 December 2000, which included the Articles developed by the ILC as an annex.

In the Articles, the ILC proposes a presumption of nationality for those individuals having a habitual residence in the territory affected by the succession of states.[31] However, in the debate in the Sixth Committee, loyalty or genuine link as known from the traditional discussion on nationality were mentioned as necessary to qualify for nationality. In this context, the ILC clarified that presumption of change of nationality was only a point of departure aimed at avoiding the problem of statelessness pending the adoption of domestic legislation on nationality. The decision in a specific case was to be taken in accordance with other applicable rules and principles and in view of the different modes of state succession.[32]

Nevertheless, it is true that the ILC at some level meant to depart from the effective link, as understood in *Nottebohm*, when identifying the criteria for the attribution of nationality in succession situations and that it essentially meant to avoid statelessness. One can witness a friction in

---

[31] Article 5.
[32] For an overview of the debate in the ILC and the Sixth Committee, see Ziemele, *State Continuity*, 212–13.

the drafting efforts, including the government comments. On the one hand, the agenda was guided by human rights considerations, which have matured since the adoption of the Vienna Conventions on State Succession. On the other hand, there were the classical considerations along the lines of the clean slate approach that pertain to events of state succession and that in matters of nationality appear to have even more appeal because of the nature of nationality as the evidence of belonging to a particular state.

Despite the sensitive nature of the topic, the ILC showed admirable efforts in *de lege ferenda* development of the rules. Interestingly, it maintained the position that the rules and principles may differ depending on the mode of state succession and they did not include in the scope of the Articles those situations that have arisen contrary to rules of international law (see Article 3). As such, the ILC confirmed that different rules and considerations apply in situations of territorial changes contrary to international law.

It can be noted that the ILC decided to distinguish between the obligation to attribute and the acquisition of nationality through naturalization, since it considered that in the former case the discretion of a successor state is more limited. This should be contrasted with the European approach described above, which leaves the choice of the methods of granting nationality, including naturalization, to the states.

As for specific principles, Part II of the ILC's Articles on Nationality lists the following for the purposes of attribution of nationality: (1) habitual residence, (2) appropriate legal connection with one of the constituent units of the predecessor state, or (3) birth in the territory. If none of these criteria would be applicable the ILC introduced a saving criterion of 'any other appropriate connection' [33] to the territory. It was explained that:

> the Commission chooses to describe the link which must exist between the persons concerned and a particular State concerned by means of the expression 'appropriate connection', which should be interpreted in a broader sense than the notion of 'genuine link'. The reason for this terminological choice is the paramount importance attached by the Commission to the prevention of statelessness, which, in this particular case, supersedes the strict requirement of an effective nationality.[34]

---

[33] See Articles on Nationality of Natural Persons in relation to the Succession of States with commentaries, para. 9, p. 34.

[34] *Ibid.*

The identification of these criteria caused heated debates within the ILC and the Sixth Committee. The ILC was criticized for having given a preference to the *jus soli* principle. There was also a criticism in relation to habitual residence criterion, even where the person has moved in the meantime, as a ground for the obligation to attribute nationality. Not all governments agreed with such a broad approach.[35]

Another important feature in the drafting carried out by the ILC was the attempt to identify the role and proper place for wishes of an individual in general or in the form of the right to choose. The ILC attributes to this issue a dual meaning. On the one hand, it is very clear that an individual's wish plays a role only where there are at least two states to which the individual might be linked. On the other hand, the ILC understands the right of option also in another sense as the right of an otherwise stateless person to apply or ask for a nationality of a state with which he or she may have a connection. Even if the ILC admits that the attribution of such a role to an individual in matters of nationality is controversial, it is here that the right of option might change the traditional approach in matters of nationality and state succession. The difficulties that the ILC encountered in the drafting of the Articles should not be underestimated. It is also true that for the time being we operate with Draft Articles that have not been turned into a binding instrument.[36] The commentary to the Articles shows the immense variety of state practice during all the relevant historical events of territorial transfers. One could have argued, for example, that the decolonization process indeed had a very specific character and choices taken by these newly independent states concerning the status of their inhabitants may be accepted as special, without giving rise to any binding precedent. However, it should not escape attention that the wave of dissolutions of the 1990s in Central and Eastern Europe, in relation to which the complexities of the decolonization process were not directly relevant, continued to raise similar difficulties and objections by successor states.

9.3.3   Conclusion

There is no question that the issue of nationality, including its political character, and the value attributed to it by states and national societies, makes the development of any international regulation complicated

---

[35] See Ziemele, *State Continuity*, 214.

[36] Document: A/RES/63/118 UN General Assembly Resolution on Nationality of natural persons in relation to the succession of States in which the General Assembly invites States to submit comments on advisability of elaborating such a legal instrument.

in general and in situations of territorial change in particular. For new states, challenges posed by the tasks of state and identity building may overshadow the interests of certain individuals or even groups of individuals. In this context, the European approach leaving a considerable space for states to choose and design appropriate procedures for granting nationality might appear a more pragmatic and sensible one.

9.4. Particular challenges posed by state succession for nationality

The foregoing sections elaborate on the overall doctrinal and legal developments relating to nationality in the context of state succession. Some significant conceptual issues remain and warrant further attention. The first of these relates to the influence of the type of state succession on the approach to nationality adopted by states or prescribed by international law. Another, more fundamental challenge is posed in this respect where there is a transition from an illegal regime. Finally, there is the specific question of state obligations with regard to the avoidance of statelessness in the event of state succession and how this has been given content in international law. These questions will be explored below.

9.4.1   Status first or relevance of types of state succession

There is no unanimity on the question of whether different rules need to be designed for each type of state succession. I submit that this is linked to a more fundamental disagreement in the international law debate as to whether international law contains, or should contain, the necessary tools to determine the continuity or disruption of a state.[37] The wisdom and practicability of distinguishing between state continuity and state succession was already rather strongly criticized in the 1960s by O'Connell[38] who 'complained that legal doctrine on succession had been derailed by the predominance of Hegelian conceptions of the State, which, from the time of Bluntschli onwards, had placed the issue of identity at the forefront'.[39] In O'Connell's view the question should be whether existing obligations survive the change and the nature and degree of change should be examined with a view to preserving obligations. However, there are scholars who

---

[37] For a good overview of ideas that have led different scholars to adopt their different positions, see Craven, *The Decolonization of International Law*, 75–80.
[38] O'Connell, *State Succession in Municipal and International Law*.
[39] Craven, *The Decolonization of International Law*, 75.

take a different view and state practice largely confirms that one cannot completely ignore the issue of identity, which remains important for the political realities of the communities concerned.[40] Indeed, many aspects of the modern state have evolved since Hegelian times. At the same time, as the process of decolonization showed and recent dissolutions of states in Europe confirmed, the self-perception of new states or the societies they represent as to their past, culture and values remains of key importance. Not all these interests are or can be captured by international law.

At the same time, international law does not easily accept the disappearance of states. After all, it is a state-centred legal system.[41] Even where elements of a state are affected or changed, it may well be that the same legal personality, even if within a smaller territory, is preserved and in the relations with new states one considers the former as a predecessor state. In view of various examples of state practice, jurists have even distinguished between two situations of the preservation of the same legal personality: (a) state continuity, despite a change in circumstances, and (b) state identity, without continuity, where a state is revived after temporary extinction. My attempt at a general definition of state continuity is as follows: state continuity describes the continuity or identity of states as legal persons in international law, subject to relevant claims and recognition of those claims determined, in principle, in accordance with the applicable international law rules or procedures when statehood is at issue.[42]

The importance of knowing whether a state has ceased to exist or continues in some form has been emphasized by James Crawford, who noted that 'the whole of the law of State succession depends on this distinction'.[43] The debate on state continuity and state succession and the importance of the issue of identity of a community is, moreover, of direct relevance for the understanding of the stakes when drafting rules regarding nationality in situations of state succession. This is discussed below.

9.4.1.1   Predecessor state continues to exist

The ILC has always taken a nuanced approach to questions of status, both in drafting the general conventions on state succession as well as

---

[40] *Ibid.*, 77, with reference to Koskenniemi's analysis.
[41] See I. Ziemele, 'Extinction of States', in R Wolfrum (ed.), *The Max Planck Encyclopedia of Public International Law*, vol. IX (Oxford University Press, 2012), 558.
[42] Ziemele, *State Continuity*, 118.
[43] See Crawford, *The Creation of States in International Law*, 400.

the Articles on Nationality. Part II of the Articles sets out specific rules or principles in relation to each mode of state succession. The 2006 European Convention only distinguishes between obligations of a successor state and a predecessor state, stating in the Explanatory Report that it uses the term of state succession to cover all modes. According to the European Convention there are important obligations on the successor state while the predecessor state should be obliged either to withdraw or not to withdraw nationality depending on decisions taken by the successor state. The Report states:

> The provision is applicable only in situations where the predecessor State continues to exist after State succession, as is the case after transfer and separation of part or parts of the territory. In cases where the predecessor State has disappeared or is not a State Party to the Convention, only the previous article concerning the responsibility of the successor State shall apply.[44]

In my view it makes an important difference whether the predecessor state survives a change, even if in a diminished form.

Indeed, territorial changes do not lead to automatic change of nationality. This change 'gives the successor State the right under customary international law to confer its nationality upon the people which are permanently resident in the territory concerned'.[45] In other words, the question was not whether the population loses nationality of the predecessor state. The question was whether people acquire new nationality *ex lege* or in any other way. Previously I pointed out the difference in approaches between the ILC Articles and the European conventions where the former build their solutions on presumption of nationality in combination with the criterion of any connection while the latter leaves such choices to states.

Andreas Zimmermann observed in relation to changes that affected Eastern Europe that practice continued to vary depending on the type of succession. In cases of transfer of territory, no clear evidence in support of an automatic change of nationality could be obtained, but some examples enabled the acknowledgment that residents were normally granted nationality. He also suggested that, in situations where a predecessor state continued to exist, nationality was looked at from a totally

---

[44] See Council of Europe Convention on the Avoidance of Statelessness in relation to State Succession, CETS No. 200, Explanatory report, para. 29.
[45] See O. Dörr, 'Nationality', in R Wolfrum (ed.), *The Max Planck Encyclopedia of Public International Law*, vol VII (Oxford University Press, 2012), 500.

different viewpoint.[46] For instance, in such situations the right to opt for nationality becomes more evident because it can be presumed that the predecessor state has no reason to withdraw nationality from nationals even if their place of residence has remained outside the territory of the state. At the same time, a successor state might be more persuaded to grant nationality to such residents.

In other words, the dynamics of the relationships and interests are different where at least in some form a predecessor state remains. Certainly, the existence of the predecessor state is also an element in the successor states' self-identification process. One should be reminded of the position adopted by the Venice Commission, which considered that there are evident categories of citizens of a predecessor state, such as civil servants and soldiers, who by any a priori measure are more linked to that state even if they may continue to reside in the territory of a successor state. For example, upon liberation of Timor-Leste from Indonesia the latter carried out a massive evacuation of about 250,000 persons among whom 70,000 were military personnel while the rest were those who Indonesia had encouraged to move to East Timor during Indonesia's rule.[47]

This example more properly belongs to the context of territorial changes as a consequence of a violation of international law discussed below. However, the Timor-Leste case exemplifies the considerations that may emerge and are legitimate in situations where the predecessor state remains and concerns the issue of genuine link with a state, either the predecessor or the successor. Indeed, there may be legitimate public interests in terms of security and peaceful development of a new state or liberated state to negotiate individual solutions for some groups of individuals with closer ties to the predecessor state or to accept the fact that they remain in the territory as foreign citizens.[48]

---

[46] See A. Zimmermann, 'State Succession and the Nationality of Natural Persons – Facts and Possible Codification', in P. M. Eisemann and M. Koskenniemi (eds.), *La succession d'Etats: la codification à l'éprouve des facts/State Succession: Codifications tested against the Facts* (The Hague, Boston, MA, London: Martinus Nijhoff Publishers, 2000), 660.

[47] See Y. Ronen, *Transition from Illegal Regimes under International Law* (Cambridge University Press, 2011), 229.

[48] Negotiations between states come up as a means to solve difficult nationality questions. For example, the Constitutional Court of Slovenia noted in one of its judgments addressing the problem of 'erased' formed Yugoslav citizens that a proposal had been made in the legislative process in 1991 for a special provision regulating the temporary situation of former Socialist Federal Republic of Yugoslavia (SFRY) citizens living in Slovenia who had not applied for Slovenian citizenship. The legislature had maintained that their situation should not be regulated by the Aliens Act but rather by an agreement between the successor states to the former SFRY.

9.4.1.2   Predecessor state disappears

Given the intrinsic link between a particular state and nationality, as noted above, the situation that arises when a previous state disappears is a complex one since the death of the state is likely to bring about the death of its nationality. Thus, when a predecessor state disappears and there are two or more successor states which have emerged in the territory concerned, different dynamics underlie the search for solutions in general and in relation to nationality of the populations. State practice in Europe shows that groups of individuals have had serious difficulties while their nationality status was determined by successor states.

The European Court of Human Rights has had to deal with this problem in relation to the so-called erased persons in Slovenia, i.e., former Socialist Federal Republic of Yugoslavia (SFRY) citizens who were legally residing in Slovenia but failed to undertake procedures that independent Slovenia established for the purposes of identifying its nationals. As a result, they were erased from the population register. It took more than a decade of various legal steps to regularize the status of these persons, demonstrating the political character and tension that the process of granting nationality in new states may entail.[49] It is interesting to note that in the context of dissolution of the SFRY the main criterion for granting nationality in the successor states was citizenship in the different republics and legal residence. Specifically there was no reference to Yugoslav citizenship of Serbia. Despite this, Serbia, for a while, continued to claim that it had inherited the rights of the former Yugoslavia and in other words continued its international legal personality. Serbia's position on continuity was not accepted with the effect that no expectations arose in relation to a possible predecessor state as a back-up option.[50]

Indeed, as the dissolution of the SFRY and similar examples show in situations where there are only new states within the territory of the former state, the identification of nationals can be a particularly difficult

---

[49] For the problem of erased permanent residents in Slovenia following the dissolution of Yugoslavia, see *Kurić v. Slovenia* (App. No. 26828/06), judgment of 13 July 2010. The Grand Chamber judgment in the case was rendered on 26 June 2012.

[50] The dissolution of Yugoslavia has been examined extensively in legal literature. See e.g. P. Radan, *The Break-up of Yugoslavia and International Law* (London: Routledge, 2002); R. Mullerson, 'The Continuity and Succession of States by Reference to the Former USSR and Yugoslavia' *International and Comparative Law Quarterly* 42 (1993), 473–93. For comments on the effects of complete dissolution of states in relation to nationality, see A. Zimmermann, 'State Succession on Other Matters than Treaties', in R. Wolfrum (ed.), *The Max Planck Encyclopedia of Public International Law*, vol. IX (Oxford University Press, 2012), 542.

process. Thus, it is no surprise that the 2006 European Convention puts an emphasis on the obligation of successor states while the ILC Articles attempt to propose that any connection is sufficient so as to not leave individuals stateless. In such a context negotiations between successor states and cooperation are of extreme importance. There are examples, such as the re-unification of Germany or dissolution of Czechoslovakia, where state succession was carried out through negotiating relevant agreements in general or on specific issues. However, this practice shows that even this approach does not answer all questions.[51]

In view of the above discussion concerning the close link between nationality and the identity of a particular community, it should be emphasized that where a predecessor state has ceased to exist and there are two or more new states in its territory, pressures and interests are somewhat different for the new states. This does not mean that they do not have their particular vision of who they are and how different they are from other states or that no conflicting and competing interests with other successor states exist. Nevertheless, the drafting efforts of relevant rules for attributing or granting nationality in such situations seem to place a particular emphasis on their obligation to grant nationality if the residents in their territory had some nationality status before.

The main question in this section was whether status or type of succession is important for appropriate choices regarding the nationality status of individuals. The reply, in my view, is in the affirmative. This is not least because the nationality issue more than any other issue touches upon the identity of the state concerned. To a great extent all drafting efforts of international rules seem to recognize that.

9.4.2   Transition from illegal regimes

It was noted earlier that situations where the changes affecting states and populations originate in an unlawful context have altogether been left out by the ILC Articles. The starting point, therefore, on whether there are any relevant rules affecting regulation of nationality is clearly different. As indeed has been argued, where a transition takes place from an illegal regime or an unlawful occupation, serious questions are raised with respect to the validity of the presence of communities who have been

---

[51] For example, upon dissolution of Czechoslovakia the question of nationality continued to generate problems. See G. de La Pradelle, 'The Effects of New Nationality Rules on the Status of Individuals', in B. Stern (ed.), *Dissolution, Continuation and Succession in Eastern Europe* (The Hague: Martinus Nijhoff Publishers, 1998), 112–13.

moved into the territory under such regimes. Even the right to remain of persons belonging to such communities may be challenged.[52]

This is linked to the obligation under international law of non-recognition of illegal regimes. While the exact scope of this obligation is subject to discussion and evolution, the importance of the obligation as such has been emphasized by the ICJ in the *Namibia Advisory Opinion* and more recently in the *Israeli Wall Advisory Opinion*.[53] The distinction between lawful and unlawful territorial changes has a whole body of international law addressing it and it is in this respect that, in my view, the distinction between the two broad categories known as state continuity and state succession might be particularly necessary if the maxim *ex injuria non oritur jus*[54] applies where unlawful territorial changes are affected.[55]

Even in the context of transitioning from illegal regimes some doubts have been voiced as to the legal importance of distinction between state continuity and state succession. A number of eminent international lawyers have taken the view that the proposition of such a distinction has always been essentially politically motivated.[56] However, it has to be admitted that several elements that are present in the conceptual discussion about state succession should be carefully reassessed when dealing with illegal territorial changes.

It was noted earlier that one of the main aims and concerns following state succession is the preservation of legal relations in force at both international and national levels. In a way, even if the special nature of nationality is recognized, the main concern in the field of state succession and nationality is the same: how to ensure that people do not lose nationality as a result of state transformations. As noted above, in the area of nationality this interest may have to be balanced against another fundamental interest of building or preserving the identity of a community. In many ways the drafting of the two Vienna Conventions on State Succession when confronted with the decolonization process already showed the conflicting agendas of continuity supporters versus self-determination and identity

---

[52] See Ronen, *Transition from Illegal Regimes under International Law*, 186 *et seq.*

[53] *Legal Consequences for States of the Continued Presence of South Africa in Namibia (South West Africa) notwithstanding Security Council Resolution 276 (1970)*, Advisory Opinion, 1971 ICJ Reports 16; *Legal Consequences of the Construction of a Wall in the Occupied Palestinian Territory*, ICJ Advisory Opinion, 9 July 2004.

[54] A principle of international law such that an unjust act cannot have legal consequences. Stern, *Dissolution, Continuation and Succession in Eastern Europe*.

[55] The Namibia Advisory Opinion in pronouncing on the obligation of non-recognition of the unlawful presence of South Africa in fact follows this maxim. See Opinion, para. 133(2).

[56] For a more recent analysis, see Craven, *The Decolonization of International Law*, 69, 77.

supporters. However, there was another dimension in the decolonization process that is relevant when discussing illegal territorial changes or transition from illegal regimes. As with illegal territorial changes which have been effected against important rules of international law (e.g. the prohibition of the use of force between states) the whole decolonization process stems from the understanding that the modern world order can no longer tolerate colonialism. In such contexts, the question is quite simple: is it just and fair to insist that something that applies to a people and has been imposed against their free will, or even by force, should remain in force?

Matthew Craven sums it up very well in stating that the drafting of the Vienna Convention shows in relation to the decolonization process 'the obvious inability of those involved in codification, to deal with the problem of succession in a way that did not draw within it questions of identity and status'.[57] The reason was the existence of the two already mentioned conflicting understandings of the purpose of the codification of the law of state succession. The first view considered that the primary aim is the maintenance of the integrity of international legal relations and thus advocated the continuity of, for example, treaty obligations of colonial powers in the territories undergoing transformation. The second view emphasized the fundamental role that self-determination played in the transformation from a colonial past and the right of newly independent states to decide for themselves what might or might not be in their interests. Craven points out that the fact that non-self-governing territories had been attributed a separate legal personality under UN law clearly contributed to the approach that dealt differently with the status and rights of colonial peoples.[58] In other words, this was important for the self-identification process of these entities.

In the end, the formulation of a clean-slate rule in the sense of the right to choose what would be inherited and what would not was the only possible compromise. Craven sums up as follows:

> What Waldock achieved was to capture, within a framework of a single convention, two largely inconsistent ideas: the first being that anti-colonial self-determination was a process, which had marked, in revolutionary manner, the end of international law's surrogate relationship with colonialism and which has also ushered in a new era in which the ideals laid down in the United Nations Charter (sovereign equality, self-determination, and equal rights) could be brought into fruition. Against

---

[57] *Ibid.*, 202.   [58] *Ibid.*, 203.

this, however, was the idea that the revolution had also been managed in a way that effectively denied its incipient radicalism.[59]

The wave of dissolutions in Central and Eastern Europe also brought about liberation of some territories from illegal regimes. The restoration of the independence of the Baltic States from illegal Soviet domination should be seen, more properly, in the context of the decolonization processes of the 1960s and 1970s and certainly as falling clearly within the area of transition from illegal regimes.[60] Craven connected the 1960s and 1970s debate with the state succession wave of the 1990s as follows:

> Certainly the events themselves were radical enough, certainly also they seemed to usher in a new era of international law, but there was no 'baggage' so to speak ... There was no reason to insist upon the radically disruptive nature of demise ... Only in case of the Baltic States were arguments about discontinuity prevalent, ... a vindication of a pre-existent international legal status that had been submerged by the violence of occupation.[61]

The nationality solutions adopted in the Baltic States and, in particular, in Estonia and Latvia gained considerable attention in international practices and academic writings.[62] The cases merit more attention for the purposes of this chapter. It should first be pointed out that many academic writings and international reports on the Baltic States have an apparent difficulty in determining from which international law perspective the cases should be examined. A few studies examine the questions of nationality in the context of the doctrine of state continuity as applied in relation to Russia and the Baltic States.

A recent study on transition from illegal regimes under international law by Yaël Ronen takes as case studies the examples of the Baltic States, Rhodesia, Namibia, the South African homeland states, Timor-Leste and the Turkish Republic of Northern Cyprus. Ronen explains that 'the main criterion for choosing these cases was that an obligation of non-recognition in response to a violation of international law was (or is) generally recognized to exist in their respect, and that a policy of non-recognition

---

[59] *Ibid.*, 263.
[60] For similar argument, see R. Müllerson, *International Law, Rights and Politics* (London: Routledge, 1994) 64–5.
[61] Craven, *The Decolonization of International Law*, 264.
[62] See among others and with further references therein, A. Lottmann, 'No Direction Home: Nationalism and Statelessness in the Baltics' *Texas International Law Journal* 45 (2008), 503 *et seq.*

was instituted in practice'.[63] This is a perfectly valid choice and indeed an important study to be carried out in international law, that is, on the effects of a non-recognition obligation in different matters of life, including nationality solutions following transitions. One can also notice how the examples naturally link the decolonization process with the unlawful use of force.

As for nationality solutions, the author observes that: 'the post-transition regime is not obliged to recognize the validity of formal status granted by the illegal regime'[64] to the settlers. 'This status is invalid *ab initio* under international law, and even if it merits partial or ad hoc recognition under the Namibia exception, the general law of State succession does not enable it to transcend the change of regime'.[65] In other words, where events might be said to fall broadly within a state succession situation, but stem from the withdrawal of an illegal regime from the territory concerned, the solutions for nationality issues are different and the codification efforts on state succession have left such situations outside their scope.

In view of the overall unlawfulness of such situations, there have been good reasons to argue that part of a population moved into such territories had no right to remain there. It could be submitted that this population is more linked to the parting regime rather than the new or restored regime in the territory concerned. However, Ronen concludes that, based on the empirical study of these cases, in such situations states have had great difficulties in making this population leave their territories. She says:

> although the implantation of settlers is one of the most visible and objectionable practices of illegal regimes, it is not an easily reversible one. Once the settler community is established in the territory, international human rights law places various obstacles on its removal, insofar as that removal is pursued on the basis of illegality of the previous regime rather than on the personal conduct of individual settlers.[66]

Since the ILC expressly removed illegal territorial situations from its consideration, presumption of nationality and other considerations relevant in typical situations of state succession do not apply. Indeed, as the example of the Cyprus conflict shows, an individual approach and the negotiation of possible special solutions in view of specific political realities of each case are more appropriate, since typically such situations also involve serious security considerations.

---

[63] Ronen, *Transition from Illegal Regimes under International Law*, 10.
[64] *Ibid.*, 242.   [65] *Ibid.*   [66] *Ibid.*, 244.

Nevertheless, solutions advocated in relation to Soviet-era settlers in Estonia and Latvia, while certainly justified by reference to such human rights as the prohibition of discrimination and of expulsion en masse, continue to raise questions as to the right balance in relation to, on the one hand, the obligation of non-recognition of an illegal regime and its consequences and, on the other hand, the legitimate human rights concerns of individuals who may have developed stronger links with the territory of these two states than any other territory.[67] In other words, the scope and borders of the application of the principles stemming from the ICJ's judgment in *Namibia* in the situation of the Baltic States is still under discussion. Undoubtedly, solutions that are (or will be) accepted will constitute important precedents in international law for some time to come.

At this stage the following summary of principles followed or rather advocated approaches may be provided. Third states seem to have accepted, as have human rights monitoring bodies, albeit reluctantly, that one cannot say that the Baltic States were under an obligation to grant nationality to Soviet settlers *ex lege*. It should also be pointed out that during the early 1990s, the question of the predecessor state, i.e., the Russian Federation and its obligations in relation to Soviet citizens, was not properly addressed. There remains a certain confusion as to whether Soviet settlers are stateless and, if so, who has caused it.[68] Nevertheless, it should be recognized that all actors pushed for and the Baltic States accepted, offering the option of naturalization to Soviet-era settlers. This could become an important clarification of the scope of the non-recognition rule, as applicable in situations where the illegal regime has managed to persist for a considerable period of time. The question remains whether this approach will be followed in other comparable situations.

Undoubtedly, stability in legal relations has been the underlying concern in relation to various state succession events, including the ones of

---

[67] See European Court of Human Rights, *Slivenko* v. *Latvia*, Application 48321/99, 9 July 2003; US Court of Appeals, Sixth Circuit *Stserba* v. *Holder*, 20 May 2011. For analysis of the *Slivenko* case in the light of applicable rules of international law on the prohibition of use of force, see I. Ziemele, 'Case-law of the European Court of Human Rights and Integrity of International Law', in R. Huesa Vinaixa and K. Wellens (eds.) *L'influence des sources sur l'unité et la fragmentation du droit international*, (Brussels: Bruylant, 2006), 199–210.

[68] The High Court of Ireland rendered an important judgment on this issue, accepting that Soviet-era settlers who did not acquire nationality of Latvia or other former republics of the USSR cannot be considered as stateless for the purposes of Irish law in view of the status and rights granted to them under Latvian law. Judgment of Mr. Justice Cooke in the case *Spila* v. *Minister of Justice*, IEHC 336, 31 July 2012.

the 1990s. This concern is equally relevant in addressing the question of the nationality of the populations concerned. On the other hand, since the establishment of the United Nations and the emergence of the idea of a new global order, there has always been unease about the preservation of those legal relations whose legitimate nature was highly questionable. In other words, the conflict between the old maxims of *ex factis jus oritur*[69] and *ex injuria non jus oritur* has become more evident with the thinking that the United Nations era strives to promote. It is evident that human rights have stepped into the midst of this conflict and somehow delineate the use of both maxims.

There is one more aspect that is particularly important in identifying the most appropriate nationality solutions in situations of territorial changes emanating in the context of violations of international law. This aspect has to do with the nation-building challenges that such entities face. The search for a strong identity for a community that has been oppressed is a huge challenge. Nationality legislation plays a particular role in determining the identity of the community as it recovers from oppression. State practice shows that nation-building is one area that, while concerned with the continuity of legal relations, has been seriously underestimated.[70]

9.4.3   Obligation to avoid statelessness

The entire drafting process of the ILC Articles shows that the ILC was prepared to strongly support the principle that statelessness should be avoided in matters of nationality in situations of territorial change. The drafters of the ECN pointed out too that '[t]here is no reason why persons who had the nationality of the predecessor State should suddenly be left without any nationality following State succession'.[71] It is for this reason that the ECN in Article 18(1) provides that the granting of nationality has to comply with the principle of the avoidance of statelessness and other human rights principles. The Explanatory Report emphasizes that 'all these principles mentioned in paragraph 1 have significance in general, although the primary concern is the avoidance of statelessness'.[72]

---

[69] This rival principle asserts that the existence of facts creates law, regardless of whether the act from which these facts stem was just or unjust.

[70] See D. Thürer, 'Failing States', in R. Wolfrum (ed.), *The Max Planck Encyclopedia of Public International Law*, vol. III (Oxford University Press, 2012), 1092.

[71] ECN Explanatory Report, para. 12.

[72] See Council of Europe 'European Convention on Nationality and Explanatory Report', Council of Europe Doc. DIR/JUR (97)6 (14 May 1997), para. 116.

It has been argued, however, that, despite numerous legislative efforts, it is difficult to prove *opinion juris* for the existence of a customary international law obligation to avoid statelessness. The obligation applies to states parties in relevant treaties.[73] Zimmermann argues that state practice shows a joint obligation of successor states to avoid statelessness, which points towards the obligation to harmonize domestic laws and to negotiate relevant solutions, while leaving a great number of details unsettled.[74] One may add here that exceptionally in relation to children, the obligation not to render them stateless combined with the acknowledged right to acquire nationality at birth can be considered as having achieved the necessary *opinion juris* under customary international law and most likely applies irrespective of the lawful or unlawful context of territorial change.[75] In other words, there is no question that strong recommendations and pressures exist within the international legal process requiring successor states to adopt such nationality laws that would avoid creating statelessness. On the other hand, it is difficult to say that there is a clear obligation as a matter of customary international law to avoid statelessness in each and every case. It is thus that in situations where as a result of state succession new states emerge, it is difficult to identify such a new state as having the obligation to grant nationality to everyone in the territory. Many different considerations come into play, as has been outlined above.

9.5.   Conclusions

The concept of nationality or citizenship has evolved over the centuries along with the evolution of political thought. It has become more inclusive, and more democratic. Nevertheless, it continues to denote a particular legal relationship and involves elements of attachment to, and interest in, a particular polity.

The fact that societies continue to organize themselves in the form of states rather than any other type of organization continues to provide the basis for the importance of nationality of the particular polity. Even the European Union with its EU citizenship has not done away with the

---

[73] See Dörr, 'Nationality', 498.

[74] Zimmermann, 'State Succession on Other Matters than Treaties', 542.

[75] See I. Ziemele, 'Article 7: The Right to Birth Registration, Name and Nationality, and the Right to Know and Be cared for by Parents', in A. Alen *et al.* (eds.) *A Commentary on the United Nations Convention on the Rights of the Child* (Leiden: Martinus Nijhoff Publishers, 2007), 25.

state system. It is true that in the long run EU citizenship has the potential to consolidate a stronger European identity and build some sort of a European demos among those living in Europe, but whether it will or should replace national identities and nationalities is another issue.[76]

Thus the view on nationality as traditionally defined by a republican position, which emphasizes that 'only citizens who are present in the polity can govern themselves by participating in making its laws' remains the backbone of how we view and organize ourselves.[77] It is true that today this premise has been surrounded by other modalities concerning non-resident citizens or aliens residing in the territory of a state.[78] Clearly the development of human rights has had an impact on the classical republican position on nationality and its role within the territory of a state. Nevertheless, broadly speaking these developments have not changed the function of nationality and even its sentimental value. On the contrary, even human rights law emphasizes the importance of nationality status and points out the shortcomings in terms of enjoyment of rights for individuals who do not have a nationality. Human rights law does not challenge the traditional way of organizing societies in states and thus the role of nationality. It is in fact dependent on states and their ability to enforce human rights rules.

In situations of state succession when states and societies go through dramatic, often painful, transformations and breakdown of their legal and economic systems, there should be space for states concerned to consolidate themselves, albeit in a non-discriminatory manner since in the long term it is a strong state that better protects individuals within its territory.[79] Clearly, the state succession context, since it involves the creation of new states and determination of new political communities, brings out more sharply the conflicting interests that directly affect decisions regarding nationality.

It is fair to say that, within the last twenty years, the number of adopted instruments of different legal characters, all attempting to regulate or set some principles in relation to nationality solutions in situations of state

[76] See D. Graus, 'Legitimate Political Rule Without a State? An Analysis of Joseph H. H. Weiler's Justification of the Legitimacy of the European Union Qua Non-Statehood', RECON Online Working Paper 2008/12.

[77] See R. Bauböck, 'Expansive Citizenship: Voting beyond Territory and Membership', *Political Science and Politics* 38(4) (October 2005), 685.

[78] *Ibid.*, at 683.

[79] For an overview on some problems of so-called failed or failing states, see Thürer, 'Failing States', 1088.

succession, is impressive. That attests to the pressure that situations of
state succession create for individuals and the concern that the problems
associated with state succession have raised with different international
actors. It is interesting to note that following the adoption of the ECN,
which has received a fairly high number of ratifications,[80] the Council
of Europe still considered it necessary to draft the Convention on the
Avoidance of Statelessness in relation to State Succession adopted in 2006.
However, the first six years of its existence only saw six ratifications among
forty-seven Council of Europe member states. Among those six only two
states are new successor states, namely Moldova and Montenegro.

Of course, one should be cautious in drawing conclusions from the
above facts. It may well be that the European states consider that state succession is no longer on the agenda in Europe. Nevertheless, it is undeniable,
as argued above, that there are not many rules with relevant obligations
in customary international law which would apply to successor states and
limit their discretion to grant or not grant nationality. Therefore, such
attempts to draft treaties have persisted. Undoubtedly, the ILC Articles
have taken the most comprehensive and nuanced approach, trying to
identify relevant criteria that would differentiate, depending on the type
of state succession, which state should attribute nationality to which individuals. The fact remains that despite multiple reaffirmations of the right
to nationality as a human right in different international law and human
rights texts, the right to a specific nationality has not evolved. As noted,
children form an exception, while at the level of state practice problems
remain even in relation to children and their nationality status.[81]

This brings me back to the questions raised at the outset of this chapter. I would maintain that in examining this area of law, it is essential to
keep in mind that the population, as identified through the link of nationality, is an essential element of a state. New states might be particularly
concerned about the strengthening of their state institutions, including
nationality and identity. There should be, and there is in fact, in international law, space for the states to do so. Interestingly, the difficulty
arises in situations when there is more than one state with likely responsibility for a group of individuals. It is in this context that all available
rules, principles and presumptions should be used to identify the primary
responsible state and the necessary exceptions to the main approach. It
is along these lines that the ILC admitted that 'one cannot consider each

[80] Out of forty-seven member states twenty have ratified the Convention.
[81] Ziemele, 'Article 7', 25.

particular State concerned to be responsible for all cases of statelessness resulting from the succession'.[82] As an example, the ILC discusses the type of state succession where the predecessor state is preserved and where, for various reasons, it may be argued that the retention of nationality for those outside the territory may lead to relationships without appropriate connection on a large scale. At the same time, on a case-by-case basis, such retention of nationality might be necessary.

There is no doubt that the latest codification efforts within the law of state succession have placed the rights and interests of individuals at the centre of their concern. However, this has not changed the classical paradigm, which accepts that in nationality matters states also have a lot to say. The main difficulty of the law of state succession is that interests of individuals and of states may be particularly vital in such situations and in relation to nationality in particular – and may not always be the same.

Questions to guide discussion

1. Why is state succession such a challenging context for questions of nationality?
2. Why has the Council of Europe taken such an interest in developing standards for the regulation of nationality in the context of state succession and what role has been given to the notion of 'appropriate connection' within these standards?
3. What different considerations are raised by the continued existence versus the disappearance of the predecessor state for the regulation of nationality?
4. To what extent is the stability of international relations the basic premise for the rules relating to state succession? How is this reconciled with the interests of individuals, especially those with no other claim to nationality?
5. Is there any obligation to avoid statelessness in state succession contexts? What issues are at play?
6. What might be the significance of a transition from an illegal regime for the application of international standards relating to nationality in the context of state succession? Do you think that such circumstances should influence the way in which states interpret and apply these international standards?

---

[82] See Commentary under Article 4, Report of the International Law Commission (1999), Chapter IV.

10

The nexus between statelessness and migration

SOPHIE NONNENMACHER AND RYSZARD CHOLEWINSKI

10.1. Introduction

Statelessness and migration are closely inter-related. Statelessness is often a consequence and cause of migration: patterns of migration contribute to the creation and prolongation of cases of statelessness while statelessness has a role in driving migration. While this nexus remains relatively understudied, there is increasing evidence linking statelessness and migration as a growing number of people around the world fall into situations of limbo and despair.

In regions of the world with high numbers of stateless persons, cross-border migration occurs irregularly as these individuals generally do not hold identity or travel documents permitting them to cross borders lawfully. Increasingly, migrants may enter another country with an effective nationality but, because of their irregular stay abroad, are stripped of the protection of their nationality. Regardless of the way they entered the destination country, individuals in an irregular situation who cannot prove their nationality may face many human rights violations, including indefinite immigration detention or a prolonged lack of any status resulting in denial of or limitations on access to important economic and social rights, and they may also be unable to return to their original place of residence.

This chapter focuses on stateless migrants and migrants at risk of statelessness. It explores the interplay between migration and statelessness in light of international law. First, the chapter considers the relationship between *de jure* and *de facto* statelessness and how both concepts impact on and are impacted by international migration, and

The ideas and observations in this chapter constitute the personal views of the authors and do not necessarily reflect or engage those of the IOM or the ILO. The authors would like to express their gratitude to Alexandra Gasteen (Regional Policy and Liaison Associate, IOM Bangkok) for her invaluable assistance in the preparation of the chapter.

irregular migration in particular. Second, the chapter examines the role played by *de jure* statelessness in patterns of irregular migration. Third, it considers how patterns of irregular migration have contributed to the creation or prolongation of cases of *de facto* statelessness. Examples are drawn from the Southeast Asian region, where statelessness is significant in terms of scale and impact. Final reflections aim to support further development of conceptual, policy and practical responses to these issues in the future.

Exploring ways to more effectively prevent migration-related statelessness has become a pressing concern for states and for the Southeast Asian region as a whole. States need to promote further international cooperation to identify specific issues and links between statelessness and migration, and adopt clearer parameters for the prevention of situations where individuals are without the protection and rights of a nationality, in accordance with state obligations in international law.

10.2.   *De jure* and *de facto* statelessness in the context of international migration

Central to the international legal framework addressing statelessness is the 1954 Convention relating to the Status of Stateless Persons (hereinafter the 1954 Convention), which defines a stateless person in Article 1 as 'a person who is not considered as a national by any State under the operation of its law'.[1] Although the 1954 Convention has achieved relatively few states parties,[2] this definition of a stateless person has been recognized by the International Law Commission (ILC) as part of customary international law and is therefore applicable to the identification of statelessness anywhere in the world.[3]

A person who is stateless in accordance with the definition in Article 1 of the 1954 Convention is commonly also referred to as *de jure*

---

[1]   The term 'nationality' refers here to the legal bond between a person and a state. It is a legal-political term and should not be confused with national origin in the sense of membership of a particular social or ethnic group. Nationality in the legal-political sense is also commonly referred to as citizenship and the terms will be used synonymously here, as is predominantly the case elsewhere in literature discussing the issue of statelessness.

[2]   Convention relating to the Status of Stateless Persons, New York, 28 September 1954, in force 6 June 1960, 360 UNTS 117. The Convention relating to the Status of Stateless Persons has been ratified by eighty states parties as at 1 June 2014.

[3]   On the legal definition of a stateless person and the interpretation of the components of this definition, see UNHCR, 'Expert Meeting – The Concept of Stateless Persons under International Law ("Prato Conclusions")' (May 2010).

stateless. A distinct concept of *de facto* statelessness has also emerged, describing the situation of people who formally hold a nationality but are similarly situated as *de jure* stateless because their nationality is in some way ineffective. Traditionally, *de facto* statelessness is considered to refer to 'persons outside the country of their nationality who are unable or, for valid reasons, are unwilling to avail themselves of the protection of that country'.[4] However, there is no agreed international definition of *de facto* statelessness, nor is there any treaty regime dedicated to addressing this phenomenon.[5] Nevertheless, in the context of irregular migration, the concept of *de facto* statelessness may be relevant and provides a means of describing the situation of those irregular migrants who are unable to rely on diplomatic or consular protection from their country of nationality – in particular if they are refused re-entry to that country.[6]

10.3.   Statelessness as a trigger for international migration

In many regions of the world, common causes of statelessness include discriminatory denial of citizenship, failure to acquire a nationality at birth, or loss or renunciation of citizenship without due regard for statelessness. These various scenarios have been explored in detail in other chapters of this book. The discrimination faced by some stateless persons in their country of residence in terms of economic opportunities, and access to health and education for their children contributes to inducing stateless persons to seek a better life abroad. Although today only a certain proportion of the population in origin countries can satisfy the admission criteria of destination countries for legal migration, stateless migrants differ from other migrants in the sense that they generally lack an internationally recognized national identity document required to cross a border. Therefore, stateless persons are constrained to move in an irregular manner due to their lack of a status at home and regardless of the admissions regime in force in the destination of their choice.

---

[4] H. Massey 'UNHCR and de facto Statelessness', UNHCR Legal and Protection Policy Series, Geneva (April 2010), p. 61.

[5] The 1954 Convention is only applicable to persons who meet the internationally recognized definition of a (*de jure*) stateless person. However, a non-binding Final Act to the convention requests states to consider extending the rights in the convention to certain persons who could be described as stateless *de facto*.

[6] For a detailed discussion of the definition of statelessness and further reflection on the notion of *de facto* statelessness, see UNHCR, 'Prato Conclusions'.

10.3.1   Statelessness triggers migration due to deprivation of rights in the country of origin

There are a variety of reasons that lead individuals to emigrate from their country of origin. In broad terms, these motivations can be categorized into:

i) Push factors, or negative aspects within the country of origin that lead individuals to seek an alternative, and
ii) Pull factors, or attractive attributes of the country of destination that make it appealing for migrants.

Push factors include a lack of educational or economic opportunities, poverty, restrictions on political or religious expression, denial of the right to property, and discrimination by the state or segments of the general population. Pull factors include economic and educational opportunities, political and religious freedoms, and the presence of family or a pre-existing migrant community. In the case of stateless persons, several of these push and pull factors are significant in the decision to migrate and may be linked to their stateless situation.

In particular, the often vulnerable position of stateless persons – namely, their inability to exercise a wide range of rights – can act as a considerable push factor and trigger migration. Stateless persons, by definition, lack the protection offered by and the rights attached to citizenship. They may not possess any regularized status in the state in which they live, namely a formal right of residence. As a result, many stateless persons find themselves deprived of even the most basic human rights and unable to fulfil their everyday needs. Migration, in the hope of finding better treatment and greater opportunities elsewhere, may then be seen as a way to address their situation. In some instances, the underlying cause of statelessness points to a wider problem of discrimination, marginalization and even persecution that may, in turn, make irregular migration in search of protection or alternative economic and social opportunities an even more likely consequence.

10.3.2   Statelessness prevents people from using regular migration channels

In general, states have the authority to determine the conditions of entry, stay and expulsion of persons who are not their nationals. This authority is an essential feature of state sovereignty. However, this may also hinder the mobility of stateless persons. Stateless persons seeking to cross borders in response to particular push factors will often face restrictions on their legal movement due either to the lack of a nationality or the lack of documentation required for migration.

10.3.2.1   Non-admission and expulsion of non-nationals

International freedom of movement in essence comprises three rights – the right to enter, re-enter and return to a country; the right to remain in a country; and the right to leave a country.[7] The right to leave a country (or the right to emigrate) is a universal human right enumerated in international law,[8] but the corresponding rights to enter and remain in a country are usually attributed only to citizens of the state. As stated by the Human Rights Committee (HRC), the supervisory body for the International Covenant on Civil and Political Rights (ICCPR), the ICCPR 'does not recognize the right of aliens to enter or reside in the territory of a State party'[9] and that 'it is in principle a matter for the State to decide who it will admit to its territory'.[10] Stateless persons do not hold any nationality and therefore they cannot rely on an unfettered right to enter or remain in any country's territory as citizens. Consequently, states may also be less willing to admit a stateless person to their territory, as there is no guarantee that the individual could be removed should there be a reason to do so, because of the absence of a country of nationality obliged to readmit them.[11]

Nevertheless, the authority of states to restrict the entry and residence of and expel non-nationals on their territory is subject to certain

---

[7] L. E. van Waas, *Nationality Matters. Statelessness under International Law* (Antwerp/ Oxford/Portland, OR: Intersentia, 2008), at 245–6.

[8] Universal Declaration of Human Rights, Paris, 10 December 1948, GA Res. 217A(III), UN Doc. A/810 at 71, Art. 13(2); International Covenant on Civil and Political Rights (ICCPR), New York, 16 December 1966, in force 23 March 1976, 999 UNTS 171, Art. 12.

[9] Human Rights Committee, 'General Comment No. 15 on the Position of Aliens under the Covenant' (1986), para. 5.

[10] Human Rights Committee, 'General Comment No. 15 on the Position of Aliens under the Covenant', at para. 5. This principle as regards admission to the territory is also clearly recognized in Article 79 of the International Convention on the Protection of the Rights of All Migrant Workers and Members of Their Families (ICRMW), New York, 18 December 1990, in force 1 July 2003, 2220 UNTS 3: 'Nothing in the present Convention shall affect the right of each State Party to establish the criteria governing admission of migrant workers and members of their families'.

[11] For the obligation to readmit own nationals in international law, see N. Coleman, *European Readmission Policy; Third Country Interests and Refugee Rights* (Leiden: Brill, 2009), 28–33.

limitations under international law. For example, the HRC states that 'in certain circumstances an alien may enjoy the protection of the ICCPR even in relation to entry or residence, for example, when considerations of non-discrimination, prohibition of inhuman treatment and respect for family life arise.'[12] This recognizes that immigration policies need to give due consideration to the situation of vulnerable persons, including those who might be stateless. States are required to observe human rights principles that prohibit collective expulsion as well as the expulsion of specific groups (i.e. nationals, refugees or stateless people).[13] Many states also devote specific attention to the family connections of migrants in a country when considering expulsion. Further, international human rights law obliges states to balance interests in very specific circumstances, such as in cases that require primary consideration for the best interests of the child under the Convention on the Rights of the Child.[14] It also places procedural conditions on expulsion, such as in Article 13 of the ICCPR.[15] However, these apply only to migrants who are lawful residents in the territory of states that are also parties to the ICCPR. This disqualifies

---

[12] HRC, 'General Comment No.15', para. 5.

[13] Collective expulsion is explicitly prohibited by Article 4 of Protocol No. 4 to the European Convention on Human Rights (ECHR), Strasbourg, 16 September 1963, ETS 46, Article 12(5) of the African Charter on Human and Peoples' Rights (ACHPR), Banjul, 27 June 1981, in force 21 October 1986, OAU Doc. CAB/LEG/67/3 rev. 5 and Article 22(9) of the American Convention on Human Rights (ACHR), San Jose, 22 November 1969, 18 July 1978, OAS Treaty Series No. 36; however, the concept of 'collective expulsion' has varied between regions. The European Court of Human Rights has interpreted collective expulsion in the context of states requiring a group of non-nationals to leave a country without considering the individual cases of the people being expelled. See *Čonka and others* v. *Belgium*, Application No. 51564/99, European Court of Human Rights, judgment of 5 February 2002. Under Article 12(5) of the ACHPR, the concept of collective expulsion appears more limited, entailing an action against groups based on nationality, race, ethnicity or religion. In international human rights law, Article 22(1) of the ICRMW effectively applies the ECHR definition to bar expulsion that is not examined case by case. See also UNGA, 'International Law Commission, 59th Session, Geneva' (7 May–8 June and 9 July–10 August 2007), *Third report on the expulsion of aliens*, by Maurice Kamto, Special Rapporteur, UN Doc. A/CN.4/581 (19 April 2007) at 33–7.

[14] Convention on the Rights of the Child (CRC), New York, 20 November 1989, in force 2 September 1990, 1577 UNTS 3, Art. 3(1): 'In all actions concerning children, whether undertaken by public or private social welfare institutions, courts of law, administrative authorities or legislative bodies, the best interests of the child shall be a primary consideration'. This legal principle is now held to be customary international law, as evidenced by cases such as *Beharry* v. *Reno*, 183 F.Supp. 2d 584 (EDNY), a case in the US Federal District Court, which determined, ibid. at p.299, that the USA, in spite of not being party to the CRC, must account for the customary principles it enumerates when considering the expulsion of an immigrant with a US-born child.

[15] ICCPR, Art. 13: 'An alien lawfully in the territory … may be expelled therefrom only in pursuance of a decision reached in accordance with law and shall, except where

from protection migrants in an irregular situation, including those who have violated the terms of their visas or residence/work permits, although such protection is extended to irregular migrants under the International Convention on the Protection of the Rights of All Migrant Workers and Members of Their Families (ICRMW).[16] Moreover, the fact of non-expulsion does not necessarily amount to regularization of a person's immigration status – it may also lead to various forms of tolerated stay without changing the individual's position as an irregular migrant.[17]

States also have particular obligations when considering the return of non-nationals under international law. The principle of *non-refoulement*, as enshrined in Article 33 of the 1951 Convention relating to the Status of Refugees (1951 Convention)[18] and Article 3 of the 1984 Convention against Torture and Other Cruel, Inhuman or Degrading Treatment or Punishment (CAT),[19] is now regarded as customary international law,[20] and prohibits the return of refugees to a state or territory where their life or liberty would be at risk due to persecution because of their race, religion, political opinion, nationality or membership in a particular social group.[21] 'Stateless refugees' may therefore have an opportunity to 'regularize' their situation, depending on how states have implemented the obligation of *non-refoulement*. Yet, *non-refoulement* does not prevent removal to a third state, including for refugees who have been

---

compelling reasons of national security otherwise require, be allowed to submit the reasons against his expulsion and to have his case reviewed by, and be represented for the purpose before, the competent authority or a person or persons especially designated by the competent authority'.

[16] ICRMW, Art. 22(2)–(4).

[17] For the position in twenty-seven member states of the European Union (EU), see EU Agency for Fundamental Rights, 'Fundamental rights of migrants in an irregular situation in the European Union: Comparative report', Publications Office of the European Union, Luxembourg (2011), Ch. 2 (Non-removed persons).

[18] Convention relating to the Status of Refugees, Geneva, 28 July 1951, in force 22 April 1954, 189 UNTS 150.

[19] Convention against Torture and Other Cruel, Inhuman or Degrading Treatment or Punishment (CAT). New York, 10 December 1984, in force 26 June 1987, 1465 UNTS 85.

[20] But states will not be obliged to keep a refugee in their territory if that individual is considered a justifiable threat to national security or has committed a serious violation of the state's penal code. See Article 33(2) of the 1951 Refugee Convention.

[21] See Article 1 of the 1951 Refugee Convention: A refugee is a person who 'owing to well-founded fear of being persecuted for reasons of race, religion, nationality, membership of a particular social group or political opinion, is outside the country of his nationality and is unable or, owing to such fear, is unwilling to avail himself of the protection of that country; or who, not having a nationality and being outside the country of his former habitual residence as a result of such events, is unable or, owing to such fear, is unwilling to return to it'.

trafficked or smuggled, although this obligation requires the removing state to ensure that the persons concerned are not subsequently subject to *refoulement* to a state where their life or freedom is in danger. Nor does application of this principle automatically lead to the grant of asylum, permanent residence, or another durable status – these matters are still left to the state's discretion.[22] Moreover, the binding nature of the *non-refoulement* principle unfortunately has not deterred states parties to the 1951 Convention from repatriating or expelling refugees, nor has its status as customary law prevented violations by non-party destination countries.[23]

10.3.2.2 Lack of documentation as an impediment to regular migration

Travel documents are required for regular migration and mobility across borders generally. The purpose of travel documents, and the passport in particular, is to identify the individual and their citizenship – providing the destination state with the guarantee that, should it be necessary, there is a country which will accept the migrant's return. Passports also inform transport carriers of the status of the person and their ability to travel legally. Without proper documentation, an individual will face significant challenges in proving their identity and establishing their nationality, leaving them at a higher risk of becoming stateless.

Migrants may be without identity or travel documents for a variety of reasons. In some cases, they may destroy (or be required to do so by human traffickers or smugglers) their documents in an attempt to gain entry to a country through an unsubstantiated claim for asylum or false identification as a vulnerable migrant, such as a victim of trafficking. Some migrants may have never possessed any form of formal identification. This circumstance arises with second-generation migrants whose parent or guardian was prevented from obtaining birth registration and/

---

[22] For the scope and content of the principle of *non-refoulement*, see E. Lauterpacht and D. Bethlehem, 'The Scope and Content of the Principle of *non-refoulement*: Opinion' in E. Feller, V. Türk and F. Nicholson (eds.), *Refugee Protection in International Law: UNHCR's Global Consultations on International Protection* (Cambridge University Press, 2003) 87–177.

[23] See the 2009 World Refugee Survey, which provides an independent evaluation of refugee treatment across four categories. Under the category 'Refoulement/Physical Protection', fourteen countries and territories in four continents received 'F' [fail] grades for forcibly returning refugees, including Malaysia and Thailand in Southeast Asia. Fifty-one countries and territories and Europe as a general category, were included, and were graded A

or a birth certificate, which would establish a connection to the country of residence or to the country of origin.

Stateless persons will at best have limited access to travel documents, making it difficult or even impossible for them to travel or migrate through regular channels. When unable to obtain passports or other travel documents, they might use fraudulent documents or pay bribes to officials in their country of origin to obtain documents. Stateless persons might also pay a human smuggler to obtain fraudulent documents and evade immigration controls in the destination country. When this occurs, stateless persons become irregular migrants, thus increasing their vulnerability to associated risks and serious human rights violations, including trafficking for the purpose of sexual and labour exploitation.[24] Indeed, various sources from the United Nations, and government and non-government agencies highlight that stateless persons and undocumented migrants (including minors) in some Southeast Asian countries (such as Myanmar and Thailand) are at a disproportionate risk of trafficking.[25]

To avoid situations that oblige stateless persons to pursue irregular migration channels, thereby increasing their vulnerabilities to trafficking and other forms of exploitation, Article 28 of the 1954 Convention obliges hosting states parties to issue travel documents to stateless

through F on their performance. US Committee for Refugees and Immigrants, 'Refugee Rights Report Card', World Refugee Survey 2009 (2009).

[24] J. Bloom, 'The Link between Trafficking and Statelessness', International Catholic Migration Commission, presentation delivered to the US Catholic Coalition Against Human Trafficking (11 February 2009).

[25] Vital Voices Global Partnership, 'Stateless and Vulnerable to Human Trafficking in Thailand', Vital Voices Global Partnership, Washington, D.C. (June 2007); 'Trafficking in Persons Report', 10th edn, US Government, Department of State, Washington D.C., (2010), at p. 320; United Nations Educational, Scientific and Cultural Organization (UNESCO) Bangkok, 'Trafficking and HIV/AIDS Project', available at: www.unescobkk. org/culture/diversity/trafficking-hiv/projects/highland-citizenship-and-birth-registration-project/, last accessed 2 June 2014; D. A. Feingold, 'Human Trafficking', Think Again, Foreign Policy, 30 August 2005, 26–32, pp. 30–31: 'In Thailand, ... studies by ... [UNESCO] have demonstrated that a lack of proof of citizenship is the single greatest risk factor for a hill tribe girl or woman to be trafficked or otherwise exploited'. The United Nations Committee on the Rights of the Child, the human rights body supervising the application of the CRC, reported in 2006 'a significant number of children residing in Thailand remain stateless, which adversely impacts their full enjoyment of rights including education, development and access to social and health services, and renders them vulnerable to abuse, trafficking and exploitation'. See Committee on the Rights of the Child, 41st Session, 'Report on the Forty-first Session (Geneva, 9–27 January 2006)', UN Doc. CRC/C/41/3 (12 May 2006), at p. 167, para. 846.

persons.[26] However, this obligation only applies to 'stateless persons lawfully staying in their territory', which excludes a high proportion of the stateless population who lack a status in their country of habitual residence. States are also encouraged to issue travel documents to any other stateless persons present in their territory and who are not permanent residents of their country, especially when they are unable to obtain such documents 'from the country of their lawful residence'. For example, the domestic law of the Philippines (the only state party to the 1954 Convention in Southeast Asia) permits the issuance of a 'travel document, in lieu of a passport', to 'a stateless person who is likewise a permanent resident … in the Philippines'.[27] However, even if travel documents can be issued to stateless persons in lieu of a national passport under the laws of certain countries, there is no guarantee that all stateless persons will be able to access this option. In addition, the stateless person will have to satisfy all the other requirements set by the destination country's immigration law.

10.4. Statelessness as a consequence of irregular migration

Today, irregular migration is a phenomenon occurring in most regions of the world. In response, states are making greater efforts to assert and control their borders, while also implementing strict immigration regimes that make it more difficult for migrants to enter countries of destination through official channels. The circumstances surrounding irregular migration and migrants' treatment in destination countries often increase their vulnerability to becoming stateless.

For a long time migration was essentially unregulated by origin and destination countries, and borders were less significant than they are today. Some of this movement dates from before the introduction of modern nationality laws. Moreover, a number of minority groups were not fully considered when states sought to establish rules, at both international and national level, to regulate transnational migration. As such, access to nationality has been problematic, leaving these ethnic groups in legal limbo and/or a situation of statelessness.

---

[26] See the travel document in the Schedule to the 1954 Convention.
[27] Philippines Passport Act 1996, Republic Act No. 8239, Section 13(e). This provision should enable stateless persons to travel regularly, return to the Philippines and avoid becoming stranded abroad. However, the implementation and effectiveness of this law has been questioned given the lack of publicly available data indicating the number of travel documents issued.

10.4.1   Conflicts of nationality laws

Migration brings with it a greater mixing of different ethnicities, languages, cultures and nationalities. With this mixing of people comes a greater risk of conflicts of nationality laws that may render people stateless. Moreover, migration may change a person's position under the applicable nationality law, making it harder for him or her to retain or access citizenship. Where migration is deemed irregular and the person lacks a legal immigration status, the risk of statelessness is increased. Irregular migrants are less likely to fulfil the requirements for acquiring a new nationality because naturalization is usually conditional upon a prolonged period of lawful residence. Yet they may lose the nationality of their country of origin. For example, a major concern under Indonesia's previous nationality law was that long-term migrants in Malaysia and elsewhere only had a limited time during which they could live outside Indonesia before forfeiting their nationality. The new Indonesian Citizenship Law, passed in 2006, addresses this problem, stating that Indonesians residing abroad for non-official purposes and without legal reason will not lose their citizenship after five years rendered stateless in the process.[28] Further, as observed in Section 10.4.4 below, under the law of Myanmar, the mere fact of migrating irregularly may be sanctioned with the loss of citizenship.

Depending on the law of the state, individuals may have the right to renounce their nationality, even if this would leave them stateless. Where states do not accept dual citizenship, renunciation may be required if an individual wants to apply for naturalization in another country, for instance following a period of residence there or after marriage to a national. Here, a potential conflict of laws may arise when the original citizenship is relinquished without prior guarantee of acquisition of a new nationality.

Children may also be placed at an increased risk of statelessness by their parents' irregular migration status as there is a greater chance of a conflict of nationality laws.[29] Where children are born to stateless irregular migrants in a destination country, they may not be able to access that state's citizenship because that country does not provide *jus soli* citizenship or contains

---

[28] Law of the Republic of Indonesia No. 12 on Citizenship of the Republic of Indonesia, 1 August 2006, Art. 23(i). See also J. Sidel, 'Indonesia: Minorities, Migrant Workers, Refugees, and the New Citizenship Law', UNHCR, Status Determination and Protection Information Section (DIPS) (March 2007), at pp. 21–2.

[29] *Case of the Yean and Bosico Children* v. *The Dominican Republic*, Inter-American Court of Human Rights, judgment of 8 September 2005.

exceptions in its nationality law for people of a particular immigration status to qualify for nationality *jus soli*. Safeguards against statelessness for children born on a state's territory who do not acquire a nationality at birth are often conditional upon the residence status of the parents and exclude children of irregular migrants. This leaves such children wholly reliant on *jus sanguinis* laws to acquire the nationality of their parents, which is immediately problematic if the parents have lost or renounced their nationality. There is also a risk of statelessness in cases where women are restricted from transmitting their nationality to their children or to their children born abroad, as is the case under the Malaysian nationality law. Furthermore, a child born abroad may be left stateless if action is not taken by the parents in accordance with nationality laws, including those of countries of origin. In such cases, the irregular status of the parents in the host country may be an impediment to accessing consular services in order to claim nationality for their children, putting them at greater risk of statelessness compared with children of lawfully residing migrants.

10.4.2   Lack of access to birth registration

Birth registration provides the basis for a state recognizing the existence of a child in its boundaries, and details information such as the date and place of birth, and family background of the child. This constitutes the foundations for claiming citizenship by *jus soli* or *jus sanguinis*. In the absence of documented birth registration and certification, a state can dispute a child's nationality claim in their territory, greatly increasing the risk that the child will not have citizenship ties to any state.[30]

Failure to obtain birth registration may be broadly attributed to either parental inaction or government administrative practices. Children of irregular migrants may face additional barriers to accessing birth registration. These factors include parental fear of arrest, detention, and deportation due to an irregular or undefined immigration status; lack of knowledge about the importance of registering children at birth; the time and financial costs involved in registration; and complex administrative or bureaucratic procedures (sometimes intentional) that impede parental access to registration. Some states have also interpreted civil registration laws in conjunction with immigration laws to disqualify irregular

---

[30] L. E. van Waas, 'Is permanent illegality inevitable? The challenges to ensuring birth registration and the right to a nationality for children of irregular migrants – Thailand and the Dominican Republic' (*Woking*: Plan, 2006) 11–12.

migrants from registering the birth of their children.[31] For these reasons, children of irregular migrants are at increased risk of non-recognition as a citizen by either the host country or country of nationality of the parents and therefore of becoming stateless.

10.4.3   Unaccompanied minors

Unaccompanied minors, including those children who are abandoned, orphaned or separated from their parents or legal guardians, without clear indication of parentage and nationality, are at greater risk of state-lessness. Children may be unaccompanied because of separation from their family while seeking asylum across borders, displacement in war zones, abandonment for social or economic reasons, or because of their parents' deportation due to an irregular immigration status. Exploitation by human traffickers also frequently results in children finding them-selves in an unaccompanied situation.

In the case of unaccompanied minors, birth registration is important. In the process of separation, registered children can lose documentation, have it destroyed by traffickers, or destroy it themselves to avoid identi-fication. However, depending on the accessibility of registration records and the circumstances of departure, these children are likely to be identi-fied, verified and sent to either a third country or their country of origin. This may not occur in the case of unregistered minors, who do not possess officially documented proof of age, lineage, or nationality, and thus face the possibility of becoming stateless without an identity or familial link.[32] To avoid statelessness among unaccompanied children, some countries, such as Indonesia, Laos and Vietnam, have crafted provisions in their domestic citizenship policies that grant nationality to children born to stateless parents, or of unspecified origin or unknown parentage.[33]

---

[31] Thailand's pre-2008 Civil Registration law (The Civil Registration Act 1991) is indicative of this practice. See van Waas, 'Is permanent illegality inevitable?'; UNESCO 'Capacity Building on Birth Registration and Citizenship in Thailand: Citizenship Manual', Bangkok, UNESCO (2008), p. 8.

[32] M. Miller, 'Birth Registration: Statelessness and Other Repercussions for Unregistered Children' in 'Nationality and the Child', 3rd European Conference on Nationality, Council of Europe, Strasbourg, 11–12 October 2004, UNICEF Innocenti Research Centre (2004), p. 8.

[33] For example, see Law on Lao Nationality, 29 November 1990, LAO-110, Arts. 11 and 12.

10.4.4   *Statelessness in the context of return*

When irregular migrants are deported or returned (voluntarily or forcibly) to their country of origin, the irregular manner of departure from their own country and entry into another can jeopardize their citizenship status and lead to statelessness. States have an obligation under international law to accept the return of their own nationals. However, countries of origin, although obliged to accept those nationals who return, may use their own nationality or immigration laws to either delay or deny readmission of their citizens. For example, under Myanmar's Citizenship Law, migrants who depart the country through unauthorized channels may be considered to have permanently left the country and have their citizenship revoked.[34] These stateless irregular migrants normally end up in a stranded situation. Moreover, for children of irregular migrants and subsequent generations of migrants, the lack of proof of nationality and the absence of birth registration can complicate return efforts. Ultimately, the universal element influencing a migrant's vulnerability to statelessness, particularly in the context of return, is the lack of access to identity and travel documentation.

10.5.   Final reflections and suggestions for a way forward

The statelessness and migration nexus should be of real concern to the international community. Whether statelessness is a cause or consequence of migration, particularly *irregular* migration, this chapter has demonstrated that there is a significant overlap between them. Examples from the Southeast Asian context have illustrated that the direct or indirect operation of immigration, civil registration and nationality laws can result in statelessness among particular categories of vulnerable migrants. Statelessness can be a direct result of birth outside the country of nationality of the parents, or of a mixed-nationality marriage where the safeguards currently in place are inadequate to deal with the realities on the ground. In other instances, the linkages are more complex, whereby irregular migration impedes access to birth registration and this, in turn, impedes access to a nationality.

---

[34] Tang Lay Lee, *Statelessness, Human Rights and Gender: Irregular Migrant Workers from Myanmar in Thailand*, (Leiden: Martinus Nijhoff, 2005), 158–9; van Waas, 'Is permanent illegality inevitable?', 14–16.

The fact of *irregular* migration remains a significant obstacle to acquisition of a nationality for both migrants and their children born on the territory of the host state. Being both an irregular migrant and stateless renders a person extremely vulnerable to human rights abuses, marginalization, and economic and social exclusion. The irregularity of migrants' status is also a barrier to resolution of statelessness in the longer term, since it impedes access to naturalization. The problem is therefore likely to be both enduring and multi-generational.

Specifically, stateless persons who are or become irregular migrants will often find themselves subject to arrest and deportation, ending up in detention facilities in countries of transit and/or destination because they have breached immigration laws. Often lacking protection from any state, with no state willing to accept their return, these persons are particularly vulnerable to human rights violations in detention facilities[35] and to violations of procedural rules.[36] Stateless migrants may face indefinite detention in immigration facilities under the condition of 'pending removal' or 'pending deportation'. In this situation, removal of an individual is improbable because often there is no country able or willing to admit them. Further, irregular stateless migrants can face repeated detention unless a legal status is issued or lawful access to another state is secured upon their release. This 'cycle of detention' could be avoided by implementing practices and policies geared towards finding alternatives to detention. When irregular migrants are also stateless, state responses need to be adaptable to their situation, given that other states may refuse to accept the return of these migrants. As arbitrary detention is unlawful under international law,[37] there are a number of alternatives to detention that could be adopted by a state while a suitable, durable solution is sought. Putting in place alternative policies would not only improve migrants' treatment and states' compliance with international human

---

[35] See, for example, provisions regarding irregular immigration under Malaysia's Immigration Act 1959/1963, as amended in 2002. Sentences for irregular entry include fines, detention, corporal punishment (caning) and deportation. Irregular migrants may therefore face 'caning' for unauthorized entry into Malaysia's territory, a practice consisting of a number of 'strokes' (hits) with a rattan cane. This could qualify as torture (or inhuman or degrading treatment or punishment) and would therefore violate international law.

[36] According to Amnesty International, several foreign nationals did not obtain legal representation when they were sentenced to the practice of caning, which is a violation of procedural rules guaranteeing access to fair and impartial justice. See 'A Blow to Humanity – Torture by Judicial Caning in Malaysia', Amnesty International, December 2010, p. 11.

[37] See UDHR, Art. 9; ICCPR, Art. 9(1).

rights standards, but could also be a way for states to avoid the economic burden associated with detention. Alternatives to detention include provision of shelter; bail or posting a bond; reporting requirements; release to non-governmental supervision; semi-open accommodation centres and restrictions to a specific area; and electronic monitoring and home curfew.[38]

Moreover, states should give further consideration to the implementation of measures that will resolve a person's statelessness, including through naturalization. Article 32 of the 1954 Statelessness Convention stipulates that states shall facilitate the naturalization of stateless persons and make every effort to expedite proceedings and reduce related charges and costs. Despite this, most states are reluctant to naturalize stateless people present in their territory. Yet, several Southeast Asian countries have gone some way to addressing statelessness in their territory through naturalization.[39] Moreover, it remains vital to recognize that where a stateless person is also an irregular migrant, it is impossible for him or her to accrue a period of lawful residence that is usually required to naturalize.

It is important, therefore, that states address the nexus between statelessness and migration more comprehensively. Recognizing and regularizing stateless persons and providing them with access to travel and identity documents will be an important means of reducing the number

---

[38] O. Field (with the assistance of A. Edwards), 'Alternatives to Detention of Asylum Seekers and Refugees', Legal and Protection Policy Research Series, POLAS/2006/03, Geneva, UNHCR, Division of International Protection Services (April 2006); 'Alternatives to immigration detention of families and children', a discussion paper by J. Bercow MP, Lord Dubs and E. Harris MP for the All Party Parliamentary Groups on Children and Refugees, No Place for a Child Coalition (July 2006).

[39] These countries include Brunei, Indonesia, Malaysia, Thailand and Vietnam. Stateless permanent residents can now obtain Bruneian citizenship by passing comprehensive tests in Malay culture, customs and language. See S. Han, 'Stateless, but a Bruneian at heart', *The Brunei Times*, 17 December 2010: 'So what does it take for a stateless person who was born and bred here to become a citizen of Brunei? Passing a test in Malay culture, customs, language and the national Malay Islamic Monarchy philosophy.' Indonesia also agreed to grant citizenship to its ethnic Chinese population; in May 2008, 139 of these ethnic Chinese stateless people became citizens of Indonesia. See 'The International Observatory on Statelessness, Indonesia', available at: www.nationality-forall.org/indonesia, last accessed 2 June 2014; and L. Yen Mun, 'Citizenship for 91-year-old', The Star Online, 9 August 2010. See also 'Viet Nam ends stateless limbo for 2,300 former Cambodians', UNHCR News Stories, 19 July 2010; and 'The National Human Rights Commission of Thailand and UN High Commissioner on Refugees to stop and eliminate statelessness problems in Thailand', National Human Rights Commission of Thailand (6 June 2012), with regard to the publication of a Handbook on Section 23 of the Nationality Act (No 4), B.E. 2551 (2008).

of migrants in an irregular situation as well as irregular migration flows. This is a shared concern and in the interest of all states, including those in the Southeast Asian region.

Questions to guide discussion

1. Explain the term 'irregular migration'. What are the factors that lead to 'irregular migration'?
2. Can you identify at least four reasons why stateless people are likely to become *irregular* migrants?
3. The rights to enter and remain in a country are usually attributed only to nationals of the state. Does this mean a state may always deny entry to or expel stateless people? What international rules offer protection against expulsion for non-nationals?
4. What might be some of the challenges for states trying to prevent statelessness among people who are irregular immigrants? Can you think of a way to address these challenges?
5. Is it possible for states acting alone to solve the issues arising from stateless people who are irregular immigrants, or is this an issue that requires the involvement of the international community? What could the international community do to help solve this issue?

More or less secure? Nationality questions, deportation and dual nationality

KIM RUBENSTEIN AND NIAMH LENAGH-MAGUIRE

11.1. Introduction

Recent trends in some countries suggest that dual nationality has made individuals more vulnerable to deportation than single nationals of a nation state. Is this appropriate and what does it mean for the meaning of nationality and statelessness under national and international law? In this chapter we argue that countries *should* commit to a broader notion of membership than nationality, drawing upon the UN Human Rights Committee's jurisprudence. By examining the meaning of one's 'own country' and the extent it protects against deportation we argue for a more secure membership for individuals with dual citizenship.

The structure of this chapter reflects the distinction between the concepts of 'nationality' in international law and the 'citizenship' created and regulated by domestic legal regimes. While both terms are used broadly to describe an individual's status as a member of a nation state, there is more than a semantic difference between the two ideas: 'Conceptually and linguistically ... the terms emphasise two different aspects of the same notion ... "Nationality" stresses the international, "citizenship" the national, municipal aspect.'[1] For the purposes of this chapter, we take 'nationality' to mean the legal relationship between an individual and a nation state that is recognized under international law, and 'citizenship' to mean the relationship created or recognized by the domestic laws of states.[2] We first

---

[1] P Weis, *Nationality and Statelessness in International Law*, 2 edn (Alphen aan den Rijn: Sijthoff & Noordhoff International Publishers B.V., 1979), 4–5. See also the contribution by Edwards at Chapter 1 of this volume.

[2] Also important are what Joseph Carens describes as the 'psychological' dimension of citizenship and Linda Bosniak's concept of citizenship as identity or solidarity, that is, 'the quality of belonging, the felt aspects of community membership' (L. Bosniak, 'Citizenship Denationalized (The State of Citizenship Symposium)', *Indiana Journal of Global Legal*

examine the concept of 'dual nationality' in terms of international law before analyzing the domestic citizenship laws of two countries – namely the United Kingdom and Australia[3] – in order to highlight the tensions between the idea of 'effective nationality' and modern, multiple citizenships. Where dual nationals are concerned, neither 'nationality', as it is currently understood in international law, nor the domestic legal status of 'citizenship', are presently capable of providing citizens with fair protection against deprivation of citizenship and deportation.

11.2.   Dual nationality and deportation under international law

Historically, exclusivity has been an essential characteristic of nationality. The concept of nationality in international law has its origins in the allegiance owed by subjects to a sovereign ruler.[4] This was an exclusive and insoluble allegiance, representing a 'debt of gratitude'[5] the subject could never discharge and which could not be renounced unilaterally.[6] Allegiance was exclusive, in the sense that a person could only be a subject of one sovereign at a time. As the sovereign nation state assumed its central position in international relations and international law, nationality came to mean the transferable allegiance owed by a citizen to the state, rather than the enduring bond of fealty or loyalty to a sovereign.[7] However, nationality was still, at least ideally, a monogamous relationship. As Peter Spiro has observed, individuals who had more than one national allegiance presented both practical and philosophical problems:

> Dual nationals represented on the one hand a constant source of international tension where one state attempted to protect its citizen from mistreatment at the hands of another state claiming the same individual

---

Studies 7 (2000) 447, 479). Later in this chapter we consider how law can enhance or defeat these elements of citizenship.

[3] We do not claim that these jurisdictions are necessarily representative of a broader trend, simply that there are parallels in the development of their respective citizenship laws.

[4] Peter Spiro, 'Dual Nationality and the Meaning of Citizenship' Emory Law Journal 46 (1997) 1412, 1420–2.

[5] William Blackstone, Commentaries on the Laws of England (3rd edn, Chicago, IL: Callaghan & Co., 1884) 117. See also Spiro, 'Dual Nationality and the Meaning of Citizenship', 1420.

[6] Rex v. Macdonald 18 Geo. 2 St. Tr. 858, 859 (1747).

[7] Kim Rubenstein and Daniel Adler, 'International Citizenship: The Future of Nationality in a Globalized World' Indiana Journal of Global Legal Studies 7 (2000) 519, 531; Spiro, 'Dual Nationality and the Meaning of Citizenship'.

as its own. On the other hand, the presumptively divided loyalties of dual nationals represented a serious potential threat from within the polity in times of international conflict.[8]

The British and Australian case studies discussed in this chapter demonstrate that the phenomenon of dual nationality continues to present the same challenges today.

In the absence of any international legal mechanism to regulate nationality in a comprehensive way, dual nationality attracted various legal responses in the international and domestic spheres. Kim Rubenstein and Daniel Adler identified several attempts in the early to mid-twentieth century to codify the international law on the topic, each of which was premised on the general undesirability of dual nationality while upholding the rights of states to determine for themselves who should hold their nationality.[9] However, as Forcese notes, one of these instruments – the Hague Convention of 1930 – cemented the conditions for dual citizenship to arise by default, by allowing nationals of one country to obtain another nationality intentionally, but not to renounce their original nationality.[10] The Hague Convention did not guarantee that dual nationals would always enjoy the same rights as their counterparts who held only one nationality; importantly, Article 4 of the Hague Convention provided that a 'State may not afford diplomatic protection to one of its nationals against a State whose nationality such person also possesses'.[11]

11.2.1   Dual nationality and deportation – problems with 'effective nationality'

The role of allegiance as the basis of nationality is echoed in the leading decision of the International Court of Justice (ICJ) on nationality in the context of diplomatic protection, the *Nottebohm* case.[12] The threshold question for the ICJ was whether, by voluntarily acquiring citizenship of Liechtenstein and thereby relinquishing his German citizenship, Friedrich Nottebohm had effectively changed his nationality for the purposes of

---

[8] Spiro, 'Dual Nationality and the Meaning of Citizenship', 1414–15.

[9] Rubenstein and Adler, 'International Citizenship', 532–3. See also Craig Forcese, 'The Capacity to Protect: Diplomatic Protection of Dual Nationals in the "War on Terror"', *The European Journal of International Law* 17 (2006) 369.

[10] Forcese, 'The Capacity to Protect', 383–4.

[11] Convention on Certain Questions Relating to the Conflict of Nationality Law, The Hague, 13 April 1930, in force 1 July 1937, 179 LNTS 89.

[12] *Liechtenstein v. Guatemala (Nottebohm)* 1955 ICJ 4.

international law. Nottebohm had emigrated from his native Germany to Guatemala in 1905, aged 24, and continued to live there, working in a family business, until the outbreak of the Second World War.[13] In 1939, shortly after the start of the war, Nottebohm travelled to Liechtenstein and sought citizenship there; when it was granted, he lost his German citizenship automatically, and returned to Guatemala.[14] Despite allowing him to re-enter on a Liechtenstein passport, Guatemala persisted in treating Nottebohm as though he were a German citizen, deporting him to the United States and confiscating his property.[15] After the war, Liechtenstein sought to challenge these actions on Nottebohm's behalf.

A majority of the ICJ did not accept that the nationality Liechtenstein had conferred on Nottebohm could validly be invoked against Guatemala for the purpose of diplomatic protection. The question for the ICJ was whether Liechtenstein, by granting citizenship, had acquired a 'sufficient title to the exercise of protection in respect of Nottebohm as against Guatemala' and was therefore entitled to seize the court of a diplomatic protection claim on his behalf.[16] The court examined the basis of Nottebohm's nationality and held that nationality is a 'legal bond having as its basis a social fact of attachment, a genuine connection of existence, interests and sentiments, together with the existence of reciprocal rights and duties'.[17] The facts of Nottebohm's case disclosed no 'bond of attachment' or 'long-standing and close connection' with Liechtenstein as a matter of social fact, but instead pointed towards Mr Nottebohm's long-standing link with Guatemala. Nottebohm had, clearly, attempted to utilize the apparent leniency of the international rules of nationality in order to avoid the operation of the laws of war.[18] In the court's view neither Nottebohm nor Liechtenstein had acted unlawfully, but Liechtenstein had granted citizenship 'without regard to the concept of nationality adopted in international relations'.[19] While Liechtenstein was entitled to grant citizenship, Guatemala did not need to recognize that citizenship as effective nationality for the purposes of providing Nottebohm with diplomatic protection.[20]

[13] *Ibid.*, 13. [14] *Ibid.*, 15–16.

[15] Cindy Buys has explored the political and, pointedly, economic context of the US detention programme, 'Nottebohm's Nightmare: Have We Exorcised the Ghosts of WWII Detention Programs or Do They Still Haunt Guantanamo?' (*Chicago Kent Journal of International and Comparative Law* (2011) 11).

[16] *Nottebohm* 1955 ICJ 4, 15–16, see also 246. [17] *Ibid.*, 23.

[18] *Ibid.*, 26. See also Robert D. Sloane, 'Breaking the Genuine Link: The Contemporary International Legal Regulation of Nationality', *Harvard International Law Review* 50 (2009), 11.

[19] *Nottebohm* 1955 ICJ 4, 26. [20] *Ibid.*, 26.

268   KIM RUBENSTEIN AND NIAMH LENAGH-MAGUIRE

While Mr Nottebohm was not a dual national, the concept of 'effect-ive nationality' expounded in his case has since been applied to resolve questions about dual-nationals' standing to bring legal claims based on one or other of their citizenships. The Iran–US Claims Tribunal, estab-lished to, inter alia, decide the claims of 'nationals of the United States against Iran and claims of nationals of Iran against the United States',[21] was asked where this placed dual Iranian–US nationals.[22] A majority of the tribunal held that it had jurisdiction to hear the claims against Iran of US–Iranian citizens, provided that their 'dominant and effect-ive nationality ... during the relevant period ... was that of the United States'.[23] As Robert Sloan has recently noted,[24] the provenance of 'domin-ant and effective' nationality is much older than *Nottebohm*, but the tri-bunal was at pains to emphasize that its decision was consistent with the *Nottebohm* decision and reasoning of the majority in that case.[25] Indeed, as Rubenstein and Adler note, the two decisions share an underlying conclusion that the legal concept of nationality is based on the existence of a genuine connection with a nation state, as a matter of social fact.[26] However, the majority of the tribunal departed from the ICJ's approach by seemingly accepting that a person could have more than one effective nationality, notwithstanding the need to identify one as 'dominant' for the purposes of standing.[27]

Although dual nationality was not squarely in issue in Nottebohm's case,[28] the decision has two important implications for dual nationality, particularly in the context of attempts to deport a dual national from one of his or her countries of nationality. First, there are suggestions in the ICJ's decision that the basis of 'effective nationality', recognized under international law, is not simply social connectedness with a state but

[21] 'Declaration of the Government of the Democratic and Political Republic of Algeria concerning the Settlement of Claims by the Government of the United States and the Government of the Islamic Republic of Iran', 20 ILM 230 (1981).
[22] 'Decision in Case No A/18 Concerning the Question of Jurisdiction over Claims of Persons with Dual Nationality' (6 April 1984) 5 Iran–US Claims Tribunal Reports 251 (*Iran–US Claims Tribunal Case*)
[23] *Iran–US Claims Tribunal Case*, 5 Iran–US Claims Tribunal Reports 251, 253.
[24] Sloane argues that the tribunal's reasons 'conferred on the genuine link theory an unwar-ranted veneer of positive legal authority', and contributed to its overestimation in inter-national law: Sloane, 'Breaking the Genuine Link', 28.
[25] *Ibid.*, 28.
[26] Rubenstein and Adler, 'International Citizenship', 537.
[27] *Iran–US Claims Tribunal Case*, 5 Iran–US Claims Tribunal Reports 251, 265–6.
[28] Mr Nottebohm was not, and did not claim to be, a citizen of any country other than Liechtenstein.

allegiance to the state, and that such allegiance is exclusive. Nationality is 'the juridical expression of the fact that the individual upon whom it is conferred … is in fact more closely connected with the population of the State conferring nationality than with that of any other State'.[29] Prima facie this view of nationality seems incompatible with the proposition that one person may hold nationality of more than one state.[30]

Second, the idea of an effective nationality or one based on a 'genuine link', may apply differently between naturalized citizens and citizens by birthright. *Nottebohm* suggests that naturalization can only be effective under international law if it is accompanied by a genuine link between the citizen and the naturalizing state, whereas no such principle has been held to apply in respect of birthright citizenship.[31] In *Nottebohm*, the majority of the ICJ focused on the particular circumstances of Nottebohm's naturalization, and on the significance of naturalization as a legal process more generally, in explaining why a genuine link was shown between the naturalized citizen and the country whose nationality was claimed.

As Robert Sloane has argued, it is important to understand *Nottebohm* as a decision about diplomatic protection, rather than as articulating a universally applicable concept of nationality in international law. Sloane is critical of what he describes as 'an unwarranted reliance on Nottebohm's romantic dicta about nationality'.[32] Sloane points out that the genuine link theory propounded in *Nottebohm* may have been 'descriptively questionable' even at the time the case was decided. In any event, it is certainly now at odds with attitudes to nationality in contemporary international law and, we would argue, the contemporary acceptance of dual nationality in domestic laws,[33] as discussed further below.

11.2.2 A broader view of 'one's own country'

Nationality in the *Nottebohm* sense recognizes that the existence of such status has an effective, social dimension. *Nottebohm* suggests that where formal legal nationality is present, but a genuine connection is lacking, the person is not to be treated as holding effective nationality (at least where

---

[29] *Nottebohm* 1955 ICJ 4, 23.

[30] Rubenstein and Adler, 'International Citizenship', 523. Cf Sloane, 'Breaking the Genuine Link'.

[31] Robert Sloane argues that, if a 'genuine link' really is the touchstone of nationality, 'the ICJ would have been obliged to find Liechtenstein's case equally inadmissible' even if Nottebohm had been born in Liechtenstein, rather than Germany, but had no other connection with that state: Sloane, 'Breaking the Genuine Link', 17–18.

[32] *Ibid.*, 4.   [33] *Ibid.*, 32.

the formal dimension of nationality was obtained via naturalization). However, *Nottebohm* does not provide a solution in the reverse where there is ample evidence of the social connection between an individual and a state, but formal citizenship is lacking as a matter of domestic law. That task falls most often to human rights law as invoked by individuals seeking some of the benefits of nationality from a nation state that either refuses to grant them legal status, or conversely labels them with a citizenship they do not want to retain.

Most relevantly for this chapter, the United Nations Human Rights Committee (HRC), constituted under the Optional Protocol to the International Covenant on Civil and Political Rights (ICCPR),[34] has received complaints from individuals who maintained long-term residence in states whose citizenship they did not hold, but who nonetheless sought to invoke the protection of Article 12, paragraph 4 of the ICCPR: 'No one shall be arbitrarily deprived of the right to enter his own country.' In the first of those cases considered here, *Stewart v. Canada*,[35] while the complaint was not ultimately upheld, it did give rise to several strong dissenting opinions, laying the foundation for a recent, successful, complaint in *Nystrom v. Australia*.[36] We consider *Stewart* briefly, and return to *Nystrom* in our discussion of dual nationality in Australia.

Stewart was a British citizen who had lived in Canada since he was seven years old. As an adult, he was convicted of over forty criminal offences.[37] The Canadian government sought to deport Stewart to the United Kingdom, whereupon he complained to the HRC that he had been arbitrarily deprived of the right to enter his 'own country'. A majority of the committee found the phrase 'own country' was not confined to formal nationality, but declined to extend it as far as people in the position of Stewart, who, it said, 'could be deemed to have opted to remain [an alien] in Canada', and who should bear the consequences.[38] In their dissenting opinion, however, Members Evatt and Ouroga wrote:

---

[34] International Covenant on Civil and Political Rights (ICCPR), New York, 16 December 1966, in force 23 March 1976, 999 UNTS 302.

[35] *Stewart v. Canada* (1997) CCPR/C/58D/538/1993.

[36] *Nystrom v. Australia* CCPR/C/102/D/1557/2007.

[37] Human Rights Committee, *Stewart v. Canada* (1997) CCPR/C/58D/538/1993 [2.2].

[38] For the majority, a decision not to obtain nationality in a country where naturalization was offered could be a matter of active refusal, or could be evidenced by a course of action that led to the state's offer of naturalization being withdrawn, by, for example, committing criminal offences [12.8].

for the rights set forth in article 12, the existence of a formal link to the State is irrelevant; the Covenant is here concerned with the strong personal and emotional links an individual may have with the territory where he lives and with the social circumstances obtaining in it.[39]

As we explain below, this approach of identifying a person's 'own country' was endorsed by a majority of the HRC in the later case of *Nystrom*. It represents a welcome expansion of the rather more limited notion of effective nationality employed in *Nottebohm*. It may also, we suggest, provide a useful way of thinking through the domestic citizenship cases of attempted deportation of dual nationals (such as the recent Australian and British cases considered in this chapter), by providing a way of determining whether, in a particular case, an individual's claim to nationality is so strong as to preclude their expulsion or exclusion from a country. It is to these citizenship cases that we now turn.

11.3. Precarious dual citizenship in the United Kingdom and Australia

We argue that possessing dual nationality can, and in some cases has, made citizenship less secure as a matter of domestic law. Drawing on the example of citizenship laws in the United Kingdom and Australia, we show how the law reflects an underlying tension in states' approaches to dual nationality between the desire to acknowledge the reality of some citizens' multiple allegiances, and to manage the risk that these multiple allegiances may be associated with undesirable behaviour. The approach adopted in the UK and Australia is a blunt one: citizens are allowed to maintain multiple nationalities, but if they do, their additional nationality weakens their grasp on their British or Australian citizenship, and makes them uniquely vulnerable to the revocation of their citizenship and to deportation. Since the UK and Australia can deprive a dual national of their British or Australian citizenship (as applicable) without violating international law by making the citizen stateless and offending the 1961 Convention on the Reduction of Statelessness, their Parliaments have expressly reserved the right to do so by conferring powers on the Executive to revoke citizenship, facilitating the deportation of former citizens.[40]

---

[39] *Stewart* v. *Canada* (1997), para. 5.
[40] It should be noted that the idea of revoking citizenship as punishment is not unique to the two countries whose citizenship regimes are considered in this chapter. Similar

11.4.   Dual nationality and loss of citizenship in the United Kingdom

11.4.1   Evolving legal attitudes to dual citizenship

Historically, British nationality law has tended to tolerate the possession of multiple nationalities by British citizens.[41] Indeed, as the common law did not recognize any right to renounce British subject status,[42] a British subject who acquired another citizenship had no option to be anything other than a dual national.[43] From 1870 to 1948, the previous attitude of tolerance towards dual nationality was abandoned in favour of a more restrictive set of rules.[44]

In 1948, a coordinated programme of nationality law reform throughout the Commonwealth commenced. Following Canada's adoption of a statutory form of 'Canadian citizenship' in 1946,[45] representatives of the United Kingdom and Commonwealth governments met and agreed that the UK and the self-governing members of the Commonwealth (the Dominions) would each adopt separate citizenship schemes, with citizens of the Commonwealth countries retaining the status of 'British subject' in addition to their new national citizenships.[46] At least as far as British law was concerned, a British subject could be a dual national. Indeed, this was the essential premise of the common scheme agreed

---

proposals are, or have been, considered actively in the United States, Israel and France. See Matthew J. Gibney, 'Should Citizenship Be Conditional? Denationalization and Liberal Principles' RSC Working Paper Series No. 75 (2 August 2011); Shai Lavy, 'Punishment and the Revocation of Citizenship in the United Kingdom, the United States and Israel' *New Criminal Law Review* 13 (2010), 404.

[41] For an overview of the history of dual nationality under British immigration law, see UK Home Office, 'Dual Nationality' (undated), available at www.bia.homeoffice.gov.uk/sitecontent/documents/policyandlaw/nationalityinstructions/nisec2gensec/dualnationality?view=Binary, last accessed 2 June 2014.

[42] Spiro, 'Dual Nationality and the Meaning of Citizenship'.

[43] While it was eventually accepted, as a matter of British law, that King George III had waived the allegiance of the revolutionary inhabitants of the American colonies that did not mean that British migrants to the United States could unilaterally absolve themselves of their allegiance to the Crown. Peter Spiro describes some of the legal and practical consequences of the English doctrine of perpetual allegiance in this context: see Spiro, 'Dual Nationality and the Meaning of Citizenship', 1421–2.

[44] Naturalization Act 1870, 33 & 34 Vict.168, ss 4–6.

[45] Canadian Citizenship Act 1946. See further Randall Hansen, 'The Politics of Citizenship in 1940s Britain: The British Nationality Act', *Twentieth Century British History* 10 (1999) 67.

[46] Hansen, 'The Politics of Citizenship in 1940s Britain'.

by the Commonwealth nations in 1948, which allowed the creation of Dominion citizenship without jeopardizing the status of the inhabitants of the Commonwealth as British nationals. The committee of experts from Commonwealth countries who designed the scheme reported that '[t]he essential features of such a system are that each of the countries shall by its legislation determine who are its citizens [and] shall declare those citizens to be British subjects'.[47] For example, as we describe in more detail below, prior to the commencement of the Australian Citizenship Act 1948, Australians were British subjects. The Australian Citizenship Act made them Australian citizens, as well as British subjects.

The substantive content of citizenship of the United Kingdom and Colonies, and British subject status more generally, varied over the succeeding decades. For present purposes, it is sufficient to note that being a 'Citizen of the United Kingdom and Colonies' did not necessarily carry with it the right to actually live in Britain or indeed to carry a British passport,[48] so that there could be dual nationals who were formally British citizens but who in practice only had a right of abode in their other country of citizenship. This has implications for the status of their 'dual' nationality at international law; the fact that a person was a citizen of the United Kingdom but did not have the right to live there, and may in fact not have lived there, suggests that either on an application of the *Nottebohm* test or the principle of 'one's own country', the United Kingdom would not have been held to be the country of their nationality.

In 1981 the category of 'Citizen of the United Kingdom and Colonies' was abolished, and replaced by three new classes of citizenship: British Citizenship,[49] British Dependent Territory Citizenship[50] (later British Overseas Territories Citizenship[51]), and British Overseas Citizenship.[52] Each of these could be held concurrently with citizenship of another Commonwealth nation, where such citizenship existed, or citizenship of a foreign (i.e. non-Commonwealth) country.[53] Since 1981 citizens of

---

[47] David Dutton, 'Citizenship in Australia: A Guide to Commonwealth Government Records' (Canberra: National Archives of Australia, 2000) 14.

[48] See Ann Dunnett, 'United Kingdom' in Rainer Baubock and Eva Ersboll (eds.), *Acquisition and Loss of Nationality: Policies and Trends in 15 European States. Volume 2: Country Analyses* (Amsterdam University Press, 2006) 551, 564–7.

[49] See British Nationality Act 1981, Part I.

[50] *Ibid.*, Part II.

[51] British Overseas Territories Act 2002, s. 2.

[52] See British Nationality Act 1981, Part III.

[53] This is more complicated where the other country does not permit dual citizenship. At the time of writing there is an unresolved question as to the status of several hundred

Dominion countries, such as Australia and Canada, have no longer been classed as 'British subjects' for the purposes of British nationality law; that classification is now reserved for those previously classified: 'British subjects without citizenship', certain alien women married to British subjects, and certain dual British and Irish citizens.[54]

11.4.2   Deportation of dual citizens and deprivation of British citizenship

Since 1948, there has been a gradual expansion in the capacity of the Executive in Britain to revoke British citizenship. The full extent of these powers does not appear to have been explored until the last decade, when deprivation of citizenship has formed part of the British government's response to the threat of terrorism.

Under the 1948 Act, the Secretary of State had legislative discretion to deprive a person, who had acquired citizenship of the United Kingdom and Colonies by registration or naturalization, of that citizenship.[55] Such an order could be made if the Secretary of State was satisfied that the citizen's registration or naturalization was obtained by means of fraud, false representation or the concealment of any material fact.[56] Naturalized citizens who lived in a foreign country for seven years (other than those engaged in government service) were required to register annually their intention to retain their citizenship, or could have it revoked.[57] However, these discretions were constrained by an overarching requirement that the Secretary of State should not deprive a person of citizenship 'unless ... satisfied that it is not conducive to the public good that that person should continue to be a citizen of the United Kingdom and Colonies'.[58]

The 1981 Act broadened the grounds for depriving individuals of British citizenship, as well as effectively ensuring that the only British citizens who could be deprived of their citizenship were those who possessed

---

people who arrived in the UK from Malaysia (which does not permit dual citizenship), who acquired British Overseas Citizen status under the British Nationality Act 1981, and renounced their Malaysian citizenship on the understanding that they would be eligible for British citizenship. In many cases these people are ineligible for British citizenship and cannot regain their Malaysian citizenship. See Emily Dugan, 'Immigration rules leave stateless Malaysians in limbo', *The Independent*, 13 March 2011.

[54] British Nationality Act 1981, ss 30–1. As we explain later in this chapter, British subject status continued to have significance in Australian law, well after Britain had ceased ascribing Australians that status.

[55] British Nationality Act 1948, s. 20.   [56] *Ibid.*, s. 20(2).

[57] *Ibid.*, s. 20(4).   [58] *Ibid.*, s. 20(5).

another nationality.[59] In addition to revoking citizenship obtained by fraudulent registration or naturalization, the Secretary of State now had the power to deprive a person of citizenship if the citizen:[60]

(a) has shown himself by act or speech to be disloyal or disaffected towards Her Majesty; or

(b) has, during any war in which Her Majesty was engaged, unlawfully traded or communicated with an enemy or been engaged in or associated with any business that was to his knowledge carried on in such a manner as to assist an enemy in that war; or

(c) has, within the period of five years from the relevant date, been sentenced in any country to imprisonment for a term of not less than twelve months.

The Secretary of State could not exercise this power on the latter ground (that a citizen had been sentenced to imprisonment for more than twelve months) if it appeared that the person deprived of citizenship would become stateless.[61] Paradoxically, the clear inference of this stipulation was that citizens could, at least in theory, be stripped of nationality on one of the other grounds even if that would result in their statelessness.

In 2002 the deprivation provisions were broadened further, to allow the Secretary of State to deprive a person of their citizenship status (including citizenship by birth[62]) if satisfied that the person had done anything seriously prejudicial to the vital interests of the United Kingdom or a British overseas territory.[63] The Secretary of State may not do this if he or she is satisfied the order would make a person stateless.[64] However, no such restriction applies to deprivation of citizenship obtained by fraud, misrepresentation or concealment of material facts.[65] The 2002 amendments provided for a right of appeal against a decision to deprive a person of

---

[59] *Ibid.*, s. 40.   [60] *Ibid.*, s. 40(3).

[61] *Ibid.*, s. 40(5)(b).

[62] As Matthew Gibney has shown, the expansion of the denaturalization power to cover citizens by birth was justified by the British government on egalitarian grounds. For as long as naturalized citizens were more vulnerable than their native-born counterparts, the former class were said to enjoy a second-class citizenship: Gibney, 'Should Citizenship Be Conditional?', 15. See also UNHCR/Asylum Aid, 'Mapping Statelessness in the United Kingdom' (November 2011) 144–6.

[63] Nationality, Immigration and Asylum Act 2002, s. 4, repealing and substituting s. 40 of the British Nationality Act 1981.

[64] British Nationality Act 1981, s. 40(4) as amended.

[65] *Ibid.*, s. 40(3), (4) as amended. See also UNHCR/Asylum Aid, Mapping Statelessness in the United Kingdom (November 2011) 144–6.

nationality, except in cases where the Secretary of State certifies that the decision:[66]

> was taken wholly or partly in reliance on information which in his opinion should not be made public –
> (a) in the interests of national security,
> (b) in the interests of the relationship between the United Kingdom and another country, or
> (c) otherwise in the public interest.

Finally, the 2006 amendments to the 1981 Act expand even further the Secretary of State's general discretion to deprive a person of citizenship where there has been no fraud or misrepresentation.[67] The Secretary of State need only be satisfied that 'deprivation is conducive to the public good' (and must be satisfied that deprivation would not make the person stateless).[68] Importantly, this language echoes the provisions of the Immigration Act 1971, which give the Home Secretary the power to make an order depriving a person of their right of abode in Britain.[69] While appeal rights remain, the provision that previously prevented a deprivation order taking effect until appeals had been exhausted has also been repealed.[70] Writing in *The Times* after the 2006 amendments were passed, Nicholas Blake QC, observed:

> Citizenship has long been a guarantee that a person is not subject to the battery of intrusive and repressive measures available under the immigration legislation, notably deportation. However, the legislative barrage of the last five years, linking immigration, asylum and terrorism, has broadened the basis for deprivation of citizenship …
>
> This increasing power for the Home Secretary to make decisions that override an individual's fundamental rights, which are protected by national or international law, for the good of the State, is alarming – particularly so if no criminal conviction or objective finding that a person has engaged in terrorist acts is required. The term 'conducive to the public good' is very broad. Not only are the criteria for stripping someone of citizenship obscure, but the means by which these criteria are established is unlikely to be fair. In cases of alleged undesirable associations brought to his attention by the security forces, the Home Secretary is likely to want

---

[66] British Nationality Act 1981, s. 40A(2) as amended.
[67] Immigration, Asylum and Nationality Act 2006, s. 56(1), repealing and substituting s. 40(2) of the British Nationality Act 1981.
[68] British Nationality Act 1981, s. 40(2), (4) (as amended).
[69] Immigration Act 1971, s. 2A.
[70] Asylum and Immigration Act 2004, Sch. 2, repealing s. 40A(6) of the British Nationality Act 1981.

to use the procedures of the Special Immigration Appeals Commission, where the person will probably not know the real case against him or her. The right of silence, trial by jury, freedom from executive detention: the ancient edifice of our unwritten constitution is being demolished brick by brick.[71]

These sentiments reflect the insecurity developing around dual citizenship.

11.4.3   Loss of British citizenship – recent cases

In recent years there have been a number of appeals from attempted revocations of British citizenship, including several high-profile cases, bringing the issue of loss of citizenship into the public domain. We examine two of these below, focusing on the difference that possessing dual nationality made for the outcome in each case.

11.4.3.1   Abu Hamza

Sheik Abu Hamza was a member of North London's Muslim community who had gained some notoriety after the 11 September 2001 terrorist attacks with his vocal praise of Osama bin Laden.[72] Hamza was born in Alexandria and acquired Egyptian citizenship at birth.[73] He moved to the United Kingdom and acquired British citizenship in 1986.[74]

In April 2003, the then Home Secretary used his expanded powers under the amended Nationality Act 1981 to inform Hamza of his intention to make an order depriving him of his British citizenship,[75] on the grounds that the Home Secretary was satisfied Hamza had acted in a manner 'seriously prejudicial to the vital interests of the United Kingdom or a British overseas territory'.[76] Hamza appealed to the Special Immigration Appeals Commission (SIAC), and before the appeal could be determined, Hamza was convicted of criminal offences, including

---

[71] Nicholas Blake QC, 'Why is there no song and dance about this Act?' *The Times*, 25 April 2006.

[72] Simon Jeffery and James Sturcke 'Profile: Abu Hamza', *The Guardian*, 15 November 2007; BBC News, 'Profile: Abu Hamza', 5 November 2010, available at www.bbc.co.uk/news/uk-11701269, last accessed 2 June 2014.

[73] *Abu Hamza* v. *Secretary of State for the Home Department* (2010) Appeal No. SC/23/2003 (5 November 2010) (Hamza) 2.

[74] *Hamza* (2010) Appeal No. SC/23/2003 (5 November 2010), 2.

[75] *Ibid.*

[76] British Nationality Act 1981, s. 40(2); *Hamza* (2010) Appeal No. SC/23/2003 (5 November 2010), 2.

soliciting murder and inciting racial hatred, and imprisoned.[77] An order was also issued for his extradition to face charges in the United States, he remained in prison pending extradition while he exhausted all avenues of appeal under domestic and European law.[78] As a result, the appeal against the deprivation of his citizenship did not come before the SIAC until 2010, and while the appeal was pending, the deprivation order could not be made.[79]

These procedural issues are significant because central to Hamza's case was the fact that between the Home Secretary's announcing his intention to deprive Hamza of his citizenship in April 2003, and his appeal being considered by the SIAC, he had been stripped of Egyptian citizenship by the Egyptian government.[80] The SIAC held that Parliament's intention in enacting section 40(4) of the Nationality Act 1981 was to prevent the Home Secretary from making a deprivation order if its effect would be to make the individual 'a person who is not considered as a national by any state under operation of its law'.[81] After taking evidence from a high-ranking legal officer in the Egyptian government, the SIAC was satisfied that an order had been made (though perhaps not published) depriving Hamza of Egyptian citizenship.[82] The Home Secretary therefore had no power to deprive Hamza of his British citizenship because that order would render him stateless.[83]

11.4.3.2   David Hicks

David Hicks is an Australian citizen who was captured in Afghanistan in late 2001 and accused of having provided support to Al-Qaeda and the Taliban.[84] Hicks was detained at Guantanamo Bay, and ultimately convicted by the United States' Guantanamo Military Commission for providing material support to terrorism.[85]

---

[77] *Hamza* (2010) Appeal No. SC/23/2003 (5 November 2010), 2.

[78] The European Court of Human Rights decided that Hamza cannot be extradited to the United States because he faces a sentence of execution there: *Babar Ahmad and Others v. the United Kingdom* (ECHR Application Nos 24027/07, 11949/08 and 36742/08) 6 July 2010.

[79] See British Nationality Act 1981, s. 40A(6) as in force before the commencement of the Asylum and Immigration Act 2004, Sch 2.

[80] *Hamza* (2010) Appeal No. SC/23/2006 (5 November 2010), 5–11.

[81] *Ibid.*, 3.   [82] *Ibid.*, 11–12.   [83] *Ibid.*,12.

[84] *R (Hicks)* v. *Secretary of State for the Home Department* [2005] EWHC 2818 (Admin) [1].

[85] The records of the Military Commission proceedings are available at: www.mc.mil/CASES/MilitaryCommissions.aspx, last accessed 2 June 2014.

While awaiting trial, Hicks applied to be registered as a British citizen, claiming entitlement to citizenship by descent.[86] He argued he should be registered as a British citizen and entitled to claim consular assistance from Britain.[87] This was particularly significant as a number of British detainees at Guantanamo Bay had been released into the custody of the British government and allowed to return to Britain.[88] The British government had demonstrated a willingness to intercede on behalf of its citizens detained on suspicion of terrorist activities, whereas the Australian government had not made strong representations on Hicks' behalf while he was imprisoned, and had indicated that Australia's position was that a military commission should try Hicks.[89]

The British Home Secretary accepted that Hicks was prima facie entitled to be registered as a British citizen but at first asserted a discretion to refuse to register him on the grounds of public policy.[90] Later, the Home Secretary accepted Hicks' entitlement to be registered but claimed that while Hicks could be registered as a British citizen he could, in parallel, be deprived of his citizenship, in effect giving him no opportunity to claim any of the benefit of British citizenship before it was taken away.[91] Speed was desirable in part because there was a concern that Hicks might, upon being granted British citizenship, seek to renounce his Australian citizenship immediately as a way of ensuring that he could not in future be deprived of his British citizenship (as to do so would render him stateless).[92]

In December 2005 the High Court of England and Wales upheld David Hicks' entitlement to be registered as a British citizen and ordered that he be registered.[93] In reaching this view, the court considered that the grounds on which citizenship could at that time be revoked did not apply in Hicks' case, so that the Home Secretary could not simultaneously give him citizenship and take it away.[94] The Act provided for deprivation of citizenship on the grounds of certain conduct – for example, showing oneself to be disloyal or disaffected towards Her Majesty. However, the High Court held that these criteria were essentially forward-looking, that is, they applied to

---

[86] R (Hicks) v. Secretary of State for the Home Department [2005] EWHC 2818 (Admin) [1] at 4.
[87] Ibid. at 2.
[88] Home Secretary v. Hicks [2006] EWCA Civ 400, [6].
[89] R (Hicks) v. Secretary of State for the Home Department [2005] EWHC 2818 (Admin), 7.
[90] Ibid., 14.
[91] Ibid., 6. See also Home Secretary v. Hicks [2006] EWCA Civ 400, [3].
[92] R (Hicks) v. Secretary of State for the Home Department [2005] EWHC 2818 (Admin), 22.
[93] Ibid., 1.   [94] Ibid., 22.

a person's behaviour once the person had become a citizen. As such, whatever Hicks had done before he applied for citizenship was not relevant to the question of whether he could then be deprived of citizenship once it was granted.[95] Had Hicks subsequently been sentenced to imprisonment for more than twelve months, even on the basis of prior conduct, that could have provided the basis for deprivation of citizenship.[96] The Home Secretary's appeal was dismissed by the Court of Appeal. Lord Justice Pill (with whom Hopper LJ agreed), did not accept the Home Secretary's submission that 'conduct of an Australian in Afghanistan in 2000 and 2001 is capable of constituting disloyalty or disaffection towards the United Kingdom, a state of which he was not a citizen, to which he owed no duty and upon which he made no claims'.[97] After the Court of Appeal's decision, but before Hicks was granted citizenship, the Nationality Act of 1981 was amended so as to allow the Secretary of State to deprive a person of citizenship if satisfied that it would be conducive to the public good to do so.[98] The day after Hicks was granted British citizenship, the Home Secretary exercised this expanded discretion.[99]

The *Hicks* case is significant not only because it demonstrates the privilege dual citizenship can provide, and how strenuously countries may resist affording that privilege to particular individuals, but also because it gives an insight into the different circumstances and experiences of dual citizens. Before the High Court, counsel for David Hicks argued that, once registered as a British citizen, he ought to be treated in the same way as the other British prisoners at Guantanamo, some of whom were also dual nationals.[100] The British government had negotiated for several prisoners to be returned to Britain, where they had not been charged with criminal offences and no effort had been made to deprive them of their nationality. Mr Justice Collins accepted the weight of a Home Office official's explanation that the differential treatment afforded Mr Hicks was justified on the basis that the other prisoners:

> all had close links with the United Kingdom, having lived here for most
> of their lives whereas the claimant had no such links and was seeking to

---

[95] *Ibid.*, 17.   [96] *Ibid.*, 18.

[97] *Home Secretary* v. *Hicks* [2006] EWCA Civ 400, 37.

[98] Immigration, Asylum and Nationality Act 2006, s. 56(1), repealing and substituting s. 40(2) of the British Nationality Act 1981 (with effect from 16 June 2006).

[99] Annabel Crabb, 'Law strips Hicks of UK citizenship in hours', *Sydney Morning Herald*, 20 August 2006.

[100] *R (Hicks)* v. *Secretary of State for the Home Department* [2005] EWHC 2818 (Admin), 26.

use his adventitious entitlement to registration to obtain an advantage which the country in which he had been born and brought up would not provide.[101]

An analogy can be drawn here with the principles applied in the *Nottebohm* case, where the ICJ looked beyond *de jure* citizenship to the social facts of membership in order to determine the applicant's effective nationality. Put another way, given his lack of connection with the United Kingdom, it could not be said to be Hicks' 'own country'.

11.5.   Dual nationality and deprivation of citizenship in Australia

11.5.1   Dual nationality in Australia

Australia is unlike some other countries with written constitutions, as the Australian Constitution does not deal directly with the concept of Australian citizenship. Until the Federal Parliament exercised its power under section 51(xix) of the Constitution to enact the Australian Citizenship Act 1948 (as part of the cooperative reform of citizenship law undertaken by Commonwealth countries and the United Kingdom, described above), Australians' nationality status was that of 'British subject'. In 1948 Australians retained the status of British subject and gained the status of 'Australian citizen'. Dutton has argued that this duality of status, which persisted until 1987 when Australians ceased to be 'British subjects', meant that 'the nationalist expectation of the coincidence of citizenship and nationality – of membership and identity – was not fully realised'.[102] Rubenstein has elsewhere suggested a different interpretation, in which dual status reflected Australians' level of comfort with dual identities as both members of the Australian community and of 'the supranational concept of Empire'.[103]

Australian citizenship law and policy has, until relatively recently, reflected a somewhat fragmented approach to the issue of dual citizenship. For almost the first ninety years of federation Australians benefited from a form of dual nationality recognized under the law of the United Kingdom. However, Australia's policy preference was that Australian citizens did not

---

[101]   *Ibid.*, 18.
[102]   Dutton, 'Citizenship in Australia: A Guide to Commonwealth Government Records', 19.
[103]   Kim Rubenstein, 'From Supranational to Dual to Alien Citizen: Australia's Ambivalent Journey' in Kim Rubenstein and Simon Bronitt (eds.), *Citizenship in a Post-National World: Australia and Europe Compared* (Sydney: Federation Press, 2008), 40.

hold any additional citizenships. To the extent possible, this was reflected in the Australian Citizenship Act 1948, which until 2002 provided that Australians who obtained another nationality lost their Australian citizenship.[104] Between 1966 and 1986, the Citizenship Act prescribed an oath or affirmation, taken as a precondition for becoming an Australian citizen, in which a person swore, 'renouncing all other allegiance'[105] to be 'faithful and bear true allegiance to Her Majesty Elizabeth the Second, Queen of Australia, Her heirs and successors according to law'.[106] However, although a person who took the oath in that form 'may well believe that, ... he or she has effectively renounced any foreign nationality',[107] in *Sykes v. Cleary (No 2)* the Australian High Court held that an oath administered in Australia under Australian law could not amount to renunciation of a foreign citizenship.[108] A person taking the oath of allegiance remains a citizen of a foreign country until that country's laws concerning renunciation of citizenship are complied with.[109] The pledge was altered in 1986, and since then new citizens have not been required to formally or notionally forsake allegiance to their other countries of citizenship.[110]

As Rubenstein observes, this disjointed approach to the acquisition and loss of Australian citizenship gave rise to a 'basic inequality in the former system'[111] – only Australian citizens who had another citizenship *before* becoming Australians were entitled to dual citizenship.[112] From 4 April 2002, Australians who take out additional citizenship are no longer stripped automatically of their Australian citizenship,[113] and may hold both concurrently (provided that dual citizenship is permissible under the law of the other state in question). There is now provision in the Citizenship Act 2007 for the resumption of citizenship lost before 2002, where a person can show that they did not realize that they

---

[104] Australian Citizenship Act 1948 (Cth) s. 17.

[105] *Ibid.* Schedule 2 (amended by Australian Citizenship Amendment Act 1986 (Cth)).

[106] *Ibid.*   [107] *Sykes* v. *Cleary (No 2)* (1992) 176 CLR 77, 108.   [108] *Ibid.*

[109] There is an important distinction between citizenship under the laws of foreign states and foreign citizenship for Australian constitutional purposes. The High Court has recognized that, under s. 44 of the Constitution, a person can be considered to have renounced their former citizenship by doing everything reasonable to that effect in 'the circumstances of the particular case' even if those steps were not sufficient to satisfy foreign processes. *Ibid.*, 108 (per Mason CJ, Toohey and McHugh JJ); 114 (per Brennan J); 128–9 (per Deane J); 138–9 (per Gaudron J).

[110] Australian Citizenship Act 1948 (Cth) Schedule 2.

[111] Kim Rubenstein, *Australian Citizenship Law in Context* (Sydney: Law Book Company, 2002) 142.

[112] *Ibid.*

[113] Australian Citizenship Legislation Amendment Act 2002 (Cth), Sch 1.

would lose their Australian citizenship by acquiring another citizenship, or that they would have suffered 'significant hardship or detriment' had they not done so.[114]

11.5.2 Deprivation of citizenship

Australia has always retained the option of depriving naturalized Australians of their citizenship under certain circumstances.[115] Before it was replaced in 2007, the Citizenship Act 1948 provided for deprivation of Australian citizenship under limited and precisely defined circumstances.[116] The deprivation of citizenship provisions (in section 21 of the Act) applied to naturalized citizens,[117] who could be deprived of their citizenship at the discretion of the Minister if convicted of making a false representation or concealment when applying for citizenship;[118] or they were convicted of an offence against an Australian or foreign law and sentenced to death, life imprisonment or imprisonment for more than twelve months, where the conviction occurred after they applied for citizenship but the offence in question was committed *before* citizenship was granted;[119] or their citizenship was granted as a result of migration-related fraud.[120] The Minister was required to be satisfied that it would be contrary to the public interest for such a person to remain an Australian citizen.[121] These provisions were substantially re-enacted in the Australian Citizenship Act 2007, with minor modifications.[122]

Whether or not an Australian citizen is vulnerable to loss of their citizenship status depends, primarily, on the basis on which they obtained their citizenship and the basis on which it is to be revoked. Citizens by descent or adoption can only have their citizenship revoked if it was obtained by fraud or misrepresentation and the Minister is satisfied that it is not in the public interest that they remain an Australian citizen.[123] At least as a matter of statutory language it is open to the Minister to make

---

[114] Australian Citizenship Act 1948 (Cth) s. 23AA.
[115] See Naturalization Act 1903 (Cth) s. 11.
[116] Australian Citizenship Act 1948 (Cth) s. 21.
[117] *Ibid.*, s. 21(1)(a).   [118] *Ibid.*, ss. 21(1)(a)(i), 50.
[119] *Ibid.*, s. 21(1)(a)(ii).   [120] *Ibid.*, s. 21(1)(a)(iii).   [121] *Ibid.*, s. 21(1)(b).
[122] Australian Citizenship Act 2007 (Cth), s. 34. A person who has obtained their citizenship by descent or adoption can no longer be denaturalized on the basis of a conviction for criminal conduct committed before they obtained citizenship; citizenship may now be revoked where it was obtained as a result of third-party fraud.
[123] *Ibid.*, s. 34(1).

such an order even where the former Australian citizen would become
stateless as a result; therefore, dual nationality does not necessarily figure
in the calculation. The same is true for naturalized Australian citizens
who lose their citizenship because it was obtained by misrepresentation
or fraud.[124] However, naturalized citizens can also lose their citizenship
if, after applying for citizenship, they are convicted of serious criminal
offences within the meaning of the relevant provisions and the Minister
is satisfied that the public interest is served by their citizenship being
revoked.[125] The Minister cannot do this if the result would be that the
former Australian citizen becomes stateless.[126] Dual citizens are therefore
more at risk of losing their citizenship under this provision than those
who, having been granted Australian citizenship, are no longer a citizen
of any other country.

11.5.3   Deportation of dual citizens

Non-citizens require a visa in order to enter and remain in Australia.[127]
Citizens do not.[128] Subject to the tightly-controlled exceptions under extradition law,[129] Australian citizens, whether or not they are dual nationals,
may not be removed from Australia against their will or prevented from
returning to Australia.

Constitutionally, it is less clear whether an Australian citizen with dual
nationality has an absolute right to remain in Australia. While the status of 'Australian citizen' is 'entirely statutory',[130] there is a constitutional
dimension to citizenship in Australia. The High Court has developed
a constitutional concept of 'membership' of the Australian community based on presumptive Australian allegiance, which has influenced
its decisions in cases involving citizenship rights, and which may have
particular application to dual citizens. If a person does not possess 'full
membership' of the Australian community, the court has held that their

---

[124] *Ibid.*, s. 34(2), (3).
[125] *Ibid.*, s, 34(2).   [126] *Ibid.*, s. 34(3).
[127] Migration Act 1958 (Cth), ss. 13–14, 29.
[128] Citizens may not be required to pay a fee in order to enter Australia: *Air Caledonie
International v. Commonwealth* (1988) 165 CLR 462, 469. As to whether Australian citizens have a right of abode in Australia, see Helen Irving, 'Still Call Australia Home? The
Constitution and the Citizen's Right of Abode', *Sydney Law Review* 30 (2008) 133.
[129] Extradition Act 1988 (Cth).
[130] *Chu Kheng Lim v. Minister for Immigration, Local Government and Ethnic Affairs* (1992)
176 CLR 1, 54.

statutory labelling as a 'citizen' does not necessarily prevent them from being constitutionally 'alien', and subject to the legislative and executive powers of the Commonwealth under s 51(xix) of the Constitution (the power to make laws with respect to naturalization and aliens).[131] This is a more generally applicable taxonomy than the case-by-case assessment of the 'social fact' of an individual's nationality status that occurs under international law.

The independent nation of Papua New Guinea (PNG) was created in 1975 from Territory of Papua and the Territory of New Guinea, which had both previously been administered by Australia. The people of Papua had previously been Australian citizens, but lost that status upon the commencement of the PNG Constitution.[132] This wholesale expatriation of a whole class of Australian citizens was upheld by the High Court of Australia in *Re Minister for Immigration, Multicultural and Indigenous Affairs; Ex parte Ame*[133] on the basis that Papuans' 'membership' of the Australian polity was of a lesser quality than that of citizens resident in the Australian States and internal Territories and they had always, constitutionally, been 'aliens' despite possessing statutory Australian citizenship. Papuans' Australian citizenship had always been 'nominal', the court decided: 'It conferred few rights and specifically no rights freely to enter the States and internal territories of Australia, as other Australian citizens might do. Nor did it permit its holders to enjoy permanent residence in the States and internal territories'.[134] In reaching this view, the court had regard to the fact that the Constitution of PNG prevents PNG citizens from holding dual citizenship. As Kirby J noted, the relevant provisions should be understood in light of their intended purpose:

> to cure the indignity of a largely nominal Australian citizenship; to abolish the differentiation between the nationality status of Papuans and New Guineans; and to fulfil the national aspirations of that new nation.[135]

As well as being a potentially life-changing decision for Australia's former Papuan citizens,[136] *Ame* has implications for the legal character

---

[131] See *Re MIMIA; Ex Parte Ame* (2005) 222 CLR 439 (*Ame*) and *Singh v. Commonwealth* (2004) 222 CLR 322, both discussed further below.

[132] See Papua New Guinea Independence (Australian Citizenship) Regulations 1975 (Cth), r. 4.

[133] *Ame* (2005) 222 CLR 439.   [134] *Ibid.*, 471.

[135] *Ibid.*, 470.

[136] As to which see Kim Rubenstein, 'Advancing Citizenship: The Legal Armory and Its Limits', *Theoretical Inquiries in Law* 8 (2007) 509, and the case described in that piece,

of Australian citizenship more broadly and in particular for Australians with dual citizenship. *Ame* suggests that it is possible for a person to hold statutory citizenship but to be, constitutionally, an alien, and thus subject to deportation and exclusion from Australian territory. The High Court went to some length to emphasize the special nature of the Papuans' position, both in terms of the effective quality of the Australian citizenship they had once enjoyed, and their role in the post-colonial formation of an independent Papua New Guinea, in order to confine the precedent being set in upholding the wholesale deprivation of their citizenship. The judgments in *Ame* suggest that there might be a constitutional impediment to revoking the citizenship of people who were members of 'the people of the Commonwealth' referred to throughout the Constitution.[137] While that idea may well afford protection to some Australian citizens, for the reasons that follow it is not clear that it shields all dual citizens from loss of their statutory citizenship, or from being treated as constitutional aliens. As we explain below, possessing dual citizenship may mean that a person is not part of 'the people of the Commonwealth'.

The category of 'the people of the Commonwealth' (that is, the cohort of federal electors who are responsible for choosing the members of the House of Representatives under section 24 of the Constitution) may exclude people who owe an allegiance to a sovereign power other than the Queen in right of Australia. In *Singh v. Commonwealth*,[138] three of the five majority judges held that the 'central characteristic' of a constitutional alien is the owing of 'obligations (allegiance) to a sovereign power other than the sovereign power in question'.[139] This definition has subsequently been reiterated by a clear majority in *Ame*.[140] *Singh* complicated the distinction then only recently drawn by the High Court between citizens and aliens. The definition of 'alien' proposed in *Singh* and adopted in *Ame* leaves the status of Australian citizens who have another nationality in some doubt. Their Australian citizen status suggests that they are non-aliens,[141] yet their allegiance to a foreign sovereign power is indicative of alienage.[142] While the proposition remains untested, it is at least arguable that Parliament is entitled to treat as a

---

Minister for Immigration and Multicultural and Indigenous Affairs v. *Walsh* (2002) 125 FCR 31.

[137] See *Ame* (2005) 222 CLR 439, 457 (Gleeson CJ, McHugh, Gummow, Hayne, Callinan and Heydon JJ), 79 (Kirby J).

[138] *Ame* (2005) 222 CLR 439.   [139] *Ibid.*, 395.

[140] *Ibid.*, 439, 458. See also *Koroitamana* (2006) 227 CLR 31.

[141] *Shaw* (2003) 218 CLR 28, 35.   [142] *Ibid.*, 395.

constitutional alien a person who owes allegiance to a foreign power, notwithstanding that they may hold the statutory status of citizen. In the event that dual citizens are capable of being considered aliens, they are at least in theory liable to lose their Australian citizenship pursuant to a law enacted under section 51(xix). At the extreme, Michelle Foster suggests,

> it would presumably be open to Parliament to legislate for the automatic removal of Australian citizenship of all persons who have or acquire a foreign nationality, regardless of the circumstances in which the foreign citizenship was acquired, and ... the individual's ability to divest himself or herself of that foreign nationality.[143]

Although the Australian Citizenship Act 2007 no longer requires a person who acquires Australian citizenship to renounce their other citizenships, in constitutional terms there is no indication in the case law that acquiring Australian citizenship automatically neutralizes the effect of allegiance to a foreign power.[144] Most dual nationals could potentially fit the *Singh* definition of an alien, unless it can be shown that a person's status as an Australian citizen effectively trumps other allegiances that the person might owe.

11.5.4 *The difference that dual nationality makes: losing one's 'own country'*

As we have explained above, when an Australian citizen is a dual national, particularly if they are an Australian citizen by naturalization, they are vulnerable, both as a matter of statute and constitutionally, to being deprived of their Australian citizenship in order to facilitate their removal from Australia. However, it is important to note that not holding Australian citizenship at all places a person in a much more immediately vulnerable state, irrespective of the nature and duration of their connections with the Australian community. As a country known to encourage immigration (albeit selectively), Australia has a population of long-term resident non-citizens, who have made lives in Australia but have not acquired Australian citizenship. The case described below shows

---

[143] Michelle Foster, 'Membership in the Australian Community: Singh v. The Commonwealth and its Consequences for Australian Citizenship Law' *Federal Law Review* 34 (2006) 161, 179.

[144] At least for the purposes of s. 44 of the Constitution, *Sykes* v. *Cleary* (1992) 176 CLR 77 demonstrates clearly that it does not.

how being a dual national in all but name has not been a sufficient basis on which to claim a right to remain in Australia, even in circumstances where Australia is arguably 'one's own country'.

Successive Australian governments have deported non-citizens who have committed serious criminal offences, even where the individuals concerned have virtually no connection with any country other than Australia, and can demonstrate that their social and family lives are enmeshed in the Australian community.[145] In one such case, *Minister for Immigration and Multicultural and Indigenous Affairs* v. *Nystrom*,[146] Stefan Nystrom was born in Sweden where his Australian-resident mother was on holiday, and he arrived in Australia aged less than a month old.[147] Nystrom lived in Australia without obtaining citizenship until he was deported to Sweden at the end of 2006, his visa having been cancelled on character grounds after he was convicted of a number of serious offences. While the Federal Court held that Nystrom had been absorbed into the Australian community and had no meaningful ties with Sweden,[148] the fact of his absorption only entitled him to an 'absorbed person visa', which the High Court subsequently confirmed could be cancelled on character grounds.[149]

Nystrom complained to the HRC, arguing, among other things, that his deportation violated Article 12(4) of the ICCPR.[150] Nystrom relied on the dissenting opinions in *Stewart*, discussed above, claiming that his strong social and family links with Australia, coupled with the fact that he had no such links in Sweden, meant that his 'own country' was Australia, notwithstanding his lack of formal citizenship.[151] In its response, Australia argued that Nystrom's 'own country' was Sweden, and that it was a matter for the state to determine the circumstances in which a non-citizen may remain in Australia.[152]

---

[145] *Jovicic* v. *Minister for Immigration and Multicultural Affairs* [2006] FCA 1758; *Minister for Immigration and Multicultural and Indigenous Affairs* v. *Nystrom* (2006) 228 CLR 566 (*Nystrom*).

[146] *Nystrom* (2006) 228 CLR 566.   [147] *Ibid.*, 566, 567.

[148] *Nystrom* v. *Minister for Immigration and Multicultural and Indigenous Affairs* [2005] FCAFC 121.

[149] *Nystrom* (2006) 228 CLR 566, 571 (Gleeson CJ), 584 (Gummow and Hayne JJ); 606–7 (Heydon and Crennan JJ).

[150] *Nystrom* (2006) 228 CLR 566.

[151] Nystrom claimed that he had assumed that he was an Australian citizen (at 2.6). The Committee attached some weight to the fact that, while Nystrom was a ward of the state during his teenage years, no attempt was made on his behalf to obtain citizenship for him. *Ibid.*, 7.5.

[152] *Ibid.*, 4.6–4.7.

In September 2011 the HRC found that by deporting Nystrom, Australia had violated his rights under the ICCPR, including under Article 12.[153] Nystrom's case is significant as it marks the Committee's endorsement of a broader concept of a person's 'own country', one not limited to formal nationality. This concept, the Committee found,

> embraces, at the very least, an individual who, because of his or her special ties to or claims in relation to a given country, cannot be considered to be a mere alien ... there are factors other than nationality which may establish close and enduring connections between a person and a country, connections which may be stronger than those of nationality. The words 'his own country' invite consideration of such matters as long standing residence, close personal and family ties and intentions to remain, as well as to the absence of such ties elsewhere.[154]

The HRC went on to observe that 'there are few, if any, circumstances in which deprivation of the right to enter one's own country could be reasonable. A State party must not, by stripping a person of nationality or by expelling an individual to a third country, arbitrarily prevent this person from returning to his or her own country.'[155]

In their dissent, Neuman and Iwasawa held that in Nystrom's case, it might have been concluded that he should be treated as an Australian national because authorities of the state party had not obtained citizenship for him while he was a ward of the state.[156] However, they preferred the approach of the majority opinion in *Stewart,* in particular the weight given in the state party's offer of citizenship and the complainant's constructive failure to take it up. This approach, in Neuman and Iwasawa's view,

> avoided making the right depend entirely on the state's formal ascription of nationality, but it preserved a relationship between the right and the concept of nationality, a fundamental institution of international law whose importance is also recognized in article 24, paragraph 3, of the Covenant.[157]

The Committee's opinion highlights the different ways in which a person can 'belong' in more than one country. For Stefan Nystrom, like others in his position, his legal status did not correspond to his social membership in Australia. The Committee declined, for the purpose of identifying Nystrom's 'own country', to privilege his legal status over the social fact of

---

[153] UN Human Rights Committee, *Nystrom* v. *Australia* CCPR/C/102/D/1557/2007.
[154] *Ibid.,* 7.4.   [155] *Ibid.,* 7.6.   [156] *Ibid.,* 3.6.   [157] *Ibid.,* 3.1.

his status as a member of the Australian community. However, Nystrom remains a Swedish citizen, and thus is a member of two national communities in different ways. His formal legal citizenship does not correspond with his lived experience and social allegiances as a long-standing member of the Australian community. The Committee's decision recognizes that this kind of formal and informal dual 'nationality' is possible and that, at least in some cases, the formal elements of nationality will not be allowed to defeat its substantive dimension.

11.6. Conclusion

Under British and Australian law, in order to deport a citizen (other than by way of extradition) it is generally necessary to first revoke their citizenship. The prospect that a citizen will become stateless if deprived of their citizenship is generally (though not universally) enough to preclude any attempt to do so. Logically, this means that if a person is only a citizen of Australia or the United Kingdom, and has no claim to another nationality, there is little prospect of their being stripped of their citizenship. Statelessness is less of a risk for most dual nationals, who, even if deprived of one of their nationalities, will have another on which to fall back. In theory, this makes dual nationals easier to denaturalize and deport. As recent British cases have demonstrated, this is more than a theoretical possibility; considerable efforts have been made to deprive British citizens of their citizenship in order to deport them or, as in Hicks' case, to ensure that they have no opportunity to claim the rights associated with citizenship in the first place.

The rightness or otherwise of punishing people by removing their citizenship has been discussed extensively elsewhere.[158] Here, we are concerned with whether it is right to make dual nationals *more* vulnerable to denaturalization than their single-national counterparts; that is, whether there is something about a person's status as a dual national that should make their claim on each of their citizenships less secure. It appears counter-intuitive that having more than one citizenship means that one can have less, or a less secure single citizenship, as a result. Indeed, in an age of globalization where the incidence of dual citizenship is rising and is being

---

[158] Gibney, 'Should Citizenship Be Conditional?'; Shai Lavy, 'Punishment and the Revocation of Citizenship in the United Kingdom, the United States and Israel', *New Criminal Law Review* 13 (2010), 404; J. M. Spectar, 'To ban or not to ban an American Taliban? Revocation of Citizenship & Statelessness in a Statecentric System' *California Western Law Review* 39 (2003), 507.

claimed as a human right,[159] it is anomalous that this vulnerability for dual citizens reflects a return to the mindset of an earlier period in dual citizenship history where that makes him or her more vulnerable.[160]

Questions to guide discussion

1. With the rise of an acceptance of multiple citizenships by states around the globe, what implications does this phenomenon have for our understanding of nationality and statelessness?
2. Is the single national more exposed to expulsion from the state and deprivation of nationality than the dual national, or vice versa? Should this be the case?
3. How should the relationship between the citizen and the state be understood, given that it can no longer be assumed to be 'monogamous'? Does dual nationality necessarily entail a division of loyalty?
4. Does the current state of law in the UK and Australia respectively privilege the legal over the social bonds of citizenship? What has been the position of the UN Human Rights Committee? Is there a distinction between an understanding of citizenship/nationality at municipal and international levels? Can (or how can) they be reconciled?

---

[159] Peter Spiro, 'Dual Citizenship as Human Right', *International Journal of Constitutional Law* 8 (2010), 111.

[160] Since this article was written, there have been several further developments in Australia and the UK in this area. In Australia, the Government responded formally to the Nystrom decision and can be viewed at: www.ag.gov.au/RightsAndProtections/ HumanRights/DisabilityStandards/Documents/NystrometalvAustralia-AustralianGovernmentResponse.pdf. In addition, the UK High Court allowed Abu Hamza to be extradited in 2012. The decision is *Hamza & Ors v Secretary of State for the Home Department* [2012] EWHC 2736: www.judiciary.gov.uk/wp-content/uploads/ JCO/Documents/Judgments/abu-hamza-others-judgment-05102012.pdf. And finally, changes to the UK law were made through the Immigration Act 2014, adopted on 14 May 2014, the relevant section of which (and full text of the immigration act) can be found at www.legislation.gov.uk/ukpga/2014/22/section/66/enacted. All websites last accessed 21 July 2014.

INDEX